A CULTURAL
HISTORY OF
THE FRENCH
REVOLUTION

A CULTURAL HISTORY OF THE FRENCH REVOLUTION

EMMET KENNEDY

YALE UNIVERSITY PRESS

New Haven and London

This publication was prepared (in part) under a grant from the Woodrow
Wilson Center for Scholars, Washington, D.C. The statements and views
expressed herein are those of the author and are not necessarily those of
the Wilson Center.

Designed by Richard Hendel
and set in Fournier type by G & S Typesetters, Inc.
Printed in the United States of America, by Vail-Ballou Press,
Binghamton, New York.

Library of Congress Cataloging-in-Publication Data
Kennedy, Emmet.
    A cultural history of the French Revolution / Emmet Kennedy.
        p.   cm.
    Bibliography: p.
    Includes index.
    ISBN 0–300–04426–7 (alk. paper)
        1. France—History—Revolution, 1789–1799—Influence.   2. France—
Cultural policy—History—18th century.   3. Politics and culture—
France—History—18th century.   4. France—History—Revolution,
1789–1799—Social aspects.   5. France—History—Revolution,
1789–1799—Religious aspects.   6. France—Civilization—18th
century.   I. Title.
DC158.8.K46 1989   88–39966
944.04—dc19   CIP

The paper in this book meets the guidelines for permanence and
durability of the Committee on Production Guidelines for Book
Longevity of the Council on Library Resources.

10 9 8 7 6 5 4 3 2 1

In Memory of

My Father

Robert Emmet Kennedy

(1905–1987)

CONTENTS

ILLUSTRATIONS

ACKNOWLEDGMENTS

The conception of this work dates back to 1975–76, when I was searching for a broader, more challenging topic than the intellectual biography I had just finished. I met Fernand Braudel at the Wilson International Center for Scholars in Washington, and in an interview he encouraged me to think ambitiously and to test his categories of the "long duration," or historical permanence and inertia, in a decade characterized by rapid transformations. The question we discussed was whether the decade 1789–99 made a lasting impact on French culture. Howard Sachar of the George Washington University History Department also encouraged me to think of a broad, far-reaching study. Jacques Godechot was most supportive of my venture, as was R. R. Palmer, who read sections of the manuscript a number of years later and offered valuable criticism. The American Council of Learned Societies, which offered me a fellowship for study in Paris in my sabbatical year 1977–78, helped to convert an idea into a project. This fellowship, in addition to giving me a year in the Bibliothèque nationale and the Archives nationales, afforded me the opportunity of discussing my conceptualization and my sources with numerous European scholars. Among them were Roger Chartier, to whom I am indebted for a critique of the original outline, Bernard Plongeron and Daniel Roche, who gave me much practical advice, and Albert Soboul, who provided me with valuable *mémoires de maîtrises* by his students and allowed me to attend his Saturday afternoon seminar on the French Revolution at the Sorbonne. Jean Adhémar of the Bibliothèque nationale's Cabinet des estampes gave unstintingly of his time, of his advice, and of his personal collection of engravings for the illustration of the book. Bernard Reilly of the Library of Congress, Prints and Photographs Division, was of great assistance in helping me reproduce from the library's substantial collection of French revolutionary materials. My friend John Reynolds did the photographing on one of Washington's hotter days. James Leith shared with me his publications on revolutionary architecture, as well as his vast knowledge of revolutionary culture in general. Marie-Laurence Netter cowrote the material that became part of chapters 6 and 11 on revolutionary education and continued to work with me on a computerized study of French revolutionary theater repertoires, which I have used in chapter 8. James Mac-Gregor generously gave of his time to write the programs for this data. My students Stavroula Lambrakopoulos and Nancy Roberts did most of the keypunching of theater performances. Son Tran and Kevin Gessler did many of the corrections. Four more students, Tula Connell, Jennifer Keene, Donny Little, and Jeffrey Lea, gave me much-needed research, proofreading, or typing assistance.

The fellowship at the Wilson International Center for Scholars, which I held in 1983–84, was an invaluable boost in getting the writing underway. My conversations there with James Billington reminded me that culture cannot be separated from the people who make and use it. Vivian Chakarian served there for six months as my research assistant and was energetic and intelligent in locating materials for me as well as in submitting a first draft of chapters 6, 7, and 8 to a word processor. Hall Gardner helped finish the research on biographies of the cultural elite.

My colleagues in the Washington Area Group of Old Regime French Historians, Robert Forster, Jack Censer, Betty Eisenstein, and Timothy Tackett, as well as Martin Staum and Dan Sherman, of Calgary and Cambridge, respectively, read parts or all of the manuscript and furnished valuable comments and suggestions. I am particularly indebted to my much regretted friend, George Armstrong Kelly, for reading through the entire manuscript and delivering to me no fewer than eighty sheets of handwritten editorial and substantive suggestions. My brother, Malcolm Kennedy, generously managed to do the same for chapters 1–7 despite his busy schedule. Patricia A. Bozzell marvelously copyedited the entire manuscript in its penultimate version with speed. Without these copyediting contributions the manuscript would lack whatever felicity it has.

Others who read the manuscript and offered scholarly suggestions in its penultimate form are Dominique Julia, Claude Langlois, Isser Woloch, and Lynn Hunt. Carol Papish did a magnificent and speedy typing job of this version from barely legible copy, and Jean Mosher typed the final draft with expertise and patience. I wish to thank my children Daniel P., Mara, and Gaëlle M. Kennedy for help in checking endnotes, Brigitte Boulad for checking accents, and the staffs of all depositories mentioned herein, especially the Gelman Library of George Washington University, the Library of Congress, and the Bibliothèque nationale. The University Committee on Research of George Washington University and the History Department offered me continued support in the form of two summer Dilthey Interdisciplinary Fellowships in 1979 and 1985 and other grants of aid for materials and secretarial assistance in other years. I am grateful to Laura Jones Dooley of Yale University Press for the excellent editing of the ultimate version and to my editor, Chuck Grench, of Yale University Press for his calm confidence in realizing that this project would come to fruition. My special thanks go to the mayor of Tart-le-Haut, Jean-Louis Aubertin, to Hilton Root, and to Dominique Julia for having obtained for me, under urgent, last-minute conditions, photographs of the revolutionary flag of Tart-le-Haut, one of which is reproduced as illustration IX.24. Finally, I would like to express my greatest thanks to my wife and children for willingly accepting the sacrifice of much of my leisure over the last decade while this book was in the making.

INTRODUCTION

The French Revolution was a profound cultural event. Two hundred years after the storming of the Bastille, the memory of 1789 and 1793 endures. Jacques-Louis David's *The Tennis Court Oath,* commemorating the destruction of the "feudal" orders and the permanent establishment of a national assembly in France, and his portrayal of the death of Marat have become icons of Western civilization, marking the springtime and sanguinary crisis of the Revolution. France's call to arms in 1792 to defend its frontiers and furrows from counterrevolutionary aggression was accompanied by a song, "La Marseillaise," that has become France's national anthem.

Historians of literature and the arts have generally preferred the Age of Louis XIV to that of the Revolution, and contemporaries of David and Marat feared that the upheavals of their generation might result in a slide back into the "barbarism" from which Louis XIV had just rescued France. The first country of Europe should not be allowed to lose its cultural preeminence.

But even the destructive aspects of France's revolution have cultural significance and warrant a history. A good example is the removal of heads from the statues of the kings of Juda at the portal of Saint Anne, Notre-Dame, in 1793. This ritual regicide by the sansculottes of the Ile de la Cité mirrored the Convention's real regicide of Louis XVI. Such dilapidation, as vandalism was then called, was often a conscious attempt to expunge the memory of royalty or "superstition" from a democracy based on "reason."

Rather than jump into the turbulent year 1789, this book will allow a privileged perspective on the long-term in cultural history—on what had been going on for decades, even centuries, and would continue, in spite of revolutionary upheaval, for decades to come. The story of the revolution in culture is framed thus to set that history in relief and to better gauge its ultimate impact.

By culture, I mean any symbolic representation of value, particularly of values that are perpetuated in time through the educational process (schools, churches, press, theater). Cultural artifacts need not consist of symbolic poetry. (The eighteenth century, a prosaic age, was bereft of good poetry.) Cultural objects can be as elementary as an almanac, for an almanac represents in some thirty pages the grand passage of time, as well as the relation between the diurnal and that extraordinary "event" which punctuates time. Or, culture can be as abstract as a treatise on metaphysics in which someone marks in words (that is, symbols) thoughts about the relation between perception and the external world—a problem that absorbed the eighteenth-century philosophes. From the peasants' almanac to the treatise on metaphysics lies the gamut of subjects that occupy the cultural historian. Their relevance or irrelevance to the Revolution is one of my constant preoccupations.

The first part of this book deals with the material environment of Parisian and rural France, with collective attitudes, or *mentalités,* and with cultural institutions, all of which existed long before the Revolution and persisted long after it. I survey such structures as the city of Paris, the main grid of which changed little during the Revolution, the corporations or guilds and such other corporate and privileged bodies as the academies, and the nonprivileged Masonic lodges and literary salons. I also look at the rural landscape and work routine and the more fluid but recurring phenomena of popular culture, such as the diffusion of chapbooks in the countryside, rural people's distrust of medicine and doctors, the struggle for literacy, and the diversion provided by popular festivals. The relation between high and low culture is also examined, particularly in chapters 2 and 3.

In part II, eighteenth-century cultural and intellectual movements of medium duration are surveyed: the Enlightenment, which began a century before the Revolution and extended into the nineteenth century, neoclassical art, and the cult of *sensibilité. Madame Bovary*'s druggist Homais is a latter-day *illuminé,* a true devotee of eighteenth-century rationalism. Neoclassicism was born in the mid-eighteenth century, of course, and it is misleading to speak of it only in the revolutionary context. A new Jacques-Louis David emerges in the 1790s, but David set his aesthetics in his *Oath of the Horatii* of 1785. A still better case can be made for situating Jean-Antoine Houdon—the sculptor of Jefferson, Mirabeau, and Condorcet and perhaps the greatest artist of his day—*before* the Revolution, when his style was fully formed and when he created the bulk of his work, rather than after 1789, when he was relatively inactive. The architects Boullée, Lequeu, and Ledoux did most, if not all, of the work that has since gained them the reputation of revolutionary architects before the Revolution. Finally, the Ecole des Beaux-Arts perpetuated the standard of classicism and neoclassicism into the mid-nineteenth century. All of these trends influenced the Revolution more than they were influenced by it. I have treated the cult of sensibility here as one long cultural continuity with changing emphases from Edward Young's *Night-Thoughts* of 1742–45 in England to Ducray-Duminil's terrible novels of the 1790s, which continued to sell extremely well into the 1840s. Sadness, melancholy, tearfulness, sympathy, terror, horror—these leitmotifs accompanied the heady rationalism of the salons. There was a literary and affective source of the Terror of 1793–94.

The culture treated in parts I and II has been described as culture of the revolutionary epoch. Quite distinct from it is the short-term "revolutionary culture"[1] proper taken up in part III, which deals with the short-term history of culture, the Revolution itself. The main thrust of this decade (1789–99) could be described as one of disruption, if not destruction, of the church, academies, schools, libraries, universities, and royal and ecclesiastical monuments. But reorganizations and creations also followed the Terror. Consider, for example, the French Institut national as a reorganization of the academies and the central schools as replacements of the old regime *collèges* after 1796. The moments of destruction correspond to the agitational phase of the Revolution, those of reorganization to the integrative phase of the Revolution. The decade was not entirely negative. Out of the confiscation and vandalism of art came public museums, including that wonder the Louvre. This is not to say that one justified the other, only that one led to the other.

Even in the acid destruction of the Terror, the Revolution followed uniform cultural laws or homologies that lend it a systematic quality. The key homology is popular sovereignty—an inversion of divine right absolutism. Not only had the living king to be eliminated as altogether incompatible with the notion of popular sovereignty (as well as for the corruption and treason for which he was convicted), but the authority and mystical qualities formerly vested in the king as an image of God Himself were transferred to the collective people. A ritual reenactment of this inversion took place in October 1793 in the execution of the sculpted kings at Notre-Dame and in the infamous play *Jugement dernier des rois* by Sylvain Maréchal ("the man without God"), in which a volcanic eruption on stage blew up the sovereigns of Europe.

Of course, religion was affected, too. After 1789 the Catholic church no longer enjoyed independence as a privileged corporate body within the body politic. Like all the cultural corporations of the ancien régime, it became part of the nation. The Revolution treated the church much as it treated the monarchy. Sovereignty in the person of the pope was inverted. The church was subordinated to the nation; Pope Pius VI was eliminated—first burned in effigy in 1791, then actually imprisoned in France, where he died in Valence in 1799. Clerics were chosen by and made responsible to the electorate created by the Revolution. The *bon curé* of the eighteenth century was ultimately subservient to the Revolution, supported the draft and nationalization of church property, took the oaths of loyalty exacted of him by successive governments, married a patriot woman, and danced the carmagnole. He was no longer the sacred person distanced from the society he served, as the Tridentine reforms in the old regime had made him. He was thoroughly immersed in a religion of man.

To accomplish this democratic inversion, it was necessary to cut deep into the tissue of the church. Everything that the ecclesiastical compromise of 1790 had sought to keep—sacraments, ritual, and doctrine—was rigorously attacked in the persecution known as de-Christianization. In this most consistent, pure, and extreme form of revolutionary ideology, the old sovereigns of church and state were eliminated and the hierarchy underneath them turned upside-down.

The attack on church and monarchy reverberated in other institutions. Such theaters as the Académie royale de musique (the Opéra) had to drop any allusion to "the former tyrant" from their names and eventually purge their repertoires. The administration of the Opéra itself went through a democratic revolution in 1793, as had the Académie royale de peinture et sculpture after 1790. School curricula were to be secularized, libraries and archives purged of any books and documents that smacked of "fanaticism" or "feudalism."

If this is what the Revolution opposed, then what did it support? I argue that it stood for a religion of man, announced by Jean-Jacques Rousseau as a "civil religion." Like those of the ancient world, this one would serve the interests of citizen and city, avoiding the conflicts of a transcendental religion like Christianity, which divided human loyalties between heaven and earth, church and state. The liberty of Rousseau's republic has been aptly described as an ancient liberty in which man is seen once again as primarily a political animal whose fulfillment is to be found completely within the state. The French Revolution consciously imitated this ancient city—David's pageantry is its visual recreation. It forsook what can be called a "modern liberty,"[2] which was introduced by Christianity and which created a private sphere of conscience and personal right, as well as a transcendental tension between the human and the divine.

The world of the French Revolution is immanent; everything is self-contained in the natural order, in a way analogous to the way the revolutionary generation in Germany was conceiving the world philosophically. If there is a God, as Robespierre and most others ardently believed, He is conceived as serving and protecting the civic order. This eradication of the transcendental dimension in the civic religion explains the elimination from the category of crimes those crimes that affect only oneself in the Declaration of the Rights of Man and Citizen (article 4) and allows one to do whatever one wishes, provided these actions do not infringe on the liberties of others. Suicide was often justified during the Revolution (in spite of Rousseau's strictures against it in the *Nouvelle Héloïse*) on the presumption of one's ultimate sovereignty over one's body.

This religion of humanity, before Auguste Comte's, found ultimate expression in the desanctification of the Church of Saint-Geneviève in 1791, the scattering of the ashes of this sixth-century patron of Paris, and the rededication of this temple "To Great Men, the Patrie, in Recognition." It was here that Voltaire, Mirabeau, Marat, and Rousseau came to rest, at least temporarily. Here the great patriots of the Revolution, like Nicolas-Joseph de Beaurépaire, were apotheosized in a truly "philosophical religion." God would no longer inhabit this erstwhile Christian sanctuary; rather, men were to become like gods, as Camus following *Genesis* would later put it.[3]

In the same line of self-apotheosis is Napoléon's act of crowning himself in 1804 in the presence of the pope, unlike Charlemagne, who had been crowned by the pope a millennium earlier. Hegel summed up the meaning of all this when in his lectures on *The Philosophy of History* he spoke of the Incarnation of Christ as a high point in history, but one in which man became God rather than one in which God became man.[4] Human apotheosis substitutes for divine incarnation. What better expression is there of the ascending principle of authority, of popular or human sovereignty?

Let us make no mistake: there is a great difference between the medieval origins of popular sovereignty, whereby a king is acclaimed in the name of the authority given to the people by God, and an implicitly original authority emanating from the nation, which, although it recognizes a supreme being, does nothing to trace its sovereignty back to Him. It is this original sovereignty of the people that makes the people quasi-divine. The pantheonization of the best among them recognizes this "divinity." Or must this be read in a purely allegorical sense? The deities in the Panthéon remain purely human—the revolutionaries were no modern polytheists. But at the same time these men were thought to have so far superseded ordinary mortality that they became like gods—hence the very terms *apotheosis* and *pantheon.* The Hébertist de-Christianizer Antoine-François Momoro explained the fragile boundary between ordinary humanity and divinity in 1793 when he insisted that "liberty, reason, truth are only abstract beings. They are not gods, for properly speaking, they are part of ourselves."[5] It was that part of themselves that the revolutionaries worshiped in the Cult of Reason in November 1793.

The revolutionaries wished to do without king and church and attempted to take things entirely into their own hands. The results were initially exhilarating but ultimately disillusioning: twenty-five years of war in which the *furia francese* unleashed itself on Europe in a conflict of unprecedented proportions—one million Frenchmen were armed in 1793. Inside France some forty thousand succumbed to the Terror, a sacrifice made more horrible because the French sacrificed their own. But these figures are dwarfed by the casualties of the foreign wars that followed: over one million, almost as many as in World War I (sustained over a much longer time but by a much smaller population).[6] Although the landscape and cities of France remained basically intact, in spite of the redistribution of church property, untold numbers of royal, ecclesiastical, and noble edifices were demolished, and little revolutionary building replaced them. Sovereign man proved sovereignly incapable of forging the heavenly city announced by the philosophes whom the revolutionaries claimed as their own but who would certainly have disowned their excesses.

Two considerations offset these implications of the most extreme forms of revolution—forms that many historians repudiate in favor of the more moderate phases, 1789–92 and 1795–99, before and after the Terror. The first is that many elements of permanence and stability in France resisted the revolutionary onslaught. The series of engravings of rural scenes by the Jacobin partisan of de-Christianization Joseph Lavallée are curiously placid—even one (fig. II.1) of a "nationalized" religious house at Nantes, near where the notorious drownings of political and religious prisoners took place in 1793. In spite of the ravages of civil war in the west, in spite of the de-Christianizing demolitions of statuary, the dilapidation of deserted buildings, the vandalism of abandoned châteaux, the desertion of fields by soldiers conscripted in the armies, and the "factories" or workshops operating at half-force for the same reasons, the physical landscape of France remained largely as it had been in 1788. This stability was reassuring. The framework of material culture remained intact. No industrial revolution accompanied the Revolution; otherwise, serious material and moral dislocation would certainly have followed. Peasants who returned to their huts after military service slipped back naturally, too naturally, into old routines. In spite of great geographical and occupational mobility during the Revolution,[7] the overall population, say, of Paris, remained much as before the Revolution: rejuvenated but essentially the same size, new births offsetting war casualties. The basic street grid of Paris, moreover, changed little.

Second, much good came of the Revolution. Terrible as were its bloodiest moments, men and women of many stripes have found in it some ultimate benefit. The bleaker moments, the darker meanings of the Terror, have now been forgotten—something that could not have been said a century ago. From the Revolution emerged a freer, more egalitarian, more tolerant society, one in which the individual and the state, rather than the order or the corporation, were the ultimate points of reference. The Napoleonic state, prepared by the Revolution and the ancien régime, stepped into the vacuum left by the intermediary corporate bodies of the old regime and established what we could call an *étatisme culturel.* It provided an anchor of stability in a politically volatile nineteenth century.

Even the ultramontane traditionalist Joseph de Maistre, who believed that the Revolution was pure evil, a revolt against God, also felt that it purged France of its corruption and prepared it for some new destiny. Alexis de Tocqueville, who mistrusted democracy, attributed its advent to the working of Providence. Though he was uncertain exactly what God had in store for humanity, he was certain that in some way the work of democracy was His work.

The society and culture that replaced the Revolution were in some respects immeasurably richer, more efficient, more variegated, if more confused, than they had been. In place of a classical unity of official culture and a deadlock between the "party of humanity" or the philosophes and the state and church came a far more individualistic culture with no special point of unity. The French Revolution left people with a hope, a hope repeatedly acted out, in a revolution that would right the wrongs left untouched or actually created by the last revolution. This hope in an ever-future revolution became a secular messianism which, when it failed to materialize, left man with that *mal du siècle* that plagued him through the nineteenth century and beyond. Or, perhaps more commonly—especially after 1870, when the Revolution had been institutionalized safely in the Third Republic—the French could look back gratefully to 1789 for what they owed it without fearing that it would threaten their present. On the other side of the spectrum are those today who refuse to "celebrate" the bicentennial of the French Revolution but who wish to simply "commemorate" it as an important, historic event with too many positive and negative characteristics to allow unambiguous rejoicing or regrets. The historian's task is to sort it out, sift the evidence, understand it, interpret it. To almost all parties, 1789 retains mythic proportions—the Great Revolution, the Great Fear, the Great Terror, the Great Nation. Its grandeur is charged with meaning that ever waits to be deciphered.

PART I

LONG-TERM

STRUCTURES

INTRODUCTION

The material environment of Paris and rural France remained relatively untouched by the fall of the old regime and the formation of the successive republican and imperial governments, retaining continuity and immobility. This material side of the nation in a sense has no history: it is mute. To it, to the inanimate buildings and streets, churches, palaces, and parks, the Great Revolution, unlike the later Industrial Revolution, was irrelevant. Inevitably, revolutionary vandalism touched everything, but the material Paris of 1815 was fundamentally the Paris of 1789. What did change were the cultural institutions, or corporations—the church, the universities and collèges, the press, the theaters. Most succumbed during the Revolution, lost corporate status, and were revived often as monopolies of the state after 1800. The flourishing literary salons and Masonic lodges, though not corporations, also disappeared, only to reappear in the Directory and the Empire.

Although Paris was a large and growing city in this period, 85 percent of France's population lived in rural areas. Peasants and seigneurs had struggled for centuries over landholdings and the exercise of collective rights over forests and meadows. This continued during the Revolution, complicated by the nationalization and sale of church and émigré property.

Many aspects of peasant life did escape the revolutionary onslaught: the tilling of soil, the harvesting of crops, the grazing of flocks in common pastures, except in such war-torn areas as the Vendée. Although feudalism had been abolished, we see in the pictures of rural life—and of a town like Nantes, where the Terror reached a paroxysm—even in those published by so pronounced a revolutionary as

Joseph Lavallée (see fig. II.1), a rather sleepy, comfortable seascape apparently unperturbed by the Terror that decimated the west.

Medical proficiency was as basic as were the primitive methods of tillage and husbandry. Differences between the elite and popular cultures can be glimpsed in both the relationships of peasants and village craftspeople and the fledgling practice of medicine. And studies have shown that elite and popular cultures differed less in the literacy-illiteracy distinction than in the reading material of each culture. The regular ritual of festivals also shaped the cultural structure. Although these festivals served as escapes from the tedium of agricultural chores, they were more than opportunities to let off steam. As Christmas in the towns of Provence shows, popular celebrations could be accompanied by elaborate symbolic decorations, the result of painstaking efforts to defer immediate gratification—and one mark of a superior civilization. The crude and the cultivated, the rural and the urbane—this mixture characterized French culture on the eve of the Revolution.

CHAPTER I

PARIS MILIEU

AND CULTURAL

INSTITUTIONS

Paris

Julius Caesar described Paris as "a town of the Parisii situated on an island in the river Seine." Its inhabitants burned their houses and destroyed their bridges rather than surrender them to the Roman legions. Ernest Hemingway, two millennia later, said he would "never be lonely along the river. . . . you knew there would always be the spring, as you knew the river would flow again after it was frozen."[1]

The Seine was one of two rivers that divided Gaul into three parts. Without the Seine, Paris would lack transport to the sea, water to drink and paint with, bridges to sing under or sell on, basins in which to wash, and a means to carry wood and comestibles. The Seine assured the city's survival and renewal through time; the Seine was the city's perennial birth.

The age of Paris could be measured by the series of rings left by successive walls that had been torn down to expand the city's limits. At the close of the old regime, the Farmers General wall ringed Paris: within lay the boulevards and the old *quartiers* of the city. Beyond extended the faubourgs, or suburbs: Saint-Germain to the west, Saint-Marcel to the north, Saint-Antoine to the east. The total urban surface encompassed 7,500 to 9,000 acres. The city's population increased from some 415,000 in 1674 to roughly 600,000 in 1789. To control this large, somewhat dangerous citizenry the police force was expanded to more than three thousand men.[2]

The distribution of the population of Paris in its various quartiers changed little during the Revolution. The crowded areas in the center remained crowded after the Revolution, and the faubourgs remained sparsely inhabited. "To compare the map of Turgot," writes historian Jean Tulard, "and that of Maire [during the Empire], the Paris of 1814 differs little from that of 1789." One can speak of roughly 160,000 new Parisians, Tulard adds, but not of a new Paris.[3]

What did this old Paris contain? Quartiers varied greatly, from the meandering, narrow streets of the center to the open fields of the faubourgs. The center around 1790 had a population density of 1,000 to 1,300 per hectare (2.2 acres), whereas the faubourg Saint-Antoine had only 26 to 75 inhabitants per hectare. Although Paris then enjoyed more social integration in many quartiers than after Baron Haussmann rebuilt it during the Second Empire (officers, merchants, and lawyers frequently lived on the lower floors; artisans, shopkeepers, and workers on the top floors), other quartiers were segregated somewhat by profession. Workers in the construction trades lived on the right bank in central Paris along the rue Saint-Denis; furniture workers concentrated in the faubourg Saint-Antoine; and the poor crowded into the faubourg Saint-Marcel in the southeast. Sébastien Mercier characterized Saint-Marcel as the most mutinous, quarrelsome, and wicked part of the city, whose denizens were "ruined men, misanthropes, alchemists, and maniacs," a description that partly reflects his own "bourgeois" outlook. By contrast, the east quartier of the Marais, he noted, was inhabited by declining, crotchety aristocrats, possessors of "half-fortunes," readers of staid periodicals, enemies of the philosophes. The Marais townhouses also housed nobles of the robe, self-proclaimed "defenders of the liberty of the people" in their obstruction of royal and ministerial "despotism" in the *parlements*. (These men voted in far greater numbers in the elections of 1789 than did the aristocratic electors of the faubourg Saint-Germain on the left bank.)[4]

The Latin quartier on the left bank housed some five thousand students, descendants of more prestigious Latin forerunners. Throughout Europe on the eve of the Revolution the university was in decay; its curriculum and discipline reflected bygone eras. Its bad reputation stemmed largely from the antipathy of the philosophes, former students. Nonetheless, the verbal skills of a Voltaire, a Robespierre, or a

Camille Desmoulins could be traced to training in the university collèges.[5]

Quartiers differed considerably in affluence. Near the Palais Royal—a neighborhood where foreign dignitaries found luxurious lodgings—Jefferson paid 72 livres for six days for a room at the Hôtel d'Orléans in 1784. Further to the east, where rooms cost 4 to 8 livres a month, thousands of newly arrived day laborers from the provinces found lodging.[6]

The north-south axis formed by the rue Saint-Martin on the right bank and the rue Saint-Jacques on the left was probably the city's most significant divider. Impecunious students, scholars, and *le peuple* inhabited the eastern part of the left bank, whereas the artisans and shop-keepers of Saint-Antoine lived on the eastern part of the right bank. The Halle aux Bleds, on the right bank, capped by a dome much admired by Jefferson, formed the central point of contact between east and west, between *poissardes* (fishwives) and aristocrats from the faubourg Saint-Germain and rue Saint-Honoré. Messenger boys hurried between these various points delivering letters (fig. 1.1). Bordering the Seine was the still unfinished Louvre, where such artists as Fragonard, David, and Vien had studios and salons were held biennially. The nobility and high bourgeois society enjoyed what the French call "external signs" of wealth—townhouses, horses and carriages, lackeys, maids, beautiful clothes, and, finally, elegant funerals. Astute contemporaries detected signs of vanishing familiarity between rich and poor—a loss of community. In the center of the city, high in the less desirable apartments, lived the poor. Many had lost their windows on the street and were no longer spectators of its busy life. Increasingly, maids of wealthy families lodged upstairs rather than in rooms within the apartments of the master and mistress. Prices, especially rents, rose far more rapidly than salaries in the second half of the eighteenth century, giving rise to itinerant tenants who would pack up and leave when rent was due, moving into other apartments vacated by well-to-do families who themselves had just moved to one of the new quartiers like the Chaussée d'Antin. The poor were also bearing more children than the rich. As had not been the case a century earlier, their families were slightly larger than those of aristocrats.[7]

The Seine watered the city, but, true to the old regime, it watered some parts better than others. The good water, or *eau du roi,* was pumped by the force of the river from the best wells to palaces, hotels, and monasteries. The less potable water, the *eau de ville,* went mostly from the Seine to ordinary citizens.[8]

I.I.
A Messenger Boy Delivering a Letter, *engraving.*
Courtesy Library of Congress, photo: John Reynolds.

Some dozen bridges crossed the Seine. The Pont Neuf bore a statue of Henri IV and the heaviest traffic: *mouchards,* or police spies (many spying on intellectuals); colporteurs, or hawkers and vendors; *racoleurs,* or military recruiters. Everyone wanted a man for something. Points of passage across the Seine or beyond the barriers were good places to arrest or draft men. But this did not discourage traffic. If you waited on the Pont Neuf for an hour, it was said, you could meet whomever you wanted. During the Revolution the successors of the racoleurs enrolled volunteers to defend the *patrie.* Controlling the bridges was crucial to controlling Paris.[9]

Another center of rendezvous was the Palais Royal, opposite the Tuileries on the rue Saint-Honoré. The Palais Royal was the creation of the duc d'Orléans and the architect Victor Louis. A vast real estate speculation, it housed theaters and restaurants, tea shops and *cafés,* wax museums and art galleries, jewelers and bookstores, and even a vast underground circus. Here gossip, news, and rumors were bandied about, and visionaries and malcontents, reformers and revolutionaries could count on an audience, if not a following. The Palais Royal contained all that was new in consumption and entertainment. Its pornography and courtesans made it unsuitable for respectable women. Inside these graceful Roman arcades could be found the most infamous forum of public opinion, as well as princely commercialism, aristocratic consumerism, popular debauchery, theft, and prostitution.[10]

Far more respectable were the Tuileries Gardens, where young women dressed in the latest fashion, wearing *coiffes* and walking arm in arm with their mothers, returned looks from admiring men (fig. 1.2). Before 1792 le peuple could enter the gardens only on the Feast of Saint Louis, the bourgeois only on Sundays. Unlike the newer Palais Royal, the Tuileries respected the hierarchy of the old regime.[11]

The court was installed in the Tuileries and Louvre apartments between the Pavillon d'Horloge and the Pavillon de Flore after Louis XVI and Marie-Antoinette were unceremoniously returned to Paris by the women of Les Halles during the October Days of 1789. The National Assembly followed and settled in the Manège wing of the Tuileries. After the king's death the Convention moved into the Tuileries proper. During the Directory (1795–99) both chambers of the assembly moved across the river to the Palais Bourbon. The crowding of more than a thousand of these deputies and the administration around the rue Saint-Honoré between the rue Neuve des Capucines and the Hôtel de Ville was one of the major changes brought by the

I.2.

The Evening in the Tuileries, *engraving.*
Courtesy Library of Congress, photo: John Reynolds.

Revolution. In addition, there were the clubs, like the Jacobin club installed in a Dominican ("Jacobin") convent on rue Saint-Honoré.[12] Paris once again became a capital, which it had not really been since the Fronde.

Few periods of Parisian history have seen so much building as the eighteenth century. The dramatic increase of land rents under Louis XV benefited courtiers, the robe, and bourgeois, who all invested much of it in new residences, or *hôtels*. The end of the century saw far more destruction of old buildings than did the beginning. Hubert Robert, one of the most intriguing artists of the academy, specialized in painting natural ruins and human demolitions (fig. 1.3). All the shops and lodgings propped up on the Pont Neuf were torn down a decade before the Bastille was besieged and demolished. The Théâtre français (Comédie-Française), the Théâtre des italiens (which took over the Comédie italienne, or Opéra-Comique, in 1762), and the Académie royale de musique, or Opéra, all moved to new buildings—the first to a structure near the Luxembourg Gardens designed by architects Charles de Wailly and M.-J. Peyre, the second to rue Taitbout on the boulevard, and the third near the porte Saint-Martin in the north of the city. Before the creation of the notorious Farmers Generals' wall and tollgates—extremely handsome constructions designed by the architect Claude-Nicolas Ledoux—the pace of construction almost tripled that of 1720, and most of it consisted of new projects rather than the remodeling of older buildings.[13]

Critics and admirers of the Enlightenment from Edmund Burke to Mirabeau have commented on the contemporary propensity to tear down the old regime structure. Burke felt it could better have been repaired, whereas Mirabeau believed it necessary to demolish "everything" before reconstructing. Building statistics show that the prerevolutionary proprietors and architects preferred the new hôtel in the new quartier to the restored "Gothic" ones of the old neighborhood.

New neighborhoods like the Chausée d'Antin and Philippe du Roule and much of the left bank were drumming from the blows of hammers and chisels—the Church of Sainte-Geneviève (transformed into the Panthéon in 1791), the Théâtre français (Odéon), the Ecole de droit, the new Ecole de chirurgie, dozens of hotels in the faubourg Saint-Germain, the Palais Bourbon of the comte d'Artois; and opposite, on the right bank, the new Place Louis XV (soon to be called the Place de la Révolution, and after the Terror the Place de la Concorde), the Madeleine, the apartments of the Feuillants, the Palais Royal, and the Halles aux Bleds.[14]

Paris changed little architecturally during the Revolution itself, in spite of ambitious plans to design a patriotic space.[15] The Place Royale, which dates from the fourteenth century and whose townhouses were built in the era of the marquise de Sévigné (the seventeenth century),

I.3.
Hubert Robert, Demolition of Houses on the Bridge of Notre-Dame
in 1786, *painting.*
Courtesy Musée Carnavalet, Paris, photo: Lauros-Giraudon.

persisted after the Revolution as the Place des Vosges. The material environment of Paris is constantly being modified, but the original grid, the warp and woof, lie intact.

The Corporate and Hierarchical Structure of Culture

It is hard to imagine a more structured, incorporated, patented, licensed, and controlled culture than ancien régime France. An examination of the official *Almanach Royal* of 1789 listing most of the official cultural organizations and their officers makes one wonder how any contemporary welfare or socialist country could be more statist. The church, universities, libraries, learned societies and academies, postal communications, transportation, printing, bookselling and hawking professions, and scriveners guild were all in varying degrees state concerns or recipients of royal privileges.[16]

The crown appointed most bishops and many abbots and abbesses, looking to Rome only for canonical investiture and for guidance in matters of faith and morals. Communications of the clergy with Rome were strictly regulated. Ecclesiastical jurisdiction had been whittled away and transferred to royal courts, while intendants had considerable authority over dioceses, parishes, and abbeys.

Secondary schooling before 1764 had been provided entirely by religious orders. Students of the primary *petites écoles* were generally taught by laity, who had been answerable to the curés and bishops since the reign of Henri IV. But state control had eclipsed pontifical authority over the universities. The most independent institution of higher learning, the Collège royal (Collège de France), specialized in languages and history and functioned throughout the Revolution. Natural history, an enlightened discipline par excellence, was pursued mostly in the King's Garden (Jardin du Roi, after 1793 the Muséum d'histoire naturelle) and administered before 1789 by George-Louis Leclerc de Buffon and later by Antoine-François de Fourcroy, both appointed and answerable to the minister or secretary of the Maison du Roi.[17]

Unlike the universities, which were ecclesiastical in origin, the seven royal academies were created by the Bourbon monarchy between 1635, when Cardinal Richelieu founded the Académie française, and 1776, when the Société royale de médecine was formed. The government not only chartered and patented each academy but appointed its secretaries and regulated the election of other members. It often prescribed research. The *directeur général des bâtiments du Roi* (in the 1780s the comte d'Angiviller) had jurisdiction over the academies and oversaw the salons, held every other year in the Louvre, where members of the Académie de peinture et sculpture exhibited their works. He was the royal Maecenas of artists. By a variety of instruments—patronage of scientific investigations, artistic instruction and exhibitions, monetary and honorific rewards and privileges—the monarchy reproduced the absolutist control and aristocratic hierarchy in culture that it had shaped in administration. Such absolutism and aristocracy was to redound throughout Europe to the glory of the king and kingdom of France.

The third cultural institution the monarchy sought to control, more tightly than either the schools or the academies, was the press. Censorship was official and explicit, rather than hidden and limited as it has been since 1884. Freedom of the press—quite foreign to the old regime—was a principle imported from England by the philosophes. Three bodies exercised censorship: the Parlement of Paris, the theology faculty of the Sorbonne, and the lieutenant general of the Paris Police. They were assisted in different ways by bishops, intendants, municipal officers, and even the Academy of Sciences. Many respectable men of letters, such as Jean-Baptiste-René Robinet, the composer André Grétry, the playwright Antoine-Vincent Arnault, a number of scientists like Joseph-Jerome Le Français de Lalande, and even a minor philosophe such as Jean-Baptiste Suard, served as censors. There was a hierarchy not only of censors but of censored material, from those enjoying the exclusive "privilege" of the king to those having permissions—*simples* and *tacites*—indicating degrees of endorsement or forbearance. Forbidden material was confiscated at the printer's shop, at the bookstore, at the author's home, or at customs. But in no period of modern French history was the monarchy able completely to control the printed word. When it tried, as during the harsh half (1685 – 1715) of Louis XIV's rule, punsters took to the streets with their *vaudevilles* and philosophes satirized the reign. Had the French not vented their feelings against the court, the ministers, and even the crown, they might well have overthrown their rulers earlier.[18]

The crown strictly regulated the number of journals. One had to obtain a license to publish and had to submit the sheets of each issue to censors before publication. As a result, the periodical and newspaper press never grew in old regime France as it had in England. In 1750 only fifty French-language periodicals were circulating, in contrast to the approximately one hundred in Great Britain and its colonies. The first French daily, the *Journal de Paris,* was printed in 1777, but the dailies did not really take off until 1789, when papers were used to influence the course of the Revolution.[19]

Other aspects of publishing were just as strictly regulated. Printers had to be licensed; in Paris in 1777 a mere thirty-six belonged to the Paris Book Guild; the number of colporteurs and posterers (*afficheurs*) had been fixed at forty since 1723 (fig. 1.4). Royal *régies,* or monopolies, even extended to the mail and stagecoach (*diligence*) services, and curés were obliged to read royal decrees from the pulpit.[20] Only pamphlets and broadsides, easy to compose and print, seemed to escape royal control.

Could this royal and bureaucratic grip on communications stifle the French spirit? In the seventeenth century, members of the Académie française commonly wrote on such given subjects as "Which of the king's virtues is the most worthy?" Playwrights were adept at flattering the royal family, and the music written at Versailles by Lully, Rameau, and Couperin was "in the service of the king." Engravers struck thousands of medals in the king's honor, and academicians paid high tribute to the crown in their reception "discourses." But this did not snuff out a century of cultural brilliance—that of the classic age, the age of Louis XIV so admired by Voltaire.[21]

But centralization is only one dimension of ancien régime culture; the corporate structure is another. Three types of corporation can be distinguished: First, the medieval Christian ideal of a harmonious body politic, the members of which perform specific functions and refrain from usurping those of others. A sixteenth-century document explains: "The head is the King. The arms are the nobility. The feet are the third estate. The arms must carry food to the mouth . . . the clergy is the heart. It is swollen with tithes. It will have to give some of them up. . . . Each must be kept in his Estate. . . . The three Estates are members of one body, of one province which is mother to all of them." One man is seen as equal to another before death and the final judgment, when, of course, no earthly rank will be considered. Although the members perform different functions, they are integrated organically in one body. Second is the early modern ideal of corporate autonomy, greatly cherished by Tocqueville, who esteemed noble, municipal, provincial, and even ecclesiastical "liberties" anterior to centralization. But this ideal could and did eventuate in a rivalrous *esprit de corps* that caused paper merchants to refuse to associate with

I.4.
The Bill-Sticker, *engraving of a painting by [Carle] Vernet, ca. 1790.*
Courtesy Library of Congress, photo: John Reynolds.

printers, and hawkers to be at odds with *libraires*. Some harmony obtains within each corps, but none among the different corps or within society as a whole. And third is absolutism and nationalism in which all the corporate bodies are subjected to the will of the state. This subjection was never total in old regime France—the Gallican church, for instance, was particularly jealous of its "liberties." The Revolution completed the process, but only after old regime monarchs had begun to look suspiciously at municipal, provincial, and clerical autonomies.[22]

A look at the academies shows characteristics of the second and third phases of corporatism. After ecclesiastical bodies, these were the highest cultural organism. The first academies were created in the reigns of Louis XIII and XIV, and many more were added in the century of the Enlightenment. By 1700 there were five Parisian academies (the Académie française, 1637; the Académie royale de peinture et sculpture, 1648; the Académie royale des inscriptions et belles lettres, 1663; the Académie royale des sciences, 1666; the Académie royale d'architecture, 1671) and eight provincial academies. In the eighteenth century the Académie royale de chirurgie (1731, 1748), the Société royale de médecine (1776, 1778), and twenty provincial academies were added, the most famous of which were the academies of Bordeaux (1703), Caen (1706), Montpellier (1706), Dijon (1740), and Lyons (1740). The academic infrastructure was well established before the great philosophical quarrels of the second half of the century.[23]

An academy, writes a remarkable historian, is "a bubble of time, arrested by one knows not what trick of history in the flow of duration." Since the eighteenth century certain academies have held their meetings on the same day. One can still find the same statutes, the same election procedures, the same routine of eulogies for deceased and newly elected members, the same *travaux,* or public memoirs, the same methods of organizing concours and prizes, the same *jetons de présence,* or attendance tokens, the same system of keeping minutes. Only the people and ideas change.[24]

The conservative historian Augustin Cochin (1876–1916) called these new intellectual institutions of the Age of Reason—academies, *chambres de lecture,* Masonic lodges—the *sociétés de pensée,* or thought societies. They were associations based on ideas, and their existence was critical to the advent of democracy. For although these academies were not fully democratic in their social composition (most members came from the privileged nobility, the clergy, and office-holding bourgeoisie), members dealt with one another as equals who shared the same ideas.[25]

Obedience to the king was clear in the *éloges* and charters of these institutions. Hardly independent in any critical sense, they strove to provide services useful to the monarchy, such as overseas exploration (Louis-Antoine de Bougainville), cartography (César-François Cassini de Thury), the first steps to unify weights and measures (Charles-Marie de La Condamine), the study of the relationship of epidemics to climatic conditions (the Société royale de médecine), or, finally, the plurisecular *Dictionnaire* of the French language (the Académie française). This last body was to arbitrate literary taste, and the Académie royale des sciences not only patented scientific inventions but censored scientific writing.[26]

Academies are pure expressions, even molds, of classicism—a rational quest for order. To separate an analysis of institutions from that of thought is unsound, because institutions are expressions, even symbols, of thought, and in turn shape thought. The network of academies—the *réseau,* or system of correspondence among them—may be seen as expressions of what Michel Foucault called the classical episteme. Foucault's "archaeology" of the human sciences finds the table—say of the genus and species of natural history, or the roots and derivatives of parts of speech in comparative or universal grammar—symptomatic of a quest for order through classification. In France, more than in Germany and England, culture was actively sponsored and controlled by the state, but this control did not make men of letters or scientists obsequious. The desired result was more a matter of "civilization" than intellectual sycophancy. Voltaire approved of the "century" of Louis XIV precisely because order, refinement, and genius radiated from its center.[27]

Masonic Lodges and Salons

The Masonic lodges formed in France between 1630 and 1790, unlike the academies, did not enjoy state protection. In theory, they were secret societies, although their existence, names, and locations were well known. Whereas the academies had sprung up in Paris and spread to the provinces, the lodges began abroad and settled in the French provinces before coming to Paris. Masons claimed that Freemasonry began in the time of Solomon. Although the pre-Enlightenment history of Masonry is obscure, by the seventeenth century Masonry was a force in England; from there it spread to the Continent. The Knights of Jubilation, an early Masonic outfit (dedicated to merrymaking), for example, arrived in Holland from England with the deist John Toland in 1710. In the eighteenth century two popes prohibited Catholics from joining Masonic orders, but many laymen, like Joseph de Maistre from Savoy, and even many clerics became brothers. (Of 210,000 Masons in eighteenth-century academic towns in France, 400 were clerics.)[28]

The Masons did not plot the Revolution. The six hundred lodges opened by 1789 were, it is true, loosely linked to the Grand Orient of Paris and to provincial orients beneath it but not to those of Scotland or England and only weakly to the German lodges. Many members of the Convention were Masons, but so were many émigrés. The Masons of Dijon were mostly *parlementaires* and feudal seigneurs reluctant to see the death of a regime under which they had prospered. A rebirth of Freemasonry took place during the Empire, especially in the army, where it had flourished in the old regime. In the nineteenth century Freemasons took credit for the Revolution as commonly as theocrats like abbé Augustin de Barruel blamed them for it. Neither seems correct. Before 1789 lodges were forbidden active involvement in politics. Freemasons were inspired rather by the Enlightenment ideal of *bienfaisance*, a kind of secular charity or do-goodism, an expression of brotherhood.

Freemasonry did not fit into the mold of the old regime's holist, corporate society; it was a voluntarist society based on the elective principle. All Masons could be elected to be masters and grand masters. Still, they evinced a "philosophical" contempt for the people. Masonic equality lay somewhere between the old regime equality within orders and the Jacobin equality of all citizens. Equality could exist among individuals of different orders as among brothers in a lodge, but this did not compromise the distinction between the orders of the old regime. Lodges themselves were often ephemeral, although foundations were more numerous after 1760, particularly between 1780 and 1789. When the Revolution came, most lodges ceased to function, because political clubs and politics absorbed the energy of many former Masons.[29]

The most recent view of eighteenth-century Freemasonry sees it as distinct from the corporate structure of the old regime; it was even anticorporate in its internal rivalries, exemplifying, like other sociétés de pensée, the divorce between society and state. Never enjoying the *privilège* of the academies, condemned by the church, and threatened with a ban by Cardinal Fleury, the lodges enjoyed a tolerance equivalent to the *permission tacite* given to unorthodox books. From the perspective of *sociabilité,* the lodges were indeed similar to the academies; the principle of association for both was merit rather than birth. And like the Enlightenment, the ideals of light and knowledge bound them tightly.[30]

The salons of Paris formed an integral part of the cultural scene and were often the sources of academic foundations, but they were unofficial, noncorporate, and unprivileged. Salons were free gatherings of men of letters, philosophes, musicians, and artists, as well as members of the court, the clergy, and the robe, held in the hôtel of a hostess with some social finesse and financial means. Individuals gathered regularly—every Tuesday at one home, every Wednesday night at another—for dinner or supper, perhaps for a musical performance, but above all for conversation.

To be boring or pedantic in a salon was inexcusable, and this set salons apart from academic gatherings. The conversational style of many Enlightenment works, such as Diderot's *Neveu de Rameau,* was inspired by the salon milieu in which they were conceived, and this style was generally light, witty, bantering, irreverent. This did not prevent participants from broaching deep and serious subjects, like freedom of will, the nature of matter, and the existence of God, provided they did not do so in too ponderous a manner. Theirs was an anti-erudite literary humanism.

Salons flourished in Paris at mid-century—salons for philosophes, salons for antiphilosophes, salons for artists, salons for cardinals, and salons for princes—but only four or five were famous. Julie de Lespinasse held a lively salon for philosophes that was impregnated by *Encyclopédisme.* Madame Helvétius held a salon honoring admirers of her late husband—Condillac, Holbach, Turgot, Chamfort, Cabanis, Morellet, Destutt de Tracy. Madame du Deffand greatly admired Voltaire, whom she succeeded in attracting to her salon for many years. Twice a week Mme Geoffrin invited different guests: on Monday a salon of artists, architects, and sculptors, on Wednesday a salon of men of letters—Diderot, Alembert, Marivaux, Marmontel, abbé Raynal, Saint-Lambert, Holbach, and the comte de Caylus. Other salon hostesses frequently held intimate dinners for court aristocrats or middle-class notables. The chief conflicts of the salons seem to have been among hostesses vying for the same clientele or those who patronized clientele that were mutually antagonistic.[31]

Women did not dominate the eighteenth-century salons of Mme du Deffand, Mlle Lespinasse, and Mme Geoffrin as had the *précieuses* of the preceding century. Less in control, they had nonetheless to orchestrate ideas, keep a balance among participants, include everyone in conversation, and see that no one became too abstruse or ponderous. Their role was well described by the Goncourt brothers, Edmond and Jules, in 1862:

> The art of conversation was the particular genius of the women of the period. . . . They ban pedantry and dispute, personalities and preemptions. They make of it an exquisite pleasure given and partaken of by all. They give it the freedom, the zest, the fleeting movement of ideas winging from hand to hand. . . . Conversation runs, rises, drops, glides and returns; rapidity gives it effect, precision lends it elegance. What feminine ease, what facility of speech, what abundant views, what fire, what verve go to make this swift-flowing conversation which sweeps every subject, veering from Versailles to Paris, from the pleasantry of the day to the event of the moment, from the ridiculousness of a minister to the success of a play, from word of a marriage to the publication of a book, from the silhouette of a courtier to the portrait of a famous man, from society to government! For everything was within the span and competence of woman's conversation.[32]

The one noteworthy salon hosted by a male was Baron Paul-Henri-Dietrich Holbach's. With a reputation for atheism, it was said to have had close connections to the *Encyclopédie* and to have bequeathed a dangerous social and political philosophy to the Revolution. But this view has recently been discredited. Only the core group of Holbach's coterie, including Holbach himself, was atheist; and few of the contributors to the *Encyclopédie* came from its ranks. Although many deplored the abuses of the old regime, they also warned against the dangers of popular resistance. As individuals they obtained the privileges of the old regime, and their works were treated with indulgence by censors like Suard, who was actually a member of the coterie.[33]

The key characteristic of these salons was not conspiracy but the promotion of an intellectual sociability similar to that of the academies and lodges. But the salons were less formal and systematic than the academies and appealed more to the imagination and sensibilities. Both salons and lodges were ends in themselves.

The salon life was social, a rejection of Blaise Pascal's austere solitude, which Voltaire had lampooned in his *Letters concerning the English Nation* (1733). Madame du Deffand felt the great enemy of happiness to be boredom (*ennui*), which Parisian society at that time, perhaps always, dreaded. "Solitude," she said, "is to the mind what dryness is to the earth."[34] The love of society, of interaction with other wits, the passion for common intellectual and moral undertakings, were the salient traits of French intellectuals in the "classic" period (1600–1800) and beyond into the nineteenth century. They were at their most intense in the decades preceding the French Revolution.

Though the salons in no sense planned the Revolution, their analytical spirit and freedom from all sense of responsibility allowed the participants to imagine how things might be if circumstances could be altered. In sapping respect for established authorities and diminishing resignation, in bending the will of the administration to favor them, they corrupted the integrity of officialdom; that is, they compromised their loyalty to the regime and helped destroy it from above.[35]

What remained of this Paris after the Revolution? A surprising amount. Cut off from the rest of Europe by the revolutionary wars and the Napoleonic Empire, the city returned to being simply Paris, the capital of France, preeminent among Europe's capitals by virtue of its superior distinction in the arts and sciences. The academies regained their specifically academic status, denied them by the Revolution and the Empire, when in 1816 the Institut royal was formed. Paramount among them, as before the Revolution, was the Académie royale des sciences, which attracted the most distinguished corps of scientists in the world. American scientists and doctors—like Peter Solomon Townsend—repaired to Paris in the Restoration to catch up with the latest medical developments. Besides the academies, a plethora of unofficial learned societies like the Athénée des arts flourished; some survived the Revolution to burgeon as they had in the old regime.[36]

Nothing changed more in the Revolution than schools of every level. After the Revolution the great royal colleges were reestablished, albeit with less autonomy, being under the control of the ubiquitous university. On the primary level, the Frères des écoles chrétiennes and other congregations once again taught city children. But only one-fourth of Paris children aged five to twelve were in school in the late 1820s. The Guizot law of 1833 would expand this instruction greatly, while leaving its content and teachers basically the same as those of the petites écoles of the old regime. As in the ancien régime, such specialized institutions as the Muséum d'histoire naturelle, the Collège royal de France, and the Ecole des ponts et chaussées, along with the Revolution's Ecole polytechnique, gave a technical education to talented students, while the Sorbonne showed more signs of vitality than it had before the Revolution.[37]

The press was greatly expanded by the Revolution to accommodate the promulgation of thousands of laws, decrees, and proclamations, and the book trade contracted correspondingly under this avalanche of ephemera. Napoléon's censorship hurt both the periodical and book trade more than any regime before it, and he bequeathed to the Restoration the Direction générale de la librairie, a reinstatement of censorship. The press of the Restoration flourished in spite of these controls. The Charter of 1814 allowed eighty royal presses and sixty private presses; some fifty clandestine presses flourished simultaneously. Works published included those of the ancien régime philosophes, which escaped censorship provided they were published in multivolume sets so as to be available only to the well-to-do. Over one and a half million volumes of Voltaire and almost half a million volumes of Rousseau were sold. Almost six hundred libraires had licenses, and prints became more available when the lithograph was introduced.[38]

In the old regime numerous royal and monastic establishments (the Bibliothèque du roi, the Bibliothèque Sainte-Geneviève) opened their doors to responsible researchers for a few hours each week. This practice was extended in the Restoration, when some forty institutions granted limited access to their collections. The Louvre, however, had become a public museum. Five royal theaters including the Opéra, Comédie-Française (Odéon), and Théâtre italien took the place of the three privileged theaters of the old regime (following Napoléon's 1807 restriction on theaters); a fourth, the Ambigu comique, had existed before 1789, and the last, the Vaudeville, was the only theatrical creation of the Revolution to survive. Theatergoers, however, continued to frequent the boulevard theaters even though the entertainment was of a "vulgar" and sensational nature. The same dialectic between high and low theater seems to have persisted.[39]

What happened to the old regime salons after 1789? As might be suspected, these institutions underwent an eclipse. The two most famous of the 1790s—Mme Roland's and Mme de Staël's—were highly political. The most famous salon of the Empire was Mme Récamier's, which actually began in the Directory. Her "affected but elegant simplicity" reigned over Parisian social life and protected young talent from the insolence of the great and the pretensions of the parvenus. The spirit of this salon was closer to that of the princesse de Salm (fig. 1.5), another hostess of the Directory, and was quite removed from the wit and coquetry of the old regime. Yet it had some of the

Je pars ... je vais rever, dans
Le poète, l'ami, l'artiste, le savi

1	M.me la P.esse	5	Martini.	10	Prony.	15	Antrieux	20	Ginguer
	de Salm.	6	Mentelle.	11	La Lande.	16	Lemontey	21	M.me
2	M.lle sa fille.	7	Pinkerton.	12	Thurot.	17	Courier.	22	Babete
3	Le Prince.	8	Langlès.	13	Clavier.	18	La Chabeaussire	23	Gudin
4	Vigée.	9	Breguet.	14	Gohier.	19	Lantier.	24	Millin

I.5.
A Soirée at the Salon of the Princesse de Salm, *drawing from* Oeuvres
Complètes de Mme la Princesse Constance de Salm, *4 vols. in 2, Paris, 1842.*
Courtesy Bibliothèque nationale, photo: Bibl. Nat. Paris.

douces soirées,

(1806)

essential qualities of traditional Paris salons: the host was a woman of influence and paramount beauty, regular weekly meetings were held, and conversation was the principal activity.[40]

The Restoration saw the rise of several salons of ancien régime style, most notably those of two court but liberal nobles, General Lafayette and the comte Destutt de Tracy. The guests of these two venerable survivors of the previous century were much the same—individuals of birth without distinction or talent and, more numerous, individuals with talent but without noble birth. In the latter category were Stendhal and Amédée and Augustin Thierry. Liberal opinion bound these people, but the aristocratic hosts set the tone. Eclipsing these institutions, however, were the more utilitarian bourgeois *cercles* where young businessmen could gather, read newspapers and journals, and discuss public affairs (as in the mushrooming *cabinets de lecture*).[41]

Though changes indisputably took place in French society as a result of the Revolution, Karl Marx believed there was nothing so similar to the society of 1830 as that of 1789, and this view has since been confirmed. As David Pinkney has argued, "The old regime lives on [in the 1830s]. . . . The Revolution of 1789 had not produced a new world or even a new France. [It] had left largely unchanged the fundamental aspects of French life—economic activity, social structure, distribution of population, language and communication."[42]

CHAPTER II

THE RHYTHM OF POPULAR CULTURE

The Rural Environment

French rural life has been marked both by structures that span a millennium and by recurring patterns of change. Wheat has been the constant produce of this most arable land of the Continent. The French climate is temperate, its rainfall abundant but not excessive, and there is variety in landscape and methods of cultivation. "Diversity is France," say historians today who prefer to study a region rather than the nation.

The north has flatlands—extensive wheat fields that are rotated triennially. In the Alpine southeast, intensive cultivation is abandoned for extensive grazing of flocks of sheep and goats. Central France, especially since the nineteenth century, has been given to raising beef. The south is another region of wheat and, like the Rhône Valley, Provence, and the area around Bordeaux, of viticulture. The rocky terrain of the west is used for dairy farming. This region enjoys the prosperity of the Atlantic seaboard, whose commerce, dominated by Bordeaux, Nantes, and Le Havre, quadrupled in the eighteenth century. In the interior of the west is the *pays de bocage* (hedged country), comprising Brittany, part of the Loire Valley, the Maine, the Vendée, and the Landes, where separate hamlets rather than the extensive villages of the north were the rule and agrarian individualism was strong. Here, collective rights and communal life were much weaker than in the north. In the south, with its biennial system of crop rotation, the scattering of holdings and the more numerous alodia, or holdings free of seigneurial obligations, meant that communal life was also weaker than in the north. Ecclesiastical landholding, prominent in the west, was minor in Toulousain Languedoc (usually less than 10 percent of the land), possibly reflecting a less devout population that was disinclined to make donations. The trade of Marseilles, the giant seaport of the French Mediterranean, links the Atlantic through the Canal du Midi (completed in 1681), which connects Sette to Bordeaux.

Well over three-quarters of the French in the century of the Enlightenment lived in villages, and if we wish to know how this majority fared during the French Revolution, how it was disposed to receive the new ideas and values that originated in the cities, we must turn first to the rural landscape, to its living conditions and mental life.

Although French rural life was divided into sundry entities, foremost was communal life: the extended family, where it existed, the parish and the village assembly of inhabitants, the common lands, and the fields "open" after the harvest (*vaine pature*).[1] "The church," writes Georges Lefebvre, "was above all the center of collective life." From parish pulpits were read royal decrees, and from among its members was formed the village assembly, endowing the village with a corporate voice. Alexis de Tocqueville in the nineteenth century pointed to a marked diminution of collective life due to monarchical centralization during the Bourbon dynasty, but villages and even a large number of municipalities and provinces continued to act as collectivities, from the open field and the village assembly to provincial estates.[2]

The land itself was divided into forestlands, wastelands (*landes*), cultivated land (*labours*), vineyards (*vignobles*), the seigneur's domain (*demesne*) (which was exempt from the principal royal property tax, the *taille*), and the *manse* (house, auxiliary buildings, and strips of land of the peasant). The villagers exercised collective rights over land that belonged to the seigneur but had escaped his control through conventions sanctioned by contract or usage. Peasants had originally "agreed" to till the lord's land in return for protection, but they thus surrendered most of their freedom and became emancipated only in the thirteenth century. Most of their labor services were then converted into feudal dues in kind and coin for quasi-hereditary rights to use the land. The basic feudal due, the *cens,* governed this arrangement.[3]

The seigneur had greater dominion over forestlands and water than over the arable land. Over the former he exercised exclusive hunting and fishing rights, and game was far more plentiful then than today. Peasants, however, did have the right to graze their flocks in forestlands at specified times and to gather wood. The seigneur could abridge these rights when he cleared a forest or drained a marsh, as could the enclosure acts of the *parlements* in the 1770s and later revolutionary legislation. Such actions were contested and litigated as late as the 1840s. In 1839 in the department of the Var, anywhere from one-third to one-half of all forestlands were still subject to such collective rights as grazing after harvest—a prime example of the *longue durée*. Maps of landowning patterns and road communications show a great continuity from Roman Gaul to medieval and modern divisions. Medieval long strips and open fields were still common in late eighteenth-century France. A map from the 1780s of Spoy in the Côte d'Or clearly depicts a medieval patchwork quilt of open and elongated fields, extended and added to by land clearings.[4]

Two tendencies working at cross-purposes prevailed in French rural history: concentration and morseling of property. On one hand, large estates continued to grow after the Middle Ages, surviving even sales of noble and ecclesiastical property during the Revolution. The Bourbonnais estate that had belonged to the comtes Destutt de Tracy since the fifteenth century lasted through the Revolution to total nine thousand acres in the mid-nineteenth century. Old regime nobles who paid the heaviest land tax often headed the departmental electoral lists of the Empire. The duc de Noailles in Eure-et-Loir and the duc de La Rochefoucauld-Liancourt in the Oise are two examples.

But concomitantly other segments of French rural land were continually being divided by inheritance, because French fiefs, unlike English lands, had become almost regularly hereditary. The revolutionary and Napoleonic inheritance codes legislated equal division among heirs (with some exceptions), and this morseled property to the point where France, unlike its neighbors, had more proprietors in 1884 than in 1780. Even at the end of the ancien régime peasant proprietors outnumbered all others, comprising well over half the total (although a little less than half the land). Middle-sized landholders often suffered encroachments by large and small holders.[5]

French argiculture traditionally followed a system of crop rotation in which one-half or one-third of the sown land lay fallow at any time. The eighteenth century remedied some soil exhaustion with the introduction of such fertilizer crops as clover, alfalfa, and especially corn. In the south farmers gradually abandoned the fallow system, and crop production increased by 50 to 100 percent.[6]

Although great landowners often introduced modernization by enclosures, evictions, the new agronomy, and road-building, at the expense of peasants and their collective rights, rural strife hardly began with modernization. Peasant and seigneurial classes have clashed throughout French history—first, in peasant revolts against seigneurial dues; second, in the seigneurial reactions, reactivating old dues that had sunk into oblivion, increasing fees and services, imposing new ones. When peasant uprisings were not directed against the *fisc,* or royal taxation, as during the administration of Cardinal Richelieu, they were directed against the feudal cens, the *banalités,* or feudal dues. When feudal dues and royal taxation grew heavy, when enclosures or other restrictions of communal rights occurred, peasants revolted. From the Great Peasant Jacquerie of 1358 to the mid-seventeenth century, communal rights and dues were at issue, whereas in the Revolt of the Croquants of 1637 and other revolts of the 1630s, it was royal centralization and taxation. The Great Fear of 1789, a third type of revolt, aimed at destroying the whole seigneurie, which had become intolerable in some regions by the increase of feudal dues, the first of which dated from the late seventeenth century.[7]

But the Great Fear and other uprisings of the Revolution did not erase the original characteristics of rural life. On the contrary, "the mass of peasants," writes Marc Bloch, "even among peasant proprietors, was far more attached to the old ways," particularly when it came to sacrificing communal rights and fallow fields. Peasant rural life epitomized the longue durée. Most peasants knew no scientific agriculture; not only were they ignorant of lime and other chemical fertilizers, they were usually unable to procure animal fertilizers due to the notorious lack of livestock. Several Napoleonic prefects after the Revolution attested to the immobility of peasant life. One of them, the comte de Luçay, wrote of the Cher: "More than elsewhere, the fermier is too removed from the capital and from the large communes, which are the centers of useful knowledge and the means of uprooting abuses. The fermier limits himself to routine and [prefers] his old habits and his prejudices to the improvements of fertile regions where agriculture is a science."[8]

The French have a dictum that Paris is not France. The capital had the greatest concentration of intellectuals, artists, and such cultural institutions as salons, theaters, academies, booksellers, convents, and monasteries. In Paris, people enjoyed the freedom of anonymity, and if they did not agree with the curé, they went elsewhere, to an abbé.[9] Provincial life was, of course, mostly rural. Thirty cities of over twenty thousand persons had academies, but one could easily be two hundred kilometers from the nearest academy, one hundred from the nearest

Vue pittorésque des ci-devant capucins à NANTES

II.1.
Pittoresque View of Former Capucin Convent at Nantes, *engraving,*
ca. 1793. From Joseph Lavallée, Voyage dans les départemens de la
France. . . . la Loire inférieure, *Paris an II [1793 –94].*
Courtesy Harvard College Library.

theater, and fifty from the nearest collège. One senses the emptiness of
much rural provincial life, its abandonment and isolation, by driving
today through small towns. But despite this and the low provincial
literacy rates (one-half those of Paris except in the major towns), rural
culture did exist and has been nostalgically preserved by historians,
painters, and engravers (fig. II.1).

Provincial rural culture was again different from Parisian urban culture. Whereas Parisian culture depended on the equal importance of
the written and the spoken word, in rural culture, the written word was
subordinate to the spoken word. At the well, brook, river (fig. II.2), or
bakery, villagers exchanged gossip. Without the anchor of the written
text, "information" grew in proportion to the fertility of the messenger
or go-between's imagination. Weather was a constant topic of conversation since livelihoods depended on it. Deviants of any kind were not
tolerated but were disciplined by family or young men in charivaris, an
uproarious serenade designed to mock offending females. In Paris censorship and society were at odds; in the village they were intimately
bound. In Paris the conflict between *gens de lettres* and the civil and

II.2.
Joseph Mallard William Turner, Saumur, *engraving of the painting.*
Courtesy Library of Congress, photo: John Reynolds.

ecclesiastical authorities destroyed old values and generated new ones; the repudiation of institutional sanctions led to upheaval and the formation of a new society. By contrast, authority *was* the village, not something erected over and against it, which helps explain the villages' perpetuation of traditions. The village was a matrix of cultural reproduction and stability. Deferential, reverential toward superiors and ancient beliefs, village life was the antithesis of the mocking spirit of Paris. Habit regulated it. Customs were honored even when harmful. Life consisted in repeating the same chores, the same festivals, the same loves, the same hates, the same stories listened to and learned by heart.[10]

Culture in this world consisted of body language, physical skills, knowledge of plants and trees—their seasonal and life patterns, their fruits and poisons. Culture meant knowing by heart every nook and cranny, every major rock, every gully, every copse and rivulet of a score of square kilometers.[11] It meant close encounters with cold, hunger, and death. If the peasant was defiant, he was defiant of nature, which he had continually to overcome both psychologically and physically. Where the urban dweller might be a bold or hardened spirit (*un esprit hardi* or *fort*) who could look death in the face without flinching, he might, according to Rousseau, also be physically effete. Not so the peasant, who, if rarely daring to question the existence of the other world, could endure physical hardships insupportable to a privileged Parisian. Whereas the philosophe had intellectual audacity, the peasant remembered that he was dust and unto dust he would return.

Paradoxically, both Jules Michelet, who argued that the Revolution was born of misery, and Tocqueville, who argued that peasants in France were better off than elsewhere, were right. The lot of rural proletariats was misery while many fortunate peasants were either increasing their landed holdings or profiting from leaseholds. The *coqs de village,* the *gros laboureurs,* were well off and could be considered rural bourgeois.[12]

Despite a modest material existence, a grinding routine, frequent subjection to injustice, a suspicion of strangers, and greed, the peasant seems to have led a fairly happy existence. Peasants were fatalistic rather than pessimistic or spiteful—looking to the stars and to the supernatural to explain good and evil. Providence, for them, overruled other forces.

The critical element in happiness is probably not what one has but whether one is content with what one has, however great or small. Contentment is often disassociated from any material criterion but linked to the level of expectations. The greater these are, the harder they are to satisfy. The *cahiers généraux* of 1789, in which peasants and other sectors of French society stated their grievances to the king and Estates General, may have aroused a certain *sense* of grievance unacknowledged earlier, when resignation before the inexorable was more common. But more on this later.

The Body and Its Illnesses

The medicine of the academies and the cities hardly penetrated the countryside, which was cared for by a widespread network of empirics, midwives (*sages-femmes*), quacks, and even an occasional sorcerer. This medicine of le peuple highlights the rule of routine and resignation. The Comité de salubrité of the Constituent Assembly in 1790 conducted a survey of country medicine, and 60 percent of the respondents claimed that charlatans were more widespread than doctors in their locales. One observer from Josselin, Brittany, said that there was only one doctor in the district and then quickly corrected himself: "I am wrong, everyone is; there is not a person of one or the other sex who does not interfere by giving his advice to the sick." At Narbonne, carpenters bandaged and bled, and a stonemason acted as dentist. At Bray-sur-Seine, "grocers" sold medicine and "surgeons" treated hernias by castration.[13]

A study of the treatment of rabies in the 1780s by the Royal Society of Medicine is revealing. Cures were rare, victims commonly resisted doctors' treatment. A five-year-old refused to cooperate with his doctor until he was too weak to resist. A woman treated at Senlis for a bite insisted that her problem was asthma; she felt that salivating helped her. When she suspected the nature of her illness, she asked to be put into a cage without air or daylight and said that her eyes and mouth were mounted backwards. Some of these fantasies were symptoms of the disease, rather than attitudes toward medicine, but an underlying distrust of the doctor is detectable. Visitors told one patient that the doctors had suffocated other victims between mattresses.[14]

In spite of occasional cures, the medical situation of most French people remained largely the same before and after the Revolution. Most people, especially rural folk, were reluctant to call a doctor. In 1857, Dr. Dunoyer of Dieu, in the Meuse, complained: "They call the doctor as late as possible, and often too late." Most patients also felt that fees were too high; cartoonists lampooned medical avarice.[15]

All sorts of interlopers—bonesetters, hypnotists, drug sellers, healers, midwives, clergy—intervened, for treatment by doctors was still often ineffective. Until the late nineteenth century, when hygiene improved markedly, cures consisted of herbal treatments, crude surgery, and potions sold by pharmacists without prescriptions. When empirics were fined and pursued for quackery they became even more popular, because popular medicine was part of popular culture; it defied the rational order of the bourgeois notables, the academies, and the universities. As late as 1953, a study showed charlatanry to be still widespread in the country. People chose to treat themselves with familiar and affordable cures. The savants and elites had supported Edward Jenner's smallpox vaccination, but peasants and workers, according to one doctor, "said that it was a poison." Only by publicly vaccinating prominent subjects in the west to demonstrate that no ill befell them could Dr. Leon Guyon persuade peasants to accept inoculation. Indeed, a study of the progress of inoculation from the Directory to the Third Republic would be as good an index as any of the resistance to modern medicine.[16]

In the Enlightenment, medicine was often pitted against religion or called the religion of humanity, doctors being its priests. But in the century after the Revolution, the French resorted more than ever to the intervention of such saints as Rémy and to the Blessed Virgin for miraculous cures. After the appearance of the Virgin at Lourdes in 1858, pilgrims visited the shrine in ever increasing numbers. Today at Lourdes, atheist doctors sit on a board to testify to medically inexplicable cures, and religion and science are seen as complementary. But only a century earlier, shrines often substituted for medicine.[17]

Throughout the nineteenth century and beyond, the sick sought folk medicine and miraculous cures for their ills. The unbelief of many doctors, which contributed to the distance between the caretakers of the spiritual and those of the body, may have exacerbated the situation. During the breach, countryfolk took care of themselves with customary means and less unhappily than had they been in the hands of doctors.[18]

Popular Literacy

It is common to exaggerate the degree of illiteracy of the French population on the eve of the Revolution. But few historians of France today believe that the Enlightenment, which the Revolution made its own, affected many more than the elites of old regime society—clergy, nobles, army officers, officeholders, and rentiers—in Paris, in the southeast, and in the Rhône Valley. Workers and peasants could not afford even the cheapest edition of the *Encyclopédie,* let alone read it. The closest they could come to the new philosophy was through conversation and hearsay.[19]

How are literacy rates for the early modern period acquired and how reliable are they? In the old regime, couples were asked to sign their marriage contracts before a notary, and the instances of these signatures as well as the failures to sign form the raw data from which literacy statistics are derived. In the 1880s a rector of an academy in Lorraine named Louis Maggiolo undertook a vast count of marriage signatures throughout France for the periods 1688–89, 1788–89, and 1814–15. These figures, compiled by schoolteachers working under Maggiolo's direction, were recently verified, rectified, expanded, and interpreted. The conclusion is that France was roughly 21 percent literate in 1686–90 during the reign of Louis XIV and 37 percent literate in 1786–90 on the eve of the Revolution. In 1830–31, another survey made by Charles Dupin and Count Adolphe d'Angeville indicated that slightly fewer than half of military service conscripts were illiterate, so literacy seems to have grown slowly but steadily following the old regime. It can be included in discussing cultural structures, although, like the concentration and division of property, it changes slowly over time.[20]

According to the studies of François Furet, Jacques Ozouf, and their colleagues, the literacy rates reflect the efforts of two centuries of Reformation and Counter-Reformation schooling. The battle for souls was also a battle for minds, for to love God one must know Him. Growth in literacy was a major consequence, although not the intended one, of evangelization, because reading was a means to faith. The eruptions of Protestantism after 1530 and of the Catholic Reformation in the seventeenth century formed the principal stimuli for catechizing the rural population, which was taught to read psalters, books of hours, catechisms, and the Bible. The Enlightenment, by contrast, had a negligible effect on popular literacy.[21]

National literacy figures, however, conceal temporal accelerations and tremendous regional variations. The "Maggiolo literacy line of Saint-Malo to Geneva" is a separation of a highly literate northern France, where male rates attained 80 percent in 1686–90, versus a southwest where male rates did not surpass 29 percent. This discrepancy persisted beyond the eighteenth century. Although the south diminished the north's lead during the Revolution, the west and southwest were hedged terrain (*bocage*) which resulted in bad communication and hence in inferior schooling and reduced literacy. In areas in which Protestantism and Catholicism conflicted or competed, the net effect on literacy was positive. This seems particularly true of Alsace, an area with large Lutheran, Jewish, and Catholic populations.

Besides regional contrast there are always the tremendous differences between male and female literacy. In 1688–89 female literacy was one-half (14 percent) of male literacy nationwide, and in 1786–89, more than half (26.8 percent versus 47.4 percent), after a century in which female growth in literacy exceeded male growth (fig. II.3). The wife in the earlier period often declined to sign her contract because she did not want to embarrass her illiterate husband. This negative attitude toward female literacy suggests why female rates were so low or were revealed so unwillingly. Molière's *Les Précieuses ridicules* (1659) satirizes pretentious female learning among the elites, and such intolerance was undoubtedly stronger among peasants.[22]

In Brittany at the end of the old regime, such a small proportion of the population had marriage contracts (fig. II.4) that the sample on which literacy rates are based may be insufficiently representative.

II.3.
[Pierre-Alexandre] Wille, Old Woman Reading, *engraving.*
Courtesy Library of Congress, photo: John Reynolds.

"Literacy," moreover, may denote many levels of skill. A Breton scholar who studied Rouennais signatures discovered a hierarchy: a simple scrawl indicated unfamiliarity with writing, and hence with reading, a more practiced signature, a greater literacy. But there is always the suspicion that the ability to sign may precede the ability to read.[23]

II.4.

The Norman Fiancée, *engraving from painting by Le Nain Brothers (Antoine, Louis, and Mathieu).*

Courtesy Library of Congress, photo: John Reynolds.

Although Maggiolo statistics refer only to rural France, comparisons can be made with urban artisans and domestics. One historian of Paris has written: "While Louis XIV reigned, 61 percent of the salaried workers signed the inventory after death of their wives but only 34 percent of women [signed that] of their husbands. . . . At the time of Louis XVI the cultural cleavage was diminished considerably to 66 percent for men and 62 percent for women." Even in the popular faubourg Saint-Marcel, the literacy rate was approximately 68 percent on the eve of the Revolution. Cities as a whole were far more literate than the countryside, Toulouse and Marseilles enjoyed rates above 50 percent, and Lyons, a publishing center, had a literacy rate of 60 percent (fig. II.5). As early as 1700, domestic servants had a literacy rate of 85 percent in Paris.[24]

If we assume what the literacy experts maintain, then what did French people of the popular classes read? Apparently, much of what has been considered strictly peasant reading in the eighteenth century

II.5.
[Pierre-Alexandre] Wille, The School Mistress, *engraving.*
Courtesy Library of Congress, photo: John Reynolds.

was actually hawked first in cities in the seventeenth century. The chapbooks, *livres bleus* (called blue books because of the color of their pages), manuals, and almanacs were not read exclusively by the peasants. The difference may have been that the popular classes read them exclusively, whereas the educated only incidentally.[25]

Reading materials distributed first in the cities were usually not books but passing literature: *images volantes, feuilles volantes,* and *canards.* Reli-

II.6.

Maxims and Prayer about the Poor and Hidden Life of [Blessed]
B[enedict] J. Labre, *engraving.*

Courtesy Bibliothèque nationale, photo: Bibl. Nat. Paris.

II.7.
Jean-Baptiste Greuze, Widow and Her Curé, *engraving from the painting.*
Courtesy Library of Congress.

gious images during the Catholic Reformation—the saint of a given confraternity, for example—were common. Book reading was rare among both the popular urban and rural peoples in the seventeenth century. The author of peasant origin Rétif de la Bretonne, in his *Vie de mon père* (1778), described his father reading aloud in the evening to the family. But the practice may not have been typical, since Rétif's family was originally Protestant and later Jansenist. Reading aloud was not practiced as regularly as the nineteenth century claimed.[26]

According to a recent work, a mass popular culture—the accomplishment of the savant or leisured class—had been created by the eighteenth century. The *Bibliothèque bleue* borrowed from elite culture, classical mythology, and medieval romances, which it adapted for mass consumption (figs. II.6, II.7). These romances, lives of saints, and fairy stories reinforced the legitimacy of the prevailing order and provided escape from the world of hardship. As such, they have been seen as instruments of elite domination and acculturation.[27]

A slightly different, but classic, account, by Robert Mandrou, sees the stories of the *Bibliothèque bleue* as escapist; they reflect not the harsh realities of peasant life but the make-believe world of adventure and happy endings or the world of salvation beyond the grave.[28] And a third account, by Robert Darnton, of peasant fairy stories, based largely on a widespread version of "Little Red Riding Hood," concludes: "The peasants of early modern France inhabited a world of step-mothers and orphans, of inexorable, unending toil, and of brutal emotions, both raw and repressed"; "French folktales demonstrate that the world is harsh and dangerous."[29] The folktales were filled with harsh and dangerous elements, but they were offset by magical happy endings—fairy godmothers, princes, and princesses. The horror of travel, the meanness of stepmothers were always overruled by the story's marvelous resolution. Every story had windfalls of riches, castles, and charms. The good fairies won over the evil ones. Morality always prevailed because "at that time there was no breaking of promises."[30]

Of the 450 titles that comprise the *Bibliothèque bleue,* some 50 were pagan fairy tales of this sort. An additional 80 books were almanacs, calendars, and popular science works, books of astrology and the occult, know-how books, and kitchen recipes. Eighty more were tales and burlesque farces. Some 50 books described society and gave advice on various professions or apprenticeships. Forty titles were devoted to the history of France—chivalric stories about Charlemagne, Roland, Oger the Dane, and Ganelon the Traitor. About 120 of the 450 were religious works, the largest single category, more than a quarter of the entire corpus. None of this dealt with the world as it was. The religious books taught the peasant how the world should be and how it would be if he or she acted according to Christ's precepts. The fairy stories offered the reader the illusory consolation of magic.[31]

It would be unfair to stigmatize the old regime peasants for reading escapist literature. Much, if not most, of the reading of the privileged orders and bourgeoisie was similar—almanacs, fairy stories, chivalric tales, pastorals, novels. Culture recreates the world according to an ideal, and this holds as much for realistic literature, which must select the most telling details from experience, as it does for fantasy. Literature and the arts must not only give meaning to life by extracting the ideal from the real but give release from the monotony of daily experience. A strictly utilitarian literature that dwelt on the mundane afflictions of everyday life would stifle the imagination.

The irony is that much popular literature *was* practical. Devotional works gave moral precepts that helped in daily living, fostered love of God, the saints, and superior beings, and promised a future happiness.

Judging the "utility" of this depends on faith. Plenty of rational Europeans from antiquity to the present have staked their lives on its reality.

The *Vie de mon père* of Rétif de la Bretonne illustrates how this devotional literature could be used in practical experience. The village schoolmaster preaches gently to his pupils before they go on vacation: "We are all brothers in the parish; we should all watch over the goods of each other. . . . when you have taken your animals to the fields, carry the abridgement of the great Bible you see here, and if you gather together read a few chapters from it."[32]

Beyond devotional literature, many books dealt with the practical matters of the various rural trades and occupations. Popular literature was often humorous. Juxtaposed against popular pious literature was the ribald and profane literature—burlesques of religious life, stories in argot of inconstant wives, cuckolded husbands, and lusty millers. A worldly philosophy of carpe diem or alternatively *tout passe, tout lasse* is expressed here in earthy Gaulois, quite foreign to the civilized refinement of the Parisian beau monde (figs. II.8, II.9).[33]

French laborers of the fields vented their frustrations and aspirations in songs probably more than in reading. Some 160 songs set to 130 tunes are found in the *Bibliothèque bleue,* and they deal with everything from war and politics to drinking and making love (these last two comprise 85 percent of the corpus). It has been said that without songs, the French would have made the French Revolution far earlier. From the *mazarinades,* or satirical pamphlets of the Fronde, to the carmagnole, peasants, poissardes, and bourgeois expressed themselves freely in prose, verse, and melody in a way they could never have done in pamphlets.[34]

By far the most used book in both popular and elite milieux was the almanac, the oldest known example of which was *Le Compost et kalendrier des bergers* (1493). A recent inventory lists some two hundred almanacs for the seventeenth century.[35] Two widely diffused almanacs in the eighteenth century were *Le Véritable Messager boiteux de Berne* and the *Almanach de Mathieu Lauensbergh.* These little volumes, miserably typeset on coarse, wrinkled paper, were sold, like the *Bibliothèque bleue* of which they formed a part, by peddlers at fairs and markets and even door to door in villages. The calendars of these almanacs could be used year after year. A typical edition consisted of a calendar proper, each day assigned to a saint according to norms of the church, and listed the phases of the moon, the beginnings of each season, and the signs of the zodiac, which were once attentively respected by the elite as well

II.8.
Jean-Honoré Fragonard, The Prearranged Flight, *painting, ca. 1770.*
Courtesy Harvard University Art Museums (Fogg Art Museum), Phyllis H. Dunlap bequest.

as by the peasants. By the early eighteenth century, *galant,* mundane, and administrative almanacs dropped the signs of the zodiac but kept the saints' days on the calendar. When the Terror came the saints were removed from most almanacs, but they gradually reappeared during the Directory and the Napoleonic era. This liturgical calendar marked the movable and immovable feasts, including Easter, Ascension Thursday, Pentecost, Trinity Sunday, Corpus Christi, the Assumption, All

II.9.
Jean-Baptiste Greuze, The Milkmaid, *painting.*
Courtesy Musée du Louvre, photo: Musées nationaux, Paris.

Saints' Day, and Christmas, as well as individual saints' days. Today most of these are observed as church and national holidays.[36]

The almanac is a product, almost a symbol, of the culture of longue durée, anchored as it is in the regular repetition of annual, seasonal, mensual, and diurnal cycles. Even the biblical chronology of the creation of the world, rejected by Enlightenment thinkers, could be found after the Revolution in some almanacs. According to the *Astrologue universel, ou Le Grand Mathieu Lauensberg* of 1837, Creation occurred in 5837 B.C. and the Deluge in 4181 B.C.

Almanacs were nature books as well. *Le Véritable Almanach de maitre Mathieu Lauensberg, mathematicien* of 1789 specifies for June: "Replant during this month cranberry trees, scallions, leeks, autumnal onions, turnips, cabbage, cauliflower, endives. In this month you pick grains, cress, chervil, pimpernel, rocket, spinach, borage, peas." This monotonous cycle is broken only by a section dedicated to "Faits extraordinaires," which provides escape from the boredom of the ordinary. *Le Véritable Messager boiteux de Berne* of 1783 includes a "continuation of the curious narration of the most remarkable things," such as the British capitulation at Yorktown, Joseph II's Edict of Toleration, the size of the European armies, an exceptional cold spell in St. Petersburg, earthquakes, and spontaneous tomb openings in Bas-Provence! Marvels were not necessarily horrors. The *Almanach historique nommé le messager boiteux* (1783) of Vievey could register amazement at the liberty of Tahitians, recently made popular by Bougainville's voyage there in the 1760s. Traditional marvels are interspersed with those of the Enlightenment. The extraordinary and the exotic momentarily checked the tyranny of the quotidian. Perhaps the ultimate release from boredom was a prediction of "the end of the world," not in Mathieu Lauensberg's almanac, as one might have expected, but in the *Nouvel Astrologue parisien* of 1820.

The Revolution did not significantly interrupt these routine entries. In the middle of the Terror, the old calendar of saints could be found, sometimes opposite the new revolutionary calendar. In 1794 Louis XVI was still seen as a good man by the *Ephémérides,* and *Le Véritable Messager boiteux de Neuchâtel* lists all the sovereigns of Europe and the princes of France (whom the Convention condemned to death or exile). The Enlightenment—decrees of toleration, useful inventions, overseas discoveries—was more easily assimilated by the popular almanac than the Revolution.

The almanacs bridged timelessness to timeliness. Their predecessor was the book of hours,[37] where heavenly prayer and earthly work were linked and beautifully illuminated. The almanac gave stability to the enormous bustle of this century of population growth, of new roads and houses and crops, of land-clearing, and of political upheaval. Unlike the philosophical novel, there was nothing controversial, nothing objectionable about these little books. The almanac was universal, anodyne, and benevolent, with the exception of its occasional racial xenophobia (against Jews, for instance). Anyone who could would read an almanac.

Statistics of sizes of editions of almanacs from 1810 reveal printings of anywhere from 500 to 60,000 copies, whereas works of literature or legislation and history ranged from 100 to 3,000 copies. Nine almanacs of the Nord (including administrative almanacs) in 1813 totaled 128,200 copies or an average of over 14,000 copies per edition, whereas twelve works of literature (again mostly fairy stories) totaled 36,500 or an average of a little over 3,000 copies. Light literature that mixed fantasy with utility predominated.[38]

To return to one of our original questions concerning literacy: Did it subvert the order that fostered it—for example, the church—or did it act as a break against radicalism? What peasants read would, it seems, have reinforced traditional values and in no way favored revolution. The Enlightenment's influence can be detected, but it is artfully woven into the threads of tradition. Reading did not foster critical thinking in rural France and may not have even in the cities. The *Bibliothèque bleue* represents what the family of Nicolas Oudot of Troyes and other publishers of popular books thought the rural folk ought to read and what they would buy. Since we know they were sold widely, we can say that *in some measure* they reflected popular culture.[39]

Festivals

Relief from the tedium of planting and harvesting could be better found in brilliant festivals than in reading.[40] In addition to Sundays, forty or fifty days a year, depending on the time and place, were feast days honoring the saints or the lives of Christ and the Virgin. But popular festivals must be measured against the refinements of elite society. The cultivated eighteenth-century gentleman moderated his life. The minuet, the swing, the coquetry of the boudoir, and the salon emphasized grace and frivolity, lightness over gravity, respectability over boorishness. The wig, the bodice, and the *culotte* all defined its politeness. Elite excess was confined primarily to ideas or private actions, like the lavish extravagance of a Saulx Tavannes or a Mirabeau. The century has been called the age of scandal as well as the age of reason.

At the height of the old regime, such ceremonies as those of the Fête Dieu or the Vœux du Roi were solemn processions of the dignitaries of the different orders and were models of "civilization" and order. Robert Darnton has reconstructed one as described by a bourgeois of Montpellier in 1768:

> A *procession générale* provided an impressive display of sound, color, and texture. Trumpets pealed; horses' hoofs clattered over the cobblestones; a throng of dignitaries tramped by, some in boots, some in sandals, some under plumes and some in sackcloth. Different shades of red and blue stood out against the lace and fur trim of the magistrates and contrasted with the dull blacks and browns of the monks. Great sweeps of satin, silk, and damask filled the streets—a vast stream of robes and uniforms bobbing up here and there and the flames of candles dancing all along its course.[41]

Each shade of color, each choice of material was made according to code and signified social rank. The ceremony was a living symbol of the highly articulated, hierarchical society of the old regime and of the order it sought to instill. It succeeded better in the top echelons of society than it did among the third estate, who were the principal participants in the popular festivals.[42]

The peasants were given to exuberance and exaggeration. In the towns where they flocked for Carnival, grotesquerie held full sway incongruously in the geometrical town squares, *jardins des plantes,* and *hôtels de ville.* But it must be noted that the Carnival, at least originally, embraced the whole population; and peasants and artisans were far from alone in behaving in wild fashion. In February came this wildest celebration of the year, when all restraint vanished. People gorged themselves with rich foods they normally could not afford, drank until they were intoxicated, accosted women whom they could not normally approach, and cavorted through the streets wearing animal masks or impersonating someone from the upper orders such as a bishop or a king.

Corpus Christi in June was the occasion of the huge Fête Dieu celebration, when the Blessed Sacrament was carried through the streets in a procession. The summer solstice coincided with the Feast of Saint John, when fires were lit up throughout the countryside and animals or straw mannequins were carried through the streets or burned. Later in the summer came the Feast of the Assumption of the Virgin and in autumn, various festivals of harvest (*moissons et vendanges*) that ended the solar year.[43]

The ritual of festivals was permanent and repetitious enough to form part of the perennial structure of culture. But ritual also meant that the celebration was raised above the level of instinct to that of symbol. Many popular festivals exhibited a degree of contrivance that could be characterized as sublimation, as seen in the archaeologue Aubin-Louis Millin's description of Christmas in Provence in 1808. During the winter solstices, the *fête des fous* or *calendes* was celebrated, and Christmas was feted with lighted candles and *bûches de Noël*—an actual log (which was burned), rather than today's log-shaped chocolate cake:

> Several days before, the food shops display all the luxury of epicurism [*friandise*]; the quais are encumbered with fruits. . . . People buy grapes in pretty pots to decorate the table for a joyous banquet. . . . They give the children laurel branches on which are hung new fruits . . . ; they give them little crêches equipped with mirrors and more or less decorated, filled with toys, among which are plaster figures of animals and of all personages that attended the birth of the Savior; they add figures of priests, popes, bishops, and saints; among the animals they place cotton or cardboard storks with a long beak of red wool. Where does this latter custom come from? Probably the Marseillais conserved this ancient symbol of filial piety, without dreaming that they received it from the Romans.[44]

Festivals meant the formalization of leisure, the ritualization of instincts, the perpetuation of ancient customs. They were not simply the notorious wild play of Carnival but an elaborate symbolic ritual. Contemporary society, by contrast, has sacrificed ritual for immediacy. Festivals constitute an important part of culture precisely because they transmit customs and beliefs in symbolic form from one generation to the next.

The Fête Dieu originated in the fourteenth century to honor the Blessed Sacrament. At the end of May 1793, when some sansculottes were expelling the Girondin moderates from the Convention, the Fête Dieu was still being celebrated all over France—almost as if the Revolution had not occurred. A municipal police *commissaire* from the section Quinze-Vingts in Paris wrote of the parish Saint-Antoine: "We found a very large crowd of citizens and citizenesses who demanded with loud shouts that the procession of the Fête Dieu take place as it had in the past." The procession took place, as had midnight Masses six months earlier when Louis XVI was being tried by the Convention.[45]

The revolutionary prohibition of popular festivals followed the earlier parliamentary prohibitions of the youth festivals in the 1780s, which themselves followed ecclesiastical restrictions of the Counter-Reformation against rowdy and drunken behavior during festivals (fig. II.10). The war to civilize and repress uncouth spontaneity did not stop with the Revolution. During the Empire the minister of Cults strove to limit popular holy days. The prefect of the Eure, like many other prefects and ecclesiastics, wrote to him on 9 April 1802: "The working men, annually salaried, see with pleasure [in a feast day] an extra day of rest to the detriment of the proprietor or the fermier."[46] The festivals were obstacles to the work regime of industrial society.

The Revolution was more of an interruption in the cycle (the Fêtes Dieu *were* suppressed during the Terror) than an obliteration of popular festivals. The Revolution's attempt to moralize forms of diversion gave way to the more traditional and spontaneous Bacchic festival, which reappeared explosively between 1801 and 1803 and lasted beyond mid-century. In 1832 in Paris, Carnival was celebrated after an outbreak of cholera with 182 public balls and 874 private balls. The same themes of egalitarianism that had leveled the old social distinctions reappeared. Poissarde language was again used as a "provisional triumph of a low language opposed to politeness." The Revolution had altered rather than abolished the old hierarchy. Carnival could survive because the conditions that caused it had largely survived.[47]

The most impressive characteristics of popular culture are its vitality and richness. Although in France at this time popular culture was distinct from elite urban culture, it was not entirely so; the two shared reading materials and festivities. Popular rural culture was not wholly illiterate, and the beliefs and emotions of peasants overlapped those of city inhabitants. Above all, rural culture was marked by routine and repetition into which was inserted the wonderful and extraordinary in the form of fairy stories, faits extraordinaires, and festivals. In reading aloud, collective pasturing, and Sunday festivals, peasants forged common ties. Although wounded by the Revolution, this popular culture survived until the third quarter of the nineteenth century, when the railroad and industrialization removed villages and hamlets from isolation. And it was strong enough in the first decade of the twentieth

II.10.
Louis-Léopold Boilly, Cabaret Scene, *painting.*
Courtesy Musée du Louvre, photo: Lauros-Giraudon.

century to provide the material from which French ethnographer and
folklorist Arnold van Gennep compiled his famous *Manuel de folklore
français contemporain*. But before this awakening of elite interest in
popular culture took place, the Enlightenment drove a wedge between
high and low culture.

PART II

ENLIGHTENMENT

AND

SENSIBILITY

INTRODUCTION

The French Enlightenment, nourished by seventeenth-century English thought, was a powerful, polemical movement that provoked "a crisis of consciousness" among the elites, many of whom ceased to believe in a divinely revealed religion. As early as 1695–97 Pierre Bayle published his *Philosophical Dictionary,* in which he said that the antiquity of a belief was no guarantee of its truth. Once that dictum was accepted, as it was by the *Encyclopédie* of Diderot and Jean Le Rond d'Alembert in the 1750s, nothing escaped critical examination. Opening the parenthesis that René Descartes had placed around politics and religion,[1] the Enlightenment released a welter of pent-up feelings and thoughts about Counter-Reformation Catholicism and divine-right absolutism that had just reached their apogee.

The movement was as complex as the regime it attacked. Voltaire (see fig. III.2) admired Louis XIV and supported an enlightened despotism yet detested the *infame*—that is, the church; Rousseau attacked contemporary European civilization yet detested the philosophe Holbach and his "clique" for their atheism. There is no one Enlightenment philosophy, but there is at least one common supposition: Reason is man's supreme faculty. Nothing must be admitted that surpasses it, not even that "knowledge of things unseen," which Paul considered the essence of faith. Although it was not greatly unified, the Enlightenment corroded the old regime by questioning the authority on which it rested.

The Enlightenment was neither so short as an event nor so durable as a permanent structure but rather something in between, which we call *conjoncture.* It spanned several generations, from that of Spinoza and Bayle around 1680 to the *Idéologues* after the Revolution. It began with the disappearance of witch trials, with Sir Isaac Newton's *Principia*

Mathematica (1687) and John Locke's *Essay concerning Human Under-standing* (1690), when comets were no longer considered portents, when the literal interpretation of the Bible was questioned, when compassion more than glory was esteemed in a monarch. The Enlightenment did not end with the Revolution but was given a last lease on life by the establishment of the Class of Moral and Political Sciences in the National Institute in 1796. The movement there known as *Idéologie* featured P.-J.-G. Cabanis, Destutt de Tracy, and the comte Chasseboeuf de Volney who tried to map out a "science of man," continuing Condorcet's and Laplace's efforts before 1789.

The Enlightenment eventually divided the elite from the people when the former scornfully withdrew from Christian worship and festivities, which had traditionally bound upper and lower classes. The elites disengaged from the people, whom they regarded with new disdain, a disdain the Jacobins never really shed. Indeed, education to the philosophes meant not to raise people above their given state in life but to enable them to perform their given duties more competently.

One movement that did try to mediate between elites and the people was Enlightened Christianity and what could be called the Christian democracy of the abbé Grégoire during the Revolution. Grégoire, a Jansenist priest from Lorraine, enthusiastically supported reform of the Constituent Assembly and the Convention (toleration of Jews, abolition of slavery, diffusion of the French language among non-French-speaking peasants). Indeed, Grégoire can be considered not only a link between the Enlightenment and Christianity but a link between ancien régime paternalism and revolutionary democracy. This spirit of mediation was strongest in the early stages of the Revolution, when Catholicism was still the state religion. During the Terror uncompromising individuals from both sides took charge, separating the rhetoric of reason from that of "fanaticism."

The thinkers of the Enlightenment sought to find for human and social behavior simple laws corresponding to Newton's great discovery in astronomy. Mathematics held promise even for phenomena so variable as election results and population estimates (Condorcet and Laplace). In chapter 4 we look first at the prerevolutionary origins of the metric system—that code that would reduce the confusion of old regime standards of weights and measures to a universal standard. Then we look at what could be considered parallel efforts in the search for elementary geometrical forms in architecture (Boullée), the fundamental traits of character in sculpture (Houdon), and pictorial simplicity using light, shade, and geometry in neoclassical painting

(David). The parallel should not be exaggerated, but the escape from the contortions of the Baroque and the frivolousness of the rococo was certainly as much a search for the natural and the true as was Newton's quest for the law of universal gravitation. Different but contemporaneous as part of the middle-term conjoncture is the quest for the true and the natural (*le vrai et le naturel*) in sentiment as opposed to reason, which we examine in chapter 5. The French Revolution derived as much from the cult of tears (Michel-Jean Sedaine and Marsollier des Vivétières), of nostalgia (Hubert Robert and Jacques-Henri Bernardin de Saint-Pierre), of terror (Edmund Burke), of horror (Horace Walpole and Ducray-Duminil), and ultimately from the cruel sexuality in pornographic literature (the marquis d'Argens and the marquis de Sade).

CHAPTER III

ENLIGHTENMENT

AND CHRISTIANITY

What does the Enlightenment have to do with the French Revolution? Traditionally, historians have ended their account of the Enlightenment with the death of the most important philosophes a decade or so before 1789. More recently, scholars have rediscovered a generation of latter-day philosophes who flourished during the Directory, the Consulate, and the Empire and whose influence can be traced into the July Monarchy. Whether one counts these Idéologues as the Enlightenment's true heirs who bridged eighteenth-century philosophie and nineteenth-century positivism, continuities with the philosophes are evident. A sensationalist psychology, which wanted to be empirical, a skepticism in religion, which wanted secularity in public education, a morality based on reason, a quest for the biological sources of human behavior or the geographical influences to which it is subject—all these were espoused and investigated by the Idéologues. Destutt de Tracy (1754–1836), Cabanis (1757–1802), and Volney (1757–1820) (fig. III.1) continued the materialist rather than the deist tradition of the Enlightenment, disengaging natural law from the clockmaker and the sensing self from the spiritual soul.

Religion

In general, the Idéologues rarely spoke of religion. If we turn to Volney's *Natural Law, or Catechism of the French Citizen* (1793)

III.1.
The Comte de Volney, *engraving.*
Photo: Lauros-Giraudon/Art Resource, New York.

we are urged to forget positive religion, the source of all strife, and live in the peace of natural law instead. Death for Volney was an eternal sleep, and morality consisted of a rational calculation of interest. Natural law was no longer that of seventeenth-century Protestant and Catholic jurists, who saw in it a moral law, knowable by reason, but rather a law of nature, a law of self-preservation. Called a counter-catechism, Volney's message matches his preference of a kind of hard-nosed sanity to the religious transports of Rousseau.[1]

Destutt de Tracy summarized Charles Dupuis's *Origine de tous les cultes* in 1804, making his most explicit statement on religion. Destutt asserted that both he and Dupuis claimed

> with great assurance that nothing is known and nothing can be known [as to whether] the first cause of the universe be blind or intelligent. . . . But we also consider it certain that, if it is blind, all prayer is without purpose, if it is intelligent, all worship is unworthy and insults it. In either case any man who speaks in its name is an impostor or a visionary; and that finally the only means of pleasing it if it is in this world, is to be just and good, that is to say, reasonable . . . and foremost, by not bending one's reason beneath the yoke of the most obvious absurdities.[2]

Rousseau (see fig. v.2), however, spoke more for the eighteenth century on religion than Voltaire (fig. III.2), David Hume, or the materialists—Julien La Mettrie, Holbach, Claude-Adrien Helvétius—and the Idéologues—Tracy and Cabanis. The standard of nature looms forth in full vigor in Rousseau's "Profession of Faith of a Savoyard Vicar": "You will see in my exposé only the natural religion: it is very strange that one should need another." Rousseau's God is not Pascal's God, hidden behind the riddles of history. "The best of all religions," Rousseau contends, "is infallibly the clearest, the religion which rids itself of mysteries and contradictions." This one religion "open to all eyes, is that of nature . . . which talks to all men a language intelligible to all minds." Although Rousseau supplied an emotional religiosity lacking in most of the philosophes and Idéologues, his "faith" was still a matter of common sense, an imperative of reason.[3]

Rousseauism of the Revolution ended up with a God-Creator, the guarantor of human rationality, morality, and the universe. Humans are creatures endowed with spiritual souls, born to serve their fellow creatures by practicing such human virtues as courage, friendship, study, work, and equality of rights. There are rewards and punishments after death, there is immortality. But this ethic has no transcendent dimension: man is born to do good on earth, virtue being its own reward. This is the deism passed on to the Jacobins of Year II, and in particular to Robespierre.

III.2.
Jean-Antoine Houdon, Voltaire, *marble bust, 1778.*
Courtesy collections of the Comédie-Française, Paris.

Nature

A firm conviction in the uniformity of the laws of nature distinguished Enlightenment thinking from both the medieval and the twentieth-century world. Newton's law of universal gravitation explained the planetary system by the mutual attraction of all matter, although Newton considered God to be *virtually* and *substantially* omnipresent, "to discourse of whom from the appearance of things, does certainly belong to natural philosophy."[4]

From the last decades of the Enlightenment through the Restoration, the great continuator of Newton was Marquis Pierre-Simon de Laplace (1749–1827). Destined by his father to become an ecclesiastic, Laplace switched early in his studies at Caen to mathematics. His first work was on calculus, on games of chance and probability, on the regularity of the universe, based on the laws of gravitation and attraction.[5]

The chapter entitled "Considerations on the System of the World, and on the Future Progress of Astronomy" in Laplace's *Exposition of the System of the World* (1796) is a departure from Buffon's speculation in *Epochs of Nature* (1779) that the collision of a comet with the sun formed the planets. Dismissing this as a chance explanation, Laplace hypothesized that the sun must have been enveloped in an "immense fluid" in the form of an "atmosphere" and that the planets "were formed at the successive limits of this atmosphere, by the condensation of its equatorial zones." Although this account could not be proved (and it leaves the existence of matter and motion unexplained), it did offer the Enlightenment scientist a hypothesis about the universe's origins.[6]

Although Laplace admitted the hypothetical nature of his theory, he was a bit arrogant about the possibilities of science. The gap between what can be known by virtue of the simple laws of nature and the incertitude of "most phenomena" can be bridged, he says, by the "science of chance or probability." All is predetermined, in that what follows is the result of what precedes. According to historian Roger Hahn, "Laplace took the final and crucial step towards an ideology of total determinism."[7]

In 1754 Diderot predicted that "we are approaching the moment of a great revolution in the sciences. . . . I would dare almost to assert that before one hundred years are up, we will not count three great geometricians in Europe." This has often been interpreted as the clue to a change, around mid-century, when a mechanistic, natural philosophy like that of Laplace gave way to a vitalistic biology like that of Lamarck.[8]

Jean-Baptiste Lamarck (1744–1829), "the most neglected among the generation of the *Idéologues,*" is the scientist who put biological transformism (that is, evolution) on a creditable basis. Educated by the Jesuits in Amiens, veteran of the Seven Years' War, he studied medicine in Paris, distinguished himself in botany, and was admitted to the Académie des sciences after the publication of his *Flore française* (1778). Beginning in 1785 he contributed to the *Encyclopédie méthodique.* He passed a totally undistinguished career during the Revolution at the Muséum d'histoire naturelle, where in 1796 he spent time contemplating the origins of living things.[9]

Lamarck's *Discours d'ouverture* at the museum in Year VIII (1800) has been termed the "birth certificate of transformism." It was reprinted in his *Système des animaux sans vertèbres* (1801), in which Lamarck justified his distinction of all living things from an anatomical or structural (as opposed to the earlier visual) vantage point. There are living things with vertebrate systems and living, bloodless things without them, called invertebrates.[10]

The concept of gradation was first presented by Lamarck in the atemporal terms of the Great Chain of Being, in which invertebrates have immeasurably simpler systems than higher vertebrate forms. But even in this early work, Lamarck's theory of evolution is suggested. Nature is seen as an active, fecund agent that fills the planet with myriad forms of life in *time* and *favorable circumstances.* Nature tends toward progression—a growing complexity as one moves up the scale—and toward interruption of the gradation. A "universal attraction" unites particular bodies, giving them consistency, whereas a "repulsive action" causes natural unities to disintegrate.

To explain the origin of life, Lamarck resorted to spontaneous generation, and to explain the movement of living things up the scale, he appealed to irritability, *need,* and effort. Although Lamarck assigned a special agency to hereditary characteristics, he also attributed much influence to environment. In one text he acknowledged God as the creator of nature and matter, but his system was basically self-operating.[11]

Lamarck never proved any of these mechanisms. He stayed on the level of pure reasoning and description rather than experimentation. But he furthered earlier trends in science—the materialism of the Enlightenment or the idea that thought and movement are inherent to matter. Descartes's radical dualism had left matter entirely "mechanical."

The *Rapports du physique et du moral de l'homme* (1802) of the Idéologue P.-J.-G. Cabanis (1757–1802) has often been considered the ultimate development of Enlightenment materialism. Age, sex, temperament, illness, diet, climate, and general sensibility, according to Cabanis, all impinge greatly on consciousness. Only one of his twelve memoirs is devoted to the reciprocal influence of the moral on the physical. Cabanis's notorious statement—"the brain in a certain manner digests thought"—suggests a strictly physiological explanation of intellectual activity. But his latest interpreter considers him, strictly speaking, not a materialist but a vitalist.[12]

Instead of reducing the psychic to the physical, Cabanis saw the psychic as emerging from the physical in a scale of life functions. Initially sharing much of Destutt de Tracy's antitheological spirit, he became open to the hypothesis of an intelligent cause of the universe. Close to death, he wrote a fellow Idéologue, Claude Fauriel, that "the stubborn claim, that causes are purely blind and mechanical, does not have the same force in light of man's sensitive nature, when it combats the contrary opinion."[13] But Cabanis did not retract his earlier work.

The mechanical heavens of Laplace, the evolution of Lamarck, and the vitalism of Cabanis were not strongly atheistic. Indeed, the irreligious sting of these works is moderated by their primary scientific aim. Laplace summed up their spirit well: "Run through the history of the progress of the human spirit and its errors: we will see final causes constantly pushed back to the limits of our knowledge." Pushed back, but not eliminated. The conclusion of the Enlightenment after the Revolution was *idéologie,* which was materialist but not categorically so, and agnostic in the style of Tracy or Cabanis rather than atheistic as in Holbach's.[14]

This spirit was related to the Revolution in several ways. Its mathematical rationality was tied to the perfection of the metric system and the codes, its episteme to a passion for classifying, its love of nature to the naturalistic revolutionary calendar and civic festivals, and, above all, its rationalism to the hostility of revealed religion. Faith in anything beyond the reasonable was pushed to the periphery of political experience—the family, the disestablished church, the private school, opinion. Science would replace religion as a method of explaining the mysteries of man and the universe. The Revolution did not bring this about, it even impeded the progress of science by disrupting the means to pursue it. But it seized the significance of science's development and acknowledged it by many institutional and symbolic expressions. It was in the 1790s that terms enthroning science—such as science of man, social science, and science of ideas—were coined. And when the old royal academies were lifted from suppression the Académie de sciences gained ascendancy over the Académie française (the Forty Immortals). When it became the First Class of Mathematical and Physical Sciences of the National Institute, it was generally recognized that science had won.

Man, Language, Society, and History

To understand fully the emphasis that the French Revolution placed on rhetoric and visual signs in the battle for men's loyalty one must understand not only the Catholic church's use of perceptual aids to belief but also the philosophes' theories about language and signs. For these theories were inseparable from sociability, educability, and power. Humans were perfectible, Condorcet argued, and malleable. This was the real promise of perfectibility. And this is what accounted for the tremendous emotional and intellectual investment the revolutionary generation placed in education.

As the Enlightenment explained the workings of nature by imminent processes, so it discarded the mind-body dualism of the Cartesians by underscoring the origins of all mental activity in experience. By 1801 Destutt de Tracy had pushed Lockean sensationalism so far that he could assert that "to think is to sense and nothing but to sense." Etienne Bonnot de Condillac and Helvétius had diminished the active role of the intellect, which Locke had retained for reflection, deduction, and intuition. Condillac's *Traité des sensations* (1754) argued that thought was "transformed sensation."[15]

The "science of ideas" of the National Institute's Class of Moral and Political Sciences proposed to unravel this successive composition and decomposition of thoughts—particularly those central to Republican life. While Rousseauists continued to use the word *soul* and Robespierre would proclaim its "immortality," the survival of the term struck the materialists of the Enlightenment as obsolete. The epistemological transcendence of the soul as the simple, immaterial source of thought, composed of different "powers" or "faculties," and distinct from the brain was thus rejected. Tracy chose to call the study he proposed not "psychology" or "study of the soul" but *idéologie,* or science of ideas. The term was wholly in keeping with a growing phenomenalism of the Enlightenment—a tendency to look at operations of the mind rather than at their substratum.[16]

This phenomenalist approach had serious consequences for human self-consciousness, for it made the self uncertain of its existence. Rousseau, Buffon, and the Swiss naturalist Charles Bonnet (1720–93) continued to insist on the unity and coherence of the self, but Hume spoke of it as a mere "bundle of sensations," and Diderot viewed it as a spider at the center of its web. Tracy compared the self to a ball in which the partners change and yet the dance persists.[17]

Faculty psychology, or the "analysis of ideas and sensations," would unravel confused sensations, would follow their progress from simple to complex ideas. The manner in which this process was conceived in the 1790s was more social than it had been for Condillac, whose imaginary statue-man received impressions in isolation. Condorcet's study of the understanding is both social and historical. Like Laplace, he was a mathematician who had ventured into calculus and applied it to human affairs, such as elections. This "social mathematics" would make human science as *natural* as possible. But of particular interest here is Condorcet's view of language as the means by which fleeting sensations and ideas are given a fixed existence in the mind. History, progress, class differences, and social interaction—indeed, the indefinite perfectibility of the human race—are all related to language. Signs make possible complex ideas like law, and thus permit the birth of society. Without signs humans are imbeciles, like wolf-children, who were described by philosophes and academicians as deprived of ideas because deprived of signs and of society. Thus, although sensual perception is individual, ideas can develop only in social surroundings.[18]

For Condorcet (fig. III.3) human progress is a function of knowledge, and knowledge a function of the perfection of language, which, as Condillac had observed, is a tool of analysis or a science itself. Civilizations are as advanced as their languages. The division of society into a learned class and an ignorant working class with separate languages appeared harmful not only to knowledge but to human perfectibility. A simple, uniform language would help communication and guarantee progress of the race. Condorcet substituted for Rousseau's naturalistic, evolutionary rise of civilization in his "Second Discourse" a linguistic-historical one, the chief index of which was analysis and science. The account of his posthumous *Esquisse d'un tableau historique des progrès de l'esprit humain* (1795) is linear and progressive. It is mechanical in its black-and-white dialectic of ignorance and reason. It is intellectualist in that progress is measured by the progress of the arts and sciences, themselves measured by language, not solely by material accomplishments.[19]

The experiences of French physician Jean-Marc-Gaspard Itard

III.3.
Jean-Antoine Houdon, The Marquis de Condorcet, *marble bust, 1785.*
Courtesy American Philosophical Society, Philadelphia. Reprinted from H. H. Arnason, The
Sculptures of Houdon, *Phaidon Press Ltd., 1975.*

(1775–1838) with the "wild child of Aveyron," discovered in 1799 in
the massif Central, conveniently sum up psychological preoccupations
at the end of the century: sensation, primitiveness, the dependence on
education and society for perfectibility, and the specific problems concerning the educability of wild children, deaf mutes, and retarded or
demented individuals. Briefly, how much could society do? How much

did man owe to nature? Itard was confronted by a report from the noteworthy psychiatrist Philippe Pinel (1745–1826), author of the *Traité médico-philosophique sur l'aliénation mentale ou la manie* (1801), who maintained that the wild child of Aveyron was an idiot, congenitally deficient, ineducable. Being a professor in the Ecole des sourds muets, Itard had trained under the direction of abbé Sicard, a Christian, who himself was indebted to Condillac's sensationalism and who had steered his school through the Terror with subsidies from the Convention, despite his priestly and royalist loyalties. Itard was the model Enlightenment doctor. He was imbued with humanitarianism and science yet was free of sentimentality and pedantry. He took the wild child into his spacious home, hired a *gouvernante* for him, clothed him, fed him, housed him, and, above all, tried to educate him. Perfectibility was inseparable from sociability.[20]

The wild child was a guinea pig in the laboratory of civilization, but much loved nonetheless. Itard sought to "determine what man is" and to "deduce from what he lacks the hitherto uncalculated sum of knowledge and ideas which man owes to his education." The child had been deprived of most senses—proof, evidently, that Condillac was right in deriving sensory powers from experience rather than birth. "He was destitute of memory, of judgment, of aptitude for imitation, and was so limited in his ideas, even those relative to his immediate needs, that he had never yet succeeded in opening a door or climbing upon a chair to get the food that had been raised out of the reach of his hand."[21]

How much could such a child learn on his own, how much did he lack when deprived of society? The wild child sensed only what he needed and heard sounds only on certain frequencies to which he was accustomed. Lacking many sensations, he naturally lacked most complex and even simple ideas. Teaching the child to read proved nearly impossible; Itard had to admit partial defeat. He was never able to bring his boy up to civilized standards because he was ineducable, and he was ineducable because he had lacked society. Without society man is incapable of civilization.[22] Itard's despondency at his pupil's failure reflected his century's concern for *civilisation,* a word it coined. The Enlightenment always feared that barbarism was knocking at its doors.[23]

French revolutionary experience called into question the very presuppositions of perfectibility. Malthus's pessimistic *Essay on Population* (1798) was a response to Condorcet's optimistic claims and Tracy's subsequent *Treatise on the Will,* or *Political Economy,* written during the

Empire, was resigned to human inequality. Confidence in the invariability of human behavior and its susceptibility to scientific laws had also begun to crumble at the turn of the century. The moral and political sciences, Tracy argued, were "very exposed to being unconsciously altered by the disposition of our sentiments, our character, our age, and the degrees of experience. . . . That is why they are so difficult and opinions are so variable." Physiological variability came to take the place of behavioral uniformity. Although the bombast of the Enlightenment is not entirely lost in the philosophes' works after 1815, there is far less confidence in the imminent reign of an age of reason à la Condorcet. The wild child stands as a symbol of the limits of reason and educability.[24]

Enlightened Christianity

Scientific explanations of the origin of the universe (Laplace) and of life (Lamarck), of ourselves, our sensations, ideas, and language (Condillac, Itard, and the Idéologues) all had their place in the coming of the French Revolution. They did this by exaggerating people's control over themselves and the environment and by stressing the concomitant oblivion of the supernatural and of transcendent obligations.

But a considerable number of reactions have been frequently overlooked. Christians hostile to the Enlightenment responded with attacks on the philosophes and with parodies of their systems. Some attempted to find a common terrain between the new rationalist discourse and Christianity. Known as Enlightened Christianity, this movement attempted to reconcile the sovereignty of reason and the acceptance of dogma not provable by reason, an amalgam that never happened and is strictly speaking impossible. But many Christians felt some of the philosophes' proposed reforms (such as the abolition of slavery, or the toleration of different religious beliefs) to be an application of the Gospel. The sanction came on Christmas 1797, when the future Pius VII, then bishop of Imola, said, "The form of democratic government adopted by you is in no way repugnant to the Gospel, it demands on the contrary all the sublime virtues which belong only to the school of Jesus Christ. . . . Be good Christians and be good democrats."[25] The priest, even more than the doctor, was the main intermediary between the Enlightened and the people. As one historian has concluded about the prerevolutionary situation: "Those most ready to see the people broadly educated and even enlightened were pious Christians."[26]

But some felt history to be moving in the opposite direction, polarizing the poor and the privileged, away from the more equal social relations that had prevailed at the end of the Middle Ages. One articulate speaker for the cause of the people was the abbé Coyer, who felt that the term *le peuple* denoted the dregs of the nation, where formerly "the people was . . . the most useful, the most virtuous and consequently the most respectable part of the nation." Coyer described satirically what many historians had noted in the relations among classes in the old regime: loss of a sense of community among seigneurs and villagers, especially after nobles removed themselves to Versailles; purchase of noble lands and titles by the bourgeois, who also repossessed peasant lands for defaults on debts; and, above all, withdrawal of the elite (nobles, clergy, bourgeois) from such communal forms of culture as Carnival and pilgrimages during the Enlightenment. All this has confirmed that elite and popular culture had divorced by the late eighteenth century.[27]

The philosophes were not beyond looking with contempt on the people as beasts of burden deprived of intelligence, as *personnes viles.* Voltaire once described a Protestant shoemaker whom he had helped release from the galleys as an "imbecile. . . . If his friends are just as dimwitted as I presume, they are as certain of paradise in the other world as they are of the galleys in this." Turgot felt that peasants would likely "miss their cow more than their wife or son." The peasants and laborers were seen alternately as ferocious, dangerous, vile, and ignorant and as miserable, pitiful toilers, necessary to provide products and services to the elite.[28]

Coyer was, of course, a Christian, and he shared Jacques-Bénigne Bossuet's belief in "the eminent dignity of the poor in the Church," indeed, in society. He lamented the chasm that separated the elite from the laboring poor. Other sympathetic clerics were abbé Térisse and the Jansenists J.-B.-L. Crevier and F.-D. Rivard, who appreciated the value of literacy for religious instruction. Indeed, most popular education was conducted by religious orders, such as the Frères de la doctrine chrétienne, whose free schools dotted numerous French cities.[29]

The Enlightened were not so blithe about popular education. If peasants moved from the country to the cities, who would work the plows? If they were to learn Latin, who would learn husbandry? How would all those products of farm labor on which the elite depended reach the towns and cities? If artisans and servants were to become poets and actors, who would perform the many manual services on which the age depended? Writers on popular education ultimately favored improvement only within a stable framework.[30]

The prevailing view was less Christian than utilitarian. Twelve volumes of the *Encyclopédie* are devoted to engravings of artisans, including highly skilled luxury workers occupied busily at their trade, the parts of their machines reproduced and identified. The ideal Christian view gave way to that of the Enlightenment—workers were regarded no longer as possessing immortal souls, equal to the great before God, but as instruments to produce wealth and pleasures.[31]

Let us look at how another priest approached the poor. At Reims the curé J.-B. Macquart thought "in 1778 to establish two schools for children of both sexes. His object was not only to remove these children from mendicity and to procure for them an education which he saw as being too neglected: He had also in mind to form good workers capable of making the mills flourish. He gave them the most intelligent masters, had spinning wheels built in a more convenient and solid manner. He demands the greatest perfection in the work and excites emulation by his rewards."[32] The curé's charity was of the useful variety—he "would work simultaneously at attacking indigence at its roots and diminishing its causes." He keeps close watch over his subjects. He visits them in their families, "sees them work, observes the strength and talent of the worker, takes the name of the master who employs him, in order to know exactly the product of the work. He calculates with them the details of their expense in food, clothing, etc. He repeats several times his investigation."[33] Work in the emergent textile *filatures* was closely supervised, and its methodical rationalization (which the *Encyclopédie*'s plates honored) established tight control, subjecting worker to master, people to elites.

The attitude of the Enlightened toward the laboring poor, which the curé Macquart partially exemplified, can be summarized as one of bienfaisance. Macquart wished to ameliorate the lot of the people within their state, to keep the poor usefully occupied, to eliminate the social danger that idleness implied, and to procure the services and products that the Enlightened so needed as members of a leisure class.

The Enlightened became cool to the workers' religion, folklore, and superstition. The fate of the *confréries* (confraternities) that had sprung up in the later Middle Ages, grouping men of all classes to perform charitable and pious works, illustrates the point. These were now deserted by the higher orders, who substituted secular, "enlightened" associations in the academies and Masonic lodges. This was part of a more general withdrawal of the elite from the elaborate complex of Catholic practices once shared with the people.[34]

The abbé Grégoire (1750–1831) is a third curé whose remarkable career was studded with service to the laboring poor as well as to black and Jewish minorities. Henri Grégoire has left a remarkable text that shows how the elite sought to transform an instrument of popular culture into one of enlightenment, however simple and "abridged":

> There is an infallible and easy method that favors the propagation of enlightenment in the lower class of society; will you believe I refer to almanacs? One can hardly conceive the extent of their auspicious or harmful influence among the lower people, according to whether they are the work of reason or stupidity. Annually forty thousand copies of [the almanac] of Basle are printed. . . . Savoyards hawk this absurd repertory which perpetuates into the eighteenth century the prejudices of the twelfth all over France. For eight sous each peasant provides himself with this palmist, astrological collection dictated by bad taste and madness. The demand, in truth, *has been less for several years, because, thanks to the Clergy of the second order, completely healthy ideas of every kind penetrate the villages.* These facts are doubtless ignored by the minister, otherwise he would seize this means of instruction to spread abundantly the result of agronomical and veterinary experiences, the paternal views of the government, etc.[35]

Grégoire himself lent peasants books from his library, and he suggested that other curés do the same. Indeed, at the beginning of the Revolution, almanacs intended to spread enlightened and libertarian principles to the people were published, such as the *Almanach du Père Gérard,* aimed at the countryside, and the *Almanach du Père Duchesne,* which, although hardly the work of a curé, aimed to put patriotism within reach of the common worker. Helvétius dedicated a chapter of his *De l'homme* (1772) to outlining a new civic catechism, whereas Voltaire and Jacques-André Naigeon both published impious catechisms, appropriating a sacred and popular form of religious instruction for Enlightenment purposes. The physiocrat Pierre-François Mercier de la Rivière asked for a "civil and political catechism," and Jacques-Pierre Brissot de Warville regretted that no "social, civil, and criminal catechism for the people" had been written. The spirit of these texts differed greatly depending on whether they were the work of bons curés or philosophes. The first enriched the peasants' savoir-vivre with practical knowledge, perfectly compatible with Christian beliefs, whereas the latter was more polemical than practical, "enlightened" rather than dogmatic. Whether this genre remained popular after being adapted by the Enlightened is dubious. But it illustrates one approach the Enlightened took to reach out to their more ignorant compatriots.[36]

The abbé Grégoire was born of a Lorrainer artisan family, close to the peasantry, where anti-Jewish feeling flourished. His mother may have nurtured him in Jansenist principles. Although he went to a Jesuit college in Nancy, he developed an antipathy to the Society of Jesus and disapproved of their reestablishment in 1814. He studied *jus gentium,* or international law, and public law and appreciated the sixteenth-century work *Vindiciae contra Tyrannos,* a justification of tyrannicide. When the works of Voltaire were presented to the Constituent Assembly, Grégoire urged that they be purged of their impieties, yet he was familiar with Enlightened ideas, for he had been "consumed by doubts from the reading of supposedly philosophical works" and had offered works on agriculture, hygiene, and the mechanical arts to the local peasants. As a parish priest, he occupied himself with the relationship of his parishioners to the Jews of Alsace. His *Essai sur la régénération physique, morale et politique des juifs* was submitted to a competition of the Royal Academy of Metz in 1785 and was awarded the prize and subsequently published.[37]

By using the term *régénération,* Grégoire accepted some sort of factual basis for anti-Semitic feelings in Alsace and Lorraine. He acknowledged the fears of those who opposed direct emancipation by agreeing that Jews were sexually more active than Gentiles, that they married very young and consequently had larger families. He also explored the problem of usury and said that Jewish antipathy for Gentiles, their tendency to form "a nation within a nation," made them "men without patrie." How could the Talmud, which, according to some authors, allowed such practices as defrauding a Christian, be allowed to coexist with national laws?

Grégoire's response to these questions was characteristically "philosophical." Men, he claimed, are what circumstances and environment have made them. "Nations," Grégoire orated, "avow while groaning that this is your work! The Jews produced the effects, you have laid the causes: who are the most culpable?" Christian beliefs, long since considered the principal reason for anti-Semitism, should justify emancipation: "Christians seeing in Jews the authors of a deicide, forgot sometimes the example of their founder, who prayed on the cross for his executioners."[38]

After the abbé Grégoire was elected by Nancy to the Estates General, he joined the third estate to sign the Tennis Court Oath, which Jacques-Louis David immortalized on an enormous canvas. Patriot poets, who saw him as more patriot than priest, lionized him:

> He carries neither cross nor mitre,
> He is proud only of his virtues,
> In our reborn empire,
> a good pastor is a great good.

Grégoire was elected bishop of the Sarthe and of the Loire-et-Cher in February 1791, and the municipal authorities rejoiced, for "true Christians see in you a defender of a pure faith, of the poor and the unfortunate, a tender and compassionate father and the truest and firmest support of the friends of the Constitution." This wedding of Christianity and patriotism foundered on the rocks of schism produced by the Civil Constitution of the Clergy and by which Grégoire had been uncanonically elected bishop: Grégoire's presumed regicide in January 1793 aggravated the situation. When the Concordat required the resignation of both Catholic and Republican clergy, Grégoire refused to submit his resignation, claiming his title depended on the people. He refused to visit Pius VII in 1804 when the pope came to Paris to crown Napoléon, and he refused to reconcile himself to the Catholic church on his death. Enlightened Christianity had early in the Revolution become Republican Christianity. The Revolution, moreover, had made Grégoire an implacable enemy of the papacy.[39]

Loyalty to the king and to the pope was superseded by compassion for the socially excluded. In 1790 and 1791 arose the issue of enfranchisement of free mulattoes in Santo Domingo, and tangentially the question of the abolition of slavery. Grégoire belonged to Brissot's abolitionist Amis des Noirs, a club that exerted great influence on the Assembly. In his *Lettre aux citoyens de couleur et nègres libres de Saint-Domingue* (1791), his egalitarianism is manifest: "God, in his tenderness, embraces all men in his love and does not admit of any differences except those which result from their virtues." Christianity, for Grégoire, was a "religion of sweetness, equality and liberty."

As late as the 1820s in France, Grégoire continued to take an active interest in what had become Haiti, serving as a cultural counselor to Jean-Pierre Boyer, the president of the republic, and describing himself to the Haitians as "a man, who is known to you by a sincere affection for men of all colors and who has devoted himself since his youth to the defense of the oppressed, especially to that of the children of Africa." Although Grégoire continued obstinately to defy Catholic and royalist sensibilities in the Restoration, his position on religious tolerance did not fall into philosophical *indifferentism,* as it was then called—making religion something "hardly distinguishable from practical atheism." "There is only one Seigneur," Grégoire added, "one faith, one baptism." The peculiar nature of Grégoire's Enlightened Christianity lay in its pronounced independence from both the philosophes and the Catholic fold. Broadening the former's humanitarianism, and finding egalitarianism in the Gospels, he tried to wed the two and ended by rejecting the formal representations of both.[40]

Relinquishing the doctrine of grace, the Enlightenment fostered a belief in natural human goodness, in malleability, educability, perfectibility. Considering man as unitary rather than dualistic, as falling entirely within the natural order, one could contemplate a "science of man" or "ideology." The Revolution borrowed heavily from the secular, anti-Christian Enlightenment. It made the Enlightenment its own; it was not brought about by it. The Revolution would frequently disdain the peuple as ignorant while proclaiming it sovereign. The initiative to close the gap between Christianity and secular Enlightenment, among the Enlightened, le peuple, and minorities, was left largely to Enlightened Christians.

CHAPTER IV

THE QUEST FOR
SIMPLICITY

The Age of Reason sought to reduce the exaggerations of the Baroque to the simplest forms and principles. This thrust has often been called the "geometric spirit," which found supreme expression in Newton's law of universal gravitation. Other sources of this quest for simplicity were classical models of sculpture, architecture, and painting, known since the Renaissance but studied with renewed vigor after the excavations of Pompeii and Herculaneum in the mid-eighteenth century. Not satisfied with the Palladian orders, the "revolutionary architects" of the eighteenth century delved further into the past to resurrect still more elementary geometrical forms.

The Problem of Weights and Measures

The unification of weights and measures of the Year III (1795) climaxed the efforts of a millennium (Charlemagne had sought it), but the system, in spite of its exportation by Napoléon's armies, is still not universal. It is taken up here as the fruition of the mathematical and astronomical Enlightenment.

Out of the old regime's hodgepodge of administrations, jurisdictions, codes, standards of measure, and religious beliefs, the thinkers of the Enlightenment and neoclassical school sought to bring order and rationality. Different as these movements were, they were inspired by the same geometric spirit that inspired the Enlightenment itself. As Tocqueville rightly showed, this was centralization, and though the Revolution in some instances brought it to completion (as with weights and measures), the origins must be traced back to the old regime. Like the Enlightenment, it may have helped cause the Revolution. More certainly it revealed a state of mind and set of goals that made the Revolution possible. One writer during the Revolution felt it was no exaggeration to speak of sixty thousand measures of weight in France before 1789. For surfaces there were the *pouce,* the *pied,* the *are,* the *aune,* the *perche,* the *verge,* the *arpent,* and the *hectare,* with their many regional variants. Eighteenth-century authors such as Alexis-Jean-Pierre Paucton felt that the diversity sprang from feudalism, for seigneurs had "low justice" over weights and measures, kept the standards in their possession, and refused to allow them to be checked by other standards. "The seigneurial monopoly of weights and measures," writes their historian, "coexisting with a *rente* in kind easily caused permanent conflicts; it created a situation propitious for the falsification of standards by the seigneurs and for the distrust, justified or not, of the peasants." The old weights and measures upheld the old regime. A common demand of the *cahiers de doléances* of 1789 was thus to unify weights and measures—not to avoid paying feudal dues but to assure an honest amount payable. The rallying cry: "un roi, une loi, un poids, et une mesure" (one king, one law, one weight, and one measure) was a slogan of equality and centralization, the chief mark of modern French history, one that the monarchy commenced and the Revolution furthered.[1]

The search for a natural standard of measures, as opposed to simple unification, was peculiar to the Age of Reason. The Dutch scientist Christiaan Huyghens had been examining the swing of the pendulum. It was believed that the duration of the swing was equal everywhere (isochronous) and could serve as a natural unit of measurement. But when astronomer Jean Richer in 1673 realized that the length of a pendulum swing varied with longitude, one longitude had to be selected. The geographer and astronomer La Condamine suggested the equator because it was equidistant from the poles and from the northern and southern hemispheres. But in Peru (in what is now Ecuador) between 1735 and 1744, La Condamine measured the arc of the meridian to determine the earth's shape. During the Revolution, a fraction of the arc of another meridian at Paris latitude (45°) became the standard of the meter. Laplace, a member of the

Commission on Weights and Measures of the Academy of Sciences (1789–93), wrote:

> It is natural for man to relate the units of distance by which he travels to the dimensions of the globe that he inhabits. Thus, in moving about the earth, he may know by the simple denomination of distance its proportion to the whole circuit of the earth. This has the further advantage of making nautical and celestial measurements correspond. . . . It is important, therefore, that one of these magnitudes should be the expression of the other, with no difference except in the units. But to that end, the fundamental linear unit must be an aliquot part of the terrestrial meridian.

During the Revolution the astronomers Jean-Baptiste-Joseph De-lambre (1749–1822) and Pierre-François-André Méchain (1744–1804) made painstaking measurements between Dunkirk and Barcelona. One ten-millionth part of the quarter (or quadrant) of this meridian was to become the meter. Area and volume were to be measured by squaring and cubing the meter respectively, and weight was to be measured by units of a cubic decimeter of water. A natural standard, albeit limited somewhat geographically, was thus adopted by the decree on the metric system on 7 April 1795 (fig. iv.1). As a consequence, France now had the universal standard. A spokesman of the Provisional Agency of Weights and Measures of the Directory stressed the new system's rational simplicity and universality: "The republican measures . . . depend on a very simple system: in each type (weights, volumes, area, length) the subdivisions are decimals, that is to say successively ten times smaller than the others." The member of the Convention (*conventionnel*) Prieur called it a "benefit to humanity. It is worthy of the Grande Nation to whom it belongs and of other civilized people, who are also probably destined to adopt it sooner or later."[2]

The meter was not the only revolutionary conquest of space. The Cassini quadrant map of France was another geometrical legacy of the old regime, and it was put to unexpected uses in the Revolution. While various expeditions set out to measure the arcs of the meridians and determine the shape of the earth, the Cassini family of cartographers—and one member in particular, César-François Cassini de Thury (1714–84)—was plotting quadrants, verifying the meridian of Paris, and undertaking the first modern map of all France. The finished product of 182 sheets placed the features of each quadrant (steeples, châteaux, hills, and so on) on a "geometric skeleton" on a scale of

IV.1.

Commission Temporaire de poids et mesures républicaines, Table of Weights and Measures Deduced from the Quarter of the Circumference of the Earth, *drawing in* Instruction abrégée sur les mesures déduites de la grandeur de la terre . . . *(Paris an II [1793–94])*.

By permission of the British Library.

1:186,400. This map, though not completed until 1815, was used to make the Academy of Sciences' population studies of the 1790s and to divide France into the revolutionary concentric departments, districts, cantons, and communes.[3]

Neoclassicism: David

The artistic counterpart of France's confusion of weights and measures in the old regime was the frivolous, decorative, cluttered rococo. The term *rococo* derived from the fantastical artificial grottoes of Versailles and suggested freedom and irregularity. For this, neoclassicism (as the eighteenth-century classical revival is called) substituted order, balance, and proportion. Mimesis, or imitation, had informed art since the Renaissance, and it inspired the instruction of the Academy of Painting and Sculpture, founded by Charles Le Brun in 1664. But eighteenth-century mimesis was no slavish imitation of nature or of models but a creative work of the artist, who extracted the generic ideal of truth and beauty from a real subject. The neoclassical artist depicted archetypal beauty and order—beauty that exists nowhere in nature but selects the beautiful from many specimens; Zeus's Helen, for instance, a composite of many beautiful women. Neoclassicism is an art of ideals, an art of principle rather than of the circumstantial, peculiar, or accidental. The arts, it was believed, could be rationally decomposed and recomposed. Anatomy, so important to the neoclassicist, was a grammar of the human body.[4]

The neoclassical artist prefers the mythological to the real because mythological figures represent archetypes. The artist uses allegory and symbols in abundance, and the individual is apotheosized, that is, raised to superhuman ideality. Time must be either classical or mythological or nonexistent—timeless. Objects and persons are generalized. This neoclassical doctrine, unlike its romantic counterpart, prefers an ethereal generality to graphic particularity.

Since the days of Francis I, young French artists looked to Italy for inspiration. After 1666 twelve of the artist-students of the Academy of Painting and Sculpture were sent to the French Academy in Rome to receive instruction, to copy the great masters of antiquity and the Renaissance, and to prepare a work of their own.

Independently of the academy at the start, the comte de Caylus (1692–1765), a progenitor of neoclassicism, voyaged widely through Europe after serving in the War of Spanish Succession, and in 1752–55 he published his seven-volume *Recueil d'antiquités égyptiennes, étrusques, grecques, romaines, gauloises*. In these he explained the ancient Greek method of encaustic painting (painting by melting in wax). In his honor, the academy established a Prix Caylus for the study of heads and expressions, and the Academy of Inscriptions, of which he was also a member, created a medal in his name for the study of the monuments of antiquity.[5]

One of Caylus's collaborators in encaustic painting was Comte Joseph-Marie Vien (1716–1809), who studied in the French Academy of Rome from 1744 to 1750. He had copied excavated paintings at Portici, near Herculaneum, and subsequently adopted an austere style. His *Sleeping Hermits* and *Daedalus and Icarus* gained him admission to the academy in 1754. Vien painted à la grecque—the new style—and it so impressed Mme Du Barry, mistress of Louis XV, that she canceled an expensive commission with Fragonard and asked Vien to paint a series portraying "young Greeks." In Rome again from 1775 to 1781 as director of the academy, Vien taught his pupils (including David, whom he influenced decisively) to paint from live models as well as to copy works of art. He himself was the first important revivalist of historical canvases.[6]

If Caylus and Vien sparked the return to the antique in painting, Johann Winckelmann became the oracle of classical antiquity, upholding its standard of the beautiful and the true for thousands of those who read his *Letters on Herculaneum* (1762) and his inimitable and popular *History of Ancient Art* (1764). Winckelmann's *Letters* detailed the discoveries in the excavated sites near Naples. He was not always complimentary—"The statues and busts of bronze of Herculaneum are for the most part mediocre or bad"—and he may even have demythologized the sites, placing their artifacts against the backdrop of great antique art, the subject of his *History of Ancient Art*.[7]

Winckelmann did not set out to prove the greatness of ancient art (by which he meant mostly Greek art of the fifth century B.C.) but to reveal and explain it. "The freedom which gave birth to great events, political changes, and jealousy among the Greeks," he writes, "planted . . . the germ of noble and elevated sentiments." The association of political liberty with moral and artistic greatness would become the credo of the revolutionary artists at the end of the eighteenth century. Winckelmann located its origins in fifth-century Athens, where he found other favorable conditions. The moderate climate of the Aegean peninsula gave rise to a "joyousness of disposition" expressed in games and festivals and physical contests. These produced beautiful specimens of humanity which inspired not only contemporary artists but Rousseau, who in his *Social Contract* sought to resurrect the games for eighteenth-century Europe.[8]

But what was this ideal of the beautiful that the Greeks discovered? Winckelmann believed that it was "impossible to conceive of beauty without proportion. . . . The observance of fixed rules will eliminate the grotesque and irregular from art. . . . The body, as well as its principal members, is composed of three parts. The body consists of trunk, thighs, and legs; the lower extremity of thighs, legs, and feet; and a similar disposition is true of the arms, hands, and feet. The same construction can be shown in other organs which are not so evidently composed of three parts. The relation existing among these divisions is the same in the whole body as in its parts."[9] He continued, following

Anton Raphael Mengs (1728–79), to explain how the three parts of the face could be divided into "twelve equal portions," a clear manifestation of geometrical aesthetics.[10]

Although Winckelmann argued that "it is impossible to conceive of beauty without proportion," geometrical proportions alone do not constitute the classical idea of beauty, which includes a certain grace, unity, variety, and harmony. The artist is an eclectic who selects "the most beautiful parts from numberless beautiful persons." The result is a general beauty that transcends the beauty of any one model. Serenity in statues and paintings is the state most appropriate to the beauty of a life of contemplative leisure. "Slow movements of the body," Winckelmann insists, are "characteristic of great minds." The Greeks brought this noble beauty to perfection; for Winckelmann, subsequent art was an inevitable decline.[11]

The imitation of things Greek, inspired by Winckelmann, did not however consist simply in geometric proportionalism. No one had described the sensuous beauty of the Apollo Belvedere as Winckelmann did in his *History:* "I am transported to Delos and the sacred groves of Lycia—places Apollo honored with his presence—and the statue seems to come alive like the beautiful creation of Pygmalion."[12] Another Hellenophile after him, however, did carry the revolutionary generation into transports about things Greek.

Abbé Jean-Jacques Barthélemy's *Voyage du jeune Anarcharsis en Grèce* (1788), a seven-volume work that ran through twelve editions by the end of the Revolution, traced an imaginary voyage of a young man through Greece in the days before Alexander the Great. The book lacked Winckelmann's insight, but, as the product of thirty years of labor, with abundant annotations from classical sources, it was a mine of information. It further fascinated the French with Greek rationality and sensuality. Barthélemy invoked the deep terror of Aeschylus's drama, the cadenced periods and inversions of Isocrates' rhetoric, the stern laws of Draco, and the lyrical qualities of the Greek chorus. Stillness was not Barthélemy's idea of Greek beauty. He chose a voyage for Anarcharsis because "everything is in action in a voyage."[13]

Classicism was not simply Euclidean or Apollonian. Grace and beauty pervade Winckelmann's and Barthélemy's works—the beauty of trim and firm bodies and graceful draperies, "thin and wet garments" that "clasped the body." The beauty of "noble simplicity and sedate grandeur," of precision, of contour—but not pure geometry, for "if this idea were geometrically clear, men would not differ in their opinions upon the beautiful, and it would be easy to prove what true beauty is." The beauty Winckelmann disclosed to his contemporaries was at once sensual and ideal, human and divine.[14]

The neoclassical school existed before David, with such artists as Jean-François Peyron and Gabriel-François Doyen, to mention only two. Historical canvases of classical subjects with a vague moral and patriotic purpose had become a quasi-official tradition, with a stylistic code (simplicity, austerity, chiaroscuro) and a repertory of treatments of the same subjects (such as *Belisarius*). The school was imitative in subject matter, frequently from Livy or another classical source, but also imitative in *treatment* of the subject, since many artists had already interpreted it. A recent interpretation of art from David to Ingres stresses both the weight of the tradition that artists inherit and the extent to which a great artist strives to overcome "the weight and authority of antiquity, of Michelangelo," the pallor of dead subjects.[15]

Jacques-Louis David reached maturity as the neoclassical school was languishing but also at the moment that the grandeur of liberty was dawning in French consciousness. His revulsion of insipid neo-classicism, as the painter Eugène Delacroix pointed out, "honors his genius, led him to the study of the antique. He had the courage to reform all his habits, he locked himself up with the *Laocoön,* with the *Antinous,* with the *Gladiator,* with all the male conceptions of ancient genius: he had the courage to refashion his talent. . . . He was the father of the whole modern school in painting and sculpture; his re-form extended to architecture, to furniture, to daily habits. He caused Herculaneum and Pompeii to succeed the bastard, Pompadour style."[16] David later described the mission of the artist as follows:

> The Arts are the imitation of what is most beautiful in nature, of what . . . is most perfect. . . .
>
> It is not only in charming the eyes that monuments of arts have reached this end, it is in penetrating the soul, it is in making a profound impression on the mind; it is then that the traits of hero-ism, of civic virtues, offered to the gaze of the people, will elec-trify the soul, and will engender in him the passions of glory, of devotion for the welfare of the *patrie*. The artist then must have studied all the springs of the human heart, he must have a great knowledge of nature, he must, in a word, be a philosopher.[17]

While in Rome, David executed his *Saint-Roch,* which did not win him entrance to the academy. The rejection nourished a bitterness to-ward that institution, which intensified during the Revolution. But in

Rome, David also did a painting that came the closest yet to his ultimate neoclassical style. His *Funeral of Patroclus,* carried out in friezelike
fashion, with some 150 to 200 figures, recounted the sad events that
followed Achilles' refusal to fight for the Greeks because he had quarreled with Agamemnon. While Achilles sulked, Patroclus gained
permission to fight in his stead and was killed. Achilles grieved
bitterly, and Patroclus's body received full burial honors. The painting's theme—guilt over the sacrifice of a friend—is similar to that of
another painting. David's *Belisarius* depicts the old soldier of Justinian,
who has abandoned him to a life of beggary, at the moment a fellow
soldier recognizes him receiving alms from an old woman. Each painting illustrates the ingratitude of a (military) superior and a hero need-
lessly sacrificed, evoking pity in the observer. In 1784 a related painting, *Andromache Weeping with Astianax over the Body of Hector,* made
David a full academician.[18]

The following year, 1785, David painted the *Oath of the Horatii in the
Hands of Their Father* (fig. IV.2)—a painting that struck observers as
completely new. The subject was from Roman history, more precisely
from Pierre Corneille's *Horace,* possibly from the historians Charles
Rollin and Livy himself. But David never hesitated to take liberties
with his sources. Here the Horatii, a famous family in Republican
Rome, are taking an oath before their father, who proffers them three
swords, symbols of male power, with which to defend the Republic. At
the left of the painting the three warriors step forward in unison, forming a pyramid of male valor and aggression. In the center, the father
takes a more retiring posture as the patriarch communicating his will
and swords to his sons. To the right, the arched bodies of the two
sisters and mother form arabesques, limp arms and folding draperies
portraying female resignation. Each composition forms a pyramid, and
additional pyramids balance the groups. The symmetry of angular
pyramids is counterbalanced by the symmetry of three Roman arches
that frame the pyramids. The arches represent femininity, the pyramids masculinity; the women on the right match the men on the left.[19]

This painting broke new ground not so much in its subject as in its
radical austerity, dull color palette, and dramatic lighting (chiaroscuro).
The taut male limbs express agility, force, and energy that will abate
only when the sole survivor returns to kill Camilla. Neoclassical painting had passed from Vien's early rococo, to more simple reenactments
of classical history, to this shocking picture of impending violence.
The Goncourt brothers later called the *Oath of the Horatii* a coup d'état.
A contemporary observer said it was "a rock against which the others

IV.2.

Jacques-Louis David, The Oath of the Horatii, *painting, 1785.*
Courtesy Musée du Louvre, photo: Musées nationaux, Paris.

crashed," having "an astonishing severity and firmness" that violated the *décence* and *douceur* of old regime sensibility. But David did incorporate those sentiments contrapuntally in the group of women in the *Oath of the Horatii,* as he did with the woman offering alms in *Belisarius* and with the women of his later *Brutus.* The *Oath of the Horatii* was an electric shock to the salon public, injecting determination for a patriotic cause right at the moment when the French were beginning to take their own patrie and its welfare seriously. Though it did not point specifically to a democratic revolution, it set the mood for such a revolution a few years later.

The same themes of *pro patria mori* (to die for one's country) are discernible in the *Brutus* of 1789 (fig. IV.3), in which a father witnesses lictors bringing in the bodies of his sons—sons he has condemned to death for conspiring against the Republic. This time the father has not commissioned his sons to defend the Republic but sacrificed their lives for betraying it. Like the *Oath of the Horatii, Brutus* contrasts agitated tenderness of women with serene strength and cruel firmness of men.[20]

IV.3.
Jacques-Louis David, The Lictors Bringing Back to Brutus the Bodies of His Sons, *painting, 1789.*
Courtesy Musée du Louvre, photo: Musées nationaux, Paris.

After 1785 David was hailed by the critics-spokesmen of the nation as a great painter who had revolutionized the art world. But he was no upstart, being well connected to the cultural elite (Sedaine, Chénier, Vigée-Lebrun). David married a wealthy woman, and she largely supported the career he judged less a trade than a "noble enterprise." His two daughters married nobles and he knew two princes of the blood (the duc de Chartres and the duc d'Orléans) through Mme de Genlis. Although a Jacobin, he was initially a moderate one, a Feuillant (he lived in the Feuillant convent). By the end of 1791, writes Philippe Bordes, "David, the idol of the day in painting, certainly had not convinced the Robespierrists that he was one of them." Nonetheless, one Jacobin, Dubois Crancé, greeted him as a French patriot, "the author of *Brutus* and of the *Horatii,* whose genius anticipated the Revolution."[21] Nothing could have stopped David from exhibiting whatever he pleased in the salon of 1789. Nothing did stop him, not even Angiviller, who had earlier commissioned paintings by David to rekindle "love of the patrie." But the fourteenth of July, Bastille Day, had exploded, and the royal administration had reconsidered its policy. *Brutus* was too powerful, too capable of igniting revolutionary feelings. Angiviller's deputy told Vien, president of the academy, that he wished to exclude *Brutus* from the salon. "One cannot be too cautious in the choice of subjects to be exhibited," he said. "Let David exhibit his *Paris and Helen*." David exhibited *Brutus*.[22]

By 1785 contemporary critics acknowledged that painting had been revolutionized. Its counterpart in theater were such plays as "Guillaume Tell," by Antoine-Marin Lemierre, and the "Mort de César" and "Brutus" by Voltaire. David's art put the Republic above personal sentiment and family attachment. These tyrannicidal plays took part of the classical seventeenth- and eighteenth-century tradition. The shrill cry of "justice" rather than grace could be heard well before the Revolution, often from voices within the royal establishment, voices the Revolution made its own.

What came to fruition in 1785 was not only a new style, a new classicism, but also a new relationship between artist and public, for this public now wielded an enormous influence on taste and the future of works of art. The academy had ranked genres in a hierarchy: historical paintings, associated with the nobility, at the top; landscapes, identified with le peuple, at the bottom. In the early eighteenth century the nobility retreated behind the private, decorative rococo, but the revival of historical paintings on large canvases by the state, specifically the *contrôleur des bâtiments du roi*, challenged this retreat in the 1740s. Paintings were honored as a result of "elite social interaction." By mid-century the public in the art world, like the public in politics (the Parlement), had become nearly omnipotent. Through the mouthpiece of the salon an artist could go public, upstage the academy, and deliver a powerful and controversial message, just as David did in 1785 and 1789 with the *Oath of the Horatii* and *Brutus*. The style that prevailed in the 1770s and 1780s was antirococo—in a sense, antinoble—but also antipopular in its stoic rejection of sensuality. It was a public taste, akin in its ideality to Rousseau's general will. Art in the reign of Louis XVI had made itself inextricable from politics.[23]

Architecture: Boullée

Etienne-Louis Boullée (1728–99) was almost a generation older than David, whose simplicity he anticipated in architecture. He was less successful than David. Although he received numerous private and public commissions as an architect (Versailles, Saint-Germain-en-Laye, Les Invalides), his most impressive designs are confined to a dossier in the Bibliothèque nationale and received little attention during his lifetime. Yet in his own unobtrusive way, Boullée's simplicity was far more extreme and unnerving than David's.

Boullée's teachers were Jacques-Ange Gabriel (1698–1782), enemy of rococo and proponent of "noble simplicity," and the abbé Marc-Antoine Laugier, who taught Boullée that only the necessary was beautiful and that geometry was the starting point of all architecture.[24] Boullée believed public architecture to be the noblest form of design. His enthusiasm for public monuments parallels the recognition given to *le public* both in the parlements after 1760 and in the civic themes of neoclassical history paintings. In the *Oath of the Horatii*, David used angular forms—orthogonal and diagonal lines, sharp, abrasive gestures, violent movement. By contrast, Boullée stressed stillness and expanses of space to rest the eyes. Circular shapes, he felt, were the most perfect of forms because of the "sweetness of their contour." Whereas the central trait of David's painting is the exchange of gazes between spectator and painted figures, as an architect Boullée's communication is limited. Where Boullée does allow for communication, as in his plans for an opera house (fig. IV.4) and a library (fig. IV.5), each element is centralized. The opera audience is seated evenly in a circular, tholuslike structure and can exit quickly from any point in the event of fire—a real contemporary concern. The library is more sinister, reminiscent of the contemporary Panopticon of Jeremy Bentham. Both have a central observation point from which to view every subject: Boullée's so that readers will not steal or deface books, Bentham's so that prisoners will not escape. Again, the structure is circular; each book is passed to a central desk by a kind of fire gang of library attendants and then dispensed. As opposed to the decentered communication of David's paintings, the library enjoys total centralization and surveillance. The revolutionary architects—Boullée, Claude-Nicolas Ledoux, Jean-Jacques Lequeu—have even been likened to Vladimir Tatlin, Aleksei Shchusev, and Albert Speer of the twentieth century in their standardizing tendencies.[25]

Like most architects at mid-century, Boullée began under the influence of Antonio Palladio. But he differed greatly from the neoclassical David, whose ancient masters had been filtered through the eyes of the "divine Raphaël." For Boullée, there was hardly a classical intermediary. In his *Essai sur l'art*, written in the 1790s, he admitted, "I

IV.4.
Etienne-Louis Boullée, Opéra, *drawing.*
Courtesy Bibliothèque nationale, photo: Bibl. Nat. Paris.

IV.5.

Etienne-Louis Boullée, National Library, *drawing, ca. 1780.*
Courtesy Bibliothèque nationale, photo: Bibl. Nat. Paris.

disdained, I avow, to limit myself to the sole study of our ancient masters. By the study of nature, I tried to enlarge my thoughts on an art which, from my profound meditations, seems to me to be still in its dawn." According to one critic, Boullée transcended classicism; according to another, he "was interested in geometrical forms rather than . . . ancient models." We might say that he dug below classicism, from massive Roman columns and arches to the primitive simplicity of the Doric order, to the Homeric era and beyond to Egypt and its most elementary forms—cylinders, cubes, cones, spheres, obelisks, pyramids. He juxtaposed these forms, abusing the classical hierarchy of orders, creating "interpenetrating masses or . . . crossings of volume and mass or . . . piles of stepped off units (motifs of contrasted sizes) or . . . assemblages of incongruous elements and [motifs of contrasted shapes]."[26]

The architect is a "fashioner of nature," one who puts nature to work, Boullée argued. Nature's simplicity enchanted him, but so did its grandeur and immensity. Thus Boullée strongly admired Gothic architecture for the consonance of its structure with its stated purpose— worship of the sublime deity—and for the concealment of the forces put to work to attain that sublimity (flying buttresses, the pointed arch). He himself stayed mostly with curvilinear structures and attempted to make his buildings show their utilitarian purposes: a tomb would show eternal repose, museums and libraries should stress com-

IV.6.
Etienne-Louis Boullée, Newton's Cenotaph, *drawing, 1784.*
Courtesy Bibliothèque nationale, photo: Bibl. Nat. Paris.

munication. Boullée's mortuary monuments, for instance, were sunk partly into the ground to suggest interment. Like David and the whole revolutionary generation, Boullée was preoccupied with death. For David, one lived only to the extent that one was willing to kill and die for one's country. Boullée sought the ultimate peace of burial.

Boullée designed an immense sphere for Isaac Newton's cenotaph (fig. IV.6), because the sphere possessed the greatest simplicity—a "flawless and endless" majestic surface that offered the utmost repose to the eye—but also because it fitted Newton: "O Newton! . . . I conceived the idea of surrounding thee with thy discovery, and thus, somehow, surrounding thee with myself." Here is Newton encompassed by the sphere whose order and universal law he discovered.[27]

Boullée peacefully endorsed the Revolution, but not the Terror, and he was denounced in March 1794 in an anonymous pamphlet for being a royalist like his contemporary Ledoux. After 1789 Boullée's work was interrupted almost entirely. A notable exception was his design for a national assembly (fig. IV.7). With its sheer, smooth massiveness and absence of pronounced articulation, it looks more like an enormous mausoleum than a legislature. Boullée's greatest moments of audacity were never far from the funereal. But the sheer size of Boullée's architecture also suggests the mass democratic culture about to dawn:

IV.7.
Etienne-Louis Boullée, National Assembly Hall, *drawing, ca. 1789–92.*
Courtesy Bibliothèque nationale, photo: Bibl. Nat. Paris.

twelve hundred deputies elected to the Estates General, several million electors in the primary assemblies of 1789—figures incomparably greater than under the old regime.

The architecture of the Revolution never went much beyond planning, due in part to its ambitious nature. But James Leith has discovered drawings by Antoine Vaudoyer, Jean-Jacques Lequeu, Armand-Guy Kersaint, Jean-Nicolas Durand, and Jean-Thomas Thibault that show characteristics already present in Boullée's architectural drawings: public purpose, massive dimensions, and elementary geometrical forms. For all these men, the new simplicity in architecture was to serve the newly discovered simplicity of human nature. Architecture consciously mirrored in space what was cherished in people's hearts: liberty, equality, fraternity.[28]

Sculpture: Houdon

Sculptors were in difficult straits by 1789. The *Mercure de France* noted: "Let us sympathize with artists who dedicated themselves to sculpture. They suffered from the Revolution twice as much as painters . . . for every rich man desires to see his features on canvas. But only a small number feel the merit of a bust."[29] Jean-Antoine Houdon (1741–1828) did not flourish during the Revolution. His submissions to the revolutionary salons were sculpted largely before 1789. Houdon's statue of Saint Scholastica, about which the Committee of Public Safety inquired with displeasure, was cleverly identified by his wife (so the story has it) as a statue of Philosophy to protect Houdon from imprisonment. Houdon had sculpted other saints early in his career—Bruno (1766–67) and a powerful John the Baptist (1766–67)—that were not exhibited in the 1790s. *L'Ecorché* (fig. IV.8), Houdon's most astonishing sculpture—a study for John the Baptist that could be called *The Anatomical Man*—was also ignored during the Revolution. His sensuous statue of 1783 *La Frileuse* (*The Shivering Woman*) (fig. IV.9) has a beauty quite unlike *The Anatomical Man,* but it is equally far removed from the patriotism of 1791, though exhibited in the salon of that year. But what of his sculptures of Voltaire in marble, bronze, and plaster, one of which was carried in front of the procession of Voltaire's remains when they were transferred to the Panthéon in July 1791? What about his remarkably expressive bust of Mirabeau (fig. IV.10), pockmarks and all, which captures both the orator's corpulence and forceful character? What about his Laplace, his Condorcet,

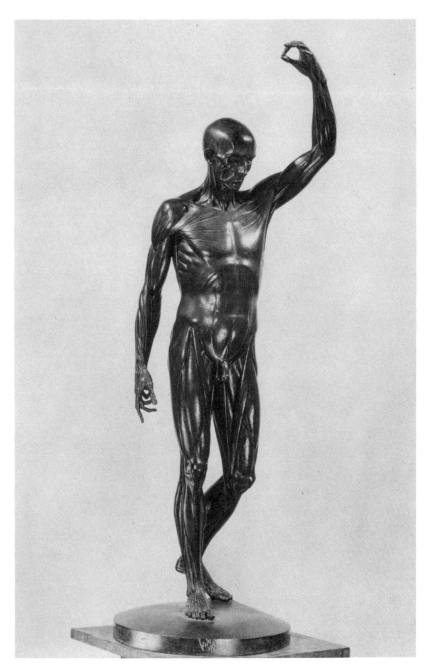

IV.8.
Jean-Antoine Houdon, L'Ecorché (The Flayed Man), *bronze statue, 1792.*
Courtesy Ecole Nationale Supérieure des Beaux-Arts, Paris.

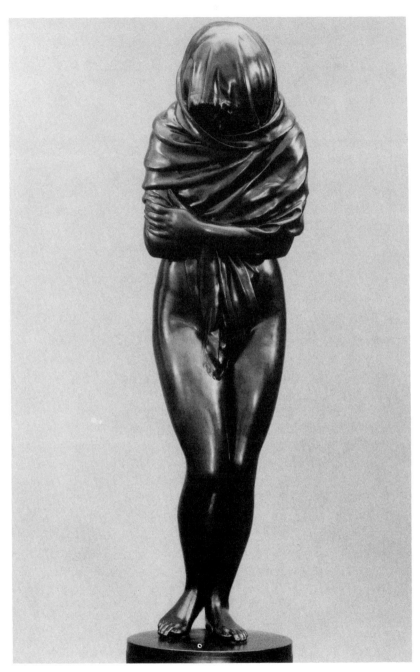

IV.9.
Jean-Antoine Houdon, La Frileuse (Winter), *bronze statue, 1787.*
Courtesy Metropolitan Museum of Art, bequest of Kate Trubee Davidson, 1962. (62.55)

IV. 10.

Jean-Antoine Houdon, Mirabeau, *marble bust, 1800. Versailles.*

Reprinted from H. H. Arnason, The Sculptures of Houdon, *Phaidon Press Ltd., 1975.*

his George Washington, which he was invited by the state of Virginia to execute in 1785 and for which he voyaged across the Atlantic? And Lafayette? And Jefferson (fig. iv.11)? And finally Napoléon, who granted him sittings, something he had refused David? How can Houdon be said not to belong to the revolutionary generation?[30]

A consummate artist, possibly the greatest French artist of his generation, Houdon *had* done patriotic subjects. But his patriotism was akin to that of Angiviller, who sought to rekindle the love of the patrie but recoiled when it flamed violently. Houdon saw greatness and force of character in Antoine Barnave, Mirabeau, Lafayette, and Napoléon. He tended to sculpt celebrities—partly, perhaps, because they brought commissions. Besides political men, they included German composer Christoph Gluck, Molière, and the actress Sophie Arnould. He exercised the classical talent of choosing the representative, the great, and the noble. He had a keen intuition about leaders and could tell who was on the crest of history's tide and not simply the object of a craze, like Alessandro Conte di Cagliostro or Franz Mesmer. Having achieved greatness by sculpting patriotic heroes, he felt a claim on them, and it pained him to submit a model anonymously along with unknown artists, as he was asked to do for the concours to choose a statue of Rousseau in 1791.[31]

Houdon was a private man, a family man, but above all an artist interested almost exclusively in art. He "remained indifferent to all the noise, all the confusion of thoughts and words." He "was a solitary individual by inclination, in no way misanthropic, but very busy and loving silence." Born to the petty bourgeoisie (son of a servant of a great household), he married for "reason" or interest, loved his daughters, lived virtuously. Calm, orderly, and industrious, Houdon went about his business without disturbing others. His personality and art lack David's combativeness; David never forgot the difficulties he had gaining recognition from the academy in the 1780s. Houdon's relations with the academy and the court were so good that he has been described as "the portraitist of the court, of the French and foreign aristocracy." For were not Washington and Jefferson wealthy Virginia planters? Was not *Diana* commissioned by Catherine the Great? Had he not sculpted Mme Adélaïde, the sister of Louis XV? Houdon stood at the pinnacle of the cultural elite of the old regime.[32]

Houdon was eventually rather passive toward the Revolution. He embraced Winckelmann's aesthetics but not David's violent patriotism. His heroes of antiquity were such mortals as Cicero and such gods as Apollo and Diana, so pure and philosophical that they soar above

IV.II.
Jean-Antoine Houdon, Bust of Thomas Jefferson, *marble, 1789.*
George Nixon Black Fund. 34.129. Courtesy Museum of Fine Arts, Boston.

fratricide. He sought replicas among his contemporaries and found them in those who were distinguished by their valor, talent, and intelligence. He sculpted these qualities in his subjects, but also their blemishes, to further characterize them. In celebrating the famous men and women of his day—the 1770s and 1780s—Houdon naturally gravitated to persons engaged in the great causes of the reign of Louis XVI: reform and liberty. In immortalizing them, Houdon contributed to the French revolutionary cult of great men—his gallery was a kind of pantheon. He continued at a much slower pace during the Revolution and Empire with busts of the playwrights Collin d'Harleville and Marie-Joseph Chénier and of Comte François Boissy d'Anglas. And later, during the Restoration, he sculpted Empress Joséphine and Czar Alexander I. But his participation in the salons fell off drastically after 1789; his floruit was over. He had participated more in the wave that brought in the French Revolution than in the current that carried the old regime out. Houdon's neoclassicism was linked more to a monarchical reform à la Louis XVI, or to a monarchical republicanism à la Voltaire the tragedian, than to Jacobinism. It expressed a cultural phenomenon that spanned the period 1750–1825. In this artistic movement, the Revolution was for Houdon largely an interruption.[33]

The Academy and the Classical Tradition in the Nineteenth Century

Did neoclassicism continue into the nineteenth century? David disassociated himself from the style of the *Horatii* after his release from prison in 1795. His *Intervention of the Sabine Women* (1799) is more humane and less masculine than the *Oath of the Horatii*—the women stand more at center stage, as peacemakers. David's *Napoléon in His Study, Napoléon Crossing Mount St. Bernard,* and *The Coronation of Napoléon* are indeed paintings of power but not of struggle, of glory but not of combat. The fire of patriotic painting is gone and in its place flickered David's increasingly private vision. The embers of neoclassicism, however, were not entirely extinguished.

Ironically, the Academy of Painting and Sculpture, which was restored to the third class of the National Institute in 1796 and received separate status in 1815, and its Ecole des Beaux-Arts were the principal heirs of a style whose champion had proscribed all academies during the Revolution. The restored academy was hardly more open to new talent and new methods than its predecessor had been. In the nineteenth century membership continued to be limited, and the average age of members, fifty-three, shows that the academy had abandoned the former practice of admitting young artists. One improvement that did take place was the emphasis on pedagogy over honorific functions—a reform the antiquarian Antoine-Chrysostome Quatremère de Quincy had demanded in 1791. The purpose of the academy was in fact to supervise the instruction of the Ecole des Beaux-Arts, located after 1818 in the defunct Musée des monuments français of Alexandre Lenoir. According to a leading authority, "the curriculum did not differ basically from that of the previous two centuries, and the sequence of drawings, from casts and from live models, had been the foundation of the academic curriculum since the seventeenth century." Copying the great masters at the Louvre was still considered essential. Wrote Dominique Ingres: "One must continually form one's taste on the masterpieces of art. To pretend to do without the study of antiquities and the classics is either madness or laziness. . . . Art never reaches such a high level as when it resembles nature so strongly that it can be taken for nature itself."[34]

From 1796 to 1863 the Ecole des Beaux-Arts sponsored the famous concours for the *prix de Rome*. Its principal category of entry was history paintings with subjects chosen from classical antiquity, although in the 1830s and 1840s numerous biblical subjects appeared. For this coveted prize, which gained recognition for a young painter, the "texts" of antiquity were quite the same as a generation earlier: *Theseus Conqueror of the Minotaur* (1807); *Briseis Mourning Patroclus* (1815); *Cincinnatus Receiving the Envoys from the Senate* (1844). Imperceptibly, the neoclassical gave way to the romantic and the realist, but in that gradual transformation, the school, the academy, and the concours of the prix de Rome served as bastions of classicism.[35]

The quest for simplicity was visible everywhere, from standards of measurement to forms of sculpture. Houdon's serene classicism, while glorifying the patriots of 1776 and 1789, transcended the politics of the Revolution and remains perhaps the best expression of the universal qualities of the school. Boullée's architecture of rudimentary cubic shapes has been called revolutionary in its geometric radicality. The simple and massive oneness of his designs, that is, shape without hierarchical articulation of parts, best expressed democracy. But Boullée did not implement these designs and stayed outside the political struggles of the art world in the 1790s. David, although he owed his career to royal protection and patronage, shook the foundations of privilege and comfort with the determination, will, and anger that he expressed both on canvas and in politics during the Revolution. Whether or not they personally became involved in politics, strength suffused each of these artists. They evinced a force that awakened and rose to the level (*hauteur*) of the problems that faced the revolutionary generation.

CHAPTER V

FROM SENSIBILITY

TO TERROR

The eighteenth century is too often thought of exclusively in terms of reason. When one reflects on how little reason ruled Candide and Candide's world, one begins to understand the irrational side of the world of the Enlightenment. Light does not exist without darkness. The century of Enlightenment was well aware of the duality of reality.[1] What is perhaps more puzzling is that often the positive is represented as welling forth from the emotional side of human nature. Certainly this is true of Jean-Jacques Rousseau's *Nouvelle Héloïse,* where the emotionality of Julie and Saint-Preux forms a welcome contrast to the rather arid rationality of Wolmar, Julie's husband.

Perhaps the best way to understand the importance given to *sensibilité* in the Enlightenment is to view it as an emotional force or energy by which people could do the good portrayed by reason. Sensibilité took the place of will, and, in the absence of original sin, makes completely natural the assent to the good (unlike grace). The sensibilité discussed here is complex, polyvalent, and treated as a pendant to the previous chapters on the Enlightenment and the geometric spirit (chapters 3 and 4).

Sensibilité may simply mean heart: spontaneous goodness and virtue, as in Fénelon's *Télémaque,* a romance about Ulysses' son, critical by allusion of the power and glory of Louis XIV. Or, it could mean awareness of the beyond, of virtue meriting eternal life and vice meriting damnation (Young, Walpole, Ducray-Duminil, and the black novel). Or, could the feeling of sensibilité be evoked by terror as well?

For Edmund Burke, terror was a sentiment that elevates the individual toward the sublime, as opposed to the trivial happiness of pleasure. Terror, Burke felt, evokes nobility of feeling, grandeur, and depth. This view differs greatly from the middle-class sensibilité that Diderot treasured as an ally of virtue and that can be found in such a play as his *Le Fils naturel* or Marsollier des Vivetières's *Les Deux Petits Savoyards.* This sensibilité is a sweet and optimistic sentimentality. We also glimpse this sensibilité in Bernardin de Saint-Pierre's *Paul et Virginie* until its conclusion, which is as melancholic about the transitory nature of human existence as are Hubert Robert's depictions of ruins. Sensibilité in music, on the other hand, represented a kind of Latin expressivity in contrast to the French classical discipline it eventually replaced. The Revolution would inherit a love of melody (Gluck) and harmony (Rameau).

At the end of the century, particularly in the popular domain, sensibilité was evoked by horror, murder, corpses in caverns, incest, and the like. This is a far cry from the spiritual archbishop Fénelon (1651–1715) or the *Nouvelle Héloïse* but perhaps not so far from the Terror and the guillotine. That these could be savored by so many and feared by so many others is elucidated by Burke's comments on the links of the fearful with the sublime. But what about the late eighteenth-century indulgence in the perverse and pornographic? Can these be linked to terror as well as virtuous sensibility? They share in that eighteenth-century fascination with whatever affects the senses. But the marquis d'Argens and the marquis de Sade display a sensuality without heart, close to greed or gluttony, and characterized above all by absolute amorality. Sade argues that if the passions exist, they exist to be satisfied. This ethic may derive from the Enlightenment's pleasure-pain principle of moral theory. The good here is identified completely with the pleasurable, however gross and cruel. Could this hedonistic sensibility have had anything to do with the Terror? Sade's world *is* a terror—a sexual concentration camp. Louis-Antoine-Léon Saint-Just's youthful epic poem, *Organt* (1789), is an unholy terror in the holy of holies—a commentary on the absence of virtue in the old regime, particularly the church. Saint-Just spells out the ultimate relations: virtue, vice, and terror. Terror draws on all the themes of sensibilité. Indeed, terror must speak to all the emotions, conditioning the individual and the nation to the requirements of the new regime. Terror is ultimately an instrument of regeneration, or so it was believed.

From Young to Rousseau

The eighteenth-century cult of sensibilité—sympathy, benevolence, melancholy, and tearfulness—was the companion to the wit and calculating spirit of the Enlightenment. Long before Rousseau's *Nouvelle Héloïse*, feeling was cultivated as strongly as reason. The century of Louis XIV did not lack sentiments to oppose the classicist's rule of reason and order. From Antoine Watteau's arcadian settings to Marie-Antoinette's bergeries runs an undoubted continuity. From Fénelon's *Télémaque* to the Revolution, the channels through which sensibility became terror are labyrinthine.

The terrible and melancholic elements of the preromantic mentality came from England. Between 1742 and 1745 Edward Young (1638–1765) published his popular *The Complaint; or, Night-Thoughts on Life, Death and Immortality,* which William Blake illustrated with eerie figures during the French Revolution. Young's *Night Thoughts,* as it was known, was a true "complaint" against the urbanity and presumptuousness of the Augustan age. More than stimulating a healthy reflection on mortality, Young introduced an appetite for gloom, out of which came an interest in the supposedly barbarous medieval past.[2] In 1757 Thomas Gray published his "Elegy Written in a Country Churchyard," which with Horace Walpole's *Castle of Otranto* (1764) launched a European cult of the macabre and the Gothic.

Horatio Walpole (1717–97), son of Sir Robert Walpole and member of Parliament (1741–67), bought the villa known as Strawberry Hill near Twickenham on the Thames in 1747, which he gothicized by adding plaster crenellation and a Catholic chapel. Dissatisfied with the results, which nonetheless helped start a vogue of Gothic constructions, in 1764 Walpole published *The Castle of Otranto,* a novel about his villa. The novel re-creates the age of chivalry, replete with knights in armor, which seemed far more interesting than the dry precepts of reason. *The Castle of Otranto* recounts crime in the towers and shadowy subterranean passages of a usurped château; the punishment for this crime is to be meted out to the third and fourth generations of descendants. Where classicism had stressed *vraisemblance*—truthfulness to life—Walpole's Gothic novel indulged freely in the grotesque and improbable. Such passages as "he sought the gloomiest shades, as best suited to the pleasing melancholy that reigned in his mind," set the mood of the supernatural, the dream, fantasy and nostalgia. Although not a great novel, *The Castle of Otranto* established a genre whose influence flowed like a subterranean current under the mainstream of eighteenth-century culture, surfacing at the end of the century in France with the black novels of Ann Radcliffe and Ducray-Duminil.[3]

It was Edmund Burke (fig. v.1), in his *Philosophical Enquiry into the Origin of Our Ideas on the Sublime and the Beautiful* (1757), who departed formally from classical aesthetics, disassociating the beautiful from the proportional and linking the sublime to pain. "Poetry, painting and other affecting arts," he wrote, ". . . are often capable of grafting a delight on wretchedness, misery and death itself."[4] The sublime for Burke is something radically distinct from the rather tame and small beautiful. Reason has little to do with the sublime, which is found in grandeur and terribleness, in oceans and mountains. Voltaire called the eighteenth century an age of prose, and countless commentators re-marked that its poetry was stillborn, due largely to a spurning of imagination, a faculty distrusted by sensationalist psychology. Burke was within the sensationalist tradition and was strongly influenced by Locke, Hutchinson, and Hume. But he developed an aesthetic that spoke to the eighteenth-century counterpassion for graveyards, caverns, irregular gardens, and astonishing mountains. For Burke, clarity was unimportant—for it "is in some sort an enemy to all enthusiasms whatsoever. . . . A clear idea is . . . another name for a little idea." The obscure in Milton's *Paradise Lost* was more conducive to terror, "which is in all cases whatsoever, either more openly or latently, the ruling principle of the sublime." In brief, "Whatever is in any sort terrible, or is conversant about terrible objects, or operates in a manner analogous to terror, is a source of the *sublime*."[5]

The philosophes, who were equating the good with pleasure and evil with pain, could have viewed Burke's writings with a jaundiced eye. Yet Diderot also spoke of terror's relation to the sublime: "Everything which astonishes the soul, everything which imparts a feeling of terror leads to the sublime. . . . Poets speak endlessly of eternity, infinity, infernal depths, darkened skies, deep seas, somber forests, thunder, lightning which tears through the clouds. . . . In all these things there is something terrible, grand, and somber."[6]

In his *Julie, ou la Nouvelle Héloïse* of 1761, Rousseau (fig. v.2) explored the emotions of unhappy love, jealousy, melancholy, and acute sensibility and produced an effect of sweet pain on readers. He left lesser writers to exploit terror. The central characters, Julie and Saint-Preux, experience the dilemmas of Enlightenment thought intellectually and morally. Saint-Preux discourses on suicide and Julie questions articles of her Protestant faith, but emotionally they are sufferers

V.I.

Portrait of Edmund Burke, *engraving by J. Jones of painting by George Romney.*

Courtesy Library of Congress, photo: John Reynolds.

V.2.
Anon., Portrait of Jean-Jacques Rousseau, *ca. 1760, engraving.*
Courtesy Library of Congress.

more than reasoners. They do not cast responsibility to the wind, which would throw them into a fatal (romantic) opposition to God, family, and society.

Saint-Preux suffers from a love that cannot be abated or requited. "If cruel fate refuses the sweet name of spouses," he writes to Julie, "nothing can take away from us that of faithful lovers; it will be the consolation of our sad days, and we will carry it to the tomb. Thus we begin to live again in order to begin to suffer again, and the sentiment of our existence is only for us the sentiment of pain." Julie's death, which deepens and sweetens this love, is preceded by the lovers' excursion with Julie's servants on Lake Geneva. A storm on the lake mirrors the tumult of their passion, a description that appealed to the eighteenth-century reader's infatuation with nature. Saint-Preux experiences a violent emotion in the boat: "But to find myself near her, to see her, to touch her, to speak to her, to love her, to adore her, and almost to possess her again, to feel her lost to me forever; that is what threw me into a fit of furor and rage which agitated me by degrees to despair. Soon I began turning around in my mind terrible thoughts, and in a transport from which I trembled in contemplating, I was violently tempted to precipitate her with me into the waves, and to finish there in her arms my life and my long torments."[7]

Although *Nouvelle Héloïse* aimed to illustrate melancholy, like most eighteenth-century novels it was also intended to edify. The exemplary chastity of the lovers after their original loss of innocence before Julie's marriage to Wolmar; their sublimation of passion into a relationship akin to the "pure love" of Fénelon; Julie's fidelity to her husband, her tender love for her children, her exemplary Christian death—all make the *Nouvelle Héloïse* a guide for life as well as an emotional experience.

Robert Darnton places this novel closer to devotional texts, which traditionally were read intensively, thoroughly assimilated, and reread, than to the new throwaway pamphlets, newspapers, and novels, which were consumed for information or distraction. Letters addressed to Rousseau after the *Nouvelle Héloïse* was published prove that readers cherished its sensibilité. A retired army officer, one Louis François, wrote: "You have driven me crazy about her. Imagine then the tears that her death must have wrung from me. Can you believe it? I spent three days without daring to read the last letter from M. de Wolmar to Saint-Preux. . . . I could not bear the idea of Julie dead or dying." The marquise de Polignac was convulsed in pain when she reached the same part, and other women wept for days.[8]

Rousseau created a revolution of his own with this novel (which had some seventy editions by 1800), as well as with his posthumously published *Confessions* (1781, 1788). A thorough bibliography for the Revolution by André Monglond contains sixty-four pages of titles by and about Rousseau, compared to forty-one listing devotional and theological works—a category that dominated publishing in the provinces before the Revolution. Almost single-handedly, Rousseau precipitated an affective revolution—one that was magnified by the political revolution of 1789.[9]

The Bourgeois Drama

Louis-Sébastien Mercier (1740–1814), in his *Du théâtre, ou Nouvel essai sur l'art dramatique,* called for a drama that would draw on the pathetic element of tragedy and the naive depiction of *mœurs* of comedy: "Let an excellent poet be an august benefactor! If he truly loves men, if he is penetrated by this divine fire which still ennobles genius, if he does not degrade it by bending his knee before the powerful of the earth, if he employs it to gather the sighs of the unfortunate, to carry them to the proud ear of those who caused them to be born, ah! with what recognition should we not pay his works."[10]

The bourgeois drama was so named because it depicted ordinary, mostly middle-class people in domestic situations. Sentiments of tenderness and compassion would be portrayed rather than the cruelty and vengeance of tragedy or the licentious buffoonery of boulevard entertainment. Classical tragedy was considered too remote from the everyday lives of most spectators. Its dilemmas and moral conflicts did not touch burghers, living comfortably and working regularly. Classical tragedy was too extravagant and too pompous.

The drama has been defined by Gaiffe as "a spectacle destined for a bourgeois or popular audience, presented with a moving and moral picture of its own milieu." Mercier described the drama as "the portrait of bourgeois life in every situation, either in gaiety, or pain, or sentiment, or morality." By bourgeois, these authors meant a class closer to Molière's "Bourgeois gentilhomme" than to Karl Marx's bourgeois. Dramas were rarely designated as such but as comedies, *opéras-comiques,* or tragedies. They could be identified by their moralizing tone, their lukewarm insistence that virtue not only prevail but be rewarded (as in the dramatization of Samuel Richardson's *Pamela, or Virtue Rewarded*), their scenes of tender recognition, and their stress on conciliation between persons of different social standing. In a sense, the bourgeois drama is profoundly unrevolutionary; it abhors violence and reconciles all differences with sentiment, that motor of virtue and proof of human goodness.[11]

For Friedrich Grimm, something was fundamentally wrong with the "false delicacy" of Parisian audiences of the 1780s—the unwillingness to permit anything unseemly or unflattering, the "excessive prudery" and basic "dishonesty" that censorship reinforced—"the most certain mark of the corruption of *mœurs*." Drama was ideological in that it portrayed not how audiences behaved but how they would have liked to believe they behaved. Audiences that wept at *opéras comiques larmoyantes* (tearful comic operas) could be convinced by their tears that they were really as compassionate, sympathetic, and benevolent as the characters on stage. Where David and Boullée alarmed and electrified audiences, the authors of the bourgeois drama lulled them into forgetting the rudeness of reality, leading them to overlook evil by making virtue seem effortless.[12]

Nor was weeping limited to fictional genres. Newspapers carried columns and printed engravings entitled "Traits de bienfaisance," which announced real acts of generosity to the unfortunate. But too much virtue in late eighteenth-century France was worn on the sleeve. The reaction came in the form of Sade's vicious world and in that of the boulevard melodramas, about which more later. Here we must try to understand how dramas may have sweetened the lives of eighteenth-century viewers.[13]

Many dramas were accompanied by music and listed as *comédies à ariettes*—Marsollier des Vivetières's *Nina*—or simply as *opéras-comiques*—Monvel's *Sargines, ou l'élève de l'amour* or Sedaine's *Déserteur* and *Richard Cœur de Lion*. Marsollier des Vivétières's *Les Deux Petits Savoyards,* in one act, with music by Nicolas d'Alayrac, was first performed in 1789. Familiar figures in Paris, savoyards performed many services, from running errands to sweeping chimneys. Mercier writes of them in his *Tableau de Paris*: "They scrimp on necessities in order to send [money] each year to their poor parents. The models of filial love are found in tatters, while gilded garments clothe denatured children. . . . They run through the streets from morning until dusk, their faces beaded with sweat, their teeth white with a naive and gay air: their cry is long, plaintiff and lugubrious." Savoyards were perfect objects of commiseration, being needy yet still self-sacrificing.[14]

The seigneur of the castle in *Les Deux Petits Savoyards* is more than grateful to find an unfortunate family worthy of the benefactions he has been yearning to bestow. In a touching song he tells how he lost his parents, how his brother is presumed dead, how he is without heirs, yet:

> I am not at all alone on earth; all the poor are my children;
> yes, I feel it, the rich man, who wants to do good,
> can still find on earth,
> both brothers and parents.

The seigneur asks one savoyard what he wants, and Michel answers, "Enough strength or money to enable my mother not to have to work."

Tender recognition, noble merit, tattered virtue, generosity, and noblesse oblige—such were some of the appealing traits in *Les Deux Petits Savoyards,* which was performed 212 times during the Revolution. Although this drama treats an ordinary subject—the savoyards and the self-made bourgeois were familiar figures—they were juxtaposed against a quasi-feudal, rustic setting, thus offering both the recognition of the familiar and the romance of the remote.[15]

The benevolence toward the lowly of the great—kings and nobles— is the touching theme of such sentimental dramas, one much exploited in the prerevolutionary years and the early years of the Revolution. Compassion is certainly admirable and necessary in any society. But when compassion becomes compulsive and its exhibition more important than the object of commiseration, when the rewards of virtue become its chief purpose, then the moral life of a people is narcissistic.

Sensibilité, or feeling, could be expressed in acting, music, and painting, as well as in literature. But the emphasis on natural feeling in acting seems curiously to have derived more from the neoclassical school of painting than from Mercier's and Diderot's theories of the drama. François-Joseph Talma (fig. v.3), the greatest French actor of the Revolution, wrote in his *Mémoires:* "Our famous painter David appeared and our painters, our sculptors and above all our young people [were] inspired by him. . . . feeling how useful this study could be to theater, I put myself into it with uncommon ardor." The imitation of David's painting meant a return to natural costuming, to simple, antique drapery and unpowdered hair, particularly in tragedies. Talma stressed that "the most sublime expressions are also the most simple. . . . Naive language is an aggrandized but exact expression of nature itself." The pompous declamations that permeated Europe's theaters gave way to Talma's natural intonation and diction. He was a master of sensibility, which he defined as "that faculty of exalta-

v.3.
Talma in the Role of Clovis in the Tragedy of That Name,
engraving, 1790.
Courtesy Library of Congress, photo: John Reynolds.

tion which agitates an actor, takes possession of his senses, shakes even his very soul, and enables him to enter into the most tragic situations and the most terrible of passions, as if they were his own."[16] Because of such techniques, the cult of simplicity drew additional force, for it was joined to the sensibility of true feelings.

Talma's words—"as if they were his own"—allude to the problem of dramatic authenticity that arrested Diderot's attention. The encyclopedist believed that there must be a conscious distinction between the artist who creates the effect of sensibility and the spectator who feels its transports. Diderot certainly believed in the "natural" and the "true," shown in his two dramas, *Le Fils naturel* (1757) and *Le Père de famille* (1758), in which he treated ordinary problems of ordinary citizens rather than the extraordinary ones of ancients. As a spectator he certainly experienced the transports of emotion. In his "Entretiens sur le fils naturel," Diderot exclaims: "The performance was so true, that forgetting in several places that I was a spectator, and an inconspicuous one at that, I was at the point of leaving my place, and of adding a real person to the scene." It would be nice, he added, if the staging were "so natural and true" that it would in effect be a painting. But this is impossible, because the nature of acting, unlike painting, is detached and deliberate. "One must remove oneself from the thing to the extent that art is more involved, where men are acting, than in a painted scene, where one sees, so to speak, only their shades." To create sensibility as an actor, one must be "cool-headed," emotionally detached. "To be true in theater, one has to do without the natural a little bit."[17]

In these writings and in the posthumous *Paradoxe sur le comédien* (1830), Diderot denies that the artist must be transparent to the public. To produce sensibility in the theater, the actor must simulate. Only when the heat of an actor's passion has subsided is he any good. Everything in acting is done for an "effect," but it must be felt only by the audience.[18]

The Musical Revolution

Artifice and control could be found in drama behind the transports of sensibility, but in French music at the end of the century, spontaneity and melody prevailed. Just as Mercier had berated French tragedy and comedy as being too remote from the hearts of contemporary citizens, so Rousseau and others complained about the formality and unnaturalness of French music in the age of Louis XIV and looked to Italy and Germany for deeper inspiration. France looked abroad in music as it had in literature for lessons on authentic feeling as opposed to classical control. In 1753, during the Quarrel of the Bouffons between partisans of French and Italian music provoked by the visit of Italian performers of opera buffa to the Paris opera, Rousseau entered the fray with his *Lettre sur la musique française.* "Arbiters of music and the Opera," he exclaimed, "men and women in fashion, I take leave of you forever." Rousseau sided with Italy against Paris, as he had sided with nature against civilization in his first and second *Discourses.* For with Jean-Philippe Rameau and Jean-Baptiste Lully, French music had lacked spontaneity, had become controlled and measured: "arbitrary beauties of pure convention," "fugues," "imitations," and "double designs." The French language, he maintained, was too irregular to be set to music, unlike Italian, which had an uncomplicated articulation, few combinations of consonants, an abundance of syllables in vowels, and few diphthongs. The French language had a didactic order, whereas the inversions of Italian made it more conducive to "good melody." Most important, Italian music had harmony, which was universal, unlike melody, which had national character. The purpose of music, Rousseau felt, was "to move, to imitate, to please and to bring to the heart the sweetest impressions of harmony and song."[19]

Music apart, such questions were not idle. Alembert assessed the political and moral significance of being a *bouffoniste:* "In the dictionary of certain men, the words *bouffoniste,* republican, *frondeur,* atheist, indeed, materialist, are all synonyms. . . . All sorts of liberties are equally dangerous. Liberty of music supposes that of feeling; liberty of feeling carries with it that of thinking, that of thinking, that of action; and the liberty of action is the ruin of states."[20] The released feeling was not only aesthetic but political.

But bouffonistes were not immediately victorious. The war was lost, at least at the opera. In 1770 Charles Burney, an English connoisseur of music, noted:

> The French are much indebted to M. Philidor for being among the first to betray them into a toleration of Italian music, by adopting French words to it, and afterwards by imitating the Italian style in several comic operas, which have had great success, particularly *Le Maréchal ferrant, Le Bûcheron, Le Sorcier,* and *Tom*

Jones. He likewise composed a serious opera, called *Ernelinde,* which is much admired by the Italian lovers of melody, but the frequenters of the great opera house of Paris are not yet suffi- ciently weaned from Lulli and Rameau to give great encourage- ment to such attempts.

Indeed, at the opera, he notes elsewhere, the "style of composition is totally changed throughout the rest of Europe; yet the French, com- monly accused of more levity and caprice than their neighbours, have stood still in music for more than thirty years [and] . . . the two great essentials of melody and expression, may still be said to be in [their] infancy."[21]

By 1774 the musical revolution had conquered even the opera.[22] In France this was the work of neither the bouffonistes nor the French Revolution but of the court of Louis XVI, in particular Marie- Antoinette. The Austrian princess, a devotee of the cult of sensibilité with her shepherds and shepherdesses, listened to the critics of the old music and imported musicians from her home, Vienna, the musi- cal center of Europe and the meetingplace of German and Italian mu- sic. Marie-Antoinette was largely responsible for attracting to Paris Gluck, Niccolò Piccinni, Antonio Salieri, Antonio Sacchini, and Luigi Cherubini—composers who continued to dominate the Paris opera long after their patroness had disappeared. Gluck won the war of 1774 over the Piccinnists, but both German and Italian music were enor- mously popular for the next several decades. By 1781 only 3 percent of the opera's repertory was "old"; the rest was composed of "modern" works. Haydn dominated the spiritual concerts, which were held in the Tuileries on feast days when the opera was closed. But motets and oratorios by Sacchini, Piccinni, Pasquale Anfossi, Felice Alessandri, Alessio Prati, Domenico Cimarosa, and Niccolò Jommelli were also performed there. Mozart made his debut at Versailles in 1763 when he was seven and returned fifteen years later, but he was neither as popu- lar as Haydn nor as Gluck, whose *Iphigénie en Tauride, Iphigénie en Aulide, Orphée et Eurydice,* and *Armide* dominated the opera during the Revolution.[23]

So great were Italian and German influences in France in the last decades of the eighteenth century that numerous conservative writers from the 1750s to the present have claimed that the Quarrel of the Bouffons was an argument between French patriots and alien con- spirators (the bouffonistes Rousseau, Grimm, and Holbach being for- eigners) bent on undermining the cultural as well as the political foundations of the old regime. "The musical quarrel of the 1750's" writes one historian, "was a prelude to the larger drama of the 1790's."[24]

Another theory points to the quarrel's impact on the development of an indigenous comic opera that in turn influenced the nineteenth-century romantic opera of Beethoven, Weber, Berlioz, and Wagner. This is the contention of music historian Paul Henry Lang, who argues that opéra-comique, not Gluck, was the main inspiration in French opera between the 1780s and Wagner. "Innocent little songs called *vaudevilles* [or *ariettes*] connected by spoken dialogue, developed into the pathetic and wildly romantic grand opera, completely devoid of comic scenes." Opéra-comique grew out of the cult of French sensibility and the *comédie larmoyante* and was supposed to be light and moving rather than actually comical. It drew from *comédie sérieuse* and sensibilité and lacked the emotional control characteristic of Rameau.[25]

Music, according to Rousseau, must express feelings. The opera buffa conveys the "truth and simplicity of nature and avoids the artificial and the recherché." Such comic operas as *Tom Jones* (1765), an adaptation by François-André Philidor of Henry Fielding's novel, were sources of romantic opera. Michel Sedaine's *Le Déserteur* (1769) anticipated romantic rescue operas after 1789. Beethoven's *Fidelio* was heir to such later revolutionary rescue operas as the *Rigors of the Convent,* in which a young woman being held in a cloister is freed (a favorite theme of anticlerical dramatists in the 1790s). The opera *Leonore* (1798) by Jean-Nicolas Bouilly and Pierre Gaveaux was an even more immediate source of *Fidelio.*[26]

If Sedaine was the father of French opéra-comique, the chief composer of this genre just before and during the Revolution was André Grétry (1741–1813), who was "bowled over" by Gluck's music during his voyage to France from Italy, where he had been studying in the Collège Liégois. Grétry does not entirely vindicate Lang's thesis: although he composed opéras-comiques, he was heavily influenced by German and Italian music. Earlier, as a choirboy in Liège, he had been complimented for singing "so purely in the Italian style." Devoted to his parents, to God, and to the Virgin, Grétry had had to tear himself from his familial surroundings. Later he wrote, "Paternal love and filial love reside no doubt in all hearts, even in the hardest ones; but people of high rank are far from knowing how much this worthy sentiment is lively among respectable bourgeois, especially in countries where luxury and debauchery have not placed barriers between fathers and their children." Grétry's moralism rings true. After some time in Rome, he felt the need for solitude and became a hermit for a few months, experiencing "the sweetest satisfaction" in his life. There he composed music for Piètro Metastasio, observing, "It is only in searching at length for fugitive effects in the wanderings of your imagination that you will manage to fix them according to your desires." Grétry's experience equaled David's "cataract operation" during his voyage to Naples in 1779. Once in Paris, Grétry focused on actors and declamation rather than on playwrights. He aimed at simplicity and naturalness—at conveying one idea per tune and fitting music to action and words to music. Instinct, an uncomplicated naturalness unadorned by wit, conveyed truth. Grétry's *Le Huron* (1768), *Lucille* (1769), *Zémire et Azor* (1771), *L'Amant jaloux* (1778), and *L'Epreuve villageoise* (1784) made him the Opéra-Comique's principal composer. Fidelity to one's feelings, authenticity à la Werther or Saint-Preux, harmony à la Gluck were ideas of sensibilité accompanying the musical revolution.[27]

Rousseau, tormented by his *Confessions,* made a point of meeting Grétry during a performance of *La Fausse Magie,* telling him: "How happy I am to meet you; for a long time I thought my heart closed to sweet sensations, but your music causes me to feel them again." A few years later Grétry composed his most famous opéra-comique, *Richard Cœur de Lion* (1784), a troubadour opera, the songs for which were widely sung (most notoriously on 3 October 1789 by the bodyguard of the Versailles garrison). Grétry composed the famous "O Richard! O mon Roi!" almost extemporaneously when Sedaine commissioned it at the last minute. When the voice of one of the singers gave out on the night of the opera's premiere, Grétry exclaimed: "That is exactly the voice of a prisoner; you will produce the effect which I desire, sing and remain at ease."[28]

Through his musical career, Grétry reflected on the connections between music, nationality, and sensibilité. He no longer appreciated French contrapuntal harmony and opted for the "sweet" melody—the song of nature—to be found more in the heat of Rome under "the influence of a burning sun" than in the cold and nervous North. Yet Grétry's sensibility was not anchored in the pre-Revolution. Fénelon's *Télémaque* was "a brook of pure brilliant water which follows its natural course, and leaves flowers and fruits everywhere"; dissonance lay in the future among "corrupt peoples." The "noisy music" came with the Revolution. Grétry did, nonetheless, write an opera on a libertarian theme in 1791: *Guillaume Tell,* libretto by Sedaine. This opera is full of local color, using cowhorns and storms to communicate "tumult and violence," fury and rage.[29]

Luigi Cherubini, who was born in Florence in 1760 and was nurtured on church music, especially Palestrina, was also an influential preromantic composer. Cherubini came to Paris in 1786 from London, where he had become acquainted with Handel's music. He lived in Paris until his death in 1842. Cherubini had always wanted to write operas, and at a young age he wrote arias for operas by other composers. Although E. J. Dent has characterized his music as "cold-blooded," his opera *Demophon* (1788) rivaled Mozart and surpassed Gluck. The formal qualities of his music preclude the label romantic, and his operas lack the emphasis of choruses, dances, and local color. With *Lodoïska* (1791, libretto by Filette de Loraux), Cherubini did enter the ranks of preromantic musicians. Like opéra-comique, *Lodoïska* had spoken dialogue, and it was closer to the English ballad than to the Italian opera. Listed as a *comédie mêlée d'ariettes,* it used duets, trios, and ensembles. These musical numbers could be lengthy, lacking proportion to the spoken parts. Cherubini's opera preceded Dejaure and Kreutzer's *Lodoïska* by two weeks and should not be confused with that production. (Several stories were made into operas by more than one composer during the Revolution; *Paul et Virginie* is a famous example.) This comedy-opera (genres are fairly imprecise here) had such romantic elements as a setting in a medieval Polish castle, a captive damsel (Lodoïska, held by Dourlinski, whose embraces she refuses because she loves her rescuer, Floreski). *Lodoïska* has been called a full-blooded romantic piece, although Cherubini himself was "something between Mozart and Beethoven." Similarities of character and situation to Beethoven's *Fidelio* have been noted, and Cherubini's vivid action (Tatar savages who beseige the castle), choruses, and orchestral color with such instruments as the clarinet and French horn were romantic devices associated with Germany but also used in the operas of the French Revolution.[30]

Another preromantic opera that captivated the contemporary imagination with characteristic "rescue" themes was *La Caverne* by Jean-François Lesueur. Lesueur had a reputation as a composer of sacred music at Notre-Dame, where he attempted to introduce orchestral music and wrote his *Essai de musique sacrée* (1787). His *Télémaque,* an operatic imitation of Gluck, used spoken dialogue like *Lodoïska* but in formal neoclassical verse. Although he wrote detailed instructions for his actors, he wanted acting to appear spontaneous. His biggest success was *La Caverne,* which, like the later successful play by Jean-Henri-Ferdinand Lamartelière, *Robert, Chef des brigands* (1792), and indeed like Nicolas-Julien Forgeot and Méhul's *Caverne,* was probably based on Johann von Schiller's immensely popular *Die Raüber* (1778). The threat of brigands was real during the French Revolution, and they were noticeably present on stage. *La Caverne* was also a rescue opera and influenced Berlioz. Its heroine, Seraphita, is abducted by brigands and taken to a cave until Roustan, a friend of Seraphita's husband, rescues her. "Romanticism is all in the play," E. J. Dent has written, "There is nothing musically romantic." Its "peasant scenes, popular dances, humorous songs and choruses" form part of this nascent romantic sensibility. Lesueur also treated Bernardin de Saint-Pierre's *Paul et Virginie* in an opera, as had Edmond-Guillaume Favières and Kreutzer before him, but without much success.[31]

Etienne-Henri Méhul (1763–1817), the son of a *maître d'hôtel* of the duc de Montmorency in the Meuse Valley at Givet, also influenced the musical revolution. Like Lesueur, he grew up in religious surroundings, studying under the organist of a monastery in Recollets and then under a German choir inspector. He renounced a religious vocation due to poor health and came to Paris, where Gluck's lyrical music made a profound impression on him. He made his debut at the Concert spirituel (the principal outlet for symphonic music) with an *Ode sacrée,* set to lyrics by Rousseau. He then collaborated with a librettist named Hoffman, an ironic and acerbic neoclassical writer who stuck with him through most of his career.

On 4 September 1790 Méhul's *Euphrosine, ou Le Tyran corrigé* premiered at the Comédie italienne. It was an immediate success. The famous duet "Gardez-vous de la jalousie" seemed to Grétry to "open the skull of the spectators with the vault of the theater." Berlioz praised its "grace, finesse, éclat, dramatic movement and explosions of passion of a violence and truthfulness truly frightening." Like operas that preceded it, this one had nothing to do with the French Revolution. Instead it was similar to such shipwreck stories as *Paul et Virginie.* *Euphrosine,* too, ended with the drowning of its heroine, who wants to marry Mélidore against her brothers' wishes. Mélidore suggests that she visit a hermitage near Messina. The hermit there has died, and Mélidore has taken his place. He shines a beacon to light Euphrosine's swim to shore. After several successful rendezvous, Euphrosine's brothers find out, and one night they shine a beacon to divert their sister from her beloved. They extinguish the light as Euphrosine approaches, and she drowns. The final act is essentially a melodrama; the music of the orchestra conveys one emotion after another, and

Euphrosine, in a breach of classical rules, prays on stage—an act that became common in romantic opera. Again, the storm, the sea, the hints of incestuous love, the peasant and sailor choruses, the explicit Christian motifs, and a finale in E major (which anticipates Weber) make this opera a foremost example of the preromantic genre.[32]

Although Méhul wrote the "Chant du départ" (1794), which has been called a second Marseillaise, and served as an inspector of the Conservatoire, he ran into occasional trouble with drama censors of the Revolution (his Adrien in *Adrien, empereur de Rome* became a general so as not to offend republican sensibilities). Perhaps his most successful opera was written during the Empire. This was *Joseph* (1807), in which Jacob arrives in Egypt and Joseph pardons his brothers. Imperial reconciliation here coincided with romantic sensibility, just as storms and shipwrecks had expressed the tensions of the Terror.[33]

Romantic opera derived exclusively from neither foreign nor French sources. Foreign composers were sponsored by such patrons as Marie-Antoinette (admittedly an Austrian, but certainly a pillar of the establishment). And the French did not compose romantic (or preromantic) opera without foreign inspiration. Grétry drew from both Gluck and the Italians, Cherubini himself was Italian, Méhul's *Caverne* was probably borrowed from Schiller and was profoundly influenced by Gluck. The opéra-comique provided a new genre with which to express such romantic themes as the rescue, but Italian and German influences, fruit of the Quarrel of the Bouffons, certainly made themselves felt through the 1790s.

Painting: Robert des Ruines

Refrains like "O Richard! O mon Roi!" in Grétry's *Richard Cœur de Lion* could evoke nostalgia of a noble, feudal past. Late eighteenth-century paintings depicting remains of the distant past triggered similar wistfulness. Hubert Robert (Robert des Ruines, 1733–1808) gained a reputation and a living as an academic painter of ruins. He began his career as a student at the French Academy of Rome. The recently discovered ruins at Herculaneum and Pompeii did not prompt him to recreate Roman history as they had David but to paint other ancient monuments in their crumbling splendor. Robert typically juxtaposed ancient monuments with scenes of contemporary life—people bathing, washing, cooking, playing on antique premises. In joining

v.4.

Hubert Robert, Demolition of Houses on the Pont au Change in 1788.

Courtesy Musée Carnavalet, Paris, photo: Lauros-Giraudon/Art Resource, New York.

V.5.
Hubert Robert, The Demolition of the Bastille, *painting, ca. 1780–95.*
Courtesy Musée Carnavalet, Paris, photo: Lauros-Giraudon/Art Resource, New York.

these two elements, Robert united the grandeur of antiquity and the charm and triteness of the quotidian. *Antique Ruins* shows persons in both antique and modern wear in front of a huge ruined arch whose pedestal is crumbling, while huge granite blocks, detached from the structure, spot the foreground. To the right is an enormous urn with the painter's name inscribed on the socle.[34]

Robert painted in silvery hues; a dull grey overcast all his compositions. Contemporaries complained about his limited palette, along with his tendency to crowd his ruins with poorly drawn figures. These detracted from the ambience of eerie solitude and prompted one critic to call him a cheerful artist. But Robert's figures languish, seeming to go nowhere and do nothing. Listen to Diderot: "The effect of these compositions, good or bad, is to leave us in a sweet melancholy. We fix our gaze on the debris of an arc de triomphe, a portico, a pyramid, a temple, a palace, and we return into ourselves. We anticipate the ravages of time, and our imagination disperses over the earth the very edifices we inhabit. For an instant, solitude and silence reign all around us; we alone remain of a whole nation which is no longer; and there is the first line of the poetics of ruins."[35]

The prerevolutionary demolition around Paris and the Revolution itself provided Robert with other melancholic motifs. The word *revolution* in the eighteenth century could signify simply the overthrow of a powerful kingdom. Robert's ruins belong to the context of such *vicissitudes*. Figures I.3 and v.4 depict the picturesque shops on the Pont au Change and the bridge of Notre-Dame being demolished to improve transportation and salubrity. But what could parallel the scene of the demolished Bastille after its siege (fig. v.5)? The immense gloom of this fortress is illustrated by myriad workmen so high on its parapet that the viewer can hardly discern them. Here was a contemporary ruin created by the Revolution. The trip to Rome and Naples was soon made unnecessary by the revolutionary ruins in the environs of Paris. The devastated churches and castles made fake ruins superfluous.

As owners emigrated, they left formerly magnificent residences unoccupied, to be sold or used by revolutionaries. Degradation inevitably resulted. Not only did contemporary and medieval structures suffer (and indeed there was an eighteenth-century interest in Gothic ruins), but the ruin of ancient edifices was hastened. In the *Ruins of the Gallery of the Emperor's Palace in Rome* (fig. v.6) what seem to be bandits (who abounded during the Revolution) camp in the subterranean remains of an ancient splendor, a rickety ladder reaching to the earth's

v.6.
Hubert Robert, Ruins of the Gallery of the Emperors' Palace
in Rome, *painting, ca. 1795.*
Courtesy Musée des Beaux-Arts et d'Archéologie, Besançon, photo: Lauros-Giraudon/
Art Resource, New York.

surface. Again the artist superimposes the present on the past, submitting it to the ravages of time and human negligence.

The Popular Literature of Sensibilité

The aesthetics of ruins announced the collapse of a civilization, but the black novel and melodrama evinced an absorption with wickedness that was peculiar to the psychology of the Terror, particularly its denunciations. François-Thomas de Baculard d'Arnaud (1718–1805), whose novels were precursors of the black novel, believed in waking his readers with "jolts of terror" and was one of the most popular authors of his time. A friend of Voltaire (for a while) and of Frederick the Great, he was enormously prolific, and his influence spread to Holland and Germany. He was the master of the sentimental novel and novella, original forms of the popular novel that were often published serially. His *Epreuves du sentiment* (1772), in four and six volumes, had gone through five printings by 1800, his *Amants malheureux, ou le Comte de Comminges,* a three-act drama, had seven printings between 1764 and 1793, and his *Epoux malheureux* (the titles speak for themselves) six printings before 1800.[36]

Arnaud's principal sources were Dante's *Inferno,* Milton's *Paradise Lost,* Young's *Night Thoughts,* and Richardson's *Pamela,* which he used for his *Fanni ou Pamela, Historie anglaise. Fanni* is the story of a virtuous country lass who marries her neighbor's son, Thaley, only to discover later that he is already married. Aghast, she departs to live in poverty with their son until Thaley, moved by remorse for his wrongdoing, takes pity on his beloved and their child. Arnaud's stories have two sides: sweet, tearful goodness and sad, horrible evil. The two are pitted against each other when female innocence and virtue is contrasted to the corruption of London.

From memoirs of criminal trials in the late eighteenth century, we know that Fanni existed in real life, because the language of sensibilité, of tenderness and horror, had reached the legal milieu. One of the most sensational cases of the century was based on charges of theft (handkerchiefs, Madeira, and money) leveled in 1785 in Rouen against a maid, Marie Cléreaux, who faced death by hanging. The parlement of Rouen took up the case, and a young, enlightened lawyer named Froudière defended the maid. He wrote and distributed a sixty-eight-page *mémoire* (which was illegal) and aroused the public to such a pitch of indignation in favor of the young woman that the parlement reversed its judgment of guilt. According to Mlle Créaux's persuasive defense, her lecherous employer had debauched another domestic, killed the child born of the affair, tried to seduce Créaux by appearing naked before her, and finally accused her falsely of crimes, to remove her as a witness to his own.

What is interesting is the language used in this case; Créaux's defense depicts the same female innocence and purity confronted by male lust and treachery as Arnaud's *Fanni*. The magistrate, to whom the memoir is officially addressed, must come to the side of innocence. He is "sensitive, honest and virtuous," whereas the plaintiff, Thibault, is a "man of immense and profound perversity" for whom "truth counts no more in his mouth than humanity does in his heart."

The defense, of course, rests on more than simple sentimentality. Froudière convincingly tested the credibility of witnesses, probability of circumstances, and consistency of accusations, all of which show the innocence of Créaux as radiating with luminosity. In surrendering his memoir to the public, he virtually wrote off the integrity of the courts of Rouen and delivered the fate of Créaux to the Rouennais. A crowd attacked Thibault's house. Sensibility and compassion for innocence combined with violence against what appeared to be utterly depraved enemies. We are very close to the psychology of the *roman noir* and the *mélodrame.*[37]

These three sides of sensibility—sweetness, horror, and terror— can be found in two of the most influential and widely read novels of the revolutionary decade: Bernardin de Saint-Pierre's *Paul et Virginie* (1787) and Ducray-Duminil's *Coélina, ou L'Enfant du mystère* (1799).

Bernardin de Saint-Pierre (fig. v.7) was a friend and disciple of Rousseau, and his tale, based on a true story that transpired in the Indian Ocean on the Ile de France (now Mauritius), resembles the *Nouvelle Héloïse* in the unconsummated love and pathetic death of the heroine. Paul and Virginie shine in filial devotion to "their parents," in their solicitude for each other, in their beneficence toward the island's slaves, and in their carefree behavior. In this tropical environment, with its verdant greenery, bananas, and monkeys, virtue is as lush as the foliage. Paul and Virginie automatically do good. A contrary desire scarcely enters their hearts. On Sundays they attend Mass at a church where wealthy Europeans, impressed with their virtue, invite them to share their pleasures. "But they repulsed their offers, always with seemliness and respect, persuaded that powerful people search the weak only to make them oblige their wishes."

Europe intrudes on this innocence. Virginie leaves the island at the

v.7.

Portrait of Bernardin de Saint-Pierre, *engraving from portrait by [Louis?]*
Lafitte, ca. 1805.
Courtesy Library of Congress.

insistence of an aunt in France to complete her education. The obstacles of fortune, social origins, and distance all separate corrupt civilization from this Eden in the Pacific.

The denouement of the novel finds Virginie with outstretched hands
on the poop of her sinking ship, returning to Paul, who braves the

waves to try to meet her. "One could see at that moment an object worthy of an eternal pity, a young lady appearing in the gallery of the poop of the *Saint-Géran,* stretching out her arms toward him who made so many efforts to join her. It was Virginie."

The novel ends bathed as much in pathos as the beginning was in sweetness, the verdant foliage replaced by the graves of almost every character. The last scene is of ruin; nature overtakes civilization. The concluding paragraph, addressed to the deceased protagonists, reads in part: "No one since you has dared to cultivate this desolate earth, nor raise up these humble cabins. Your goats have become savage; your orchards are destroyed; your birds have flown away, and only the sounds of sparrows who circle above this basin of rocks are heard." Nature takes over as it does in the paintings of Hubert Robert. And here the political moral: The civilization of Paul and Virginie, a fragile enclave of virtue in the worldwide ancien régime, collapses.[38]

Louis Fontanes, a publicist of the Empire, ranked *Paul et Virginie* next to *Télémaque,* one of Bernardin's sources of inspiration. Dupont de Nemours and Louis and Napoléon Bonaparte all wept on reading this match for Goethe's *Werther.* Bernardin's sentimentality can be just as powerful when dealing with the disintegration of the illusory world he creates in the first part of the novel as with the illusions themselves of that world. Cruel chagrin follows naive optimism as necessarily it must. Before the end of the Revolution, this "novel of rose water" went through twenty editions and reprints; by 1850 sixty-nine more had appeared,[39] extending the sway of sensibilité well into the nineteenth century.

A more "popular" form of sensibility, one closer to Arnaud in its exaggeration, violent contrasts of good and evil, and taste for terror, is the work of François-Guillaume Ducray-Duminil (1761–1819), editor of the *Petites Affiches* during the Revolution. Ducray wrote a dozen novels and plays that also went through innumerable revolutionary and nineteenth-century reprintings, allegedly purchased by coachmen and chambermaids. They lead from the world of the sentimental to that of the full-blown black novel.

The Black Novel and the Melodrama

In the introduction to his novel *Alexis, ou La Maisonnette dans les bois* (1789) Ducray-Duminil laments the man with a sensitive nature: "Oh! how he is to be pitied, the sensitive man." Pursued by fate and misfortune, he must suffer; an unlucky star overhead spreads evil influences wherever he goes.

Alexis is the story of a presumed orphan placed in the Collège de Navarre by his anonymous, mysterious father, who wishes to conceal his relationship to his son, and of Clairette, born out of wedlock. Illegitimacy haunts Alexis as it did Paul in *Paul et Virginie*. Alexis falls in love with Clairette, but before he can marry her he learns the terrible story of Clairette's birth. Each night a coffin containing the remains of Clairette's mother is removed from a cavern underneath the maisonnette of Clairette's stepfather.

This four-volume novel leaves nothing out and is as much a horror story as a tale of terror. Ducray-Duminil's morbid fascination with corpses and funereal caverns is far less delicate and less sweet than the melancholic *Paul et Virginie*. Virtue for Ducray-Duminil comes in the form of mail-fisted justice and revelations of infamy. What could be further from classical bienséance than a man impaling his wife and child and burying them beneath his house?

Ducray-Duminil and Arnaud (who published his *Epreuves du sentiment* in serial form) can be said to have introduced the popular novel— one that, as the critic Jean-François de La Harpe said, is not a "blue story" (referring to the bibliothèque bleue of Troyes) but a "black story." Ducray-Duminil's characters are not free agents. Their lives are interwoven by the mysteries of fate, occasionally identified with Providence. The result is a strong, pre-Dickensian penchant for coincidence. Ducray-Duminil explains his novel as "a tissue of adventures linked together . . . which taken separately, are very credible. One does not give them credence because, as they say, it is impossible that they all happened to the same person. What does it matter to me if that is so? If instead of one hero, this story had two hundred, the facts are no less true and no less interesting to me."[40]

Ducray-Duminil's most famous novel was *Coélina, ou L'Enfant du mystère*, published in no fewer than six volumes in Year VII (1799) and reprinted twenty times in the nineteenth century, for an estimated total of 1.2 million copies.[41] It resembles *Alexis* in its preoccupations with illegitimacy, corpses (a woman buried alive and preserved for a generation), mysterious identities, greed, inheritance, criminality, even murder. Throughout, merciless fate seals the characters' destinies by punishing vice. Those who pretend with the philosophes that man is in control are the villains, whose vices Ducray-Duminil says he paints "with large strokes to make a greater impression." This world is only partly imaginary. Illegitimacy, banditry, vagrancy, and a generally high degree of geographical mobility were characteristic of France during the 1790s.[42]

Seven editions of Ducray-Duminil's prerevolutionary novel *Lolotte et Fanfan,* nineteen of *Alexis,* and twenty-one of *Coélina* (not to mention René-Charles Guilbert de Pixérécourt's widely popular dramatic adaptation of it) made Ducray-Duminil a formidable popular novelist. The cult of horror and ineluctable fate separate him sharply from the brighter, sweeter vein of eighteenth-century sensibilité of Rousseau and Bernardin de Saint-Pierre. Dark presentiments loomed over the 1790s.

The melodramas on the eve of that decade, accompanied by music, portrayed similar embodiments of persecuted innocence, with complicated intrigue and a denouement by some quasi-miraculous intervention. Melodramas highlighted assassinations, shipwrecks, brigandage, and terror. They were somber in mood and infused with a high degree of moralism. Though commonly thought to have evolved from the bourgeois drama of the 1770s, melodramas had other origins. (The drama did not succeed as well in the Revolution as these lugubrious productions or the frivolous vaudevilles.) One source of the melodrama was the *pantomime héroïque,* which flourished on the boulevards in the 1780s.[43]

Jean-François Arnould-Mussot's *Héroïne américaine* (1786), which had 120 performances during the Revolution, is a pantomime taken from a presumably true story borrowed from the abbé Raynal. It tells of an English officer who, having escaped from the savage Caribs, is secretly nourished by a young Indian girl (the *héroïne américaine*). He falls in love with her but later sells her into slavery. His betrayal notwithstanding, she saves her former lover from torture. The success of this creation was attributed to "the multiplicity of episodes, the incessant variation on the theme of persecution, . . . the particular and general combats, [and] above all, the vast and picturesque decors."[44]

Some dramas bordered on the melodramatic. The caverns found in Ducray-Duminil are present in *Camille, ou Le Souterrain* of Marsollier des Vivetières, in *Le Château de diable* of Joseph-Marie Loisel de Tréogate, and in Larmartelière's adaptation of Johann von Schiller's *Die Raüber* in *Robert, Chef des brigands,* which was very popular during the Terror.

Forêt noire, situated in Calabria, was an enormously popular pantomime throughout the Revolution. It dramatizes the conflict of a daughter who marries against her father's wishes and conceives a child by one of her brigand kidnappers. This pantomime in Loisel de Tréogate's version of 1797 performed at the Théâtre de la Cité was the first to be called a melodrama.[45]

The black novel, which followed the drama and the heroic pantomime, helped crystallize the melodrama. *The Monks* by Hector Chaussier became a melodrama at the Théâtre d'émulation in December 1797. Other melodramas include Alexandre Curmer's *La Laitière polonaise,* Ducray-Duminil's middle revolutionary novel *Victor, ou L'Enfant de forêt,* Alexandre Duval's *Montoni, ou Le Château d'Udolphe* and Pixérécourt's *Coélina, ou L'Enfant du mystère. Coélina* was a veritable triumph of the melodrama in spite of the aghast reactions of theater connoisseurs. With the close of the Revolution, melodrama had emerged as the new popular entertainment.

One critic has argued a connection between the terror of exaggeration, bombast, and grandiloquence in the assemblies on the one hand, and the emergence of a fiction of melodramatic terror focusing on caverns, brigandage, medieval castles, and primeval forests on the other—the latter transposing the former on stage. A mood and language may well have translated itself from politics to stage after having migrated from the novel to politics. The melodrama rocked the boulevards in the first decades of the nineteenth century, long after the Revolution had ended.[46] Psychological terror outlived political terror.

Pornography and Terror

The black novel and the melodrama are only half of the somber side of the eighteenth century. The other half is libertinism, the inverse of hypermoral sensibility. *Thérèse philosophe* (1748), a pornographic, "philosophical" novel thought to be the work of the marquis d'Argens (1704–71), displays clerics in obscene "mystical scenes." Spurious "philosophic" observations are made, such as that passions "are the work of God. You would like to destroy these passions and restrain them within limits. Senseless men. You pretend to be second creators, more powerful than the first." Man is weak; to the libertine he is a slave of his passions. Since free will is illusory, men should simply follow their natural inclinations. Any countervailing moral injunction is hypocritical. "Most men are dupes of the idea that they have vices and virtues." One can only make a calculus of pleasure and pain. Distinctions between good and evil are meaningless, for they are "only relative to the interest of established societies among men." In fact, all is good, because all results from our organization, which is God's will. Thus, pleasures pursued in secrecy and "decency" are harmless.

The marquis de Sade (1740–1814) read *Thérèse* and employed many of its arguments in his novel *Justine, ou Les Malheurs de la vertu* (1791), which is a kind of anti-*Pamela*. Here virtue does not pay. Lustful men, including monks, sodomize and persecute the innocent Justine, the heroine-victim who is not rewarded in the end. *Justine* lacks a plot or turning point. It is a boring novel of sexual terror in which Justine is abused until she is almost insensible. Sade contrives a kind of sexual concentration camp within a monastery, where machines are used to help satisfy demoniacal perversities. The monotony of this novel well describes the futility of feeding insatiable appetites (it could have been written about gluttony). Its mechanical descriptions reflect perfectly the materialistic philosophy on which it is predicated and the libertine world of the Provençal upper aristocracy from which Sade and Mirabeau came. As in *Thérèse,* no moral order or freedom exists in *Justine.* We are all creatures of the passions God created. Only necessity exists.[47] Sade's *Justine* is a direct riposte to the cult of virtue in Richardson and Bernardin de Saint-Pierre. It unleashes perversity, which sugar-coated sensibility had never acknowledged but perhaps did much to provoke. Revolutionaries inherited both the secular piety of virtuous sensibility and the libertine apologies of bestiality.

If there is any freedom in this dark world of the Enlightenment, it is a negative freedom from restraint. Whereas sensibilité was eminently moral, the black novel, still moral in its message, anticipated the French Revolution's atrocity and violence. It perhaps found fulfillment in Matthew Lewis' *Ambrosio, or The Monk* (1795), whose sexual liberation has been interpreted as a parable of the Revolution's political liberation. Sade certainly felt that *The Monk* was "the inevitable result of the revolutionary shocks which all of Europe had suffered." The unrestrained sexual libido in Argens's and Sade's work before and during the Revolution was, according to this view, the instinctual drive that lay beneath the rational facade of the Enlightenment. Thus, "the popularity of Gothic fiction in the 1790s and well into the nineteenth century was due, in part, to the widespread anxieties and fears in Europe aroused by the turmoil in France, finding a kind of sublimation or catharsis in tales of darkness, confusion and horror." Tearing down a civilization meant more than political violence. After *The Monk,* the best literary representation of the Gothic revolutionary specter was Mary Shelley's allegory of the French Revolution. *Frankenstein* (1818) replaced God with man, destroying family, property, and human life.

The Gothic novel and sadism, while predating the Revolution, may have derived another two generations of life from it.[48]

Like *Thérèse philosophe*, Sade's *Justine* is a work about sexual necessitarianism, in which some critics see the Enlightenment reduced to its logical consequences while others see it parodied in a reductio ad absurdam. By contrast, the pornographic *Organt* of the young revolutionary Saint-Just (1767–94) is usually dismissed as an adolescent prank. The poem was published anonymously in 1789, but he wrote it earlier as a satire of the Diamond Necklace Affair involving Marie-Antoinette and the cardinal de Rohan. This mock-heroic poem is a good deal more confusing than Argens's and Sade's work, with its rather baroque Heaven, God, angels, devils, and members of the clergy damned for peculation and pederasty.

Organt seems to contain an element of freedom, however, something missing from Sade's mechanical obsessiveness. God is the God of love, but he sells miracles. The keys to Heaven are bought from devils, and a guardian angel tells of beauty's perishability. A prelate parades with a cross and a scepter representing "stupidity." Besides clerics, the privileged and semiprivileged members of the old regime—doctors, sophists, charlatans, sectarians—are lampooned. *Organt* does espouse a certain determinism. Man is defined "in a word as an animal" (chant 16). But the gross sensuality is not amoral as in Argens and Sade; here its practitioners are tormented. *Organt* may be best understood as representing a regime brought down by sensuality and greed. In the general Fall, no one is saved. All warrior nations come together in the Last Coming: "There heaven paints its image in blood."[49]

If sensibilité was imagination soaked in sweetness, and if the black novel haunts that imagination with the horror of vice and persecution, both preserved the moral order of the Christian universe. But for Sade and Argens, virtue has no meaning; for Saint-Just it exists, but no longer in its erstwhile strongholds mired in corruption, lassitude, and selfishness. To raise France to the level of a republic (which was more difficult than making a revolution), it was necessary to create institutions. Saint-Just's posthumous *Fragments on Republican Institutions* and some of his speeches are haunted by the inertia of an unregenerated France, whence his distinctions between the revolution that had been accomplished in government and the one that lamentably remained to be worked out in society.[50]

Mirabeau wrote in 1791: "There is no one who does not avow today that the French nation was prepared more by the sentiment of its misfortunes than by the progress of its Enlightenment." Saint-Just went into the Revolution with perhaps a keener sense of the reality of these misfortunes than of the promise of reforming them. He conserved a touch of melancholy in his later political writings. "A republican government has virtue for its principle; if not terror. What do those want who want neither virtue nor terror?" Without virtue, the republic cannot survive. Sensibilité impels man to virtue, it affirms his natural goodness; it does for him what grace did for Christians. If it does not well forth, then terror must take its place.[51]

INTRODUCTION

The old regime was a hierarchy of honor and birth. It was also a corporate society; members of a profession or of a social order, like the nobility and the clergy, enjoyed privileges peculiar to that order. Privilege by definition was inegalitarian and accorded to some what it denied to others. But the old regime did countenance equality in two ways. Within orders and among corporate bodies, members were equal. Carpenters felt close to and supported one another—in their work, services, and prayers. The ancien régime corporation was as much a moral as an economic entity. In addition, all members of the old regime, from princes to paupers, enjoyed a spiritual or moral equality in the sight of God, regardless of the functional and honorific inequality that separated them for the good of society. This Pauline medieval image of society was patterned after the human body; the king is the head, the plowmen the feet, the administrators the hands and arms. All occupied different places, with different degrees of honor, but the cooperation of all was essential to the good of the whole.

According to the abbé Coyer, the old regime's corporate identity was crumbling as all but manual laborers seceded from what had once been le peuple. Enlightenment forces contributed to this fragmentation. Physiocrats, for instance, attempted to abolish the guilds or corporations, to remove internal tolls and barriers, and to free the land from collective use for open commerce and private enterprise, particularly farming. The philosophes constituted a "republic of letters," what Voltaire called the "little flock," who, through reason, cast off the "self-incurred tutelage" of tradition and authority to "dare to know," to use Immanuel Kant's language.[1] These new individualisms, both economic and intellectual, were incompatible with the corporatist mentality of old regime society. The French Revolution was in large measure a war of newfound equality against ancien régime privilege.

Beginning with the Assembly of Notables in 1787, the privileged nobility resisted equality of taxation. Later, during the Estates General, the assembly refused with much of the clergy to meet and vote by head with the third estate. On the night of 4 August 1789, however, fiscal and political privileges were attacked at the root, and the tenacious hold on privilege began to weaken. With the Declaration of the Rights of Man and the Citizen, all privileged bodies that stood between the nation and the citizen were denied political legitimacy. All men were declared equal before the law, and only those distinctions sanctioned by social utility were allowed. Those of birth and order were eliminated.

The attack on the cultural corporations of the old regime began before the attack on the king, largely because, like the church, the corporations had fewer defenses than the crown, which had the courts, police, and army. The academies, the church, and the theaters had been exposed to ridicule before 1789. The Chapelier laws of 1791 dissolved such economic and cultural corporations as guilds and privileged theaters, withdrawing all protection from them. With the regicide of January 1793, all royal protection vanished. The ensuing liquidation left a vacuum, which the Terror and the Directory strove to replace with republican schools and pedagogy, secular festivals, a civic and patriotic religion, a subsidized press, and republican music.

CHAPTER VI

THE MEN AND THE
INSTITUTIONS (1)

CHURCH AND SCHOOLS

Church

The revolutionary attack on the Catholic church in
France began with the attack on feudalism. Tocqueville notes that anticlericalism before the Revolution stemmed from the entanglement of
religious and ecclesiastical structures with feudalism, rather than from a
hostility to religion itself. On 4 August 1789 the men of the National, or
Constituent, Assembly (created in consequence of the Tennis Court
Oath of 20 June) abolished feudalism and the privileges not only of
seigneurs but also of provinces, municipalities, officeholders, and the
church, which lost a principal means of support—the tithe. Fiscal equality and equality of opportunity replaced privilege. When all privileges,
which erected so many intermediary powers between crown and subject, were abolished, there remained only the individual, invested with
sacred rights, and the nation, invested with the equally sacred authority
of the "general will," specifically invoked in the declaration.[1]

The long-term reasons for the attack on the church included Richerist
egalitarianism (rights of priests vis-à-vis bishops), Jansenist *étatisme*
(or Erastianism), philosophe anticlericalism, rationalism and utili-
tarianism, popular antipathy to clerical tax exemptions and the tithe,
and resentment over the moral failings of clerics. The "good conscience" of 1789 wanted the church to be purer, poorer, more apos-

VI.I.

Honors Rendered to the Poverty of the Church of Saint-Jacques of
the Butchery, *engraving, ca. 1792.*
Courtesy Library of Congress, photo: John Reynolds.

tolic, more responsive to the indigent, and more removed from the
court and aristocracy (fig. VI.I).

Confiscation of church property (2 November 1789), unlike the suppression of the tithe, did not stem from popular discontent with the
church. Few of the 1789 general *cahiers,* or statements of grievances,
collected in the *baillages* and *sénéchaussés* (electoral districts) demanded
confiscation. Besides, the Declaration of Rights had declared property
a sacred right (article 17). How, then, did the confiscation come about?

Both Mirabeau, the principal orator of the Constituent Assembly,
and Talleyrand, its most influential cleric, charged by the finance committee to float a loan, believed that since the assembly had abolished
one source of ecclesiastical revenue (the tithe) another had to be
found. Church property, Talleyrand argued, was different from that of
private citizens, since the church merely held it in trust for such public
purposes as divine worship, charitable works, and education. If the
state could provide these services, the intention of the benefactors who
contributed the property could be honored. On 2 November 1789, the
assembly voted 568 to 346 in favor of Mirabeau's proposal to put the
property of the clergy at the disposition of the nation. The French

church, now merely an organ of government, had ceased to be independent. The distinction between church and state, which originated with Western Christianity, the root of what Benjamin Constant would call "modern liberty," was eclipsed by a more "ancient liberty." In this rediscovered pagan liberty, the Christian dualism of the spiritual and the temporal would disappear before the absolute dominion of the temporal.[2]

The Enlightenment made universal tolerance and the brotherhood of all men the centerpiece of a new order—"a party of humanity." Before the Revolution, Protestants had no legal right to hold public office (Louis XVI's most famous minister, Jacques Necker, was excepted because he was a foreigner). The many Protestants who had not left France following the revocation of the Edict of Nantes were presumed to have converted, and attempts were often made to educate their children as Catholics. The edict of 1787, which the government of Louis XVI passed in the face of opposition by the clergy and parlements, recognized Protestant marriages but required that they be validated before a judge or priest. Fewer than half the general cahiers that broached the issue approved of tolerance, whereas 60 percent (weighted heavily by the clergy) wished to maintain Catholicism as "the only public cult." The deputies of 1789 tried to satisfy both constituencies. Article 10 of the Declaration of the Rights of Man and Citizen stated: "No one may be disturbed on account of his opinions, even religious ones, provided they do not disturb the public order established by the law."[3] The following article assured "free communication of thoughts and opinions" by speech and by the written or printed word. Law would restrict only abuses. Yet before the Terror, no official measures were taken to disestablish or separate the Catholic church from the state. Indeed, a Benedictine deputy, Dom Gerle, provoked a heated debate on 12 April 1790 by suggesting that Catholicism be declared the state religion. The motion was defeated with the assurance that the provisions in the budget for the Catholic cult indicated the nation's solicitude.[4]

It would seem that Catholicism was recognized de facto as the paramount but not sole religion of the French. The idea that all men are "born free and equal in rights" and that "liberty consists in the power to do whatever does not harm another" (articles 1 and 4 of the declaration) included religious liberty. Such liberty was grounded in the recent theory of natural law, which spoke of individual rights as claims against society and the state. The part of the natural law that spoke of obligations was played down in the 1789 text and would not reappear until after Thermidor, and then strictly in a social rather than a religious context.[5]

For both Protestants and Jews, emancipation came in stages. After the limited liberty granted to Protestants in 1787, a decree of January 1789 gave them the electoral franchise, which they used to elect fifteen deputies to the Estates General, among them Rabaut Saint-Etienne from Montauban. On 24 December Protestants were made eligible for any public office; nearly one million Frenchmen gained *droit de cité.*[6]

In 1784 Louis XVI suppressed a personal tax (*péage corporel*) on Jews, and Chrétien-Guillaume de Lamignon de Malesherbes sought to expand his liberal 1787 edict on Protestants to cover them. But continuing hostility toward Jews was expressed in the cahiers of 1789. In December 1789, the assembly discussed civil rights for non-Catholics. Robespierre spoke of expiating crimes against the Jews perpetrated by France and other nations. "How can the social interest of society be founded on the violation of eternal principles of justice and of reason, which are the foundations of any human society?" But the proposal to grant Jews equal civic rights was postponed. In September 1791, after interventions by Mirabeau, abbé Grégoire, and radical journalists like Antoine-Joseph Gorsas, as well as the active participation of Jews of the east in the Revolution, the assembly granted civic rights to those Jews who would take an oath of loyalty to the constitution. This oath was administered simultaneously to other categories of Frenchmen, such as clergy and teachers. Emancipation came for the Sephardic Jews of the south in January 1790. Granting civil liberties to Protestants and Jews was less a sign of Christian tolerance than an indication of the secularization of French state and society, which no longer could be called officially Catholic. The new communitarian bond was the nation rather than the church; it was no longer necessary to belong to the church to belong fully to the nation.[7]

On 13 February 1790, following a law abolishing religious vows the previous autumn, all religious orders—except those performing teaching or such other useful public services as hospital care—were dissolved. Vows of perpetual obedience, poverty, and chastity appeared to the men of 1789 to violate the inalienable rights of personal freedom embodied in the Declaration of Rights, just as monasteries violated its anticorporate ideology.[8]

There was a real connection between newly discovered liberty and democratized license in the early years of the Revolution. A popular print (fig. VI.2) represented libidinous nuns joyously leaving their convents to fall into the arms of gallant national guardsmen. But few nuns

VI.2.
The Frock to the Wind and Liberty to Monks and Nuns, *engraving,*
ca. 1790–92.
Courtesy Bibliothèque nationale, photo: Bibl. Nat. Paris.

left voluntarily. One mother superior was shocked at the prospect of
expulsion, arguing that the caprice of legislators disrupted the nuns'
charitable occupations. Indeed, charity of all kinds suffered during the
Revolution.[9]

The exodus from the monasteries was often followed by active engagement in new careers opened up by the Revolution. Following the
philosophes' hostility to celibacy, the Legislative Assembly resolved
that marriage, since it was of natural law, was compatible with the
priesthood. (That marriage was not an obligation of natural law seems
to have eluded the legislators.) It went on to say "that the law no
longer recognizes either religious vows, nor any other engagement,
which would be contrary to natural law and to the constitution, that
the quality of French citizen has lost any affiliation with any corporation which demands religious vows."[10] Religion was henceforth to
exist entirely within the confines of the civil order of society, of which
marriage was a "primary unit," whereas celibacy was a condition fit
only for a transcendental order.

The Civil Constitution of the Clergy, voted by the assembly on 12

July 1790, helped simultaneously to disorganize the French Catholic church and establish a new church tied to the state. Since clerical salaries now depended on the state, the state necessarily intervened in the church's internal organization. The number of parishes was to be reduced, and dioceses were made coterminous with the eighty-three new *départements* (provincial administrative districts) that divided up the old *généralités*. Both priests and bishops were to be chosen by the electorate—that is, the active (propertied) citizens who voted in civil elections. Those not paying the minimal property tax were excluded, but non-Catholics and nonpracticing Catholics who met the property qualifications could vote. The state was defining the religious *ecclesia* by civil criteria, substituting the democratic principle of sovereignty for the Catholic apostolic succession. The Gallican precedent, whereby the king nominated many of France's abbots and bishops (who were then canonically instated by the pope), was being extended beyond recognition. As the bishop of Aix put it during debate on this issue on 29 May 1790: "We are certainly astonished to see disappear in this way the holy canons and title deeds of the Church. . . . It is possible for some retrenchments to be made in the Church; but the Church must be consulted." The church was not consulted. Article 19 of the constitution went so far as to forbid a bishop to communicate with Rome for confirmation of his appointment.[11]

It is characteristic of the spirit of 1789 that revolutionary measures were presented as time-honored. Such deputies as Jean-Baptiste Treilhard, who supported the radical church reforms, described these new measures as reflecting early Christianity. The primitive church, with its resistance to civil authority and relative lack of hierarchy, became a foil with which to criticize the contemporary church.[12]

Violence mixed with love—assaults on persons and property alternating with protestations of fidelity—characterized the mood of 1789. The cahiers, which had asked for little that was done after the first month of the Revolution, attacked none of the fundamental laws of the church. To convince themselves and the public of their rectitude and of the legitimacy of their actions, the revolutionaries stressed the compatibility of old and new. Popular sovereignty was proclaimed, but the king was to remain king. And although the church was dispossessed and reorganized unilaterally without Rome's consent, everyone who approved it insisted that it was in union with Rome in matters of doctrine.[13] The general feeling of 1789 was expressed in "Ça ira" (see fig. IX.10): everything would work out. Fraternity would be universal: such nobles as the vicomte de Noailles and the duc d'Aiguillon had sacrificed their feudal dues, wives of artists had donated their jewels to the national cause, priests volunteered to sacrifice their tithes, bishops had sacrificed the silverware of churches, and (although this example is more dubious) on 2 November a bishop (Talleyrand) led the assembly to sacrifice all ecclesiastical property—10 percent of the land of France—to liquidate the national debt. At the very moment that the king was being stripped of his sovereignty and made a public servant like the clergy, dozens of songs were being sung in the streets of France about "le Bon Roi, Père du Peuple."[14]

Such euphoria could not conceal the cleavages among the French caused by revolutionary legislation. An oath of November 1790 to the Civil Constitution of the Clergy was required of all ecclesiastics. The clergy, far from unanimously supporting the new measures, was sorely divided. Only 7 of 160 bishops took the new oath, which read: "I swear to be faithful to the nation, to the law and the king, and to maintain with all my power the Constitution determined by the National Assembly and accepted by the king." Since an integral part of the new but still incomplete constitution would be the Civil Constitution of the Clergy, bishops, who were well versed in canon law and responsible to the pope for both their office and tenure, could not be expected to approve it. Almost all bishops were noble, which perhaps made them less disposed to accept democracy in the church.[15]

The overall rate of acceptance of the regular clergy (those belonging to religious orders) has not been tabulated completely, but figures for Paris show a weakening of resistance as the Revolution progressed. Some 468 of 916 religious records remain. Of these 468 clerics, 33 percent took the oath by 1791, 45 percent by 1792, 54 percent by the time of the Terror, and 62 percent by 1796–97.[16] For the parish clergy nationwide, the latest figures show 54 percent of the parish clergy approving the oath, but with wide regional variations: the Basses-Alpes, the Loiret, and the Var exceeded 90 percent approval in the initial oathtaking. The majority in the Rhône and Saône areas, the center, and the Ile-de-France (the region surrounding France) took the oath, but other regions refused en masse: the west, especially the Vendée (65 percent) and Morbihan (90 percent); in the east, the Bas-Rhin in Alsace (90 percent); and parts of the massif Central, the Nord, and Pas-de-Calais (the last two over 80 percent).[17]

The confused laity resented illegitimate pastors and often challenged their right to dispense sacraments. The authorities, for their part, took forceful measures to install those who swore to the constitution. Little by little, they prevented those who refused the oath, the "refractory" clergy, from practicing. Attempts to explain why certain curés or vicars took the oath and others refused have not produced simple answers. Economic considerations may have motivated some clergy. The age of the oathtaker is also revealing. Refractory vicars and curés were younger than their "swearing" counterparts in the Vendée and Alsace—two areas of overwhelming refusal. Yet, overall, refractory clergy tended to have lived longer in their parishes and thus probably had closer bonds with their parishioners than did the oath-taking clergy. The latter often took the oath after replacing an evicted refractory priest and were consequently seen as "intruders" (*intrus*).

The level of education also may have influenced clerics' choice. In rural areas no pattern is evident, but in towns, where clergy tended to refuse the oath in larger proportions than in the countryside, many clerics had university degrees. These educated urban clergy may have been more aware than their rural counterparts of the conflict between the principles of the Enlightenment and the Revolution and those of the church.[18] Oathtaking must ultimately be seen as a consequence of the new religious liberty enunciated by the Declaration of Rights.

The exceptions to any pattern are so numerous that one cannot rely exclusively on social and geographic explanations. Individual conscience played a vital role. And parish influence or local administrative propaganda and pressure could sway a cleric. The effect was to divide the church of France: towns versus country, episcopacy versus lower clergy, east versus southeast, west versus center, and even neighbor versus neighbor or brother versus brother.[19]

The Revolution, which had begun by removing all religious barriers to create one nation, had managed to erect a formidable divide that set many of the French against the Revolution. A spate of catechisms sought to sway Catholics to one side or the other. The Catholic catechisms stressed the unity and apostolicity that marked the church. Schism was "the greatest of all the crimes," and those who perpetrated it were "ravishing wolves." The assembly's civil jurisdiction was acknowledged, but not its ecclesiastical pretensions. The authority of the Civil Constitution of the Clergy was thus nil, and the civil oath of the clergy an "act of the most atrocious despotism."[20]

The constitutional catechisms, in contrast, cited past cases of civil intervention in church matters, apostolic precedents of poverty, elections of bishops, and rights of the laity to speak out on matters of faith (much of this dating back to late medieval conciliarism, if not antiquity). Papal bulls on these matters, it insisted, were to be ignored. The Catholic authors, once confident in combat with the philosophes, became strident, having been put on the defensive and legally excluded, whereas the constitutional catechist, with the backing of the government, could adopt a more tolerant tone.[21]

Claude Le Coz, the constitutional bishop of the department of Ille-et-Vilaine, was a good example of a churchman complacent about a marriage between church and revolution. He assured the pope of his "true sincere, inalterable intention of living in the most perfect communion with the Seat of Rome," but he told the municipality of Rennes that he believed "more firmly than ever, Sirs, that our holy religion will gain much from this revolution."[22]

Some curés went beyond a patriotic submission to the new ecclesiastical regime to promulgate a revolutionary gospel. Jacques Benoît, curé of the commune of Bourgueil of Indre-et-Loire, preached "altogether incendiary words" in January 1790. Benoît evidently told his parishioners that they "were obliged to give a quarter of [their] revenue to the poor" and that "the poor could present themselves with the Gospel in hand and claim their property." Such language was as unsettling to the new revolutionary mayors as to churchgoers.[23]

Apprehensions of a coming conflict soon became apparent to both constitutional and refractory clergy. In a pastoral instruction for Lent, the constitutional bishop Luc-François Lalande spoke of the specter of civil war and urged the refractory clergy, who were being legally repressed and thus emigrating in great numbers, to return to "the heart of their motherland." He prayed that God would "snuff out all the hatreds and all the divisions which trouble and tear apart our cities and countryside; that He fill our hearts with this spirit of union and fraternity which alone can assure public happiness. . . . The greatest crime is to light up the flame of civil war and to wish to bathe oneself in one's brother's blood." Gabriel Legouvé's moving *Mort d'Abel* at the Comédie-Française in 1792 also evoked, in a pastoral setting, the tragedy of fratricide.[24]

For the sake of peace, Louis XVI had approved the Civil Constitution of the Clergy on 24 August 1790 and had implored the pope to do likewise. But the king heartily disapproved of the Civil Constitution in principle and declined to approve the ecclesiastical oath of 27 November 1790 until the end of that December, when he temporized, in the hope that revolutionary enthusiasms would abate.[25]

Pope Pius VI (1775–99), after months of delay, took the opposite course. On 10 March and 13 April, he published two briefs that condemned the Civil Constitution of the Clergy and various principles contained in the Declaration of the Rights of Man and the Citizen.

These briefs reveal a vision of man and society diametrically opposed to that of the Revolution and are valuable in explaining some of the issues of the civil-religious war that broke out in France and Europe within a year.

The first brief, *Quod aliquantum,* addresses the philosophical underpinnings of the Civil Constitution of the Clergy and of the Revolution. It calls "monstrous" the "absolute liberty which not only assures the [individual] the right not to be disturbed for his religious opinions, but which accords [him] even more this license to think, to say, to write and even to print with impunity anything that the most disordered imagination can suggest in matters of religion." *Quod aliquantum* does, however, recognize the assembly by maintaining that these rights spring from a natural liberty common to all. "But what could be more insane than to establish among men this unbridled liberty which appears to suffocate reason, the gift of others' help and that of helping in their turn those who should ask their support." Original sin, the pope continued, imposes limits to our freedom. Man still has the power to choose good and evil, but he needs precepts and commandments to help him. Paul spoke of the need of every individual to submit to the powers that be; because man is fallen, he needs to be restrained by society. He cannot exercise rights as if he were created for himself alone, "but rather to be useful to his fellowmen."[26]

These comments would appear to sanction the hierarchical and corporate character of old regime Europe, to find it more compatible with the Christian view of authority and mutual dependence. But the pope explicitly disavowed any hopes of a restoration: "We do not intend by recalling these maxims to provoke the reestablishment of the old regime of France." Indeed, Pius VI had made it clear earlier that France's elective, representative system was unobjectionable when limited to civil institutions.[27]

The second brief, *Caritas,* unambiguously condemned democracy in the church. The pope urged those who had brought about the schism by "changing the universal discipline of the church, combatting the judgments of the church fathers and the decrees of the councils, overthrowing the hierarchical order, changing at their pleasure the manner of electing bishops, destroying episcopal seats, and ultimately substituting a vicious and new form [for] another that was better and far older" to "repent and abjure their errors, to come back to the church, which like a good mother, receives them with open arms."[28]

Some clerics retracted their oath, and the king turned more decisively against the Civil Constitution, refusing to sanction a law deporting refractory priests, but the schism continued to worsen. The competition between constitutional and refractory clergy contributed to the secularization of the state, as had granting toleration to Protestants and Jews. Each clergy held separate registers of births, marriages, and deaths and contested the legitimacy of any other. The state took the opportunity in September 1792 to step in and create the civil registers, or *état civil*. Henceforth, sacraments would not define citizens but would be options only for those who wanted them. The nation, not the church, was the new communal bond. "Ancient liberty" meant incorporating competencies of the church into the civil sphere. This caused a rift with the Catholic remnant, who had to be married, first civilly—at the *mairie*—and then in the church. The Revolution effectively created "two Frances." The civil state of marriage, moreover, was not indissoluble. This same law introduced divorce by mutual consent.[29]

Even before the publication of the papal briefs, the National Assembly made a decision that symbolized France's secularization. On 4 April 1791, two days after Mirabeau's death, the assembly approved a proposal that the Church of Saint-Geneviève, which Louis XV had commissioned in gratitude to the patron saint of Paris, be converted into a pantheon to honor great men of the *patrie*. The marquis de Pastoret, who initiated the act of secularization, explained that "the temple of religion should become the temple of the *patrie*; the tomb of a great man should become the altar of liberty." On 11 July, in an elaborate ceremony attended by some 200,000 people, the remains of an implacable enemy of Christianity were transferred to the former church. Voltaire, who had been denied a Christian burial in 1778, came to repose in the Panthéon, the erstwhile temple of Saint-Geneviève, the fifth-century nun whose remains would soon be scattered in the Seine.[30]

Schools

Critics of the church often denounced prevailing educational practices based on Catholic doctrine. The playwright Louis-Sébastien Mercier denigrated the Catholic catechism, the basis of French primary instruction, as "unintelligible" and filled with words that the children repeat "the rest of their days without having a comprehension of what they say." In the place of catechisms based on dogma, Mercier, Helvetius, and Holbach advocated one based on "reason and natural law." Some authors, repelled by the unreasoned, au-

thoritarian character of dogma, actually penned prerevolutionary catechisms of this nature.[31]

Mercier painted a bleak picture of little schoolchildren, force-fed
Latin, paddled, and even lashed when they resisted. If a teacher was
Catholic, "he could be brutal, hard, ferocious." Madame Roland, by
contrast, recorded her childhood catechism classes in Paris fondly,
even after she had abandoned her faith. Mercier's philosophic indignation is difficult to explain when one thinks of the idyllic catechism
lesson of a Burgundian schoolroom, which Rétif de la Bretonne depicted in his famous *Vie de mon père* (1778). But Mercier's disdain was
far more characteristic of the philosophes and legislators of the Revolution than was Rétif's nostalgia.[32]

Critical as they were of existing schooling, no noteworthy Enlightenment figure advocated free public education for peasants and
workers (see chapter 3). One desideratum, however, was to make
French education truly public and national, if not universal and com-
pulsory. Even if the teaching corps continued to be largely clerical
(religious orders were recognized as organized and efficient), and even
though not everybody should be taught, the educational system of
France should cease to consist of so many corporate micro-units and
become truly national. These views concerned mostly secondary education; when the Jesuits were expelled in 1764, their schools were administered by public boards or councils, presided over by Rolland
D'Erceville, a parlementaire and advocate of national education. Although clerics were frequently appointed as teachers and bishops sat
on the new boards, the precedent was set for public, state, and largely
lay control over educational institutions, a precedent that paralleled the
demands of the philosophes and Jansenists for state control of the
church.[33]

Critics of the collèges could be as merciless about its curriculum as
could critics of the catechism. Alembert's article "collèges" in the
Encyclopédie both captured and inspired much of the criticism of the
Enlightenment and Revolution in a classic caricature: he complained
that rhetoric consisted of "flooding two pages with [Latin] verbiage,"
but that the knowledge of Latin acquired was "very imperfect," as was
that of religion and philosophy. Alembert found this Latin education
useless. Mercier found it positively harmful, for it made one want to
resuscitate the Roman republican world one was studying, while remaining the subject of a monarch—something he felt was nigh impossible. A student who is taught Latin ten years before he learns French,
he expostulated, comes to know Rome but is a stranger to Paris. For

Alembert, the education of the old regime was dying of obsolescence. For Mercier, classical education contained the seeds of the regime's destruction.[34]

When the tithes were suppressed on the night of 4 August 1789, it became apparent that schools and collèges would suffer, since a certain (as yet undetermined) proportion of their revenues derived from them and from the income from clerical property. Educational property was originally to remain exempt from the sale of church property. The original impulse of the constituents was not to interrupt the schooling of youth (or, for that matter, the relief of the poor or the care of the sick) before new "national" institutions were created. But the intent of three of the most famous authors—Mirabeau, Talleyrand, and Condorcet—who had published plans for educational reform before the Terror, was to create a new system independent of the old regime. As Mirabeau put it: "In order to reconstruct everything, it was necessary to destroy everything." The effect of much of the legislation of the early 1790s, intent notwithstanding, prevented the old educational institutions from functioning normally. By 1793 many had disappeared.[35]

The material losses of schools, collèges, and universities came early and can be measured by a survey (*enquête*) of educational resources nationwide made by the first Comité d'instruction publique, which was created by the Legislative Assembly on 14 October 1791. Such surveys were numerous during the Revolution and expressed a passion for the geometric already evident in the Cassini quadrant maps of France and in the prerevolutionary work to standardize weights and measurements. The new division of France into eighty-four departments and over five hundred districts, designed for administrative coherence, formed the framework for the educational survey of 1791–92. To create a single, uniform national system of education meant also to assure the equality and uniformity of component parts.[36]

Any survey must be scrutinized with reserve. That of 1791–92 covered only 217 of all 527 districts (with roughly 6 districts per department). Administrators, beset by the problems of the Civil Constitution of the Clergy and the sale of national property, often neglected to respond, and the accuracy and thoroughness of the reports of those who did may be questioned. Would an administrator want to report that the land of a collège had been alienated or sold if a decree of 1790 forbade such action? Would he not be apt to exaggerate the extent of financial loss from the suppression of the tithe or *octroi* (a municipal entry tax, part of which went to education), in order to make a case for a subsidy?

A summary of responses shows that fewer than half the secondary and higher educational institutions reported loss of income. Most schools presumably continued to enjoy their property incomes (*rentes*), endowments, and other incomes. As has been shown for Auch, tithes continued to be collected long after their suppression, some into the twentieth century.

The petites écoles and elementary schools run by religious congregations were affected least by the legislation of 1789–91, because most functioned on student fees and municipal subsidies rather than endowments. Throughout France administrators noted the presence of teaching sisters and masters. In the district of Gex in the Ain, for example, the district Directory observed: "There exist in most of the country municipalities schoolmasters who teach how to read and write and teach the young their catechism." The overall picture given by this survey of primary education is one of continuity with the old regime, in spite of certain local anticlerical administrations.[37]

Secondary schools also continued to function, but they suffered greater financial loss than the primary schools. Most continued to enjoy their rentes, endowment incomes, tithe revenues, or substitute indemnities, but some lost large amounts of their income: the Grand Séminaire at Rennes lost almost half when barracks were built on its property, the Collège Py in Perpignan three-quarters. By contrast, the famous Collège La Flèche in the Sarthe, where Descartes had been educated, lost only 10 percent of its revenues. The Paris collèges, according to this survey, experienced no losses, but a case study of the Collège Louis-le-Grand presents other problems of an equally serious nature.[38]

Significant student radicalism did not attend the Revolution of 1789 as it did later revolutions. Students did become involved—mostly as soldiers after 1792—but the Revolution had a greater impact on them than vice versa. At the Collège Louis-le-Grand and elsewhere, a certain amount of "fermentation" or "effervescence" took place, according to Louis-le-Grand's director, Jean-François Champagne. Philosophy students petitioned the rector of the University of Paris in late 1789 to protest the practice of taking dictation in notebooks: "Written almost always without being understood, preserved without being read, initialled by the professor without being looked at." Another petition called for the exclusion of "ministers of the Catholic religion" from the university faculty. Demonstrations could turn out two hundred students. One by philosophy students in May 1791 demanded a holiday to commemorate the taking of the Bastille. "Most of [the stu-

dents]," wrote Champagne, "are giving up their classes from boredom." Professors, meanwhile, were leaving to avoid taking the oath,
expected also of educators, and the Directory of the department of
Paris grew more hostile to the old regime educational establishments.
In a statement of November 1791, they termed the collèges "Gothic
institutions" and complained of the expense of maintaining them and
of litigation by professors who refused the oath. "Out of prudence,"
this Directory closed down the theology faculties (the first faculties
everywhere to be suppressed) at the Sorbonne and Navarre collèges.[39]

Further legislation to suppress the last of the religious orders—
those for women and teaching—passed on 4 and 18 August 1792. On
8 March 1793, at the suggestion of Joseph Fouché, more expropriations were scheduled—of school endowments and other property,
excluding buildings and lodgings actually in use. This law, Fouché
bragged, would overcome the timidity of previous legislation, which
had been "afraid to overthrow the foundations of past errors with one
blow." Fouché's bill delivered that blow, but his description of the
existing state of education in 1793 makes one wonder whether it was
necessary. "Surely, any regime might be stigmatized by the spectacle
which France now presents. . . . The houses of education in our departments offer nothing but ruins to our eyes; the collèges are almost
entirely abandoned."[40]

The Terror set in over the summer of 1793 after various events: the
proscription of the Girondin deputies on 31 May, the assassination of
Jean-Paul Marat on 13 July, the rise of the sansculottes, the first *levée en
masse* in European history, price controls (the "general maximum" on
staples), and a general mobilization of the workers for war against
the first coalition of European allies. A declaration prompted by a
sansculotte deputation to the convention on 5 September 1793 announced: "Terror is the order of the day."

War and the Terror furthered the deterioration of education. The
Collège Louis-le-Grand functioned lamely with approximately one-
tenth its former student body. Its library was confiscated, and its curriculum, students, and faculty denounced for "aristocracy," counterrevolution, and even corruption. On 17 September police commissioners
inspected the collèges of the University of Paris (which had been suppressed, along with all universities, on 15 September 1793) to put on
seals—which were lifted and reimposed in the following months with a
great display of legality.[41]

As endowments were confiscated and collèges closed, thousands of
teachers sought other employment or pensions from the state. Many

enrolled in the army or went into the republican administration. Many who continued to teach were rarely paid. Writing in 1796, the chemist and academician Jean-Antoine de Fourcroy remonstrated: "You have taken away the property of the collèges; what are you doing for instruction if you do not pay the professors?" Joseph Lakanal, a conventionnel and educational reformer, summed up the situation bleakly in a proposal in July 1793: "Thus, for nearly four years, youth has been practically abandoned to itself. Although I do not believe in the excellence of the old methods of education . . . I cannot avoid deploring the effects of such a long absence of instruction, and fearing that it will be too noticeable on the generations which are beginning to replace us."[42]

The effects of the interruption of education have concerned historians of right and left for roughly a century. Contemporary praise or indictments of the situation in the 1790s are valuable as original sources, but they are not exempt from interpretation by the historian. Was the speaker trying to laud the Revolution by giving an unrealistically optimistic picture of its education? Or was he pointing to the decline of education to indict the Revolution? Must all contemporary or subsequent writings on the cultural work of the Revolution be dismissed simply as expressions of one's antipathy or enthusiasm for the Revolution itself? It would seem not, in this instance, for it is clearly documented that numerous supporters of the Revolution unreservedly criticized its educational record.[43]

The Bouquier Law, the first to establish a new system of universal primary education, passed on 19 December 1793. Although it established free, public instruction and the "liberty of teaching" (that is, it envisaged no state monopoly), teachers were nonetheless obliged to produce a "certificate of civicism" and good morals, signed by local authorities, and were subjected to supervision by municipal as well as familial figures. Teachers were to be salaried by the government and were to use state-commissioned textbooks. Attendance at school was obligatory for three years, and parents who neglected to send their children to school could be denounced before the police and forced to pay a fine. The obligatory and state supervisory character of this plan were striking when compared to the local and voluntary petites écoles.[44]

What were the results of this legislation? The records of a survey carried out in October 1794 show information from 350 of 557 districts. Of these, only 32 had a full quota of schools; 41 had some schools; 227 either gave no report or reported no schools or few. In Grenoble only 4 teachers out of a needed 250 were active. In

Paris only 250 teachers were active for a school-age population that we can estimate at roughly 100,000, or 1 teacher for every 400 pupils. Clearly, most student-age children were not attending school during the Terror.[45]

Four years later, Minister of the Interior François de Neufchâteau conducted another survey after a second major educational plan, the Daunou proposal of 3 brumaire Year IV (25 October 1795), had been partially implemented. This plan allowed private schools to compete openly with public schools, which on the primary level were not subsidized by the state, except insofar as teachers were occasionally lodged in former rectories. Attendance was not obligatory. Appointment and supervision of teachers were placed in the hands of local juries of public instruction and municipal governments. The reimposition of student fees after provision for free instruction was frequently decried as retrograde both at the time and later.[46]

Neufchâteau's survey of Year VI under the auspices of directorial *commissaires* has left records of eleven departments (for which figures for both public and private primary schools were available), and in these slightly fewer than half the cantons replied. The 285 that did had 1,400 schools, or approximately 5 per canton. Since the average canton contained at least ten communes, an estimated half the communes in 1798 had no schools, although many sent pupils to communes that did. School attendance varied from 2.9 percent of the population for the poorly schooled Gers in the southwest to 11.8 percent for the highly schooled, pluralistic Bas-Rhin in Alsace (16 percent would represent full attendance, since this represented the approximate school-age population). For half the communes of France to have schools, as opposed to one-quarter under the Bouquier plan, would indeed have been a definite improvement.[47]

During the Consulate, counselors of state were sent out to survey the state of France since the Revolution. Their reports confirm that education was on the mend, that enrollments and the number of schools were increasing, but that many communes had no schools and that attendance was still low (one-tenth of expectations for Paris, with only twelve public schools—but many private schools—in operation). Fourcroy, who greatly influenced the Napoleonic school reforms of 1802–6, reported that Normandy had "organized" fewer than half (177) of the prescribed 425 schools in the Manche and that in three Breton departments, "two generations of children are threatened with ignorance of knowing how to read, write or learn the first steps of arithmetic."[48]

The Republic lacked the means to finance its educational policy. Much of France refused the ideology of the Revolution, enshrined in its education, by supporting the traditional parish schools (petites écoles) that had survived the Terror. The Revolution did dent this two-century-old school network by establishing for the first time hundreds of public primary schools, with rights of inspection and even appointment, and by attempting to impose a secular morality. State monopoly of education had begun to emerge, in principle if not wholly in fact. Yet educational opportunity probably diminished somewhat in the interim between the old Catholic "public" education and the free secular education, because the financial support for all education had been greatly weakened by the confiscation of endowments.[49]

Universality, gratuity, and secularity had not been achieved on the primary level, but secondary-level schooling more closely met the objectives of the Daunou law. Old libraries and religious houses or collèges in the capitals of each department had been converted into central schools. Students often failed to pay minimal tuition, but professors were salaried and appointed by the state. Faculties were often impressive, since they included many distinguished local savants. Professors in Paris included the biologist Georges Cuvier, Lakanal, and Laplace, and in the provinces such local intellectuals as Edmonde Mentelle and Louis Ramond (the Hautes-Pyrénées), the mathematician Genty (the Loire), and professor of literature Joseph Droz (Besançon).

Although nearly half the professors of the central schools had taught in the old regime collèges (one-third as priests) the two institutions were quite different. Admission was open at the central schools—there were no financial or scholastic entrance requirements. Students could enter at age twelve, and unlike the collèges the central schools had no classes. Courses were divided into three groupings, each with theoretical age minimums that were often waived. No maximum age was set, and some students were in their forties. Those twelve and older began with drawing, ancient languages, and natural history. From age fourteen they studied mathematics, physics, and chemistry, and from sixteen they devoted themselves to "general grammar," belles lettres, history, and legislation. With this latitude of age groupings and the absence of classes, the central schools became a great medley of students of varying ages and preparation. Instructors had to divide their students into groups *within* their courses and teach at more than one level.

Students of the central schools generally lived within thirty kilometers of the departmental capital, which was the seat of the school, although some came from neighboring departments; the geographical recruitment was much more local than it was for the collèges. Similarly, the students' social origins were considerably higher than had been the case at the collèges—a peculiar irony when one considers that a democratic revolution had intervened. Most students of the central schools were sons of officeholders and professionals (40–50 percent) or children of men in business or commerce (20–30 percent). Children of fermiers and laboureurs were scarcely represented. The shopkeeping and artisanate classes were also less well represented in urban écoles centrales.[50]

What was the educational experience at a central school like? Classes opened at the end of October (1 brumaire), accompanied by ceremonies organized by the department, which, with the local school board ("jury of public instruction"), was constantly involved with the administration of the school. These were solemn affairs much like the observances of the *decadi* (tenth day) and festivals. Officials gave high-minded speeches on the virtues of republican education and the value of study and science in the formation of character.

Ten thousand students were enrolled in the central schools in 1799, one-fifth of the 50,000 who had been enrolled in the collèges at the end of the ancien régime. One scholar has termed this a "brutal descolarisation," and this is even truer when one considers that these students took on average only 1.7 courses. The most popular course in the central schools was drawing, which accounted for 6,038 of 17,626 enrollments. Many students took drawing in their first and only year. Students could draw for vocational purposes, as for carpentry or surveying, but drawing also could be artistic—landscapes, anatomies, and still lifes. The rationale for this training had been developed during the old regime in such vocational schools as the Ecole des arts, Amiens, where students learned to train the senses, coordinating eye with hand. Drawing fit perfectly with grammar or "ideology" courses taken in the third group of offerings, where the link between sensation and abstract ideas was analyzed.[51]

The central schools, minimally controlled by the central government, exhibited little regularity or uniformity. Although the Directory established a central secondary system of education on paper, it was a far cry from when, a century later, the minister of education could look at his watch and know exactly what was going on in each grade throughout France. At the central schools some professors met their courses eight of ten days in the revolutionary week, whereas others met only every other day. Some held classes for longer than two hours, others for just one. Professors taught only one course, but if they had a hundred students, as could be the case in drawing and mathematics (the second most popular course), the load could be heavy. Most professors used some form of the Socratic method, but after the ministers of the Interior demanded to see the professors' cahiers, notes were also used. Teachers do seem to have avoided the old regime method of dictating notes to their students. Professors' cahiers, moreover, often displayed great learning, drawing from the latest scientific and Enlightenment sources. Condillac, Locke, Garat, and Beauzée were used in general grammar in a study of the generation of faculties, language, and knowledge from elementary sensation. Virgil, Ovid, Horace, Lucian, and Anacreon were studied at Besançon in ancient languages in the first group of courses. Stendhal studied Sallust at Grenoble. But students frequently entered these courses with little or no preparation. Professors of general grammar and Latin were thus obliged to teach the rudiments of French and Latin grammar to their charges. At Besançon the mathematics instructor Demerey divided his auditors into three groups. Each had a separate lesson every day in the same classroom with the other groups in a three-year sequence; Demerey gave twenty-four lessons per ten-day week (until his health gave out in 1798). The first level consisted of arithmetic and algebra, the second of equations, geometry, and plane trigonometry, the third of students preparing for the école polytechnique, although they learned conjointly with those struggling with arithmetic![52]

Few students enrolled in natural science courses, considering the emphasis the central school pedagogues intended to give to science. Texts and the professors may have been excellent, but only 1,156 pupils studied physics in 1799, compared to some 5,000 students in the old regime. Although that education had been based on Latin and rhetoric, it did impart a fairly solid education in the natural sciences that was not generally recognized by the revolutionary legislators and has often been ignored since.

Natural history, with 1,664 inscriptions, and chemistry, with 1,156 (an average of about 16 and 10 per school), were preoccupied, as was the eighteenth century in general, with classification. Linnaeus was used at Besançon in botany; there, students made excursions into the countryside to collect herbs and other plants. Zoology centered on the classification of animals, using the method of Cuvier. Physics concentrated on the properties of air, light, electric fluids, and chemical affinities, as well as on mineral, vegetable, and animal properties. The chemistry professor used the world's most brilliant chemists, most of whom were French—Fourcroy, Lavoisier, Chaptal, Morveau, and others.

From a twentieth-century perspective, the teaching of history in the central schools was peculiarly doctrinaire. Viguier of Besançon described ancient monarchies as "shaped in a time of barbarism [and consequently] offering little of interest to republicans." History was thought to be a dangerous subject laden with errors that had to be expunged before it could enter students' minds. It was the historian's duty to draw moral lessons from the past, eschewing its "prejudices" and "errors." A broad sweep—even of the "centuries of ignorance"— was typical of history courses in the central schools. Viguier thus began with the ancient world and continued through medieval and modern history, synthesizing his course at the end.

A course in legislation drew the fewest students (462), which is unusual, since the purpose of this education was to instill republican values. The authorities wanted this course to be grounded in recent natural law theory and moral philosophy. The professor at Besançon, Prud'hon, was a Catholic and gave more of a straight course in law and jurisprudence until he was reprimanded and altered his cahier.

Religion was not taught in the central schools. Instruction was to be entirely secular, although not atheistic. God was mentioned from time to time in the third group of courses as the foundation of the moral and natural law, but this certainly did not equal the religious and theological education imparted by the Jesuits and Ortorians in the old regime. Catholic parents distressed by the prospect of their children growing up with no knowledge of God often refused to let their children attend these schools, instead sending them to private schools and pensions. Criticism of this lack of religious training and an overall lack of structure were major reasons for the system's demise after 1802.[53]

The students of these schools tended to come from republican families, or at least families with a strong republican member. Stendhal recounts how his grandfather, a member of the local jury of public instruction, evidently prevailed over Stendhal's more conservative father to send Stendhal to the central school of Grenoble.[54]

In Year IX the 500 students of Besançon, the 492 of Quatre Nations in Paris, the 395 of Dijon, the 236 of Nancy were far fewer than their collège counterparts of the old regime (Besançon's Jesuit school had had 800 students), but enrollments were generally rising in the final years before the schools were nipped by Napoléon.[55]

Students did not live at school, as they had in the ancien régime. Efforts to establish boarding facilities connected with the schools were generally unsuccessful. Students thus did not identify themselves with the school as much as if they had lived there together with their masters and classmates. Moreover, on average students did not study at the school for more than two years, further minimizing any strong ties.[56]

As in Jesuit schools, emulation was encouraged. Those distinguishing themselves in the concours, or competitive exams, usually oral and administered by the jury of public instruction, received prizes at the end of the year and at the Festival of Youth in March. Prizes consisted of books by Enlightenment or classical authors or objets d'art from the depots of confiscated property. As at the beginning of the school year, much was made of these ceremonial events. It often seemed as if the whole republican administration showed up to declaim how much the future of the country depended on the students' efforts.[57]

In the end, the shortcomings of the school system caught up with it and exposed it to the criticism of Bonaparte, who had something far more structured in mind. Stendhal recalled his enthusiasm for the abbé Gattel's grammar lessons at Grenoble yet his ultimate disappointment with the whole experience and how at age fourteen he would wander up to the deserted third floor of the school to daydream. This was one aspect of the student liberty that came under fire in 1802. Nobody seemed to take charge of these boys who drifted in and out of class at will. One talked of a "dissipation inseparable from a revolution" at Besançon and deplored the teachers' lack of authority even to expel unruly students, who might appeal this action to the departmental authorities. Surely no one wanted to restore the corporal punishment of the old regime, but the reluctance to give teachers sufficient sanctions to assure discipline was symptomatic of the revolutionary critique of authority. Napoléon did not simply call back the collèges of the old regime but reestablished authority in new state schools based on a military model and allowed private and religious schools to continue.[58]

By 1811–12 the 337 *collèges communaux* and 36 lycées had a student population of 35,130—triple that of the Directory yet still less than in the old regime. Recovery and renewal had begun, but previous levels of scholarization had not been reached. Furthermore, the reduction of free education—the combination of tuition and fewer scholarships—was met by abandoning the idea of universal education at all levels. Destutt de Tracy argued that there were two classes, the *savante*, or propertied, class, able through leisure to pursue higher levels of instruction, and *la classe laborieuse*, which had neither the leisure nor the resources to do so. Although *sélectionnisme* had been admitted even in the Spartan plan of national education by Louis-Michel Lepeletier de Saint-Fargeau (whose plan was sponsored by Robespierre after Lepeletier de Saint-Fargeau's assassination), in 1801 Tracy presented it baldly in terms of social distinctions. The bourgeoisie was the immediate beneficiary of the nationalization of education.[59]

Napoléon accentuated the scientific tendencies of French revolutionary education in the twenty-three state lycées founded in 1806 and restored religious education in all but higher education by granting a large role to the religious congregations in primary and private secondary education. Moreover, he systematized this effectively for the first time in a pyramidal two-track system under state monopoly of the university—a broad primary system and restricted secondary and higher ones.

Nationalization, centralization, greater standardization, competitive exams (concours) or testing for entrance to higher scholastic and professional opportunities, and a weakening of the administrative control of bishops and religious orders over education (but not of religion itself) were the primary effects of the Revolution. The consequences on literacy of the temporary disruption of schooling seem statistically negligible, for they were counteracted by the priority placed on reading by the Revolution.

The effect of revolutionary legislation on the church and the schools, which were heavily entwined, was similar. The legislation of 1790 that reorganized—in effect, disorganized—the church had to lead to the equal disruption of educational institutions that depended on the church. But the revolutionary legislators after 1792 were more eager to find a republican substitute for the old schools than to organize a republican church. The church was left to its own devices, to languish without public support or means of its own, waiting as it were for the Napoleonic restoration and the Concordat. It is amazing that religion experienced a revival in the Directory without the institutional "infrastructure" and that literacy seems to have grown at its previous pace during the Revolution and Empire despite the shortage of schools.

CHAPTER VII

THE MEN AND

THE INSTITUTIONS (2)

THEATERS, ACADEMIES, AND

SCIENTIFIC COMMITTEES

Theaters

The exclusive privileges of established theaters were much criticized before the Revolution. In education, reformers demanded greater national or state control and a coordinated network and hierarchy of teaching institutions. But reformers of the theater worked to disestablish their corporate, privileged status. Deregulation, they felt, would allow talent to flourish.

Old regime privileges separated popular from high theater. Popular theater led a tenuous existence on the fairgrounds, where lewd clowns, stuntsmen, mimes, and monsters caused crowds to howl, whereas high theater dealt in spoken drama, Alexandrine verse, and classical themes. Before 1759, only privileged theaters could exist. The Comédie-Française "owned" classical French tragedy and comedy; the Opéra "owned" all opera and ballet; the Théâtre italien "owned" the *commedia dell'arte* and, after 1762, the opéra-comique. The crown tolerated smaller theaters and entertainment booths by "permissions" similar to those accorded certain Enlightenment books. After 1759, several important popular theaters were established on the boulevards—the Grands Danseurs du Roi (1760), the Ambigu comique (1772), the Variétés (1777). But different literary genres were tailored for different social classes: tragedy for nobles, farce for the people, and comedy for the bourgeoisie. This caused many problems. Such entrepreneurs as Jean-Baptiste Nicolet and Nicolas-Médard Audinot, for example, wanted to perform some of the repertoires of the privileged theaters, which of course opposed such requests by bringing legal action against little theaters that infringed on their "property rights."[1]

Louis-Sébastien Mercier abhorred the cultural separation of le peuple from the elite. The occasional free spectacles given le peuple in the great theaters, he felt, demonstrated how unnecessary this separation was. At a play celebrating the birth of a dauphin, for example, poissardes sat beside the queen and a coal merchant next to the king. "This populace applauds at the right places, even at the delicate passages," Mercier exclaimed somewhat naively. Passing to the little theaters, he observed: "The theaters for farces are almost always full. There, obscene or detestable plays are put on because [these theaters] are forbidden to perform any work which might have some salt, wit or reason to it." What these theaters needed were "agreeable . . . and moral plays."[2]

Defenders of theater privilege were not deliberately degrading the people of Paris with rubbish or even necessarily catering to vulgarity. They simply needed protection for their theaters to exist, and they did not feel the people were capable of appreciating the higher forms of entertainment. But these privileges began to erode before the Revolution. Audiences were more mixed, as both defenders and critics of privilege acknowledged. Nothing could stop a hairdresser from buying a ticket to the *parquet* (orchestra) of the Comédie-Française (fig. VII.1). High-ranking nobles, courtiers, and bourgeois, moreover, frequented the boulevards, whose curiosities were as exotic to them as anything found in foreign lands. Such newspapers as the *Journal de Paris* began to include bourgeois and boulevard theaters in their lists, although in proper hierarchical order—the privileged theaters were printed high on the page and were separated from the popular theaters by a line.[3]

The decrees of 4 August 1789 abolished feudalism and substituted right for privilege in French life and thought. This eventually included abolishing the corporate monopolies enjoyed by the Comédie-Française, the Académie de musique, or Opéra, and the Comédie italienne. The law of 13 January 1791 revolutionized entertainment by granting theatrical liberties: any theater now had the right to open without the blessing of one of the privileged theaters, and any theater

VII.I.

François-André Vincent, Joseph-Jean-Baptiste Dazincourt, Sociétaire (Shareholder-Actor) of the Comédie-Française, *engraving of a painting.*
Courtesy Musée des Beaux-Arts, Marseilles, photo: Lauros-Giraudon/Art Resource, New York.

could perform any genre. No longer did works belong in perpetuity to certain theaters; they became public domain five years after their authors had died. The entire patrimony of the Comédie-Française, which had hitherto meant the exclusive right to perform Molière, Corneille, Racine, and scores of others, became national literary property.[4]

This Chapelier law established a regime of free competition in conscious contrast to the old system of privilege and protection: "When,
in order to compensate humanity a bit and occupy people's minds,
despotism takes upon itself the task of encouraging the arts, competition in theater can be a greater cause for quarrels than a means of
perfection: There are only protectors and protégés; and the protégés
have talent only in proportion to the influence of their protectors. Under
liberty, it is merit which prevails, competition only stimulates it."[5]

Privilege had been defined in the *Grand vocabulaire françaix* of 1767–74
as the "power accorded to a person or a Commonality to do or to
enjoy something to some advantage to the exclusion of others." *Rights*
in 1789, in contrast, were powers to do or enjoy something accorded
universally without distinction. Actors in old regime France had no
civil liberties, including rights of ecclesiastical marriage or burial, because of the church's long censure of the theater. If the ideology of
Diderot and Mercier were to gain ascendancy, actors and theaters
would be sources of moral edification as much as the school and the
church. In September 1792, when the civil state established wholly
secular baptisms, marriages, and deaths, actors finally obtained civil
equality. No longer were "comedians" deemed immoral, ignoble
persons.[6]

The Chapelier law of 1791 equalized theaters, and the law on the
civil state made actors citizens. Authors were the third party and audiences the fourth in the complex world of the stage. Authors traditionally received little payment for their manuscripts, which they had
great difficulty getting read by theater *sociétaires,* or share-holders (usually the actors themselves). Olympe de Gouges complained bitterly
and picturesquely in a pamphlet about the Comédie-Française, which
had read her play *Slavery of Blacks* (1789), adopted it, and then shelved
it when colonists and their deputies opposed it. She was promised a
"turn" for her play, but it was delayed. She gave François-René Molé
(fig. VII.2), a leading actor and sociétaire, two orange trees, which he
liked, but they failed to produce the desired effect. In her "Address to
the Representatives of the Nation," she explained that, in spite of her
sycophant behavior, the "comedians" and the colonists "continued
to hold me in humiliating dependency." Jean-François Cailhava de
l'Estendoux, who made similar complaints about the treatment of
his plays, welcomed the Chapelier law, which stated: "The most
sacred, the most legitimate . . . the most personal of all properties is
[a writer's] work, fruit of [his] thought." Writing to the Comédie-
Française at about this time, Cailhava stated that he wished to "with-

VII.2.
François René Molé, Sociétaire-Actor of the Comédie-Française, as
the First French Hamlet, *engraving, ca. 1770.*
Courtesy Library of Congress, photo: John Reynolds.

draw" from the Théâtre national his works, which they "disdain, so that I may give them to Sieur Nicolet, if fancy so moves me. My works are my property, [which] is sacred."[7]

The usual "rights" or royalties of playwrights were a specified fraction of the net receipts of the performances or a lump sum paid by the theater for perpetual rights to a script. Before the January 1791 law passed, the shareholders of the Comédie-Française argued for their repertory rights on the grounds that they had paid for them, and they listed payments made to Molière and Corneille. Madame Denis, Voltaire's niece, stated unambiguously: "I cede and abandon all my uncle's [literary] property to Messieurs les Comédiens Français." Referring to all these rights, the comédie beseeched: "If these are not properties, we ask you to tell us what is meant by this word?" Such rights were equity for the comédie—the livelihood of such great actors as Mlle Clarion and Dangeville.[8]

But authors' interests differed from those of actors. On 3 July 1777, seven years before his *Mariage de Figaro* (figs. VII.3, VII.4) opened at the Comédie-Française, Pierre-Augustin Caron de Beaumarchais established the Société des auteurs et compositeurs dramatiques—the counterpart of the Société des comédiens français—a society that from the Revolution to the present has protected authors' rights vis-à-vis theater managers, other authors, and publishers. During the Revolution, it was helped as well as chaotic financial and legal conditions permitted by the Bureau de législation dramatique. Surviving records show that only about 1 or 2 percent of operating costs went to authors. Beaumarchais's pamphlets on behalf of his impoverished and frustrated clients enunciate the language of commercial capitalism. To directors who claimed they could not afford to pay more royalties, Beaumarchais responded with an analogy of the cloth merchant. Can the merchant not pay for his cloth because the cost of spinners and overhead are too great? If directors are going bankrupt, let them put on the old repertory. And if the public does not want the old repertory, let them pay for the new one.[9]

The debate over theater mirrored the ongoing debate over society and the state. In both, the principals were the individual and the nation versus the corps and the king, free competition versus regulation, equality versus privilege, individual rights versus collective rights. The theater debate cannot be viewed independently of the physiocratic debate over proprietary capitalism: the artist's rights, or proprietary individualism, versus the old regime's cultural (and proprietary) privileges. Although Beaumarchais, Chénier, and La Harpe's campaign for

VII.3.
Beaumarchais, *engraving, ca. 1784–88.*
Courtesy Library of Congress, photo: John Reynolds.

theatrical liberties was a success, numerous playwrights, among them
the future Vaudeville author Jean-Baptiste Radet and the Revolution's
favorite comic author, L.-B. Picard, felt that the theaters' proprietary
rights were favored. But a copyright law did issue from the fray. Proprietary consciousness hung thick in the air.[10]

The history of the theaters themselves during the Revolution illustrates how these disputes developed. As many as thirty-five theaters
opened by late 1791, the most famous and long-lasting being the
Vaudeville of Pierre-Antoine-Augustin de Piis and Pierre-Yon Barré.

VII.4.
A Performance of Beaumarchais's "Mariage de Figaro" at the
Comédie-Française, *engraving, ca. 1784–88.*
Courtesy Library of Congress.

Others included the Louvois, and the Théâtre français, rue Richelieu, which sponsored a repertory similar to that of the Comédie-Française.

Most theaters changed names at least once during the Revolution, reflecting political change. The new name for the Comédie-Française was Théâtre de la nation. In 1793 the schismatic Théâtre français, rue Richelieu, became the Théâtre français de la liberté et de l'égalité and then the Théâtre de la république. The Théâtre national de Molière became the well-known Théâtre des sans-culottes, and so forth. But frequent name changes also reflected instability.[11]

The Chapelier regime created intense competition. Since the plays of Molière, Crébillon, or Marivaux were performed simultaneously in several theaters, each theater garnered greatly reduced receipts. Financial records during the Revolution show a general decline in revenues. Receipts of the Comédie-Française dropped 20 percent in 1789, picked up in 1790, but plunged after the Chapelier law passed. When it was finally closed in 1793 for political reasons, receipts were one-half their 1787–88 level. Most of this loss was due to the emigration of the nobility, who had habitually rented boxes (*loges*) (fig. VII.5). The Théâtre italien, or Opéra-Comique, lost an even greater proportion of its receipts from the loss of box rentals (from 306,000 livres in 1789 to about 7,500 livres in 1794), but its overall losses were on the order of 15 percent. The Opéra was and always has been in deficit. In 1787–88, when it was partially subsidized by four little theaters and by the Opéra-Comique in exchange for grant of privileges to perform sung parts, it still ran 150,000 livres in the red. Internal administrative and political chaos, marked by the indiscipline of actors and dancers, led to an increase in the deficit. A "Report on the Opéra" by municipal officer J.-J. Le Roux, dated 15 February 1791, shows a deficit of 465,800 livres, or close to 70 percent of receipts.[12]

Not only were theater finances in deficit, but factionalism and democracy brought administrative chaos. An engraving (fig. VII.6) shows the "people" of Paris closing down the Opéra, which they regarded as a bastion of aristocracy during the uprising of July 1789. In 1790 a Comité d'opéra was created to allow actors and staff to participate in the administration. As in the academies, quarrels over precedence, rights, and equality became heated. The playwright Poisson de La Chabeaussière wrote to the minister of the Interior to complain of the "petty intrigues backstage in favor of dance against singing. . . . What is more, Citizen Minister, experience has proven that the theatrical administrations never prosper in the hands of actors." During the Terror the two directors of the Opéra were imprisoned for oppos-

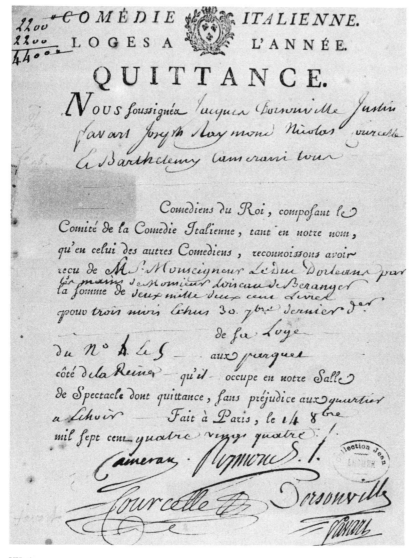

VII.5.
The duc d'Orléans's receipt for payment for his box at the Comédie italienne in 1784.
Courtesy Library of Congress, photo: John Reynolds.

VII.6.
[Pierre-Gabriel] Berthault, People Causing the Opéra to Be Shut Down,
12 July 1789.
Courtesy Library of Congress, photo: John Reynolds.

ing an irreverent opera on the Passion of Christ by the conventionnel
Philippe-François-Nazaire Fabre d'Eglantine and one of the authors of
the new French revolutionary calendar. In 1794 the Comité d'instruction publique decided to subsidize the Opéra and to tighten the financial controls around the institution. But administrators continued to be
replaced during the Directory and finances worsened.[13]

The closing of the Comédie-Française in September 1793 was due
more to politics and ideology than to deficits. The Comédie-Française
was the most important theater to be turned into a political arena during the Revolution, and this first occurred with the premiere in November 1789 of Marie-Joseph Chénier's explosive play *Charles IX.*
Chénier followed the philosophe version, indicting the monarchy and
the church for historical conspiracy, despotism, and fanaticism. The
privileged theater of the state understandably balked, and such actors
as Saint-Fal refused to play in the tragedy. But Talma made his acting
career by playing the role of Charles IX. Audiences were in tumult
over the play. When the *Réveil d'Epiménéide* was being performed one
night in 1790 in place of *Charles IX,* Mirabeau shouted for Chénier's

play from the audience. Talma appeared and agreed to perform it. Pandemonium broke out, and Danton, future member of the Comité de salut public, was arrested. The divisiveness spread to the comedians—some appealing to the king, others to the revolutionary municipality. Eventually (28 September 1790), Chénier withdrew the play in order to press the Assembly to legislate authors' rights, and the "blacks," who opposed *Charles IX,* refused to speak to the "reds," who were forced to move to rue Richelieu.[14]

The Comédie-Française survived for two years. When the Terror took hold in early September 1793, the Comédie was performing François de Neufchâteau's adaptation of Carlo Goldoni's *Pamela.* The play was deemed suspect because Pamela, a servant, married Mylord Bonfil, a *ci-devant,* or former noble, and all former nobles were prime "suspects." Certain lines in the play, moreover, had "aristocratic" overtones. The Jacobin *Feuille du salut public* denounced theater and audience ("The room was filled with women who displayed a truly monarchical luxury. The impure royalists were legion"). Neufchâteau was far from having aristocratic sympathies, and he had written this play before the Revolution in 1788, but the Comédie was closed on the play's ninth performance (2 September 1793). Neufchâteau was locked in the Luxembourg for the duration of the Terror and the actors were imprisoned in La Force.[15]

The Opéra survived amid internal conflicts and external control by compromising its traditional repertoire with the *Hymne à la liberté* by François-Joseph Gossec or with the *Offrande à la patrie* by Pierre-Gabriel Gardel. But the Comédie-Française failed to compromise its repertory sufficiently to shed its "black" reputation. The surrender of its privileges had not translated to a surrender of its aristocratic character.

A third theater, that of La Montansier, differed from the troubled Opéra and the refractory Comédie-Française and is somewhat more illustrative of a certain, perhaps feminine, entrepreneurial survival. Marguerite Brunet, known as Mlle Montansier, was the daughter of a pinmaker from Bayonne. Born in 1730, she had mastered the inner world of theater directorship in Rouen and in Versailles, where she ran the queen's theater, well before the Revolution. Her financial troubles, her run-ins with authorities, her conflicts with the public, her quarrels with her lover and partner, Bourbon-Neuville, established her as a colorful yet somewhat raucous and unrespectable individual. Ironically, her connection with Marie-Antoinette fostered this reputation. In the first years of the Revolution she kept her nose free of politics, abandoned Versailles, and established a theater (the former Beaujolais) in the Palais Royal. Here she bought eleven arcades, occupied as usual by book dealers, prostitutes, and gamblers. No one ever knew where Mlle Montansier got the money to pay for her theaters, but it was supposed that Marie-Antoinette was one source.

The Théâtre de la Citoyenne Montansier in the Palais Royal put on mostly comedies (3,766 performances), operas (835 performances), and comic operas (346 performances). When the Terror broke out, Mlle Montansier's heart and business instinct taught her the value of patriotism. Like many others, she naively believed in natural goodness and in the compatibility of personal and public interests. Her biographer writes that "she played the same role with the governing democrats that she had played earlier with the proud Marie Antoinette to become ultimately directress of theaters in the Republic, as she had earlier with the Court."[16]

In November 1792 La Montansier (the "La" made her a social institution) wrote the minister of Foreign Affairs proposing that she be authorized to set up a patriotic theater in Brussels, with public support, in order to educate ignorant Belgians in the principles of French republicanism. She adopted the language of the Revolution—a language of passwords among the revolutionaries who created it. "The Brabançon heads," she explained, "are still crammed full of prejudices." And Minister Pierre-Henri Lebrun-Tondu replied on 27 November: "I can only applaud your laudable design to propagate in Belgium, with all the means at your disposal, the principles and love of Liberty and of Equality, just when the success of our armies free the inhabitants of servitude and slavery under which they have bent for so long." In Brussels she put on a more patriotic repertoire than in Paris, whereby she hoped to "remove the blindfold" from Belgians' eyes.

She failed. The government paid 53,320 livres, of which 33,000 livres went to her, but the public resisted the propaganda: Gen. Charles-François du Périer Dumouriez, with whom she had close, possibly amorous, relations, defected to the Austrians, and the French armies began to retreat from Belgium. Mademoiselle Montansier returned to Paris on Good Friday 1793 and proceeded to put on plays during a season when theaters had been traditionally closed (*Clôture de Pâques*). She raised money and bought another theater on the rue Richelieu, which opened as the Théâtre national with public subsidies for patriotic plays. But she was not well liked by the *enragés,* who denounced her in November 1793 for questionable loyalty. Since La Montansier's Théâtre national was next to the Bibliothèque nationale,

Pierre-Gaspard Chaumette and Jacques-René Hébert claimed that she intended to set fire to the building! Montansier was clapped into prison, and the site of her theater was given to the Opéra, which moved in in August 1794, a few days before Mlle Montansier was released from prison. With the help of a lawyer and her partner, Neuville, she addressed a grievance to the Convention protesting the arbitrary closing of her theater at a time when it was flourishing with patriotic plays. She and her creditors were indemnified for a substantial part (1.3 million francs) of what she claimed to have lost (close to 1.8 million francs), but the Convention refused to give her back the theater, which it felt had become "a rallying point for counterrevolutionaries."[17]

The name of her Variétés Montansier in the Palais Royal was changed to Péristyle du jardin égalité and then Maison égalité. This theater at the Palais Royal kept its reputation for courtesans and pornography during the Thermidorean reaction and the Directory. In 1798 it became the Montansier-Variétés; and in 1807 Bonaparte spared La Montansier in his Réunion of theaters. The Théâtre des variétés opened on 24 June 1807 and remains open today.

La Montansier was deferential to political authorities, although she had difficulties staying in their good graces. Her life was one of short-lived arrangements (save her abiding ties to Neuville), big debts, and shallow political commitments. She and her theaters stayed afloat during the Revolution by giving audiences what they wanted and by half-convincing the authorities that she was giving them what *they* wanted.

The careers of other theater directors during the Terror were equally chaotic. The tacit censorship of the Commune (which became explicit in the hands of the Commission of Public Instruction on 1 April 1794), denunciations for lack of civism, visitations from police commissioners and secret agents of the Ministry of the Interior—all made imprisonment a constant threat. Directors walked a tightrope between authorities and audiences, who were more vocal than ever. Several of the most important directors were imprisoned: La Montansier, and Dorfeuille and Louis-Joseph Francœur of the Opéra (for refusing Fabre d'Eglantine's *La Passion du Christ*). Barré, François-Pierre Léger, Monnié, Radet, and François-Georges Fouques, dit Desfontaines—directors, actors, and authors of the Vaudeville—were arrested by the Committee of General Security on 20 September. Barré, director of the Vaudeville, was inculpated by an army officer who stated during the trial of Marie-Antoinette that he had seen Barré go in and out of the Tuileries during the night of Louis XVI's flight to Varennes.[18]

The exposure of directors to censorship and imprisonment meant that, in spite of the Chapelier law, they could not establish any repertoire at will. The revolutionaries' wishes had to be accommodated far more than those of the old royal censors. The constant melée of stage personnel and the insecurity of property also destabilized operating conditions. Still, theatrical disruption was considerably less than that of the church, collèges, and academies, which disappeared temporarily as institutions.

If directors were more often than not at odds with the new order, many actors and authors joined forces with the revolutionaries. In 1789 comedians became National Guardsmen, to the dismay of many who revered this new revolutionary institution. Theaters made patriotic contributions to the war effort of 1792, and many actors broke their contracts and joined the army: J.-B.-Henri Gourgault, dit Dugazon was an aide-de-camp of Antoine-Joseph Santerre, commander of one of the *armées révolutionnaires*; Saint-Preux and Jean-François Boursault-Malherbe joined the regular army; and Nourry dit Grammont and Charles-Philippe Ronsin, both playwrights, were high-ranking officers of the terrorist armée révolutionnaire. Talma was a member of the Jacobin club, and the popular playwright Monvel presided over the Cult of Reason in Saint-Roch on 30 November 1793.

But numerous actors were also imprisoned, among them: Dubois, Emile Gavaudan, Pagès, Mari-Labron Mezières, and Rose Niceumann. Several more were guillotined—Fabre d'Eglantine, Collot d'Herbois, Babin Grandmaison, Anne Leroy, Loison—and Mme Fusil emigrated to Russia.[19]

Repertory changed after Thermidor, as Thermidorean plays succeeded the Jacobin variety. *Cange, le commissionaire de Saint-Lazare* and its variants made a hero of a jail keeper who secretly aided a detainee and his family. Entrepreneurs and actors enjoyed greater security, although audiences now became agitated by the antirevolutionary "gilded youth" (*jeunesse dorée*). But even after Thermidor, officials continued to expect theaters to be "écoles de civisme et mœurs républicains." Police commissioners installed themselves inside theaters to keep public order. The theater, unlike newspapers, was for them a public institution—a place where the public gathered, where keeping public order and inculcating the proper *esprit public* was necessary. Without public vigilance, institutions that should be sources of morality could turn into centers of corruption. Judging from the reports on the Théâtre Feydeau, the police presence increased after Thermidor. Censorship became more regular, although incidents of actual suppression lessened. The bulk of this correspondence relates to matters of public policy: proper fire prevention and lighting for safety and decency; exclusion of public women ("a public nuisance") from the theater; maintenance of the proper decor (tricolor flags); encouragement of benefit performances for the poor; and the revival of the old (but not voluntary) "poor tax" on entertainment, which had been eliminated by the more "liberal" Chapelier regime.[20]

Robespierre, in a discussion on the liberty of theaters in January 1791, declared the presence of any authority inside theaters repugnant to free men. But theaters and much else came to be policed by the military. A year after the coup d'état of Brumaire, the central administration of Paris assigned twenty fusiliers to Sargeret's Théâtre Feydeau. In the provinces, as in Paris, police officials were responsible for seeing that a song prescribed by the Directory ("Veillons au salut de l'Empire") was sung without commotion and that its counterrevolutionary counterpart ("Le Réveil du peuple") would not be sung at all. They also inspected repertories, keeping personages and symbols of the old regime as well as those of the Jacobin "tyranny" off the stage. Everything—fire, prostitutes, riots, finances—was a police concern.[21]

During the last years of the Revolution, mayhem on stage decreased markedly, yet legislators, including Chénier, now a member of the Council of Five Hundred, were unhappy with the results of the theatrical revolution. These deputies complained that the theaters were not truly republican, citing the continuing indecency at such theaters as the Gaieté of Nicolet, the festering nests of royalism and counterrevolution here and there, and the pitiful dramatic quality due to a decline in public taste. Many attributed this to the abolition of theatrical monopolies. So much competition prevented any one theater from achieving excellence. Talents, artists, repertories, and audiences were overly divided.

On 9 floreal Year VI (28 April 1798) a resolution was introduced in the Council of Five Hundred (the lower house of the Directory government) to reduce the number of theaters and revivify their civic spirit. The measure was defeated a month later. Those who had supported the bill, however, spoke for the future as well as for the past. Chénier had signaled the end of the theatrical revolution with a speech in the council in November 1797: "Today, the exclusive privileges having been abolished, there is only the inconvenience of an infinite multiplicity of theaters, which destroys simultaneously the dramatic art, true competition, social mores, and the legitimate surveillance of the government." Theaters, he argued, should be proportionate in number to the population: cities having fewer than 100,000 people should have only one theater; such larger cities as Marseilles, Lyons, and Bordeaux could have two.[22]

A little known theater critic, Mauduit Larive, published a short pamphlet entitled "Some Reflections on the Decadence of Theater" in which he pointed out that London, although twice the size of Paris (1.1 million inhabitants), had only four theaters to Paris's twenty. The division of the old Comédie-Française into three troupes and the mushrooming of many more theaters resulted in "continual war" and "ruinous competition." The size of some theaters (3,000 spectators) made impossible demands on actors' voices. Theatrical liberty had resulted in "the loss of the art, the corruption of public spirit and the ruin of entrepreneurs."

A moral problem also existed. Larive revived the old charge against actors, claiming they were incapable of playing tragedy, because, being given to libertinage, they were incapable of portraying virtue.[23] A deputy from the Oise named Porthiez agreed that the classical tradition had declined on stage: "For too long a time, the friend of French literature has become indignant at seeing actors in tragical [costume] recite mindlessly the immortal verses of Racine and Corneille, of Voltaire and of Molière. . . . In a few more years the damage will be irreparable." Amaury Duval, the editor of the *Décade philosophique,* the organ of enlightened opinion during the Directory, published a short pamphlet entitled "Observations on the Theaters," in which he complained: "The repertories contain, for the most part, only formless productions by a swarm of so-called dramatic authors, who are ignorant of the human heart, the world . . . , the rules of the art, [and] even the language in which they dare to write. In brief, mediocrity in every respect has taken over the theaters, and has made them practically worthless."[24]

In the final months of the Revolution many of the best-known and most performed playwrights of the period—Legouvé, Arnaud, Laya, Demoustier, Picard, Beaumarchais—signed a petition asking for a reduction of the number of theaters to two state and two private and seeking to give control to "artists" rather than government officials. The *Décade philosophique* had called for an Institut dramaturgique to exercise control over theaters and repertory. The petition was rejected. In December 1802 the consular government of Napoléon imposed a fairly tight surveillance on the Opéra-Comique, which had to submit its repertory every Saturday for consular approval. On 8 June 1806 a comprehensive law governing the operation of theaters called for censorship of the repertoires of the newly restored, formerly privileged theaters (Opéra, Comédie-Française, and Opéra-Comique), which enjoyed exclusive rights over their repertoires. Each theater had an assigned genre that it had to perform. Of the theatrical creations of the Revolution, only the Vaudeville was allowed to survive. In the provinces, twenty-five theater arrondissements were created in each of which one ambulatory company could rove. Only Paris, Lyons, Bordeaux, Marseilles, Nantes, and the annexed Turin were allowed several theaters. In cities with permanent theaters, exclusive rights to perform certain types of repertory were set up, and new theaters were submitted to a *police des spectacles* (in itself not new). Two "conquests" of the Revolution—the liberty to establish a theater at will and the right to adopt any repertory at will—were lost. Censorship became official, thorough, and regular, although the right of authors to contract with directors for the use of their plays was recognized and protected.[25]

The French theater world, in short, returned to a regime of state protection and control more rigorous than that of the ancien régime. Theater artists and critics concluded that artistic quality was not bound to individual rights, democracy, and free enterprise. When Napoléon created a new theater monopoly, he did not restore the old regime corporate entities with their endowments and privileges but created a new system of state theaters under private management. In theater, as in education, the state's role increased greatly. Etatisme, not liberté or égalité, again became the guarantor of the cultural supremacy that France nearly lost under the regime of theatrical liberty.

Academies

The academies—particularly the Academy of Sciences—were resented fully as much as the privileged theaters by those who were excluded from them. The academic aristocracy was redoubtable in the 1780s when talent and privilege were joined to high birth. One- to three-quarters of the members of the Parisian academies were noble when one includes the noble cleric. Such a combination of advantages exposed academicians to the envy and ridicule of those who did not belong.[26]

Jean-Paul Marat (1743–93) is the most notorious of the rejected would-be academicians. Although Marat did have scientific credentials, they were judged insufficient. He had earned the sobriquet "doctor of incurables" in England and had studied with some success the causes of farsightedness, but, according to one excellent analysis, he had shown indications of "the grandiose and the scornful." The work that would have crowned his reputation was an unfounded critique of Newton's theory of light refraction and the existence of an igneous fluid in heated bodies (Book I of the *Optics*). Marat held that the academy rejected his work because of its blind adulation of Newton, on whom it based its reputation. The academy, for its part, accused Marat of being an ignorant charlatan: "a man who promises great things and who is incapable of filling any of his engagements."[27]

Marat's rebuff doubtless contributed to his revolutionary temper, but his angry personality was well shaped before his quarrel over Newton. His confrontation with the academy was a confrontation with the old regime. He insisted that he had been wronged by men who were protecting their reputations rather than honoring the truth. He, Marat, was the pure devotee of science—austere, living humbly, willing to sacrifice his small fortune to finance experiments, respectful of authority and religion. His qualities were quite unlike the sham of the academicians whom he attacked in *Les Charlatans modernes* (1791). They, not he, were the charlatans.

Although Franz Mesmer (1734–1815) had less of a claim on established scientists than Marat, his career and ambitions paralleled Marat's. Mesmer arrived in Paris in 1778, the same year Marat presented his papers on fire to the academy. He was an Austrian physician who believed that he had discovered a fine, invisible fluid universally present in all bodies. Mesmer argued that the harmonious flow of this fluid was the key to good health and moral peace. His system was called "animal magnetism" because the flow of the fluid occurred magnetically and, when manipulated by a mesmerist in a *bacquet,* or tub, could cure "dropsy, paralysis, gout, scurvy, blindness, and accidental deafness," according to a contemporary announcement. The beau monde of Paris was taken in by this medicine, and the Société de l'harmonie universelle, with 430 members, spread its practice throughout France. Like Marat, Mesmer cured the incurable and dumbfounded the academy, which was unable to explain his success.[28]

In 1784 two sober commissions were appointed to investigate the mesmerist phenomena. After numerous observations, the Faculty of Medicine concluded that "Mesmer's fluid did not exist," and the Société royale de médecine proceeded to condemn animal magnetism. Mesmer does not seem to have lashed out against these two bodies à la Marat. But J.-P. Brissot, another would-be academician who was also a police spy, found a political cause in Mesmer's fluid. Like Marat, he was a frustrated aspirant of the Republic of Letters and Science, and he defended mesmerism as follows: "Don't you [academicians] see, for example, that mesmerism is a way to bring social classes closer together, to make the rich more humane, to make them into real fathers of the poor? Wouldn't you be edified at the sight of the most eminent men . . . supervising the health of their servants, spending hours at a time mesmerizing them?" The real academicians were, for Brissot, "base parasites" and "oppressors of the fatherland," "vile adulators" of magnates. The revolutionary message Brissot extracted from Mesmer was the promise of a republic in which distinctions between ill and healthy, patient and doctor, rich and poor would cease to exist.[29]

Although the Academy of Sciences bore the brunt of criticism from aspiring and frustrated savants, the Académie française was also lampooned. In his *Tableau de Paris,* Mercier flatly stated that it was ridiculous to allow forty men—the members of the academy—to judge a country's taste, since wit, or esprit, was too widely spread to be arrogated by the so-called forty immortals. The academy was therefore an offense to men of letters and "all men are themselves the judge of the arts."[30]

Simon-Nicolas-Henri Linguet (1736–94), a maverick journalist, was refused admission to the Académie française in 1770. He described himself as "a simple and unknown man" who would have nothing to do with intrigue and "partisanship." Like Marat, Linguet accused the academy of a "philosophical" irreligion or antireligion: "It's a novitiate that prepares them for imitation. It's the promise of a blind devotion, the courage to keep oneself firmly attached to the *Masters* . . . who admit into it only the elect."[31]

Not only the academies and individuals but the academies and amateur societies had conflicts. Each academy acted as a corporation with a monopoly in its field. Rival organizations—agricultural, medical, and scientific—appeared after 1750, and some were eventually recognized as "royal," like the remarkable Société royale de médecine. Other unofficial societies for learning included Musée de Paris of Court de Gebelin; the Lycée of Pilatre de Rozier and La Harpe, a popular center with an excellent reputation for adult education; the Lycée des arts of Charles-Emmanuel-Gaullard Desaudrais, in which scientists and artisans rubbed shoulders; the Société encyclopédique; the Société philanthropique; dozens of Masonic lodges, of which the most notable was the Loge des neuf sœurs, to which many men of letters and future deputies belonged; the Guild of Saint Mark for artists, suppressed by Turgot in 1776; and many others. The multiplication of these societies in the second half of the eighteenth century testified to the public's desire for knowledge and *sociabilité* and to its refusal to be controlled by privileged bodies.[32]

Why were the academies abolished in 1793? The rhetoric of the Revolution paid homage to the arts and sciences, and such new institutions as the Muséum (the Louvre) and the Commission on Weights and Measures were established in recognition of their importance. But the "Report and Proposal for a Decree on the Abolition of the Academies" by the abbé Grégoire of 8 August 1793 (fig. VII.7) led to the abolition of the academies on the same day. Drawing from arguments put forth over a number of years, Grégoire faulted the academies' esprit de corps and the egoism of its members. The Jacobin Gilbert Romme had referred to some of them as "guilds of the Fine Arts," which, he implied, should go the way of all guilds. Marat in his *Ami du peuple* of 17 August 1790 had called them "pure establishments of Luxury," useless, censorious, and discriminatory in their publications and admissions policies. Grégoire thus concluded: "For the good of the sciences and letters, it is important that there be no more academic corps in France." Throughout history the academies had unjustly excluded such men as Molière, Nicolas Poussin, Pascal, Jean-François Regnard, Helvétius, and the abbé de Mably. Distinctions between academic and nonacademic scientists and men of letters ought not to exist, because it was the same as distinguishing bourgeois from nobles, which the Revolution had ended. Education had after all become "public," and Grégoire wanted the highest learning publicly expounded in public forums: "The heart of the legislative body will be the tribune for harangues." Genius does not arise from guilds from the body of free people. Academic privilege is inconsistent with democracy. "The human mind, having attained its virility, can take flight without the aid of an academy." Only merit should distinguish free men.[33]

Jacques-Louis David's speech the same day in the Convention seconded the abolition of the academies for similar reasons (although David wanted to abolish the Académie des sciences, whereas Grégoire wished somehow to save it). He, too, was shocked by the academies' esprit de corps and arbitrary teaching methods. According to one historian, David attacked the academy for excluding the painter Jean-Germain Drouais, whom he had long admired. According to another, David became embittered toward the academy when L.-B. Pierre, of the office of the Direction of Royal Buildings, refused him admission in 1782 on the basis of his Roman painting *Saint-Roch*.

On 27 September 1790 David formed the (revolutionary) Com-

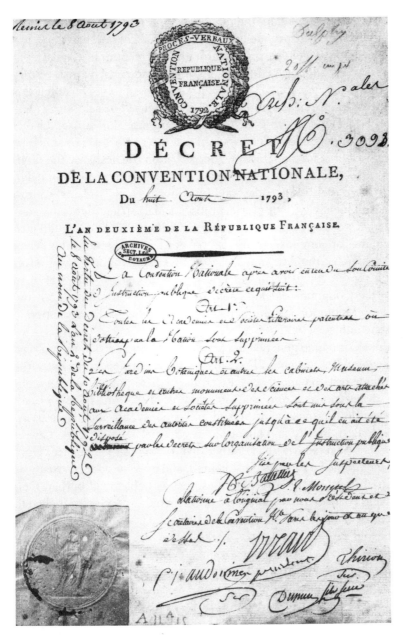

VII.7.

Decree of National Convention of 8 August 1793 abolishing the academies, document.

Courtesy Archives nationales, photo: Archives nationales.

mune des arts, peopled by the dissidents who met in his quarters and considered him their president. It had no official charter, like the Commune de Paris, which had arisen through insurrection. In August 1791 David actively supported the demand of nonacademician artists to representation in the Salon of 1791—a prior impossibility. David felt this to be a logical extension of the equality of rights. The salon was to be entirely open and to avoid favoritism toward academic artists. In October, Quatremère de Quincy assured that the number of nonacademic judges would equal the academic ones. Within the academy the dissidents refused to accept the academicians' self-reform and continued to try to usurp their space, titles, and functions. "Our dissidents want to abolish all hierarchy," the president Joseph-Marie Vien (fig. VII.8) complained. "No state, no society can exist without it. Even children in their games appoint leaders and obey." But David was no child. When the "Bastille of the Academy" was removed in 1793, following Grégoire's report, its space in the Louvre was given to what was then called the Commune générale des arts.[34] The enemies of the academy worked a revolution in cultural institutions parallel to the revolution in the state and society.

In the Commune générale des arts, equality and patriotism replaced privilege and precedence. The only requirement needed to enter the Commune des arts and its successor, the Société populaire et républicaine des arts, was a *carte de civisme* and proof that one lived off one's artwork. Both provisions were still exclusionary, but they were based on republican loyalty and financial integrity (as defined by the Law of Suspects of September 1793) rather than on talent or influence. Only well-intentioned patriots were admitted, and every academic artist was expected to burn any academic titles, just as nobles had burned their titles and coats of arms and just as priests would soon be compelled to surrender their letters of priesthood as tokens of their repudiation of the old regime. In the six weeks following 25 September 1793, seventy-four titles of members of the old Royal Academy of Painting and Sculpture were burned, while batches of new artists joined: twenty-nine on October 9, twenty on December 30. The salon, open to all artists since 1791, would now be judged by concours, or contests, rather than by academic judges. The jury des arts, which some had wanted the competing artists to select, included Ronsin, a member of the Revolutionary Army, Hébert, the enragé editor of the *Père Duschesne,* and Jean-Nicolas Pache, the mayor of Paris. As one observer put it, "Patriotism should have the upper hand over art."[35]

Projects were undertaken to redesign Paris and create monuments

VII.8.
Madame Adélaïde Labille-Guiard, Portrait of Marie-Joseph Vien,
painting, ca. 1783.
Courtesy Musée Fabre, Montpellier, photo: Lauros-Giraudon/Art Resource, New York.

to commemorate and glorify the Revolution and its heroes. Auto-da-fé made short shrift of counterrevolutionaries' works. The émigré François-Xavier Fabre's painting of Louis XVII, one member urged, should "be immediately dragged to the foot of a liberty tree, where it will be mutilated by each of the members of the Society. . . . Let its debris be burned and its ashes thrown to the wind at the sound of a thousand repeated cries of *Vive la République*." The academy had been purged—or rather rebuilt—in such a way that nothing inconsistent with the Revolution (members, customs, regulations, forms of recognition, and subjects of artwork) could survive.[36]

The future of the Academy of Sciences was debated quite publicly in the national assemblies and in the Committee of Public Instruction. The Assembly debates bore on all the academies, but the Academy of Sciences received close and prominent scrutiny. As we have seen, this academy performed a major public role, from censoring scientific publications to issuing patents for inventions. Unlike the Academy of Painting and Sculpture, internal organization had already been partly settled by Antoine-Laurent Lavoisier's reforms of 1785. The real issue was the academy's relation to the wider world of artisan and amateur scientists. Many expected the academy to become more useful and less speculative. Its standardizing weights and measurements may not have warranted such criticisms. But a challenge to the academy's exclusive leadership—begun at least two decades earlier—came to a head in August 1793. Several scientific journals—the *Bulletin des sciences,* the *Magasin encyclopédique,* the *Annales de chimie*—had been founded without academic approval, as had such private societies as the Société philomatique and the Société d'histoire naturelle. The government's Bureau de consultation des arts et métiers (1790) and the more recent Bureau de brevets et inventions ended the Academy of Sciences' exclusive roles in issuing patents and prizes for science.[37]

Government-appointed committees and such organizations as the Commune générale des arts formed by egalitarian-minded artists themselves took over the work of the academies. The destruction of the academies was the inevitable consequence of the anticorporate thrust of the Revolution and its war against privilege. To have tolerated academic distinctions when those based on birth were being suppressed would have been entirely inconsistent with the general razing of the old regime.

Scientific Committees

After the dissolution of monasteries and religious houses, after the closing of the collèges and academies, and after the de facto suspension of schoolteacher salaries, the newly declared republic had a choice. Either it could agree with the regicide *conventionnel,* the painter and playwright Gabriel Bouquier, who said: "Free nations have no need of a cast of speculative savants. . . . The sciences of pure speculation remove from society individuals who cultivate them, and become in the long run a poison which undermines and destroys republics." Or, it could agree with those who feared that the destruction of the arts and sciences in France fueled the accusations of counter-revolutionaries throughout Europe who charged that France had become barbaric. A compromise was attempted. Savants were forced to join such official commissions as the Observatoire de la République, which became the Bureau de longitudes in 1795. There, such men as Joseph-Louis Lagrange, Laplace, Lalande, Cassini, and Bougainville were recognized as savants (implicitly on the basis of their former membership in the academy) but were stripped of their speculative and honorific functions. Most scientists were safe, provided they served the immediate practical needs of a nation at war, performing more "applied" or artisanal jobs. They frequently mixed with artisans who had helped bring down the academy.[38]

Until the Academy of Sciences was abolished, it controlled the Commission of Weights and Measures, which then became an independent commission chaired by Lavoisier and staffed by members of the Observatoire: Laplace, Charles-Augustin de Coulomb, and Jean-Charles de Borda. The task of this committee was to introduce a standardized system of weights and measures and create an actual physical standard that would be kept under lock and key in Paris. On 23 December 1793 the commission ousted Lavoisier, Laplace, and several others. A new commission, which included Lagrange, Gaspard Monge, and Claude-Louis Berthollet, was formed—only true Republicans, as Monge put it.[39]

In addition to serving on these commissions, scientists could be made to inspect the various arms manufactures in Paris, Saint-Etienne, and Meudon. Men like Jean-Henri Hassenfratz were sent to the provinces to inspect saltpeter production. On 24 December the country was divided into eight powder (to produce gunpowder) arrondissements, which were directed by the chemist Jean-Antoine Chaptal. Almost all distinguished scientists were enlisted in the national defense: arms and powder, *aérostation militaire* (balloon reconnaissance for the Belgian frontier), the Chiappe telegraph (to communicate war news from the front to Paris), and all kinds of metallurgy. During the Terror, applied science survived, but little scientific research was published.[40]

VII.9.
First Meeting of the National Institute, *engraving, ca. 1796.*
Courtesy Bibliothèque nationale, photo: Bibl. Nat. Paris.

The Revolution liberated theaters from the privilege and censorship of the old regime. But, in doing so, it exposed the venerable protectors of the classical tradition (the three privileged theaters) to severe competition in a new theatrical marketplace as well as to such dangerous revolutionary bodies as the Committee of Public Safety, whose demands for revolutionary drama conflicted with public taste. Theaters survived, but poorly, in the vise of contrary pressures. Monopoly and protection would reappear under Napoléon.

The academies, by contrast, were exposed to attacks by revolutionaries; unlike theaters, they were not simply controlled by privilege but were unthinkable without privilege: exclusive bodies with the right to co-opt members, confer honors and prizes, and arbitrate the cultural life of the nation. In the revolt against all old forms of authority, the academies, which had excluded so many from their ranks, were prime targets for destruction. In their absence, the temporary committees and commissions linked learning to the state. After the Terror, when the tide of ruin had ebbed, the academies were reorganized in the National Institute (fig. VII.9). Not a corporate body, this was a central, national institution, in which old and new savants were called to further the science, the social science, and the belletristic and artistic endeavors of the nation. If there were any cultural victims of the Revolution, they were the cultural corporations of the old regime; and if there was a beneficiary, it was the nation and state, which exercised greater control over less independent cultural bodies than before.

CHAPTER VIII

VANDALISM AND

CONSERVATION

The French Revolution was caught in the throes of destroying one civilization before creating a new one. Contrary to what is sometimes thought, it did not wipe the slate of the old regime clean but attempted to salvage from the past those works of art and literature which, like an old testament, might be seen to announce a new, or even more surprisingly might be considered worthwhile in themselves. But these reasons for conservation did not preclude the destruction of many works of art (thought to be insidious reminders of royalty, feudalism, and superstition). Official commissions appointed by the successive national assemblies carried out the work of liquidation (and conservation), when vandals did not beat them to it.

The Commission of Monuments and Notre-Dame

The Commission of Monuments, created to conserve artistic and scientific objects on nationalized property, was at times called the Council of Scholars or the Commission of Four Nations. It was organized by decree on 13 October 1790 and was joined to other municipal commissions with similar objectives. It was succeeded on 17 December 1793 by the Temporary Commission of Arts, which had existed since August 1793 and was itself succeeded during the Directory by the Council of Conservation.

The Commission of Monuments first met on 8 November 1790 and sent its views on conservation to all eighty-three departments. The minister of the Interior and the Commission itself then drew up instructions on what should be retained, what conserved, and what transported to a depot such as archaeologist and conservator Alexandre Lenoir's Petits-Augustins (4 January 1791), which later gained fame as the Musée des monuments français (fig. VIII.1). Religious objects or objects reminiscent of the Bourbon monarchy, like the statue of Richelieu at the Sorbonne, could be preserved, in spite of their tainted provenances. Museums—basically eighteenth century in origin, although revolutionary in their public, pedagogical emphasis—made their preservation possible. The placement of a statue of a monarch or a saint in a museum instructed the public that it existed now only for artistic and historic reasons, as Lenoir emphasized in the many editions of his *Description historique et chronologique des . . . monuments français.* Stripped of its former living power, a statue of a king was now a reminder of the tyranny of the old regime; the equestrian statue of Henry IV on the Pont Neuf could no longer act as a source of inspiration for a living king. A statue of a saint or of the Virgin was no longer a physical sign of a living person to act as a channel of grace and material favors. All were now regarded merely as symbols of a dead cult, a repudiated past, shells of ritual, objects of curiosity.

The members of the Commission of Monuments did not consciously carry out these deep acts of desacralization. But in the writings of Alexandre Lenoir and in the memoirs of his fellow commission members, a clear philosophy of conservation and exhibition takes shape, one that closely resembles Condorcet's in his *Sketch of an Historical Outline of the Progress of the Human Mind* (1795). Both stressed that historical progress consists in growth of human reason—through epochs for Condorcet, through centuries for Lenoir.

Who were these commissioners of monuments?[1] A *compte rendu* of the commission on the eve of its disappearance in late 1793 lists twenty-five members, of whom twenty-three can be identified with reasonable certainty, with two more deduced from the minutes of attendance of 1793. These men were significantly older than the average *conventionnel.* Ten were over fifty; only four were under forty. They had acquired their reputations under the ancien régime and were considered savants—a venerable title. Over half (twelve out of twenty-three) were born in Paris, and of those born in the provinces, most were from the north. These savants spanned a variety of learned professions. Hubert-Pascal Ameilhon and abbé Gaspard-Michel Leblond

VIII.1.

Hubert Robert, The Visit to the Museum of French Monuments,
painting, ca. 1796.

Courtesy Musée du Louvre, photo: Lauros-Giraudon/Art Resource, New York.

were librarians; Dom Poirier, a Benedictine monk, was the archivist
of the Abbey of Saint-Denis; Armand Camus was a canon lawyer,
archivist, and conventionnel who organized the archives of France
after the Terror; Guillaume Debure l'Aîné was a *libraire,* or publisher–
book dealer, for the Académie des inscriptions. Several were professional antiquarians, archaeologists, or classicists: Barthélémi, Joseph
Dacier, and Puthod Maison-Rouge. David, J.-B. Regnault, Annicet-
Charles-Gabriel Lemonnier, and Gabriel Doyen were painters, whereas
Augustin Pajou and Louis Boizot were sculptors. Two were scientists:
Nicolas Demarets was a physician and Alexandre Vandermonde a
mathematician. Finally, Anne-Louis-François d'Ormesson de Noyseau
was the son of a *président à mortier* of the parlement of Paris, a position
he himself occupied just before the Revolution.

A striking characteristic of these men is their academic backgrounds
before the Revolution. No fewer than thirteen belonged to one of the

great Parisian academies, eight to the Académie des inscriptions et belles lettres, of whom three also belonged to the Académie française. Four more belonged to the Académie de peinture et de sculpture and one to the Académie des sciences. A significant proportion of the commission members (six, or almost a third) were clerics or defrocked clerics. They were Ameilhon, one of the most ardent revolutionaries of the commission, Joseph Dacier, Dom Poirier, Leblond, Barthélemy Mercier abbé de Saint-Léger, and Antoine Mongez.

The fate of these commissioners in the Revolution was not, on the whole, direful. Only Ormesson was guillotined; five were imprisoned at various times and by various factions; and three evidently lost their fortunes. But fourteen appear to have carried out their work as commissioners undisturbed. Most were political moderates and concentrated on their work as savants, although Mongez, François-Valentin Mulot, Camus, Antoine-François Sergent-Marceau, and David were ardent revolutionaries. The last three were also regicides.

Three of the most active members deserve a further look. Ameilhon (1730–1810) was a member of the Académie des inscriptions et belles lettres as of 1766, librarian of the city for thirty-eight years and of the arsenal for fourteen. He was the most active member of the commission in its destruction of "signs of feudalism" on monuments. He also connived to conserve thousands of books from official vandalism at the Bibliothèque de Saint-Victor, whose contents he transferred to a nearby hospital rather than see them thrown out the windows. He converted some vacant churches into depositories for books and saved several Jesuit churches from being sacked. He is perhaps the best example of a savant alternately playing the role of vandal and conservator.

Louis-Simon Boizot (1743–1809) was a sculptor and a *dessinateur* of the manufactures of Sèvres. He received the prix de Rome in sculpture and was admitted to the Academy of Painting and Sculpture in 1778. In 1792 he became a member of the Commission on Monuments, where he was very active and was in charge of verifying objets d'art in the Salle des Antiques at the Louvre. Boizot had submitted ten inventories of objets d'art between 1 September 1793 and 16 March 1794, when the commission was effectively replaced by the Commission temporaire des arts.

Lemonnier (1743–1824) was a painter of Vien's school and had received the grand prix in 1770, had studied monuments at Rome, and had been elected to the Academy of Painting and Sculpture in 1789. He painted a famous picture of Louis XVI receiving the merchants of Rouen on his return from Cherbourg, which he hid during the Revolution and the Empire. He was a member of the academy in 1789, lived in the Louvre during the Revolution, and was active in saving objects from vandalism.

Boizot and Lemonnier seem to have led rather ordinary, unperturbed lives during the Revolution. Ameilhon was caught up in its drama, but his role was exceptional. As for the rest of the members, the majority went about a routine of meetings and inventories. All were clearly devoted to antiquities and monuments, attested by their willingness to work without pay.

An instruction issued during the conscientious Roland ministry in 1792 enumerated types of objects the commissioners were to conserve: "1. Any object of artistic value, whose worth is greater than the value of metal it contains . . . were it melted down . . . ; 2. All monuments anterior to the year 1300 . . . because of the costumes; 3. All beautiful monuments . . . ; 4. Any monument which sheds light on the history and epochs of art or on mores . . . ;" and "9. . . . Inscriptions, stones and cloth from monuments or relics to be destroyed."[2]

Once clerical and royal property was nationalized, mobile property was left in place, demolished, or conserved. The history of monuments and of objets d'art during the Revolution is a story of a struggle between the agents of demolition and the agents of conservation. Such state agencies as the Administration of the National Domain and the Committee of Public Safety (which thought that the copper roof of the Abbey of Cluny "would be a precious resource for naval armament") wanted property nationalized for other than artistic reasons. The Commission of Monuments tried to forestall confiscations by other state bodies by getting to the object and having its own demolitioner, Scellier, do the job first.[3] The commission's participation in the confiscation and demolition could be called official vandalism.

If a demolitioner acting for a public agency reached a monument before the Commission of Monuments, or if an auctioneer sold a painting, manuscript, or vase at a derisory price, he would be duly criticized. But the real opprobrium of the term *vandal* fell on those who wantonly destroyed or stole objects of artistic value. A decree of 13 April 1793 penalized with two years' imprisonment those who, "by malevolence, destroyed or damaged monuments of arts and sciences." A decree of 6 June 1793 stipulated two years' imprisonment for anyone who degraded the newly public Tuileries Gardens and other public places, or monuments of art. The Jacobin Gilbert Romme denounced vandals who had misinterpreted a 9 October 1793 decree that ordered the removal of emblems of feudalism from statues, books, and other objects.

Removing the fleurs-de-lys, he argued, could damage the objects to which they were attached.

The problem illustrates the commission's dilemma in simple, almost symbolic, terms: How to remove vestiges of the old regime from an object one wanted to conserve? Two weeks after the decree of 9 October was issued, Thibault reported to the National Convention that municipal officers had visited individual homes, where they "burned some books and engravings on which were found some of these signs [of feudalism]." The Jacobin M.-J. Chénier protested that "it was to books that we owe the French Revolution,"[4] and a new decree stipulated that objects from which the signs of royalty could not be removed without damage should be placed in a museum. Vandalism may have been revolutionary, but, contrary to the abbé Grégoire's famous reports on the subject, it was not solely Jacobin.

An "Instruction on the Manner to Inventory and Conserve . . . Proposed by the Temporary Commission of the Arts . . ." illustrates how officials appropriated the popular right to destroy feudalism:

> Citizens who are wholly unacquainted with the study of the arts must not be permitted to destroy monuments, of which they know neither the value nor the design, under the pretext that they think they have found emblems of superstition, of despotism, of feudalism. At one time, a mighty people could avenge its chains, crush its oppressors, and strike with rightful anger; but today it has entrusted the care of its fortune and its vengeance to legislators, to magistrates in whom it confides; now that enlightened citizens have been appointed by judges and by curators of artistic masterpieces, which are in their control, does it not suffice to watch over their conduct and should not [the people] at least always listen to them before making a decision?[5]

Only the republic and its officials could destroy monuments, statues, and selected works of art. The people enjoyed limited participation.

Countering deeds of vandalism was a means of refuting counterrevolutionary accusations that revolutionary France had lapsed into barbarism. Dominique-Joseph Garat, the minister of the Interior in the summer of 1793, urged his commissioners to show that the arts were "flourishing more and more among us in the midst of terrible storms of a revolution." Like Louis XIV, the revolutionary administrators saw the prestige of art and learning as a chief ingredient of national glory.

In Year II Jacobins were in alliance with sansculottes, allowing no easy scapegoat for vandalism. In Year III the abbé Grégoire put the blame on the Jacobins: "We should be frightened by how rapidly the conspirators demoralized the nation and brought us back by barbarism to slavery at the moment of total regeneration. In the space of a year, they almost destroyed the product of several centuries of civilization." Grégoire himself was largely responsible for the legend of "le complot vandal," a story fabricated in the general Thermidorean detraction of Jacobinism.[6]

Before Grégoire's reports, vandalism was usually called *dilapidation*—a term that describes the passive death of a monument rather than its willful destruction by humans. Much of the revolutionary deterioration of such châteaux as Versailles, Sceaux, and Marly was the work of nature and human neglect rather than human violence. Fire, humidity, leaking roofs, broken windows, and a general lack of upkeep proved ruinous. Madame du Barry's treasure-filled château at Louveciennes suffered several of these mishaps by the time of her execution in December 1793. In May 1792 the Commission of Monuments visited the Tuileries and urged the removal of objets d'art that were "deteriorating day by day." On 23 July 1794 Alexandre Lenoir complained that the roof to his Petits-Augustins had caved in. At Chantilly a member of the commission complained of neglect of the armor, and at Versailles, where the members of the commission had procured most of their paintings for the Louvre, some 228 that remained were taken out of their frames and "scattered around in haphazard fashion on every side of each room." Ancien régime France was passing into ruins, which Hubert Robert romanticized (see figs. I.3, v.5, v.6) as Piranesi had romanticized the remains of Imperial Rome.[7]

Unauthorized sales of valuable works of art at bottom prices were another enemy of conservation. Lenoir spoke of "quantities of little painted portraits" in an art merchant's shop, Place des Quatre Nations, whose frames were similar to those officially removed from the Grands-Augustins. Lenoir was convinced that they were a "subtraction" from this "precious collection," a "theft from the nation." David complained that "artistic monuments [were] wasting away, [that] departments, municipalities, plain agents arbitrarily place orders for works of art and many national riches disappear." Sales were often organized before commissioners could arrive. Leblond complained to Lemonnier on 18 May 1793 that two works by Louis Carracci had been sold before he could get to them. Popular demand was great for such sales, causing an agent of the Ministry of the Interior to express fear of "insurrection" or arson if the paintings of the academy were not sold immediately.[8]

Officials themselves engaged in petty vandalism, more or less authorized by the law. On 25 November 1792, David urged that the post of director of the Academy of Rome be abolished and that artists at the French Academy "make an auto-da-fé of its busts, and I am sure that the people will applaud." Lenoir informed the commission in November 1793, in the middle of the campaign of de-Christianization, that he had "decided . . . to have three poorly sculpted stone figures which are situated above the door of the provisional depot of monuments knocked down to the ground. The bad statues, which you know as well as I, represent some grimacing monks and a sort of Virgin. I thought it necessary to take this wise and patriotic measure to assure the tranquility of the depot confided to me." This tactical vandalism, which sacrificed only "bad" art, was meant to forestall popular vandalism. But municipalities sometimes interpreted their assignment more crudely. In the same period of de-Christianization, statues were pulled from the portals of churches and even pillars and columns were destroyed, as at the cathedrals of Cambrai, Valenciennes, and Arras. On 4 October 1793 the town of Sarcelles in the Seine informed the commission, "We have executed the law which destroys all the monuments in the churches."[9]

The fate of Notre-Dame illustrates the conflict between official vandalism and conservation and merits a detailed account. On 30 October 1792, Louis-Pierre Manuel, procurator of the Paris commune, wrote to David, then deputy of the National Convention, informing him that Citizen Vonarmes, a committee member of the Section de la Cité, had drawn up a list of objects to be removed from the metropolitan cathedral. Vonarmes's list was long, comprising tombs and statues of kings and nobles, notably those of Louis XIII, Louis XIV, and the duc d'Harcourt. The list of exterior objects specified: "Above the doors, at a right angle to the base of the towers, [is] what is called the gallery of 22 colossal kings, poorly sculpted in stone, with their crowns and sceptres." The work is "very difficult and very costly." David passed this document on to the Commission on Monuments on 6 November 1792 with no annotation. Apparently he had no objection to the proposal—not even to the description, "poorly sculpted," of what are now recognized as extraordinary thirteenth-century heads of kings of Judah (not France).[10]

The Commission of Monuments quickly grasped the matter and appointed some of its members to examine the objects targeted by the Section de la Cité, which they did with Vonarmes on 8 November. On 15 November, two days after they made their report, Vonarmes visited

Leblond and informed him of the "haste in which they [the Section de la Cité] were going to demolish all the designated objects, if measures were not taken very promptly to remove them according to the accustomed forms." The following day Leblond reported back to the minister of the Interior. A sansculotte sectional committee was pressuring the Convention and its commission, which strove for procedural correctness. This failed to satisfy the section, which announced that it would take care of the matter itself. The ministry partly complied. On 26 November 1792, Minister of the Interior Jean-Marie Roland de La Platière ordered this sectional committee to proceed with the Commission of Monuments to demolish the objects in question. The minister excluded from his list, however, the tombs of the two Bourbon kings and Harcourt, some epitaphs, and the Gallery of Kings which the commissioners' report had warned against destroying: "As to the exterior of the portal, the 22 kings in the gallery seem to be placed simply like saints in their Gothic niches and their suppression could damage the overall decoration and would cost a great deal as it would be necessary to scaffold the whole facade in order to destroy them, even if [only] the sceptres and crowns were suppressed." Still, the commission recommended that "all stained glass windows and paintings with coats of arms . . . must be suppressed with all the necessary precaution to avoid damaging the objects to which they are attached."[11]

On 2 December 1792, Leblond wrote to Roland de la Platière that he had presented a demolitioner to a member of the Section de la Cité and to the guardian of Notre-Dame. The demolitioner prepared to go to work, and Leblond was confident that the minister's "authorization to suppress in Notre-Dame and its vicinity everything which could offend Republican eyes will produce a good effect." Official vandalism was like amputation: members were cut off to save the body. Leblond doubtless intended limited demolition.[12]

The actual destruction of the Gallery of Kings and the west portals of Notre-Dame did not begin for almost another year and then was undertaken by masons and marblers under orders from the Commune, the Section de la Cité, and the Commission of Monuments. An entrepreneur named Bazin, working for the Revolutionary Committee of the Cité and approved by the Commission des travaux publics, erected scaffolding fifty feet high and thirty-six feet long between 10 September and 4 October 1793. After 16 December, Scellier undertook the demolition, with the help of Citizen Daujon, a municipal officer, and one Bellier, much experienced in removing "emblems of feudalism" from monuments. He tore down the kings and a large number of other sculptures, including one of the Virgin. The bill covered seventy-eight large statues and twelve small ones. The rubble was dumped in a little alley on the east side of the cathedral. Some of it was even used in street repairs. Writing in his *Nouveau Paris,* Mercier asked: "Do you know what became of them? Heaped behind the church, one on top of the other, they remained buried under the filthiest refuse. Their distorted figures attract attention, and when one sees them yet another time, their great sceptres in hand, their varied and comical mutilations elicit smiles of pity, but one soon reflects on the curious interruptions in time and the strange twists of fate." Mercier's melancholy was not unlike that of Diderot, Hubert Robert, and Bernardin de Saint-Pierre on the fate of civilizations.

The rubble of kings was sold in 1796 to a contractor near the Hôtel Dieu, who in turn sold it to a lawyer, Jean-Baptiste Lakanal, who was building a mansion in the Chaussée d'Antin. Lakanal was a Catholic royalist; when he perceived that he had bought desecrated statues, he buried them according to the dictates of canon law. The Banque française du commerce extérieur bought the mansion in 1977. Its manager, François-Giscard d'Estaing, had the wall opened and discovered the magnificent heads. These were later donated to the Musée de Cluny, where they are now on display.[13]

Official bodies of conservation were implicated in desecrating the extraordinary works of art that passed through their hands. The commissioners had proved no match for a sansculotte section in 1793.

Saint-Denis

The story of the basilica of Saint-Denis during the Revolution—infrequently recounted in spite of its symbolic and anthropological significance—is even more shocking. Denis, who came from Rome and became the first bishop of Paris, was the patron saint of France, just as Sainte-Geneviève was the patron of Paris. The Abbey of Saint-Denis had been the mausoleum of French kings since the sixth century, commemorating and sacralizing royalty. It suffered routine desecration during the early days of the Revolution when royal troops were stationed there. After the fall of the monarchy, the Assembly authorized the municipality to melt down a number of its bronze and copper statues of former kings. *Les Révolutions de Paris* published the following:

While we are in the process of effacing all vestiges of royalty, how is it that the impure remains of our kings repose still intact in the former Abbey of Saint-Denis? . . .

On the 22d of September 1792, the day after the abolition of royalty and the establishment of the Republic, why did not the sansculottes of the 10th of August go to Saint-Denis to have the hand of the executioner exhume the vile bones of all the proud monarchs, who from the bottom of their tombs still seem today to defy the laws of equality; Louis XIV, Louis XV await their successor there in peace? One would say that the Revolution respected them. . . . The piled stones of the building consecrated to their burial should not remain.[14]

That month the monks vacated the basilica, which now stocked flour and wheat. The body of Louis XVI was not interred in the royal sepulcher, or anywhere else known to the public, in order to prevent a martyr's cult from developing. Like the corpses of other victims of the guillotine, his was consumed in quicklime "in order to efface even its slightest traces." Meanwhile, the roof of the basilica was stripped of lead, exposing it to rain for a decade. According to one account, the Commission temporaire des arts, the successor to the Commission des monuments, decided to destroy the building but never carried this out. As the anniversary of the overthrow of the monarchy approached (10 August 1793), the terrorist Bertrand Barère de Vieuzac, a member of the Committee of Public Safety who harbored an obsessive hatred of royalty, alluded to the royal tombs of Saint-Denis in a tirade against the First Coalition and the French royal family: "During the monarchy, even the tombs learned to flatter kings. [But] pride and royal pomp could not be sweetened in this theater of death; and the scepter-holders who did so much harm to France and humanity, seem even in their tombs to show pride in a vanished grandeur. The powerful hand of the Republic should efface these haughty epitaphs pitilessly and demolish painlessly these mausoleums which bring back frightening memories of kings."[15] Following Barère's report, the Convention declared on 1 August: "The tombs and mausoleums of the former kings . . . all over the Republic will be destroyed on 10 August." On the 6th Saint-Denis was filled with soldiers and workers armed with picks and chisels (see fig. VIII.1) under the direction of the same Scellier who demolished Notre-Dame. A letter of 8 August from Garat to the commission stipulated such "precautions to be taken in the demolition of monuments in the tombs and existing mausoleums in the church of Saint-Denis" as informing savants of the department and administration. Garat left office retaining simultaneously the desire to demolish and to conserve. On the first days of desecration (6–8 August 1793) the Merovingian, Carolingian, Capetian, and Valois tombs were opened— Dagobert, Pépin, Carloman, Hugh Capet, Charles the Bold, Charles V, Charles VI, Charles VII. The tombs bound for the Petits-Augustins in Paris included those of Philip the Bold, Philip the Fair, Blanche of Castille, Charles VIII, Henry II, and other "morsels which will be destined to enrich the Museum of Fine Arts."[16]

According to Lenoir's *Musée des monuments français* (1800), he and the commission had been able only to pick up the pieces left from "the furor of barbarians." The new minister of the Interior, Jules-François Paré, found no reason to leave any remains: "It is urgent that the remainder of the monarchy disappear"; and the commission responded: "Tomorrow the hammer will strike the remains of royalty." But three weeks later, it asked the minister of the Interior for two hundred printed notices "of the law that condemned those who damaged monuments in public edifices with two years imprisonment." Casual looting had become a problem throughout the republic. In the end, the attack on Saint-Denis in autumn 1793 involved three forces: conventionnels and a ministry eager to stage auto-da-fé of royal effigies, local vandals who looted indiscriminately, and the Commission of Monuments, which procrastinated in following official instructions in hopes of saving artistic monuments.[17]

By the beginning of October, Scellier and his workers were ready to demolish the royal tombs. From 12–25 October the Terror took one of its most macabre turns. The guillotine was to rid the earth of living traitors—a purification through human sacrifice. But the kings of Saint-Denis could not be guillotined. Their tombs had to be demolished or placed in museums, and their embalmed bodies had to be exposed to disintegrate or tossed contemptuously into a common pit—for kings were now commoners and their former subjects sovereign. Only then could royal thaumaturgical powers be considered extinct, the last traces of a millennium of monarchy annihilated.

The kings' corpses were to be consumed by a chemical, but their tombs would be saved to illustrate the centuries of art from the Middle Ages to modern times. The fleurs-de-lys would be removed from the statues. The operation was one grand task of sorting (*triage*) and classification. "The remains of the princes and princesses were also in this grave, sealed in lead and deposited under trestles which lay over the coffins; they were carried into the cemetery and the entrails were thrown into the common pit with the cadavers; the lead seals were put aside to be taken with the rest to the foundry, which had just been established in the cemetery itself in order to found the lead as it was discovered."

Corpses, lead, and bronze were removed from coffins, statuary from tombs. The first were reinterred in common, like plebeians or like guillotined bodies. The metals were added to the nation's reserves for national defense, the statuary taken to the Museum of Monuments. Nowhere so much as at Saint-Denis does the desacralizing, analytical character of conservation appear. Lenoir observed in his "Notices historiques sur les exhumations faites en 1793 dans l'abbaye de Saint-Denis": "The graves and sepulchers of approximately one hundred and fifty princes and princesses of three races and of other notable personages buried in the church of Saint-Denis cannot help but furnish matter for observations relative to history, to antiquities, to the arts, to costume, to anatomy, to physiology, to chemistry." Dom Poirier recommended not only that the statues of kings and queens be saved as illustrations of the history of costumes but that the corpses themselves "furnished abundant matter for observation of anatomy and of chemistry by the progressive state of dissolution of the human body over a large number of centuries, by the different manners of embalming, and the singularity of seeing quicksilver employed in the embalming process of some fifteenth- and early sixteenth-century bodies."[18] Bystanders were more immediately impressed by the powerful stench that emanated from these corpses and filled the basilica for days.

Scellier and his workers began with Henry IV, France's most popular king. Once uncovered, his well-preserved "fresh" face was recognizable, his skull embalmed, his body propped up in a shroud. An adept bystander made an impression of his face on a cloth. A soldier cut off part of his beard. Two days later, the corpse was thrown unceremoniously into the Bourbon pit. But another eyewitness could not resist taking a last relic—a toenail—which he later gave to Louis XVIII!

When the coffin of Louis XIV was opened two days later, he, too, was discovered to be well preserved, but the crowd could not tolerate his presence, and he was thrown at once into the Bourbon pit on top of Henry IV. The same eyewitness jumped in after him for a tooth; unable to extract it, he settled for another nail. On the fifteenth, twenty-one coffins were opened; on the sixteenth, twenty-seven, including that of Louis XV, whose corpse Lenoir described as follows: "His skin was white, his nose violet, his backside red like that of a newborn child." On the nineteenth, medieval kings were disinterred; on the twenty-first, Saint Louis's body was thrown into the Valois pit. On the twenty-fifth, writes the historian of this ghoulish ritual, "satiety and boredom" descended. One savant who had not received an invitation in time to attend the exhumations expressed special regret, because he had been studying "the composition and decomposition of human bodies."[19]

It took months for them to arrive at the Petits-Augustins. The most exciting loot—symbolically as well as monetarily—were eleven crowns, eleven scepters, two diadems, and two rings.[20]

The one cadaver not reburied in quicklime was that of the vicomte de Turenne, military hero of Louis XIII and Louis XIV. It was kept for several months at Saint-Denis, thanks to Lenoir's reluctance to bury him. Turenne's body was eventually handed over to the guardian of the abbey, who eked out a living for eight months by showing the corpse and selling relics to visitors. In June 1794 this scandal ended abruptly and the remains were transferred to the Muséum d'histoire naturelle. There the corpse lay exposed for four years until a deputy of the Council of Five Hundred named Dumolard protested in 1796, and it was sent to Lenoir's Museum of Monuments. Finally, Bonaparte, in recognition of Turenne's military genius, laid him to rest in the Invalides in September 1800. Turenne alone survived the desecration of Saint-Denis, just as Napoléon alone retained power after the *épurations* (purges) of the Revolution. Turenne's honored body symbolizes the victory of the army in the French Revolution, even as the desecration of a millennium of kings marks the death of royalty.[21]

But the Commission of Monuments was also a casualty of the Terror, partly because of its procrastination in demolishing the tombs of Saint-Denis. A Commission temporaire des arts had been created in August to take over the scientific and artistic artifacts of the defunct academies. This new commission soon began to criticize the old for not ridding Saint-Denis of some royal tombs on the one hand and for not conserving artistically valuable items on the other. (Had the Commission of Monuments restricted itself to removing feudal signs and statues it could have kept the monuments.) Six weeks earlier, Deputy Mathieu had urged the Convention to abolish the Commission of Monuments, charging that the commission's zeal had slackened. Bibliography, once its real strength, had been neglected, and the sciences had never received the attention they deserved. Furthermore, he had continued, the nation had suffered unpardonable losses under the commission's maladministration. Objects that should have been transported to a depot, like the marble and porphyry columns at Saint-Denis, had been left in place. Cargoes of émigré art (that of Marie-Gabriel Choiseul-Gouffier) had nearly been shipped to Marseilles. Tables of petrified wood, objects of natural history, paintings by Sébastien Bourdon—all could have been sold far above the prices the commission had fetched, whereas the depots were filled "with useless items."

The same day the Convention voted a decree dissolving the Commission of Monuments and transferring its functions to the Commission temporaire des arts, which Mathieu had praised and whose members, at David's suggestion, would be salaried, unlike previous commissioners. Although the principal criticism of the Commission of Monuments was its alleged incompetence, the civic loyalty of its savants was mentioned: "In the present and general movement, the civism of several members of this commission has seemed stationary, and that of others backward."[22]

The moribund commission might have refuted some of the charges, but in fact the enormous transfer of art from private to public hands was too much for this largely volunteer body, whose task, to execute the demolition and conservation policies of the Revolution, was in any case ambiguous. What control did the commission have, for instance, over Citizen Potiers, who had bought the castle of Grèves in the Seine-et-Marne, which contained 368 paintings of the royal family? In a letter of 13 August 1793 Potiers recommended that these paintings of "the family which reigned until recently" be "slashed and thrown to the fire." Potiers's "civism" was rewarded with an indemnity. But did Potiers wish the legitimate destruction of the "signs of royalty," or was this vandalism of the highest sort? How could the Commission of Monuments, with such sparse information, be held responsible? Likewise, depredations due to the negligence or absence of palace guards were beyond its control, yet it was held responsible for them by its enemies, as, for example, at Marly, where the Venus of Medici and the "beautiful copy of ancient Diana were broken in spite of the surveillance of the national guard."[23]

Bureaucratic formalities slowed the commission's work. Lenoir informed the commission in December 1793 that he could not remove objets d'art without the specific authorization of the Directory of the department and before the municipality made an inventory. Moreover, one of the constituted authorities had to accompany him. The difficulty of getting so many bodies to agree to remove one historic object was a central cause of delays, which in turn invited dilapidations and sales.

Finances were another problem. The Convention had appropriated 300,000 livres for art in 1792, and the minister of the Interior regularly paid the "mémoires" submitted by the dutiful, hard-working, and enterprising Scellier for demolitions and transports. Although most commission members were not salaried, they were reimbursed for traveling expenses, including substantial meals and on occasions three or four bottles of wine. But the enterprise was definitely carried out at the level of a commission rather than of a ministry; thousands of workers and officials could easily have been employed, as they later were by ministers of culture.

The departments and provincial towns, moreover, resisted expropriations by the commission, whose limited staff and resources resulted in inadequate surveillance. The commission simply could not handle the volume of work involved in a nationwide expropriation of objets d'art. Three examples illustrate the tug of war between Paris and the provinces over this question. In August 1793, Mulot, a member of the commission, wrote from Auxerre to the commission that he and the local authorities were unaware of the need to pay for the excavation of an ancient tunnel underneath the Church of Saint-Julien. The department overruled the district and authorized the expense, but after thirty-six *arpents* (approximately thirty-six acres) had been dug, they decided to stop wasting money. In the district of Nogent-sur-Seine (department of the Aube) the little commune of Quincy protested the "removal of the tomb of Héloïse and Abelard." Notwithstanding, this tomb was soon in Lenoir's museum. On 14 September 1793 the administration of Versailles petitioned the minister of the Interior to leave the precious objets d'art in the town, since they were its principal attraction. But the major part of Versailles's holdings had already been transferred to the Louvre for its opening the previous month.[24]

Libraries and Archives

Objets d'art were only one concern of the Commission of Monuments. Another was the huge collection of books and manuscripts in the royal and noble castles and in the thousands of monasteries, convents, churches, schools, and academies. As early as 14 November 1789—just two weeks after the confiscation of church property—a decree ordered chapters and monasteries to deposit catalogs of their libraries and archives at municipal or royal courts. The entire enterprise, soon to be called the Bibliographie générale de France, was directed by the Bureau de bibliographie of the Commission of Monuments and its successor. The undertaking proved Herculean. One commission member, Mercier de Saint-Léger, wrote in early 1791: "We asked for the catalog of provisional depots in two or three months. I will make you a prediction that it will not be done in two years, and that even then it will be done by salaried copyists who will understand nothing and who will be poorly directed."[25]

Later reports bore out Mercier's prediction. Grégoire estimated the nation's patrimony of books at 10 million—over thirty times the holdings of the Bibliothèque royale in 1790 (300,000 volumes). First this national patrimony had to be inventoried and cataloged, a task that presented an uninterrupted series of difficulties. Districts resisted cataloging lest their books be taken to Paris, which was the commission's intention when books found in the departments were unobtainable in the capital. Such persons as Debure, a member of the commission, were devising systematic cataloging principles, using an alphabetical catalog by author—except for anonymous works, which were cataloged first alphabetically by title and later by subject. Each month, twelve copyists sorted the several thousand cards they received at the Bureau de bibliographie from the provinces. Urbain Domergue of the bureau and then Grégoire in the Convention criticized clerical incompetence in reports on the overall operation.

Near utopian aspirations quickly turned into bitter, denigrating commentaries on the state of culture in the world of books, as well as in the world of art, academies, education, and theater. The loftiest idealists, the most effective organizers like Grégoire, fell far short of their own expectations and became acerbic about what they perceived was responsible for their failure—the public, bad taste, ignorance, cupidity, superstition.

Grégoire complained of the ills of "dilapidation" and the failure of most departments to send appropriate bibliographic cards: "Inept copyists . . . have tampered with the titles of rare books, changed their dates, confused editions, and sent useless catalogs in notebooks instead of in cards, the only ones the law asked for, the only ones which we can use." Grégoire found that the "editors" were selecting books on the basis of their covers instead of their contents. Genealogies bound in Morocco leather were saved, and "the immortal books of Hubert Languet, Althusius, Milton, and William Allen only escaped . . . censure . . . through obscurity, hidden under a modest parchment envelope." Furthermore, treasures of the ancient world and of foreign countries—sometimes old parchments—were counted rather than identified in detail, "because it would have taken too long to describe them."[26]

Domergue raised another problem, parallel to the one the commission had already considered regarding paintings and sculpture. How much of the printed mass originating in the old regime and the Christian Middle Ages should be kept? What should be sold? What should be burned? Only the commission was supposed to choose, but often the copyists and local authorities did so themselves, and with little discrimination: "To the prejudices of the moment, the authors of the bibliographical plan joined their own professional prejudices: the furor to accumulate books caused them to collect with equal care Maria Alacoque [a seventeenth-century saint], and Voltaire, the *Guide for Sinners* and the *Social Contract,* some miserable lawsuits of novices against monks and the lawsuits of peoples against tyrants. How many works [were saved] which are not worth the squares of paper on which the title was copied!"[27]

Too many books, too many corpses, too many statues. Domergue would purge the nation's libraries as the Section de la Cité had purged the portal of Saint Anne at Notre-Dame. The ritual decapitation of the kings of Judah was to be repeated in a symbolic execution of feudal authors. "Our libraries," Domergue explained, "also have their counterrevolutionaries; I vote their deportation. Let us channel the poison of our books about theology, mysticism, royalism, feudalism, and oppressive legislation to the enemies' camp." France would be purged of error; counterrevolutionary Europe would be inundated with it and become delirious.[28] The "index of reason," Grégoire agreed, would be used to reduce the national collection of books from 10 million to 5 million volumes. The balance would be either sold or traded abroad for more appropriate books "for the libraries of free people."[29]

If Domergue conceded that "we must conserve one or two copies of all the productions of human stupidity," he was a good deal less indulgent than Lenoir toward the remnants of the execrable past. One senses that Lenoir liked some of the Gothic virgins and kings. Domergue, on the contrary, proposed to save "bad" books in the same spirit as "the botanist [who] places the lethal aconite in his herbarium, among a lot of salutary plants. But let us have our tablettes of pr[o]scription like the ultramontanes. The bishop of Rome puts the philosophes on the index of fanaticism, let us put the theologians on the index of reason."[30]

Books seem not to have been exchanged much with foreign nations. What then happened to the proscribed books? If they were not poorly identified, ineptly selected, summarily or erroneously cataloged, they were collectively dispersed or destroyed. Municipalities often sold libraries before the commission arrived. Entire convent libraries were sold in Paris as early as August 1791 "under the eyes of the National Assembly," because convent members were often selling their libraries or taking them with them to avoid confiscation. In December that year, a sale of books, supposedly of an abbé, turned out to be books belonging to the provincial convents of the Capucins of Besançon and the Bernardins de Fontaine and therefore national property. Buried with a heap of unappreciated breviaries and missals were copies of Titus Livius, Florus, and an Aldine Polybius from the early sixteenth century. Convents apparently sold valuable books by the item and the remainder by the pound. Due to the paper shortage during the Terror, the famous printer-publisher Firmin Didot, charged with the nation's publishing, asked the commission to sell him discarded books, such as missals, by the pound so that he could recycle them for luxury paper.[31]

Grégoire made his most damaging charges after Thermidor. At Paris, Marseilles, and elsewhere, he claimed, persons had proposed to burn libraries: "theology, they say, because it is fanaticism; jurisprudence, chicanery; history, lies; philosophy, dreams; sciences, none are needed." In subsequent speeches against Jacobin vandalism, Grégoire repeated his allegations of "book burning." Hanriot was cited as proposing to set fire to the Bibliothèque nationale, a proposal quoted by an anonymous "Doléances Républicaines" (Republican Grievances): "Burn all the books . . . they are useless and harmful." Such statements reinforced allegations of Jacobin anti-intellectualism. Indeed, as noted, the words "The Republic has no need of savants" were actually pronounced by the conventionnel Bouquier. Mulot, a member of the Commission temporaire des arts, supported the petition of the Lycée des arts "to stop the disastrous effect of a decree which condemned to fire all books inspired by what they then called superstition." But which decree was that? Similar allegations about widespread burning of counterrevolutionary prints and engravings have been made—and with similar lack of concrete proof—by a twentieth-century authority who has claimed that the "traditional imagery of engravings was destroyed by the millions."[32]

The threat must be distinguished from the act of book burning. A raging fire burned the library of the Abbey of Saint-Germain on the night of 19–20 August 1794. This was not an intentional act of arson, however, but was caused by the explosion of a saltpeter depot situated too close by. Intentional acts of burning unwanted books in one or another district probably occurred—at Evreux Saint-Pierre le Bitry, for example—but documentation of such acts is scarce. As already noted, Ameilhon, one of the commission members, saved the Bibliothèque de Saint-Victor from destruction by the Ministry of the Interior, yet he himself handed over hundreds of valuable volumes of noble titles to be destroyed by the Directory of the department of the Seine. "It is up to the Directory," he wrote, "to choose the day which is most suitable for the burning." He is estimated to have been responsible for the annihilation of 632 volumes. Lesser forms of vandalism also occurred, as attested by a district in the Ardennes (8 December 1792): "We cannot hide the fact that ignorance, cupidity, and, above all, negligence have permitted libraries to deteriorate."[33]

The legislators' intention, of course, had been to establish a national network of district libraries holding books of "reason" parallel to the network of schools teaching true republican principles. Some felt that, like the national bibliography itself, this was an impossible project whose aims might be better accomplished by simply distributing unwanted books among the population at large. This was, in fact, the course of action adopted in an unconcerted manner. It might conceivably have accomplished precisely the opposite of the Convention's bibliographical aim—to keep from the public books proscribed by "the index of reason."

The bibliographical efforts of the Revolution were declared a failure. On 31 October 1794 the Committee of Public Instruction made the Bureau de bibliographie a responsibility of the Commission of Public Instruction. A year later (26 February 1796), Pierre-Louis Ginguené, then in charge of public instruction in the Ministry of the Interior, suggested that the bureau be dissolved, which was done by Bénézech, the minister of the Interior. When Grégoire scathingly attacked the bureau's record in a postmortem account in April 1794, he indicated that only 1.2 million cards out of a projected 10 million had been completed. When émigrés returned and regained civil status, they reclaimed their houses *and* their books! These books, incidentally, had surprised the catalogers by their enlightened modernity. Even with contemporary methods of compilation—word processors, duplicating machines, computers, sophisticated communications—Grégoire's task would have foundered. The cashiering of the Bureau de bibliographie expressed a general dissatisfaction that sprang from the exaggerated expectations of legislators and the intractable sluggishness of local agents.[34]

But the significance of the Bibliographie de France was not simply its failure. The project of "cultural revolution" expressed one aspect (classification) of what Michel Foucault has called the classical *episteme* (*Les Mots et les choses*). The comparative tables of general grammar, natural history, and chemistry graphically analyze parts of speech, species and genera of plants and animals, and chemical properties, respectively. One can thus visualize relations of derivation, affinity, and difference. Parallel to these are the systematic tables of weights and measures of the metric system and the bibliographical classifications according to author and subject (broken down in Baconian or Encyclopedic manner), edition, places of publication, and provenance. The reality is that France still lacks such a national bibliography. This project has been described as "a gigantic work of Penelope, the termination of which became impossible to foresee" but which nonetheless helped clear "the way to the civilized world."[35]

Although most historians describe the Convention decree of 27 January 1794 creating a network of local public libraries as as great a failure as the Bibliographie générale, it did have some success. The Republican historian Benjamin Bois made a case for Angers. In this provincial town of 34,000 inhabitants at the close of the old regime were libraries in abbeys, seigneurial houses, and some parishes. Monastic libraries held one thousand to ten thousand volumes, principally sacred and philosophical works. But, unlike many others, these monastic libraries were not open to the public and their content was hardly suited to the general public. No public library existed in Angers until 1798, two years after the Bibliographie de France ceased to exist. A document in the local archives describes the confiscated religious books as "a dead collection which nobody wishes to use and which is deteriorating from humidity and dust." This library, consisting of the collections of religious and émigrés, was placed in the bishop's palace and included more than forty thousand volumes in Year VII (1798–99). According to the prefect, in Year X (1801–2) it contained sixty thousand volumes of religious works. When it was cataloged according to the system of Debure l'Aîné, a former member of the commission, it included the *Encyclopédie* of Diderot, the *Mémoires* of the National Institute, the *Journal des Savants*, the *Dictionnaire* of Pierre Bayle, and other Enlightenment works. An ex-Benedictine headed the library, which was open on even days of the *decade* (the ten-day week inaugurated in 1793) from 10 A.M. to 1 P.M. Both the collection and its availability evidently met the demands of the public and the central school of Angers.[36]

Local initiative, responding to promptings from the various ministers and committees in Paris, thus succeeded in creating local public libraries, in spite of the collapse of a centrally directed system in Paris. All over France, with varying degrees of success, public libraries were formed on the ruins of the old private, corporate, religious, and royal libraries that had escaped "book burning" or the "index of reason." The Christian heritage (like classical theater) was put in the public domain rather than annihilated. Throughout Paris, former royal and monastic libraries were opened to the public: the Bibliothèque royale, the Bibliothèque of the marquis de Paulmy, and the Hôtel de Soubise became, respectively, the Bibliothèque nationale, the Bibliothèque de l'arsenal, and the Archives nationales (1794).

A recent account of library history during the Revolution by Paul Priebe credits the nationalization of printed and manuscript material emanating from religious and émigré property with the quintupling of the size of the Bibliothèque royale, making it the largest library in the world. Its close supervision by the legislature served as a model for the library systems of other European nations. Prièbe asserts that in spite of chaotic conditions, "the period 1789 to 1794 marked the most important single era in the history of the Bibliothèque Nationale."[37]

Not only did the Revolution make a Herculean effort to create a national bibliography and a national library system, its Commission on Monuments and a Commission on Titles (1794) sought to select, classify, and house or destroy millions of documents conserved in castle, monastic, and royal archives. None of these archives was public, least of all the best ones, which had been carefully preserved by the church since the tenth century.

Fortresses and castles contained hated "despotic" and "feudal" titles, which had to be destroyed to prevent their serving as the basis of new claims or as painful reminders of things that had been destroyed. Titles of nobility and of feudal dues numbered in the millions and were top priority for elimination. Judicial records of odious legal procedures or tax records of monarchical extortion fell into the same category.

During the Great Fear of July 1789, insurrectionary peasants burned many châteaux archives. Official public burnings followed spontaneous popular ones. On 12 May 1792 the National Assembly decreed: "The papers deposited in the [monastery of the Great] Augustins, belonging to the former orders of chivalry and to the nobility, will be burned under the orders of the department of Paris, after property titles, whether national or individual, and items of interest to the arts and sciences have been removed by the municipality and the Commission on Savants under the department's surveillance."[38]

The former Benedictine Dom Poirier, a member of the Commission on Monuments, addressed a sensible and courageous letter to the Committee of Public Instruction in July 1793 that typified the commission's conservationist attitude: "Many of the acts and registers which the Convention has just abolished . . . are valuable because they contain [information] relative to history, to customs and usages of centuries preceding ours, to dates, to geography and to the topography of France, to the glossary of our language, to paleography, diplomatics, the price of necessities, and to the value of money, to weights and measures, to commerce, agriculture, and to the arts."[39]

As one proceeds through the list of partially destroyed archives, Poirier's lonely protest carries greater weight. Not only were feudal titles sacrificed. The municipality of Tours burned the famous cartulary of Saint Martin. The Ministry of War made cartridges out of three thousand pages of documents relating to the kings of France of the fifteenth and sixteenth centuries, out of papal bulls and patent letters of Saint Louis (from the church of Meaux), and out of artillery and budget records from Flanders and Artois (five hundred items). A great and valuable store of documents belonging to the Maison du Roi—decisions of the French kings, letters of the lieutenant general of police, minutes of royal councils, and one hundred cartons relating to the high magistracy and lower courts in which "absolutely nothing useful was found"—were all destroyed in the Year III (1794–95). The Temporary Agency of Titles described this historical treasure as "a monstrous, disgusting heap of letters, orders, imprisonments (*cachets*), commands to Parlement (*jussions*), recommendations . . . provisions of benefices, petitions of every kind, ecclesiastical disputes, old letters of exchange, bank notes . . . records of criminal affairs and proceedings . . . which procured for the Republic more than two hundred thousand papers and parchments for scrap."[40]

From the chancellery archives, sixty-four registers of former "secretaries of the king" and most of the papers of the Direction de la librairie—the papers of the clerks of civil and criminal affairs of the Parlement (totaling 170,000)—were disposed of. Documents to be discarded from the Chambre des comptes were designated by the metric foot. Counted up by the Bureau de comptabilité for the Ministry of Finances, they amounted to 11,760 volumes.

"Almost everything was saved" in the ecclesiastical archives under the pretext of historical or domainal interest: the officialdom of the Revolution burned "feudalism" rather than "superstition." The Christian past survived in archival as well as in printed form. Inventory, selection, conservation, or destruction were the steps in this last judgment of books and documents that proved more merciful than the fictional last judgment of kings.[41]

The Louvre

Before the invasion of the Tuileries on 10 August 1792, the Louvre had been a royal palace, but it had also served as a gallery—a salon of paintings and sculpture with studios and residences for artists, among them, Boucher, Vien, and David. Several ministers—Colbert, Marigny, Angiviller—had hoped to make it into a national library or museum, but the dream was never realized during the old regime. Shortly before the Revolution the *Mémoires secrets* of Louis Petit de Bachaumont recorded: "The Famous Museum retreats instead of advancing; we thought we would be able to enjoy it in 1787, and nothing has been done this year."[42]

This dream recurred after the October Days but ran against the need for a royal palace. Barère de Vieuzac expressed the tension between these conflicting aims in the Constituent Assembly: "Do not believe that the king has asked you for the Louvre as a residence, he wants the Louvre as a palace of the arts." The Assembly tried to reconcile the two objectives in a decree on 26 May 1791: "The united Louvre and the Tuileries will be destined for the residence of the king, for the reunion of all the monuments of the sciences and the arts." The seizure of the Tuileries, the incarceration of the royal family, the abolition of the monarchy, and the nationalization of royal property settled the question. One day after the overthrow of the monarchy, 11 August 1792, the Assembly created the Commission of the Museum, whose "function was to collect paintings, statues and other precious objects from the Crown possessions," as well as from "the churches and national houses and from those of the émigrés." The clear-sighted Roland de La Platière, minister of the Interior, conceived the enterprise as follows:

The Museum must see to the development of the great riches which the Nation possesses in drawings, paintings, sculptures, and other monuments of art. As I conceive it, it should attract foreigners and compel their attention. It should nourish the taste of fine arts, rejuvenate amateurs, and serve as a school for artists. It should be open to everyone. This monument will be national. There should not be an individual who does not have the right to enjoy it. It will have such an influence on minds, it will elevate souls to such a height, it will warm hearts so much that it will be one of the most powerful means of giving the Republic distinction.[43]

The objectives of the Louvre had been discussed during the monarchy. But the Louvre—a public museum whose collections consisted of expropriated national property—actually opened as a national museum under the Republic (not without failure, lapses, and committee squabbles) on the anniversary of the overthrow of the monarchy: 10 August 1793. Six commissioners were appointed: Nicolas J.-R. Jollain, J.-B. Regnault, François A. Vincent, Charles Bossut, Pierre Pasquier, Pierre Cossart. All except Bossut, a geometrician, were painters, and the first three were academicians. Already 125 paintings had been removed from the château of Versailles and installed in the Louvre. Included in this collection of masterpieces were Lodovico Carracci's *Martyrdom of Saint Sebastian,* two landscapes by Claude Lorrain, *A Pastoral* by Giorgione, Leonardo da Vinci's *Virgin, Child Jesus, and Saint John,* four Raphaels, a Rembrandt self-portrait, Titian's *Pilgrims of Emmaus,* and Michel Vanloo's standing portrait of Louis XV. The bulk of the collection (970 paintings) was still being inventoried at Versailles in June 1793.

The depots of the Commission on Monuments, notably the Petits-Augustins under the direction of Alexandre Lenoir, were another logical source for the museum's collection. The Commission on the Museum ran up against Lenoir's proprietary tenacity in the face of claims from a fledgling museum. Between December 1792 and 24 July 1793, Lenoir repeatedly refused to hand over forty-seven paintings in his collection that the commissioners wanted for the Louvre. Only the minister of the Interior's decision to open the Louvre moved Lenoir to surrender all but three paintings. Among those he sent were Raphael's *Christ in the Tomb* and *The Samaritan,* and five paintings by Philippe de Champaigne, which had probably been confiscated from churches.

Clearly, the best paintings belonged to the royal châteaux and to such favorites as Mme du Barry, to such dukes as Orléans, most of whose collection had been sold in England, and to such former ministers as Angiviller. The lists of paintings confiscated from all the dispossessed aristocrats can be found in the commission's papers.[44]

Two questions naturally arise: Where had these paintings come from, and where did they go after they were confiscated? It is not surprising that princes of the blood or royal mistresses should possess Italian masterpieces. Madame du Barry, daughter of a dressmaker and mistress to the comte du Barry, later became mistress to Louis XV, who showered her with diamonds and perhaps gave her paintings. As the official administrator of all royal art collections, Angiviller had rare access to paintings and other objets d'art.

Lenoir himself was an avid collector of, among other things, royal portraits, which he began to assemble before the Revolution. He offers a rare glimpse into the art of collecting, as well as into the peripatetics of objets d'art, during the Revolution. Interrogated by Citizen Seignette, judge of the Highest Court of Appeals (Cour de cassation), about the provenance and history of a statue representing *Justice,* Lenoir explains:

> Citizen, it is with much pleasure, that I endeavor to satisfy the demand you made of me relative to the tomb of Boulenois, Place des Carmes. This monument, rich in beauty because of the marbles which compose it, was sold in 1791 to Citizen Boulenois, son of the jurist-consult who erected a tomb to the memory of his father. Since then, he has sold it to several marblers, with the exception of two mosaics which I think he still possesses. The beautiful porphyry vase passed into commerce. I have since seen it at the [store] of a man named Huet, rue Beaubourg. I bought the deep blue eagle from a marbler; the other debris of the tomb as well as the sarcophagus are still in the Panthéon; they belong to Citizen Scellier, marbler, rue Saint-Jacques. This, citizen, is the state of this magnificent monument today, richer still, by virtue of the materials which compose it, as well as by the execution of the sculpture. My entire desire is that these notes satisfy you. I consider myself very happy that this occasion has afforded me a conversation with you. Be assured of my perfect esteem.[45]

Some émigré art escaped confiscation and was put on the market by relatives. This was the case with the collection of the duc de Choiseul-Praslin, which included Rubens's *Portrait of a Flemish Woman,* for which the commission paid 7,750 livres, Rembrandt's *Interior with the Holy*

Family (17,120 livres), Jacob Jordaens's *Meal of a Family,* and a rare
iron helmet and gold shield (4,800 livres). The Rubens portrait was the
only one of the three verifiably in the Louvre collection (as no. 281)
when the Commission du muséum drew up an inventory in November
1793. The Jordaens may possibly be no. 438. It is unclear where the
Rembrandt ended up.

More significant from a cultural standpoint is the largely religious
character of the Louvre collection in 1793. Of the 537 paintings listed
in the inventory of 1793, 303, or 56 percent, are unmistakably religious. Most depict scenes from the life of Christ. As one entered the
Louvre, the first painting in view in the bay on the right was Nicolas
Poussin's *The Israelites Receiving Manna in the Desert,* the third was
L'Espagnolet's *Saint Paul,* the fourth Leonardo da Vinci's *Holy Family
with Saint Michael,* the next Pietro Bernini's *Saint John Preaching in the
Desert.* Other bays contained landscapes or paintings of classical mythology, such as Correggio's *Jupiter and Antiope,* and all forty-one
sculptures listed were of classical republican or mythological subjects.

Why did the revolutionary officaldom (the Convention, the minister
of the Interior, and the Commission of Monuments) choose to fill its
national museum with paintings of sacred Christian personages just as
de-Christianization was being launched? One could conjecture that the
art confiscated from religious houses dictated the character of the exhibit. But a register of paintings taken from such houses does not
match those in the Louvre, so they could not have been the principal
source of the Louvre's holdings.

Did either the commission or Garat establish a deliberate principle
of selection and arrangement for the Louvre? On 21 April 1793, Garat
addressed reflections on this matter to the Commission on the Museum: "You have to examine whether you should adopt as the criterion [of selection] that of diverse schools, that of history either chronological or progressive, that of genres, that of styles, or that of simple
pictoresque variety. . . . You should also discuss . . . whether the exclusion of all works of living artists would not tend to give [those
works] a more august character and remove their production from all
corrupting influences of self-love and petty intrigues. This idea was
suggested to me by an artist who stands to lose should this [idea] be
adopted."[46]

To avoid self-promotion, favoritism, and rancor among artists,
the Louvre policy during the Revolution was to reject paintings of
living artists. The 1793 catalog (fig. VIII.2) contains no Davids,
Hubert Roberts, or François Gérards but many Poussins, Titians, and

CATALOGUE

DES

OBJETS CONTENUS

DANS LA GALERIE

DU

MUSÉUM FRANÇAIS,

Décrété par la convention nationale, le
27 juillet 1793 l'an second de la
République Française.

De l'Imprimerie de C.-F. PATRIS,
Imprimeur du Muséum national.

VIII.2.

Frontispiece of the Louvre catalog just before the museum's opening,
July 1793.

Courtesy Archives nationales, photo: Archives nationales.

Rubenses. The absence of Mme du Barry's collection, and the presence of the Versailles collection, which was almost entirely religious in nature, is explicable by this selection principle. The provenance of the Louvre's religious collection was primarily secular, traceable to the royal and émigré châteaux rather than to monasteries and churches, whose collections were far poorer. But the irony remains: republican and revolutionary subjects, which were officially sponsored for concours in painting and sculpture, were, if contemporary, deliberately excluded from the national museum and, curiously, sent back to the former royal palace, Versailles, which became a museum for the French school.

The historical character of the museum necessarily excluded the Revolution, which was attempting to abolish history and begin time anew. Figures of the Christian past in the museum were cut off from the present and future, so there was no danger in their being enshrined. The Louvre and Lenoir's Museum of French Monuments became depositories in which to quarantine the past lest it exercise a pernicious influence on the present (though the salons of contemporary artists were held in the Louvre). The curators and commissioners, that is, could cautiously acknowledge the greatness of the past without imposing it on the Revolution. But these paintings were secretly held in high regard. Many informed judges felt that, as a whole, the contemporary generation of artists and poets had not lived up to the preceding one, however much rhetoric and the work of Antoine-Jean Gros, Girodet-Trioson, and David might belie it.

The official opening of the Louvre on 10 August 1793 appears to have been uneventful. No descriptions of it have been found. Instead, the treasurer of the Commune of Arts, Jean-Guillaume Bervic, wrote on 25 August 1793 to the new minister of the Interior, Jules-François Paré, urging that the museum be closed along with the salon at the end of September. The idea of a permanently open public museum had not yet arrived. The Louvre was reopened by order of the same minister on 8 November 1793 for "the last three days of each *décade*" for the public and "from 9 to 4 the first five days of the *décade*" for artists. A year later (29 January 1794), the *Décade philosophique* published a critique of the museum. Its author criticized the inferior lighting of the galleries, the practice of indicating the provenance of paintings, which evoked the odious memory of tyrants, and the absence of any progressive arrangement of paintings within schools ("With what pleasure could one observe art, rising up gradually from the dryness of the Italian School, from the timidity of the Gothic taste of Cimabue or Giotto, to the graces of Guido [of Siena], to the energy of Michel-angelo"). "We must agree, the arts are in need of a great reform and, so to speak, of being revolutionized. Why should painting, for ex-ample . . . offer us only oil canvasses . . . ? Will not the time come when we will see frescoes painted on the walls of public monuments, entire poems, moral allegories? The porticoes where people gather to discuss public affairs, or private matters, will be decorated someday with the painting of events from their own history; the palace in which their Senate reigns will doubtless contain the history of their whole Revolution." Yet the popularity of the existing museum gratified him: "We saw with great interest the people flock there in crowds: they observe with avid curiosity, ask questions, admire or reprove appro-priately. Soon the Museum will be our most popular promenade. Men and women of all classes seem to give each other rendezvous there in the morning to spend a few hours. So much the better."[47]

Not only did this critic favor contemporary revolutionary paintings over historical or religious ones, but he seems to have esteemed the art criticism of the public over that of the connoisseurs. The public was well informed, whereas the critics, he claimed, mistook Greek for Ro-man and Roman for Hebrew busts. David himself claimed that the people were the best judges of art, and the museum's conservators defended themselves by claiming that "all citizens are conservators, which is why they, the official conservators, mingle with the pub-lic daily so as to be enlightened, and even corrected by them if necessary."[48]

The Parisian cultural elite generally scorned those who failed to live up to its standards, to win the approbation of those whom Stendhal later called "the happy few" of broad knowledge and finely tuned sen-sibilities. The Enlightenment made this scorn formidable. The requi-site erudition consisted in a mastery of language and technical skills. To be ignorant of Alexandrine verse, to be puzzled by classical allu-sions, to lack a grasp of history, to mistake editions or make a wrong attribution—all were signs of cultural barbarism. Denunciations, so common in the Revolution, could focus on political-ideological loyalty or on competence. Generals were cashiered in autumn 1793 for losing battles. Their accusers had difficulty accepting military failures at face value and usually ascribed ulterior anti-Republican motives. Failures in the conservation of monuments, books, and especially art provoked similar accusations against connoisseurs.

The attacks on the Commission of the Museum began just a few months after its formation and perhaps manifested Jacobin hostility to this Rolandist commission as much as an interest in conservation. On 4 March 1793, J.-B.-P. Lebrun, an art dealer (*marchand de tableaux*) and the husband of Elisabeth Vigée-Lebrun, who had been left off the list of members of the Commission of the Museum by Roland in August 1792, complained to the minister of the Interior that the restoration of works deposited in the museum should stop immediately until a concours could select competent artisans. Two days later, a reputable restorer and artist named Picault denounced the commission a second time for "alarming restorations" and "irregular procedures taken with the most precious paintings by ignorant artists who, like harpies in the fable, spoiled everything they touched." Picault was thinking of Raphael's *Holy Family,* Correggio's *Jupiter and Antiope,* and various Veroneses, Titians, and Rubenses.[49]

Meanwhile, Lebrun published a pamphlet, *Observations sur le Muséum national,* raising still another troubling problem for art lovers in these months: The Raphael bought by the commission, he charged, was only a copy, one of various erroneous attributions. Four Flemish and Dutch paintings, Lebrun claimed, had been attributed to Italians, four French paintings to Flemish masters, and four paintings by students to their masters. On 18 December 1793, David, who certainly had thoughts of his own on the matter, made this grist for his mill. After he had delivered two scathing reports, the Convention passed a decree replacing the Commission of the Museum with the Conservatory of the Museum: "If one examines the credentials of restorers of paintings and of the persons who have been employed to destroy the paintings of the Republic, one will see prizes [commissions] arbitrarily distributed, without order, without principles, without any rationale; in such hands, the more costly the restoration of the paintings, the more they are ruined."[50] A triangular struggle among painters, art merchants, and bureaucrats had emerged; David wanted the job to go to painters rather than to Roland appointees.

The following month, on 17 January 1794, David returned to lash the expired commission, listing the Poussins, Lorrains, Vernets, and Correggios that had been lost by its bungling "dilapidations." But David did not see the disaster that sprang from official vandalization: all the art depositories of the old regime, thousands of objets d'art, being transported from castles and monasteries to republican depots and from there to Parisian and provincial museums. Instead, David saw the problem in terms of competence and artistic professionalism. "The people," he said, "will know how better to appreciate artists."[51] David was more concerned about who was making the decisions than about what decisions were being made. He did not question involvement of the great Revolution in artistic property that lay at the heart of the art world's problem.

The issue became even more pressing after the republican armies spilled over French borders. France reoccupied Belgium in spring 1794, and on 11 August paintings began to be shipped from there to Paris by several members of the Commission temporaire des arts. Grégoire joyfully contemplated these treasures in his first report on vandalism. In addition to trunks full of books, maps, and scientific objects, he rejoiced that "[Gaspard de] Crayer, Vandyck, and Rubens are en route to Paris, and the Flemish school is coming en masse to decorate our museums."[52]

The Italian campaign brought back the greatest artistic treasures to the Louvre, of course. Cecil Gould has described the result as "the finest collection of old masters . . . which has ever been assembled." Napoléon himself was not artistically inclined and tended to levy objets d'art by decimal figures—usually one hundred. He left the selection of works to a commission of art connoisseurs, including the now vindicated Lebrun, Barbier, and Tinet (who had been active in Belgium), the engraver Jean-Baptiste Wicar, the painters Gros and Barthélémy, and the sculptor Jean-Guillaume Moitte. The spoliations succeeded one another: in May–June 1796 armies ransacked Parma, Modena, Milan (fig. VIII.3), and Bologna. Rome followed a few months later, and in May 1797, it was Venice's turn. Practically nothing was taken from Naples, in spite of its wealth of sculptures, because it did not fall within the sphere of original conquests.

Elsewhere, the French were oblivious to paintings of the fifteenth and eighteenth centuries and concentrated on the Raphaels, the Titians, and the Correggios of the sixteenth century. But the real treasures were such Hellenistic and Roman sculptures as the *Apollo Belvedere,* the *Dying Gaul,* the *Laocoön,* and the *Farnese Hercules.* Lebrun drew up catalogs in advance of the armies and the commissaires of art. The commissaires received carte blanche to take whatever they wanted within the numerical limits set by Napoléon and his treaties.

Transportation of these trophies was a formidable task but seems to have been carried out (on sea and by land, even over the Alps) carefully and with only minor damage. Controversy did break out, however, over whether the objects had been carefully packed and whether the upkeep by the original Italian owners had been so poor as to warrant their removal by the French.

VIII.3.
Entry of the French into Milan, 25 floréal an IV [14 May 1796].
Courtesy Bibliothèque nationale, photo: Bibl. Nat. Paris.

After the Belgian, Italian, and later German booty was deposited in
Paris, the Louvre experienced a veritable glut of works of art (some
1,390 foreign paintings). Consequently, Napoléon directed that a
certain number be transferred to the Luxembourg Palace, recently
reopened as a museum, with contemporary paintings of the French
school to go to Versailles. Additional paintings went to the museums
in major French cities, some (114 paintings in 1806) were returned to
Parisian churches, and some objets d'art even went to foreign imperial
cities—Brussels, Mainz, and Geneva, in particular.

The Louvre had opened in 1793, but the Grande Galerie was obliged
to close from 1796 to 1799 (part of it until 1801). One major problem
was bad lighting. Hubert Robert had envisioned skylighting, and
lights were duly cut in the base of the curvature of the vault, but lighting remained a problem. After the acquisition of so many objects, the
impact of the Louvre on visitors was overwhelming as well as exhilarating. The English who visited this embarrassment of riches after
the Treaty of Amiens in 1802 found the collection extraordinary but
excessive—"a chaos of confused forms." But few could doubt that the
conquests had established the Louvre as the world's greatest art museum.[53] The booty included one of the most famous paintings of the

time—Rubens's *Descent from the Cross*—among some forty works by Rubens removed from Belgian churches and sent to Paris.

On 27 July 1798 a "Festival of Liberty and Triumphal Entry of Objects of the Sciences and Arts Collected in Italy" was held in Paris: "The cortège was divided into four parts, each accompanied by members of the Institute, savants, and artists, who were interested in the riches. Chariots . . . some with manuscripts, others with books, cages containing ferocious animals, were shaded by exotic plants [from Egypt]; others had cases on which one read: Transfiguration of Raphael, Christ of Titian, the last more massive, more solid carrying the Apollo Belvedere, the Laocoön . . . paraded under the eyes of Parisians."[54]

The museum survived the Revolution, even flourished, and can be considered one of the period's most lasting achievements. Vivant Denon became the directeur général des Musées impériaux under the Empire, when more and more European masterpieces were brought to France as the Napoleonic armies marked up victory after victory. As early as 1795 the conservator of the museum said that the French nation, "having crushed its enemies, must enchain them again by admiration, forcing them to bear voluntary tribute to it every year. . . . What a spectacle the National Gallery will be to every onlooker." The Empire fulfilled his words. Imperialism in the arts formed the cultural counterpart of France's legal and administrative imperialism. France took Italy's paintings and in return gave Italy constitutions and kings when Italian republics became ungovernable. This exchange lasted until the Congress of Vienna, when France returned most of these paintings to Italy.[55]

In France, objects from ecclesiastical and other national property continued to flow into Lenoir's museum and various depots until decade's end, although the volume decreased sharply. And art no longer flowed one way. On 8 March 1799 several Gothic statues were taken from Notre-Dame, but two years earlier a white marble tabernacle from Ville l'Evêque was restored to Notre-Dame. In his 1799 catalog, Lenoir published a long "List of Objects Removed from the Depot of the Petits-Augustins and Restored to Their Rightful Owner Following Orders of the Magistrates in Exercise."[56]

When Bonaparte came to power, the current was strong in both directions. Lenoir was confirmed as director of the Museum of Monuments, which continued successfully until it was closed during the Second Restoration. But the whole attitude toward conservation changed with the Concordat, which reinstated the Catholic church in France. A *statuaire* of Notre-Dame, Louis-Pierre Deseine, published this in an *Opinion on Museums*: "To save monuments of art from the furor of vandalism was assuredly a praiseworthy thing, but for such an enterprise to become useful to the public . . . and to the entire nation, it would be necessary to conserve these same monuments as sacred objects, which should be surrounded with a profound respect as belonging entirely to history, to morality, and to the politics of the different ages of an Empire."[57] Deseine rightly felt that an artistic object was not wholly "conserved" once it had been removed from its original, possibly sacred, setting. The whole museum craze, Deseine argued, had begun before the Revolution when artists went to Italy to collect. Deseine's naturalism valued milieu over display. He was opposing a deep thrust of eighteenth-century culture: *representation*, by which the sign of an object takes distance from the thing-in-itself, and *classification*, by which an object is removed from its natural order and placed in a logical but artificial system. For Deseine, art, particularly religious art, retained a mystical bond with the object represented: "How can the numerous foreigners in our cities believe," he argued, "that the French government means to reestablish the Catholic religion, if the temples in which the cult is practiced remain forever in the state of degradation in which the revolutionary furor left them?"[58] A choice had to be made between the museum and restitution.

In fact, a final choice never was made. Lenoir's museum survived the Restoration and the Louvre flourished. In 1816 the tombs of the royal line were ceremoniously returned to the Abbey of Saint-Denis (fig. VIII.4). Lenoir himself restored statuary piecemeal in the Restoration. But in spite of the efforts of the architect Eugène-Emmanuel Viollet-le-Duc later in the century, the churches never recovered all their original artistic treasures; many surviving objects remained in Paris and in provincial museums.

As the political revolution wrested political powers from the privileged orders, the French revolution in culture wrested the artistic patrimony from the same elites and gave them to the nation. The Louvre exhibited to a broad public paintings of Christ's life that had originally belonged to the crown, the church, and the nobility. The cultural ideals and texts of the old regime did not cede place to those of the Revolution. Rather, the Revolution nationalized the high culture of the past. Inventories of ancien régime libraries and archives segregated books

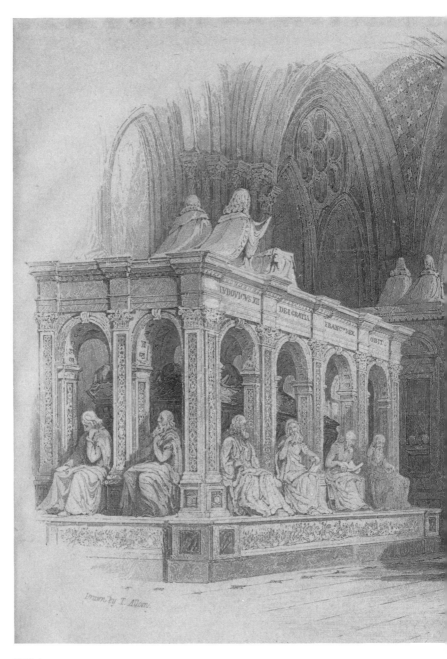

VIII.4.
Visitors in Abbey Church of Saint-Denis near the Tomb of
Louis XII, *engraving, ca. 1840.*
Author's collection.

Engraved by W. Floyd.

of reason from books of unreason. But since most books were confiscated from monasteries, the public libraries that emerged in the nineteenth century were paradoxically rooted in a monastic past. Many unneeded monastic books were even dispersed at random among the public. The cultural property of the old regime was largely redistributed rather than burned, as some would have preferred.

CHAPTER IX

THE FINE ARTS

AND THE

REVOLUTIONARY

IMAGINATION

MUSIC, ART, AND DRAMA

The revolutionaries employed music, art, and theater to persuade a vacillating public of the rightness of the revolutionary cause and the villainy of counterrevolution. Since the time of Condillac and Diderot creative artists and their patrons had been aware that the average person depended on the aural and visual senses for ideas. For the Revolution to succeed, a similar revolution in human outlook had to take place, one brought about with the help of the arts.[1]

Statistical Overview

The surprise is not that the Revolution used the fine arts to further the revolutionary cause but that the arts, or rather artists, resisted revolutionary themes and principles as strongly as they did. Statistical studies of the genres and subjects of art submitted to the salons in the Louvre after 1789, a study of the theatrical repertoire of revolutionary Paris, and a statistical study of songs based on the catalog published by Constant Pierre at the beginning of this century reveal that only in music did revolutionary themes prevail—more, perhaps, the result of the compiler's selection than of the songwriters' predilections. Constant Pierre includes virtually no songs or, more accurately, no lyrics from the ancien régime in his catalog. The revolutionary trend was to put new lyrics to old tunes (no more than 5 percent of revolutionary songs were set to new music), on the assumption that well-known melodies would catch on more easily. Thus P.-J.-B. Nougaret, one of the leading songwriters of the Revolution, described his penchant for old tunes: "So that my hymns would be more popular, more generally useful, I desired not only that learned composers embellish them with harmonious chords, but even more I put them all to well-known airs."

Production of songs connected in some way with the Revolution rose from almost 150 in 1789, to over 300 in 1791–92, to 600 in 1793, and peaked at 700 in 1794, dropping to under 150 in 1795–97 and to under 100 in 1798–1800. The most frequent themes of the first lines of these songs (table A.1) were the Supreme Being, Liberty, and Peace. French heroes were Marat and Lepeletier, whereas Louis XVI was both hero and villain. The favorite republican date in song was the Tenth of August—the day of the invasion of the Tuileries—and the most popular institution, the National Convention. What these statistics omit is how often these lyrics were set to old tunes.[2]

Theater statistics compiled under my direction show that, unlike music, approximately two-thirds of the plays performed during the Revolution were composed during that time, but the most frequently performed plays of the decade tended to be those written during the old regime (table A.2). This is corroborated by a list of the top forty-five authors, which places Molière third with 1,800 performances and Robineau de Beaunoir, a popular playwright well before the Revolution, atop the list with 1,891 performances. Beaunoir's famous play *Jeanette, ou Les Battus ne paient pas toujours l'amende* was a much performed play during the last decade of the ancien régime and received more than 80 performances during the Revolution. Dorvigny, Anseaume, Voltaire, Marivaux, Dancourt, Rousseau, P. Baurans, Marmontel, and Favart were other old regime authors performed from 331 times (Favart) to 1,264 (Dorvigny) (table A.3). How much the legacy of the old regime weighed on revolutionary theater is still in doubt, but we know it was considerable.[3]

Another way to answer how much the theater of the Revolution transmitted revolutionary ideas draws on the nature of play titles. An analysis of *titles* (table A.4) indicates that a growth of revolutionary titles in relation to nonrevolutionary *titles* peaked in 1794 (2,400 of 4,900), dropping to below 1790 levels by 1799, thus following the rhythm of the Revolution itself. This count lists the incidence (favorable, unfavorable, or neutral) of revolutionary themes, events, or persons. Only a content analysis of plays can go further. This has been done on the top fifty plays of the decade, and more than half have nothing to do with the Revolution. The weight of the old regime on theater would seem to be as great if not greater than on songs.[4]

When we turn to the art salons of the Revolution, we naturally ask: How much was the style of Jacques-Louis David, and of the neoclassicists generally, represented at the Louvre salons of the Revolution? Unfortunately, it is impossible to study all the paintings and sculptures themselves, since many are lost or otherwise inaccessible. A study of Stanley Idzerda more than a generation ago, however, based on the salon *livrets,* or guides, and other sources, shows a decline in didacticism between 1787 and 1795 from 11.1 percent to 7.5 percent of the number of works, the very opposite of what one would expect. Religious themes did decline from 17.7 percent before the Revolution to an even smaller 3.5 percent in 1795, which is not surprising.[5] But another scholar, James Leith, found that classical themes, as opposed to neoclassical works, nearly tripled between 1789 and 1793; this figure includes erotic, mythological, and didactic themes. Representations of contemporary political events, political caricatures and allegories, and portraits of politicians, generals, and philosophes account for only 5.1 percent.[6]

Two other studies[7] and my study of the Desloynes Collection confirm the statistics of Idzerda and Leith, but with slight differences. The overwhelming trend of the Revolution—from 11.9 percent to 27.8 percent between 1785 and 1793—was toward landscapes and portraits, neither genre of which lends itself to revolutionary propaganda. M. W. Brown explains the upsurge in portraiture as the desire of the middle class, the main beneficiary of the Revolution, to commemorate itself as the new elite. The hierarchy of paintings placed histories first, then allegories, portraits, landscapes, still lifes, and battle scenes. Although the Revolution does not seem to have won out in the salons on didactic or neoclassical themes—at least not quantitatively—it did upset hierarchy by substituting bourgeois portraits and landscapes for grand historical canvases. William Olander has found further that contemporary historical paintings supplanted the traditional historical paintings of antiquity.[8]

To sum up the comparison of these three fine arts: Musical lyrics may have been revolutionary, but song tunes were often inherited from the past. In theater, most plays performed during the Revolution were contemporary, although the majority of the fifty most performed plays were written during the old regime and many of the leading playwrights had died before the Revolution. The Revolution seems to have made an unintended impact on the art salons, adding works of art at the lower end of the hierarchy of genres—that is, popularizing or democratizing art—but failing to vindicate the genre the Revolution wanted (didactic, civic, or neoclassical). This last analysis, like that of music, rests on incomplete evidence, for we are comparing the open salons of the Revolution with the closed academic ones of the old regime. All that can safely be said is that differences existed between the salon art that the public saw in the old regime and the art that the art world as a whole was showing in the salons of the Revolution. The lacunae in the evidence in all three arts (nonacademic art proper before 1789, traditional songs of the Revolution, *content* of most plays of the Revolution) illustrate how the historian must complete a puzzle in which pieces are missing.

Reconciliation

The early Revolution, from 1789 to 1791, could be called the patriarchal stage. Louis XVI remained in good standing with his people, and an aura of good feeling and reconciliation prevailed. The nation took the place of the three orders—clergy, nobility, people—whose members were now brothers. This fraternity expressed itself in the greatest festival of the Revolution, the Festival of the Federation, which combined deputations of the National Guard from every federated department of France on the Champ de Mars, where the old order (Talleyrand and sixty chaplains of the National Guard) said Mass in honor of the Revolution. The nation thronged a vast amphitheater constructed by French citizens. Michelet considered this the high point of the Revolution. Certainly the sentiments of brotherhood and regeneration were never stronger than in 1790.[9]

This conciliatory spirit was a quest for unity amid centrifugal forces generated by the Great Fear of 1789, the nationalization of church property, and the Civil Constitution of the Clergy, which would split the Revolution into factions. The principal motif, conciliation, controlled much art in this period, though not all.[10]

Most ancien régime musicians had ties to the church, since church music, in the days before public concerts, was their main outlet. Indeed, musical education hardly existed apart from the *maîtrises de chapelle*, where musicians learned voice and instrumentation. The one major concert of the old regime was the Concert Spirituel, which was held at Easter and other religious holidays when the Opéra and theaters were closed. Not all the music in these concerts was relegated to the organ or choir, but, as its name indicates, it had a religious character.[11]

A number of the most famous composers of the Revolution had a background in church music. François-Joseph Gossec (1734–1829), who was born in Belgium, worked in the private orchestra of a wealthy farmer-general and wrote a Mass for the dead in 1761. Late in the 1770s he became director of the Concert Spirituel. Florentine composer Luigi Cherubini (1760–1844) lived in Paris after 1786 where he composed a Mass and a Credo in D minor. Although neither of these composers specialized in sacred music, it is curious that Gossec wrote any at all, considering his career as a musical de-Christianizer in 1793. Etienne-Nicolas Méhul (1763–1817), who also wrote for the Concert Spirituel, learned composition as a lad in a Franciscan convent in Givet, near the French border of what is now Belgium. Jean-François Lesueur (1760–1837) was born in Picardy and served as choirmaster at a number of provincial cathedrals before filling that post at Notre-Dame in Paris.[12]

The themes of songs written in June and July 1789 express confidence in the unity of the three states under one "father of the people"—Louis XVI—even though some of his actions, such as calling up troops around Paris, seemed to threaten the Revolution. More time would elapse before this father-king would be replaced by the female Marianne, the emblem of the Republic.[13]

The mixture of old authority and new order can be found in an extraordinary work written in 1790 by a little-known composer named Marc-Antoine Desaugiers (1742–93). He called his work a *hiérodrame,* or sacred drama, intended to commemorate the storming of the Bastille the preceding year. He cleverly delved into sacred scripture, especially the psalms, where he thought he found biblical analogues of the French people's current struggle for liberty. The hiérodrame reads in part:

WOMEN
O God, cast a compassionate light on us and on our children.
(Ps. 113, 14)

CITIZEN
Regain your courage and fight: You are called to liberty! Our
enemies have drawn the sword to destroy the weak and
indigent; Let their sword enter into their own hearts. (Kings 4.9;
Gal. 5.13; Ps. 36.14, 15)

CITIZEN AND CHOIR
May our enemies blush and be dispersed; that they flee, and that
they may perish. (Ps. 6.14; Ps. 67.1)

CHORUS OF WOMEN DURING THE PRECEDING
O God help us! (Ps. 78.9)

THE CITIZEN AND THE CHORUS
Yes God will come to our help.

THE CITIZEN
The Lord rejects the councils (or counsels) of the princes. Let us
run and destroy their odious fortress. God will combat for us.
Let it be. (Ps. 32.10; Isa. 51.22)

Desaugiers's drama was performed by six hundred musicians of the
Académie royale de musique (the Opéra) and by several theaters, including the Théâtre italien, the Théâtre Montansier, and the boulevard
theater of Audinot and Nicolet. It was a major production.[14]

The hiérodrame, although full of the combativeness of the storming
of the Bastille, can still be interpreted as conciliatory in that it re-
spectfully used a church genre (the sung psalm) to celebrate pa-
triotically the fourteenth of July, which of course was in turn made
sacred by the music. The hiérodrame presumes a consensus in the ·
nation on the first phase of the Revolution.

A Te Deum for the Festival of the Federation was also celebrated at
the same anniversary of the storming of the Bastille. A huge deputation of six hundred to seven hundred of the National Guard was sent to
the parish of Saint-Germain-Auxerrois, where the king listened to a
"cry of love and recognition" mingled with shouts of "long live the
king." The National Guard entered the church without any order of
precedence, as a tribute to equality. "The chain of deputies stretched to
the dais, several were confounded with the ministers of the altars and
religion; marching thus side by side, the law inspired the most profound veneration." This sanctification of the profane was characteristic
of the Federation mood of 1790.[15]

Gossec (with Gardel the director of the Opéra) continued in this same vein in the autumn, composing an "Offrande à la Liberté, scène religieuse," which was an adaptation of liturgy for theater to sanctify liberty. This piece was performed 130 times on different stages during the Revolution, especially between 1792 and 1794 at the Opéra.[16]

The National Guard gradually replaced the maîtrises de chapelle and de cathédrale as the main musical establishment of the Revolution for two reasons: music was increasingly designed to serve the patrie rather than glorify God, and the two revered beings—God and patrie— were being wedded. Under the direction of Bernard Sarette, secular music flourished successively in the Band of the National Guard, the Ecole de la garde nationale (1793), the Institut national de musique (1793), and the Conservatoire de musique (1795)—a national music college that was later imitated throughout Europe.

Other hymns for patriotic purposes in these same years included Gossec's "Hymn to Equality" (1793), "Hymn to Humanity" (1795), and "Martial Song for the Festival of Victory" (1796). Cherubini alone wrote hymns to Fraternity (1794), to the Panthéon (1794), to Victory (1796), and to "Republican Saltpeter" (1794). Méhul, for his part, wrote a "Hymn to the Eternal" (1794) and a "Hymn on Peace" (1797).

This constant sanctification of the patrie and the profane was done without explicit sacrilege before the de-Christianization movement, but it tended to idolize the new revolutionary world. The sacred space for the Revolution was no longer what lay beneath cathedral vaults, although these could be used, as when Notre-Dame hosted (probably in July 1790) the blessing of the flags of the National Guard (fig. IX.1). The usual setting for patriotic celebrations was in the open air, as on the Champ de Mars during the Festival of the Federation (when, incidentally, it poured!), and in subsequent festivals when the heavens served as the ceremony's vault.[17] Humanity was to be at peace with nature.

The song that best expressed the hopes of the early 1790s was the tremendously popular and optimistic "Ça ira." The expression was Benjamin Franklin's, and a composer for public balls named Bécourt put it to instrumental music that was difficult to sing. His original title was the "National Carillon," and the original words, by a singer named Ladré, seem to have been simply "ça ira, ça ira, ça ira!" expressing the revolutionary confidence that, in spite of such obstacles as rain on the day of the Festival of the Federation itself, things would work out. Until the composition of the "Marseillaise" in 1792, it served as the principal song of the Revolution, even as its anthem. Beyond these words, looking for the urtext of the "Ça ira" is futile, claims J. Tiersot.

IX.1.

Pierre-Gabriel Berthault, Benediction of the Flags of the National Guard at Notre-Dame, *engraving, ca. 1790.*

Courtesy Library of Congress, photo: John Reynolds.

One can substitute for Ladré's version two lines mentioned in the July 1790 issue of the aristocratic *Mercure de France.* "The music and the cries of joy are mixed with commonplaces about the aristocrats. The refrain of the majority of these songs runs: 'Ça ira, les aristocrates à la lanterne! Crèvent les aristocrates,' which can be translated: 'It will work out, the aristocrats to the lantern! Die aristocrats.'" The *Mercure* adds that there were "other fraternal jokes which ladies enchanted with democracy [sing], and which the journalists under the influence of wine call *patriotic hymns."* Another version not cited by the *Mercure* runs simply, "Les aristocrates à la lanterne; Les aristocrates on les pendra!" (The aristocrats to the lantern; we will hang the aristocrats).

It is hard today to understand how these words could have been the principal refrain for a festival of fraternity as the Festival of the Federation certainly was! Yet that seems to have been the case, and the evidence for it is again the *Mercure de France,* which calls the song a *facétie*—a joke, which Tiersot describes as "more bantering than seriously menacing." The expression *lanterner* had entered French after the storming of the Bastille, and apparently one could talk about it without causing excessive fright. Three months after the Federation, these words could be heard sung in an adaptation by a gathering of officers:

Ah! Ça ira, ça ira, ça ira!	Ah! It will work out, it will work out, it will work out!
Les démocrates à la lanterne!	The democrats to the lantern!
Ah! Ça ira, ça ira, ça ira!	Ah! It will work out, it will work out, it will work out!
Tous les députés on les pendra.	We will hang all the deputies.

One notices immediately the similar mixture of reconciliation and vindictiveness (however jocularly represented) as in Desaugiers's hiérodrame, although the "Ça ira" had nothing sacred about it but came straight from the streets.[18]

Similar buoyant optimism and hopes for reconciliation can be found in works of fine art and in popular prints. In one such print, a woman holding a crucifix (fig. IX.2) appears to members of the three estates, who stretch out their arms to her; the caption reads, "By me you are all brothers." The woman represents the Virgin Mary or the figure of Religion, which binds people together in binding them to God. Themes of fraternity and of the compatibility of religion and patriotism are found in a print that illustrates divine truth in the form of broad shafts of light and in the caption lists verses from Luke 21 warn-

IX.2.
Reunion of the Three Orders under the Protection of the
Virgin Mary, *engraving, ca. 1789.*
Courtesy Library of Congress, photo: John Reynolds.

ing Christ's disciples of being persecuted for His sake (fig. IX.3). The symbol of light as truth figured prominently in the Enlightenment, in Freemasonry, and in the Revolution, as it had, of course, in Christianity. Note that here a specifically Christian text illustrates the National Assembly's spirit of reform.

The print subtitled "The Regeneration of the French Nation" represents Louis XVI holding a sword, facing the scales of justice, and looking beyond to American Indians overseas. Behind him stands a female figure representing liberty (fig. IX.4). That the king was a popular figure before the escape to Varennes is undeniable. A print from the radical *Révolutions de Paris* shortly after the October Days of 1789 shows the king giving alms to a young boy who calls him "chevalier" (fig. IX.5). The guard accompanying the king tells the lad to keep the money, for the donor is not a "chevalier" but the "oldest of the family." Such illustrations of "traits de bienfaisance" were common before as well as during the early days of the Revolution, when a high premium was placed on social and political reconciliation. This print, although published in a radical newspaper, could pass as royalist.

Another print (fig. IX.6) shows a member of the Third Estate addressing a noble and a clergyman. The caption—"Touch there Sirs, I knew you would be one of ours"—expresses the overriding desire of the three orders for unity, a feeling that had given rise to the National Assembly and to outbursts of fraternity. These feelings, like those promising that things would turn out all right ("Ça ira"), grew in direct proportion to fears of social antagonism and breakdown of the old order. If one wanted to avoid a complete collapse, other bonds of unity had to be formed. Even the well-known print portraying a woman of the people carrying a woman of the aristocracy and a nun on her back ("This game had better end soon") is playful rather than resentful.

The appeal to religion was also meant to still tremors of unrest. The print *Jesus Christ on the Mountain* (fig. IX.7) depicts not a sansculotte Jesus but a Jesus of the early Revolution who warned his audience to watch out for false prophets, love the king, and respect the law of sages. In such prints as this, religion is the ally of revolution—a theme touched on from another vantage point in chapter 6. Similar situations today raise the question whether such eighteenth-century cases were not the beginning of an immanentist religion of revolution and of human emancipation rather than a religion bridging the human and the divine. These are the nuances, important nuances, that separate an involvement of religion in such blessings as coronations and civil ceremonies

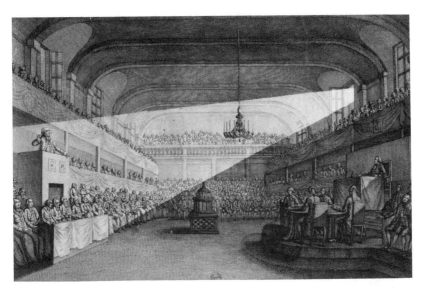

IX.3.
From the Gospel of Saint Luke, Chapter XXI, *engraving, ca. 1789–90.*
Courtesy Bibliothèque nationale, photo: Bibl. Nat. Paris.

(figs. IV.1, IX.8) from an opportunistic use of religion to further purely sociopolitical objectives. There are moments in history when people of purely worldly, often evil, objectives will speak in the language of religion to gain approval for nefarious causes; and there are religions with purely political objectives garbed in holy robes. These are the wolves in sheepskin referred to in the caption of *Christ on the Mountain.*

Contemporary historical painting originated not with the Revolution but in the seventeenth century. The engravers Moreau père and fils exhibited such contemporary commemorative works as the marriage of Louis XVI and Marie-Antoinette, the coronation of Louis XVI (fig. IX.8), and the opening of the Estates General.

The cult of the Tennis Court Oath (an oath of 20 June 1789 by which the deputies of the Third Estate, together with a number of clerics, bound themselves together in disobedience to the king as representatives of the nation, never to separate until a constitution should be written) developed in the winter of 1789–90. Moreau was commemorating the seventeenth of June in copper, and David became interested in painting *The Tennis Court Oath* (fig. IX.9) on canvas. Three years later, on 5 February 1792, David exclaimed: "O my patrie, Oh my dear patrie! We will not be obliged any longer to go looking in the history of ancient peoples to use our brushes. . . . No, for no history of

IX.4.

The Regeneration of the French Nation, *engraving, ca. 1789–90.*

Courtesy Bibliothèque nationale, photo: Bibl. Nat. Paris.

ATION FRANÇAISE en 1789.

comme pouvant être le modèle d'un *Monument Public*

......

Le Roi traversant la Place de Louis XV, un enfant qui balayoit le passage, lui demanda quelque piece de monnoye, en l'appellant M.ʳ le Chevalier. Le Roi lui donna 6.ˢ Je n'ai pas de quoi vous rendre, dit l'enfant. Un des personnages qui suivoient S. M. dit, gardez l'écu, ce Monsieur n'est pas Chevalier, il est Laire de la famille.

Au Bureau des Revolutions de Paris, rue Jacob, t.⁰.8.ᶜ. N.⁰.3

IX.5.

Act of Bienfaisance of Louis XVI, Revolutions de Paris, *engraving.*
Courtesy Library of Congress.

no people offers me anything so grand, so sublime, as this oath of the
Tennis Court, which I must paint. No, I will not have need to invoke
the gods of the Fable in order to warm my genius. French nation! It is
your glory that I want to propagate."[19] This attitude saturated everything surrounding the Tennis Court Oath, represented as a cosmic
event (observe the storm outside the windows). David's compatriots
saw the event as so significant that as of 1790 the Jacobin clubs subsidized the painting through subscriptions. The theme of reconciliation
stands out—particularly between the First and Third Estates, who join
in the National Assembly never to separate until "the constitution of
the kingdom shall be laid."

The gestures of the deputies are dramatic: Robespierre, to the right,
clutches his breast and throws back his head; Edmond Dubois-Crancé
(center right) stands with outstretched hands like many other deputies;
Barère (foreground left), legs crossed, takes notes feverishly. All but
one deputy (Martin Dauch, extreme right, head bowed in shame) take
the oath. At center stage (for this is a theatrical portrayal of a dramatic
event if there ever was one) stands Jean-Sylvain Bailly, the astronomer

IX.6.
Touch There, Sirs, I Knew That You Would Be One of Us, *engraving,*
ca. 1789.
Courtesy Bibliothèque nationale, photo: Bibl. Nat. Paris.

soon to be mayor of Paris, who administers the oath. Below him several clerics of different faiths and orders (Dom Gerle of the "regular"
Benedictine clergy, left; the abbé Grégoire, the Catholic curé, center;
and Rabaut Saint-Etienne, a Protestant pastor, right) embrace one another. Seated to the right is the abbé Sieyès, who catalyzed the declara-
tion of a National Assembly on 17 June. The new order spells toler-
ance among different kinds of Catholic clergymen as well as between
Catholics and Protestants. Unity is being sworn to in the new National
Assembly in contrast to the rivalrous esprit de corps of the old regime.
In one of David's studies for the painting, a lightning bolt strikes the
Chapel of Versailles, signifying divine anger with religious intolerance.
The reconciliation here is between the clergy and the Third Estate, or
National Assembly, which part of the clergy had already joined. The
remainder, along with the nobility, came over on 26 June. This was no
longer a reconciliation with the old order but the cataclysmic birth of a
new order.[20]
    The dramatic expression of these ideals of social reconciliation

IX.7.
Christ on the Mountain, *engraving, ca. 1790–91.*
Courtesy Bibliothèque nationale, photo: Bibl. Nat. Paris.

and bienfaisance, which abound in prerevolutionary bourgeois drama, compensated for the social conflicts that did exist and were amply dramatized by Alexandre-Louis Robineau de Beaunoir and Louis-Archambault Dorvigny. *Richard Cœur de Lion* by Michel-Jean Sedaine (a close friend of David) is a three-act comedy in prose first performed at the Comédie italienne in 1784 and popular in the first years of the Revolution. In chivalric fashion, Richard has gone to conquer the Holy Land, which is being held by pagans. The play stresses the theme of mutual service of king and subjects; peasants interact easily with their seigneur. *Richard* was one of many idealizations of a feudal regime which, though it no longer existed, was perpetuated in the imagination of readers of the *bibliothèque bleue.*[21]

Auguste et Théodore, ou Les Deux Pages, by Nicolas Dezède, Ernest Baron Mantauffel, and Louis-François Faur, is a two-act comedy that ran fifty-five performances between 1789 and 1792. The setting is contemporary, not medieval; the pages live and work in the court of Frederick the Great, who is depicted as a benevolent monarch. The pages are as devoted and honest as their master is benevolent. The "intrigue" revolves around the parents of the pages. The father was killed in the service of the king at the Battle of Riesberg, and the

IX.8.
Jean-Michel Moreau [le jeune], The Coronation of Louis XVI at Reims,
11 June 1775, *engraving, 1780.*
Courtesy Library of Congress.

mother was left to support six children, whence the need of employment for the two oldest boys and the gratitude of the family toward the king for providing such an opportunity. This model of enlightened monarchy "listens to all his subjects. All have an equal share in his goodness and justice; he is the guardian angel of his subjects. He will be sensitive to our misfortunes." Ruminating on the nature of government, Frederick declaims: "If the weak were always meant to cringe and feel crushed by the powerful, one would never dream of making laws. There is no real person, no powerful one where I reign. My power is for the oppressed and my presence is for all my subjects."[22] And when Auguste's mother, on a visit to her sons, is being pursued for debts at an inn near the court, the innkeeper's wife implores her husband to satisfy the mother's creditors for the sake of a "brave officer who died defending us, and whose children will defend us again. Let us pay my friend, it is a sacred duty, let us pay in the name of the patrie." Bienfaisance, patriotism,[23] sensibility, commiseration—all contributed to make this play a great success.

Les Deux Petits Savoyards of 1789 by Marsollier des Vivétières, which we examined in chapter 5 and was such a hit in the early years of the Revolution (over two hundred performances), is similar to *Auguste et*

IX.9.

Jacques-Louis David, The Tennis Court Oath, 20 June 1789, *engraving of the unfinished painting at Versailles, 1791.*
Courtesy Musée Carnavalet, Paris, photo: Art Resource, New York.

Théodore in several respects. Each play has a seigneur, two urchins, and a mother to whom the urchins are devoted, and in each the monetary honesty of the urchins earns them the confidence of the wealthy. *Les Deux Petits Savoyards* also displays a penchant for coincidences and recognitions, as in the novels of Ducray-Duminil.

Many early plays of the Revolution stress "comic," familial, and social harmony, in the tradition of didactic bourgeois drama. Marsollier des Vivétières's *Nina, ou la folle par amour* (premiere 1786) is another immensely popular one-act comedy with music. Its protagonist is a young woman who loses her reason when her father breaks off her engagement to her true love on the appearance of a wealthier suitor. Naturally, paternal avarice is conquered and the lovers united. One scene portrays Nina holding hands with children and old people. Love flows beyond the couple to other generations.

Most contemporary dramas stressed love and reconciliation and often bore as their titles the names of two lovers, such as *Philippe et Georgette* (1791) and *Blaise et Babette* (1783), both by Monvel, and Kreutzer's successful adaptation of *Paul et Virginie* (1791). After the

Terror several versions of a story circulated about a prison guard named Cange who helped a destitute couple—the husband was in prison—by giving each a gift of fifty livres, supposedly from the other, but actually without the other's knowledge. These plays were much performed in the aftermath of the bloody Year II, doubtless because they depicted mercy and hidden generosity.

Another play, *Nicodème dans la lune* (1790), a "folly in prose" by Cousin Jacques (Louis-Abel Beffroy de Reigny), presented a fabulous figure of popular culture during the Revolution. Beffroy subtitled his play "the pacific Revolution." In *Nicodème* the civilization on the moon is an empire with a titled, propertied nobility, represented by a duke; a clergy close to the people, like France's lower clergy; peasants groaning under taxes and feudal dues; a well-meaning but remote emperor; a court minister (read "ministerial despot"); and women of the court who are given to Nicodème as baubles to take back to earth. In other words, Beffroy projected onto the moon a France of the old regime— of oppression and deception—and assigned Nicodème, an astronomer and balloonist, the task of judging the lunacy. The emperor is much like the good monarchs Frederick II and Louis XVI, who, as we have seen, are benevolent, eager to make direct contact with the people and quick to provide a magic remedy.

Beffroy gives the curé a central role as the peasants' spokesman, reflecting the prominent role the curés of the old regime played during the early days of the Revolution. He is a "brave man who likes to laugh . . . not a scoundrel like those with a sweet face and a wicked heart."[24] Ally of the people, the curé circumvents the nobility to appeal to the monarch, much like the patriot curés of 1789. Nicodème promises better days to come: "The days of gladness will change hardship into pleasure."[25] But he insists that there must be real cause for gladness to cheer the villagers.

The social struggle in *Nicodème* occurs primarily between the seigneur (the duke) and the peasants, who are allied to the curé, "a partisan of the lowest class of people," and ultimately to Nicodème, who lands on the moon to act as an independent observer and counsel the emperor about the "pacific revolution" on earth. The emperor confronts the "dangerous fermentation in his estates."[26] He tries to distance Nicodème from what the earthling sees as the "terrible" condition of the moon by offering him a choice of the girls of his court to accompany him back to France.

Nicodème comes to no satisfactory denouement. The emperor is warned of falling like a victim into an abyss. The whole problem is reduced to one of communication and generosity. If the emperor listens to "honnêtes gens," they will put him on the right road. The clergy then voluntarily surrender all their prerogatives, which alarms a prelate: "All names become confounded, what chaos in the world."[27] But Nicodème is far more nonchalant—he even refuses to kneel before a messenger, reserving that honor for the Creator.

This play, which was performed at the Théâtre comique et lyrique for two years, presumably succeeded because of its pleasant style of revolution, its portrayal of concern for all on the part of benevolent persons in power, and its interesting focus on the problem of information and communication among oppressed, oppressor, and reformer. Inasmuch as these scenes mirrored the France of 1789–90, they struck sympathetic chords. The play is more about noblesse oblige and sensibilité than about revolution. It idealizes the Revolution as a revolution stripped of violence. As such, *Nicodème dans la lune,* like *Les Deux Petits Savoyards,* is a good illustration of the noble sentiments, good feelings, optimism, and hope that characterize the years 1789–91.

The first stages of the Revolution were marked by a great outpouring of generous sentiment, fraternal feeling, noble effusiveness. Groups antagonistic to one another before the Revolution—clergymen of different faiths or deputies of different estates—were reconciled. All joined in what Cousin Jacques in *Nicodème* called "a peaceful revolution." This phenomenon of conciliation has been described by one author as The Spirit of 1789, which is a far cry from that of 1793. The prevailing belief was "ça ira"—everything would come out right. Ruling over all this commotion was God, with His shafts of light beaming on the Tennis Court, the National Assembly, and the king, who prevailed over all as "père du peuple." Social harmony, as Barnave, Duport, and the other Feuillants foresaw, depended largely on the king, the linchpin of the social edifice. Should he be removed, all security of persons and property would vanish. The optimistic monarchist song in theater, music, or art would then appear as a swan song.

Satire: A Weapon of Revolution

The fraternity of the young Revolution, with its healing oils of reconciliation, was soon shattered by factionalization. The clerical oath split the church, and the royal army divided into groups loyal to the king, to the princes on the frontiers, and to the Assembly and nation. The king's authority began to devolve to the Assembly and the Commune of Paris, and the clubs infringed on the Assembly by preparing legislation at meetings. Tempers rose, accusations abounded, and character assassinations were carried out in pamphlets and newspapers. Conflicting passions meant that each individual and institution, royal or patriot, had to struggle to survive. The Revolution was a torrent that strew the ruins of the old regime in its path.[28]

In this destruction (Saint-Simon and Comte called it the "critical" as opposed to the "organic" phase of civilization), humor—acid, satiric humor—was enlisted in the arts to undermine the old order. Certainly the subversion of ancien régime culture was more noticeable than was the creation of the values and structures that were meant to substitute for it.

Satire often took the form of music. Many satirical songs directed against the court and the formerly privileged orders were crass parodies of sacred hymns. One such was the "O Filii," which likened the pope to "a turkey" (doubtless because he had condemned the Civil Constitution of the Clergy) and called the archbishop of Paris a "criminal, Alleluia." One version of the optimistic "Ça ira" of 1790 runs:

> O it will work out, work out
> . . . .
> In spite of the saboteurs
> All will succeed
> We no longer have nobles or priests
> . . . .
> The Austrian slave will also die out,
> Ah ça ira
> And all their infernal gangs
> Will fly off to the devil.[29]

The "Carmagnole" is a far more bloodthirsty song, written just before the king's overthrow in August 1792. The juxtaposition of violence and merriment is jolting:

> Mrs. Veto had promised
> To have all Parisians' throats cut
> But her plot miscarried
> Thanks to our gunners.

Let's dance the Carmagnole,
Long live the sound of the cannons!

. . . .

Antoinette had resolved to make us fall on our rear ends.
But the effort missed—
She fell flat on her face.

Her husband, thinking himself a winner,
Little knew of our valour,
Go, Louis, fat Austrian boor
Into the tower of the Temple.[30]

This invective is characteristic of the last days of the king and queen. It does not hesitate to defile them, invade their bodies, leaving her "flat on her face" and likening him to a "fat boor." Such abusive songs accompanied a spontaneous desacralization of royalty.

An illustration (fig. IX.10) shows a group of tattered peasants dancing around a liberty tree crowned with a liberty cap. All sing such patriotic refrains as "Dansons la carmagnole" and "Ça ira."

The note of gloating irreverence at the humiliation of the king and queen pervades many other songs, such as:

Vous savez que je fus Roi	You know that I was King
. . . .	. . . .
Je suis Lou lou lou, Je suis	I am Lou lou lou, I am
oui, oui, oui.	oui, oui, oui.
Je suis Lou, Je suis oui,	I am Lou, I am oui,
Je suis Louis Seize	I am Louis sixteen.
Bien mal à mon aise.	Very ill at my ease.

A few months later circulated a more sinister and prophetic song, "The Death of Louis Capet":

It could be happy
Being king on earth,
For him it was unfortunate
That he was without character:
You need a head to be crowned
Being weak and too stupid
He was guillotined.[31]

When the revolutionary calendar was created in Year II (September 1793–September 1794), lyrics cheered the return of time to its natural

IX.10.

Dansons la Carmagnole, *engraving, ca. 1792–93.*
Courtesy Bibliothèque nationale, photo: Bibl. Nat. Paris.

course and reviled "charlatan pontiffs [who] made every day a holiday." The "Awakening of the Père Duchesne" and the "Hymn of the
Versaillais" ridicule the allied sovereigns of Europe in a fashion not
unlike the play *Le Jugement dernier des rois* by Sylvain Maréchal. There
were songs on prices, songs on surveillance ("Each one of us will
watch over those who are suspected, Trala Déridéra [bis]"), songs
on the guillotine. Counterrevolutionary Girondin and Thermidorean
songs were also penned, although they are not numerous in the collections. These ridiculed the National Assembly, the *assignats,* the Declaration of Rights, and the Jacobins.[32]

Simple satirical and parodic themes inspired period caricatures. *The
Patriotic Hunt of the Great Beast* (fig. IX.11) is an allegory of the storming
of the Bastille. The beast represents the troops surrounding Paris on
the eve of the storming. The citizens, alarmed by the cries, "To arms!
To arms!" forged weapons as redoubtable as those swallowed by the
animal. The patriots cut off the many heads of the beast, who retreats,
spreading in its path desolation and famine, despair and shame.

The appeal to bestiaries and allegory to recount the fearful episodes

IX.11.
Patriotic Hunt of the Great Beast, *engraving, ca. 1792.*
Courtesy Library of Congress, photo: John Reynolds.

of the Revolution is more the rule than the exception. Only the mytho-logical—a huge beast or a modern Gargantua—can hope to represent the enormity that the counterrevolutionary enemy represented to the popular patriot imagination. This antiroyal, anticlerical satire is evi-dent in *The Former Great Dinner of the Modern Gargantua with His Family* (fig. IX.12). Rabelais's legendary hero, famous above all for gastro-nomical extravaganzas, is here represented as Louis XVI, seated at the center of the table with an entire piglet on his fork (Louis was called a "big pig" after his flight to Varennes). Marie-Antoinette, to his left, is completely décolletée (since the Diamond Necklace Affair in 1786, radicals had regarded her as a loose woman) and adorned with ostrich feathers, a play on her Austrian origins. To her left sits the comte de Breteuil, who as an émigré in 1790 headed the king's diplomacy with the courts of Europe. Here he impales a soldier whose blood the queen collects in a glass, symbolizing the bloodshed she caused through her support of the counterrevolution.

To the king's right are the princes of Provence and Artois (with their wives), one replete from eating and about to play a game, the other with pockets full of money. All are stuffing themselves in some way. Forming a border around the sides and bottom of the table are servants bringing fruit, climbing a ladder to the table of the giants. Another group staggers beneath the weight of an elaborate three-tiered plate of lobster and fish, and still others transport kegs of wine. In short, the privileged orders are parasites who live off the produce of the people. By one reading, the French Revolution was an attempt to connect work and its fruits more closely and to make leisure less respectable. This was at least implied in the law of suspects of September 1793, which required citizens to give proof of their means of subsistence.

The *March of the Modern Don Quixote for the Defense of the Mill of Abuses* (fig. IX.13) features a troop of counterrevolutionaries in search of a mill (rather than a windmill) that represents all the abuses of the banalités, or utility dues, of the old regime. Atop the mill is a picture of Louis XVI, identified as a "hoarder" (*accapareur*). Around the two cen-tral figures—Don Quixote and the Mill of Abuses—stand various bishops and nobles and soldiers with their cortèges, one on stilts to the left carrying news of Varennes. All are portrayed in ridiculous disarray.

A print entitled *Anti-Patriotic Federation of Former Aristocrats* (fig. IX.14) has as its emblem at the bottom a drawing of the Bastille with the inscription "It was time." The figures in the federation are bestial, fantastical, and infernal, convoked "by discord, received by ambition."

IX.12.

The Former Great Dinner of the Modern Gargantua with His Family, *engraving, ca. 1791–92.*
Courtesy Library of Congress, photo: John Reynolds.

What crimes do the patriotic artists attribute to the Blacks, or counter-revolutionaries? The attempt to dissolve the National Assembly; fanatical protest; the Saint Bartholomew Massacre, a crime for which Voltairians would always hold religion responsible; an auto-da-fé in the name of God of peace and mercy, reminiscent of the days of the Inquisition; and the sins of hypocrisy, tartuffery, and conspiracy.

This is far from the unanimity of the Federation of 1790. The temper of the French has slipped from the reign of grace, by which Michelet characterized the old regime, with benefits bestowed from above as favors rather than claimed from below as rights, to the realm of the bestial, the diabolical.

Most prints aimed at ridiculing counterrevolutionaries feature similar themes. It is not godless France (as Burke would have it) that was to blame. For the patriot-artists, the fatal discord was sown by the counterrevolutionaries in alliance with the European powers. That the

IX.13.
March of the Modern Don Quixote for the Defense of the Mill of Abuses, *engraving, ca. 1789–91.*
Courtesy Bibliothèque nationale, photo: Bibl. Nat. Paris.

counterrevolutionaries might have had valid reasons for opposing the Revolution (such as defending the king, the church, and the property of the "ci-devants"—former nobles—which the constitution guaranteed), was not countenanced by these caricaturists. The idea was to vilify the perceived enemy.

The prints *The Frock to the Wind and Liberty to Monks and Nuns* (see fig. VI.2) and *The Very Credible Life of the Monks* (fig. IX.15) are both hostile to the religious way of life. The first espouses a naturalistic philosophy: what pleases the senses (sociability, marriage) is good, what opposes them (celibacy, seclusion) is bad. It is no secret that the Enlightenment and the Revolution held monastic orders and religious vows in low esteem—they were abolished in February 1790. Contemplation was not considered useful, and only the useful would be tolerated. But the main motif of this print is liberty—to dispose of one's self as one chooses—as shown by the legislation on corporations (abolition of guilds), marriage (divorce), and authorship (copyright).

The Very Credible Life of the Monks satirizes the discrepancy between clerical appearances and presumed reality. To the left, churchgoers

IX.14.
Anti-Patriotic Federation of Former Aristocrats,
engraving, ca. 1790–92.
Courtesy Bibliothèque nationale, photo: Bibl. Nat. Paris.

flock to listen to a monk preach about fasting and penitence. To the
right, the monks feast and drink in the presence of flirtatious, finely
dressed women. The caption reads in part: "To provide for your feast-
ing, the farmers and artisans live in indigence, and they are like con-
victs chained to work. It is the people, in truth, who do the penitence
for your vices and sins."

The king, clergy, and aristocracy were not the only butts of revolutionary propaganda. After the war broke out, the English were also
ridiculed. In the print entitled *The Great Sharpener of the English Knives,*
attributed to David (fig. IX.16), Prime Minister William Pitt the
Younger sharpens his daggers on a stone turned by a conveyor belt
operated by George III, here identified as George Dandin, or George
Turkey (probably a pun on Molière's play *George Dandin*). A bunch of
daggers and money are destined for the assassins in Paris. The French
imagined two things about Pitt during the Revolution: that he subsidized the European coalition against France with England's great
wealth and that he kept a string of informers, spies, intriguers,
and henchmen inside France during the war. Both views had some
foundation.

The counterrevolutionaries, for their part, were not idle in using

IX.15.

The Very Credible Life of the Monks, *engraving, ca. 1789–92.*
Courtesy Library of Congress.

propaganda against the Revolution. One authority in the field has
claimed that millions of "traditional" prints were destroyed during the
Terror, leaving the record lopsided.[33] But enough examples survive in
French and American collections to piece together their strategy. (Excluded here are the marvelous caricatures by the Englishman James
Gillray, probably the most talented satirist of his day, who is well
known and in any case not French.)

The print entitled *Last Procession for the Burial of the Civic Oath* (fig.
IX.17) is a satiric look at the constitutional church from the perspective
of the Roman or the refractory clergy. To have "a foot of nose," as
Archbishop Gobel of Paris is represented as having, is a sign of being
mocked or taken in. The lesser clerics have lesser (but still long) noses,
and the sacristan, in the shape of a devil, carries the civic oath in a
coffin.

Two prints portray the Terror of the Year II in a particularly bad
light. In the first (fig. IX.18), a revolutionary surveillance committee is
staffed by unsympathetic, even malevolent men wearing liberty caps
and reading certificates of good conduct and civicism. An old petitioner-

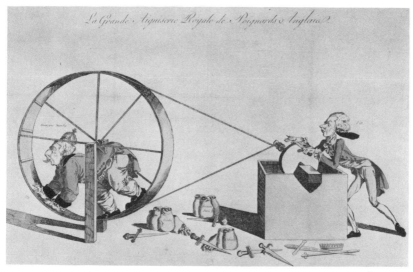

IX.16.
[Jacques-Louis David?], The Great Royal Sharpener of the English
Knives, *engraving, ca. 1793–94.*
Courtesy Bibliothèque nationale, photo: Bibl. Nat. Paris.

suspect, certificate in hand, is instructed to place it on a pile of like
certificates. Justice seems doubtful.

The title of a larger print (fig. IX.19) on the same subject was also
the name of a popular satiric play by Charles-Pierre Ducancel in 1794.
Here Fragonard's son as painter and Berthault as engraver portray
a much larger committee whose members regard with hostility the
woman and child entering on the left. To the extreme right are bottles
of wine responsible for at least one committee member's drunkenness.
Prospects of the woman's acquittal are as dim as those of the old man
in the other print. Both prints are meant to show the cruelty of surveillance and denunciation during the Terror, especially toward the
weak and defenseless (see chapter 12).

The anarchist in the print of that name (fig. IX.20) is portrayed as
two-faced, deceiving the woman of the people with one face and the
well-dressed gilded youth with the other. To the youth he wears
breeches, to the woman he is a sansculotte. The print demonstrates the
poor image the Jacobin "anarchists" enjoyed after Thermidor. The
duplicity for which they were blamed belied the Rousseauist simplicity
and transparency they were supposed to exemplify.

IX.17.
Last Procession for the Burial of the Civic Oath,
engraving, ca. 1790–91.
Courtesy Library of Congress.

The patriotic calculator (fig. IX.21) satirizes the terrorist-execu-
tioner, "the drinker of blood" as he was called after the Terror. On his
desk lie six heads, on the wall a gun and bullet case. He calculates that
he has fourteen "to shave." The atrocious irony is that patriotism is
measured by decapitations.

The targets of satirical prints were also ridiculed on stage. *Le Convalescent de qualité* of Fabre d'Eglantine is similar to *Nicodème dans la
lune,* to the *Jugement dernier des rois,* and even to *Le Noble Roturier* (of
which more presently) in that it transposes a character of the old regime into the Revolution. It capitalizes on the brusque change of circumstances to create situations—unforeseen and incongruous—in the
old regime.

In the *Convalescent* we have a noble who has been absent from Paris
since the days of the old regime. He returns to find everything about
him changed. Although he reacts with stubborn incredulity and indignation, he must come to terms with the new order of things: his
daughter, a nun, is marrying his overseer, his doctor has sworn loyalty
to the new regime, his servants are no longer in livery, his peasants

IX.18.

The Committee of the Year II, *engraving, ca. 1794–95.*
Courtesy Bibliothèque nationale, photo: Bibl. Nat. Paris.

have become unmanageable, and money can no longer be procured from tax farms, abbeys, rentes, lotteries, or loans. "Reason has reduced your calculations to zero," his creditor tells him. As his doctor puts it:

> I tell you, talking sense—it is time to surrender. The whole state
> has changed. Men are equal; there are no more seigneurs, there
> are no more vassals. The parlements are dead; so is the high
> clergy;
> The army has sided with this supreme Law;
> The king, in agreement with everything, has captivated our
> hearts and is the father we have chosen.[34]

The play's punch springs from the marvelous, unconscious transposition of the marquis in time (Nicodème's had been in space). The highly structured corporate and privileged nature of the old regime is incongruously violated before the eyes of the protagonist. Although the above quotation shows that the king is still considered the father of the people, this play cashiers the old regime rather than reforming it as had *Nicodème.*

IX.19.

[Alexandre-Evariste] Fragonard [fils] and [Pierre-Gabriel] Berthault, The
Interior of a Revolutionary Committee under the Reign of Terror,
engraving, 1794–95.

Courtesy Bibliothèque nationale, photo: Bibl. Nat. Paris.

IX.20.

The Anarchist: "I Trick Both of Them," *engraving, ca. 1798.*
Courtesy Library of Congress, photo: John Reynolds.

Another transposition of a noble into the reign of equality is even more humorous. The vaudeville by J.-B. Radet called *Le Noble Roturier (The Noble Commoner)* is as successful at role reversal as is Fabre's earlier play. Here a noble joins the scramble to find a sansculotte genealogy, a coveted mark of respectability in Year II. A noble genealogy, by contrast, would get one in trouble. The genealogist in the play is experienced. Having found noble genealogies for pretentious commoners before 1789, he will have no difficulty proving that the same parvenus were descendants of fruit merchants. The marquis dresses as a sansculotte, a noble commoner, the inversion of Molière's *bourgeois gentilhomme.* The genealogist explains: "When on old parchments I hinted recent nobility, it required a good deal of skill to achieve our ends. But today . . . it is easy for me to furnish proofs of common birth." When a friend asks the marquis, who is dressed as a cobbler, whether he really is one, he responds wryly: "By gosh, at present one better be."[35]

IX.21.
The Patriotic Calculator, *engraving, 1789.*
Courtesy Library of Congress, photo: John Reynolds.

Radet and Desfontaines's play, like the *Convalescent,* is funny, but where the *Convalescent* applies the derisive note of social conflict, *Le Noble Roturier* has softened edges. The *Convalescent*'s humor comes from the triumphant new rule overthrowing the ancien régime by befuddling the marquis. *Le Noble Roturier* instead pokes as much fun at the prestige of sansculotterie as at the vanity of noble titles. Although the new order is victorious, one senses that folly will prevail in whatever regime people devise.

Not only the nobility but the whole old order was satirized on stage. Anticlerical plays called convent plays were the staple of many Parisian theaters, particularly on the boulevard, during the Revolution. This distressed the authorities, including the Committee of Public Safety, which considered them "garbage" and wished that a healthier, more uplifting republican fare could be fed to the people. But reports of the agents of the Ministry of the Interior in the autumn and winter of 1793–94 amply testify to the popularity of this garbage.

The great comic playwright of the Revolution was probably Louis-Benoît Picard, whose play *Les Visitandines* ran from 1792 to 1794 at the Feydeau. It features two bumbling Quixotes, picaresque rogues, who in their intoxicated state mistake a convent for an inn. Through a series of stunts they wake up the sisters and cause bedlam. One of the travelers finds his true love of yesteryear.

The ariettes made this play popular, but so did the lines of the drunk rogue: "Each one chases after happiness, and I find it at the bottom of my glass." Later, the mother abbess says: "I believed the Lord had a particular predilection for [our home] . . . all our sisters are so virtuous, so worthy, which is not to say that I regard them as perfect. For example, Sister Saint Anne is a bavarde, Sister Josephine is a coquette, Sister Augustine is a prude. I who talk to you have a giddiness, a vivacity . . . but we mutually tolerate our little faults."[36]

Two plays by Pigault-Lebrun, *Les Dragons et les bénédictines* and *Les Dragons en cantonnement,* differ in spirit. In the first, republican dragoons scale a convent wall "to make love" to the nuns under the pretext of coming to praise their virtue. Unlike Picard's innocent and apolitical play, here the old regime is assaulted. And Pigault's nuns are not silly like Picard's but cocksure accomplices in the dragoons' seduction. One nun is wholly bereft of belief and talks like a bold freethinker. The nuns marry the dragoons, bring up their children for the patrie, and live a happy, wholesome family life.[37]

Like demons, fairies, and monsters, infidel clerics, ribald monks, and coquettish nuns were not inventions of the Revolution. What was new was the enthusiasm with which playwrights and the public matched and married their clerics, had them dance around liberty trees, and made them into "good citizens"—fathers, soldiers, mayors, teachers—as indeed many clerics did become. Fodder for revolutionary propaganda was transformed into pure amusement. In the *Sœurs du pot,* a mother superior falls in love with a young apothecary. Is the aim of the author to vilify nuns? He says: "The tender humanity of the sisters merits a too sincere homage for the author to have had any other aim than to banter, to please, and to divert." Other plays also capitalized on the comic reversal brought by secularization, among them, *La Sainte Omelette* (sacrilegious), *La Confédération du Montparnasse, Mélanie, Les Réchappées du couvent, La Sainte dénichée.* The first serious historian of boulevard theater claims that a popular anticlericalism there was more playful than malicious. Month after month the "indecent remains" of the old regime, as one official put it, kept the boulevards popping while the Committee of Twelve grimaced.[38]

Le Convalescent de qualité and *Le Noble Roturier* satirized the nobility; *Les Visitandines* and *Les Dragons et les bénédictines* ridiculed the regular clergy. And a clever play by Joseph Aude, *Cadet Roussel* (1793), mocked the hierarchy of theatrical genres. This extremely popular play, which was performed eighty-two times at the Théâtre du palais variétés, consisted of two plays within a play—a play upon plays, for the characters perform a comic opera and then give a tragedy in verse. The whole skit, particularly the tragic half, is a clear spoof on the pompous language of high theater: "Devoirs! . . . Amour! Jour du sang! Jour affreux! Incomparable ami" ("Duty! . . . Love! Day of blood! Horrible day! Incomparable friend"). When Plumineux, the tragic hero, threatens to drink a vial of poison, the audience jeers, "Let him drink it," while the actor's father (also in the audience) shouts fearfully, "No, no, let someone else drink it."[39] *Cadet Roussel* turns comedy against tragedy. Indeed, the theaters of the Revolution were filled with comic plays that satirized what the revolutionaries held in contempt—nobles, émigrés, priests, nuns—so drama turned out to be less noble than the revolutionaries would have liked.

Each of the above-mentioned plays spares the monarch. A direct, hostile treatment can be found in Sylvain Maréchal's play *Le Jugement dernier des rois,* which Maréchal described as neither comedy nor tragedy but "prophecy." This play had only twenty-two performances at the Théâtre de la république in late 1793 and early 1794.[40] It may well have been too radical for the Committee of Public Safety, which was then moving against the most extreme forms of de-Christianization. The hero of Maréchal's play was a sansculotte who had been unjustly exiled to a volcanic island in the last days of the old regime. But the Revolution comes and with it the last judgment of kings. George III, Catherine the Great, Pope Pius VI, Francis II, and Charles IV are all chained and transported to the island by sansculottes who have brought them there just before liberating their aged comrade. The sovereigns are submitted to extreme indignities—the pope is to marry and Catherine II is to visit a Cordelier or a Jacobin club—and then blown up by a volcanic eruption, caused by saltpeter allegedly provided by the government.

The *Last Judgment of Kings* is the ultimate theatrical piece because it touches the untouchable—kings and queens, the pope, the pinnacle of the old regime. The world is truly turned upside-down in this play. The lowliest of the old regime, the sansculotte, becomes master and judge of the former sovereigns. Far from limiting retribution to one king in one country, the judgment extends to all kings throughout Europe. Unlike many revolutionary plays, this one has no indulgence for its victims. Its judgment is relentless, final, and complete. A revolution has been staged in which subjects make sovereigns scramble for their bread and sentence them to death. The aged sansculotte exclaims on learning of the execution of Louis XVI, "The French have then become men. . . . This people, like the God that is preached to them, only have to will [to become free]." This work of an "homme sans Dieu," as Sylvain Maréchal styled himself, is more blasphemous and vindictive than any previous play. It attacks the old regime dead center, lauding regicide a year after the execution of Louis Capet and just a few months after the exhumation of the royal remains at the Abbey of Saint-Denis.

We have looked at two modes of viewing the Revolution—reconciliation and satire. In the former, the fatherhood of Louis to his people and the brotherhood or fraternity of all men were celebrated, half in joy that these two sentiments actually existed and half in hopes that they would endure. In revolution as satire, the arts became vehicles to criticize and mock various orders, constitutions, and figureheads of the old regime—from the clergy and nobility to the monarch himself. The satiric mode lost the tone of reconciliation and passed to the offensive. Nothing was spared, and the gimmicks of transposition in space or time contrasted prerevolutionary France with France after the Revolution.

Commemoration

One mode of the Revolution, self-commemoration, remains. We have glimpsed it in Desaugiers's hiérodrame, a work of reconciliation but also one of commemoration. Like the Festival of the Federation of 1790, the hiérodrame was designed to commemorate the storming of the Bastille of the fourteenth of July.

"La Marseillaise" was composed by Rouget de Lisle to give the French courage to defend France against the Austrians and Prussians. Written in Strasbourg at the request of the city's mayor in April 1792, just four days after France declared war against Austria, the "Marseillaise" was known first as the "war song of the Army of the Rhine." The song caught on, went through innumerable editions, and soon became *the* song of the Revolution, sung at performances, at festivals, in the army, and in schools. Its words evoke the threat of the enemy, identified with tyranny and bloodshed. The rural and agricultural dimensions of the conflict—the risk of defilement of France's furrows as well as its wives—are illustrated by popular crockery and the popular flag of the Revolution from the Tard and Saône (figs. IX.22, IX.23, IX.24). The French armies represent the new liberty. France was at war almost continuously for a generation after the "Marseillaise" was composed; the "Marseillaise" was a success partly because it was always relevant.[41]

Although the "Marseillaise" was composed to rally patriots around the tricolor, it soon became an ode to the Revolution and its triumphs over aggression and oppression. The "Marseillaise" became a commemorative hymn conjuring a beleaguered country, a unifying anthem even more emotive than the "Star Spangled Banner."

"La Marseillaise"

Stanza 1	*Stanza 1*
Allons, enfants de la patrie,	Rise up citizens of the patrie,
Le jour de gloire est arrivé!	The day of glory has arrived!
Contre nous de la tyrannie	Against us the bloody standard
L'étendard sanglant est levé! (bis)	Of tyranny has been raised! (bis)
Entendez vous dans les campagnes	Do you hear in your fields
Mugir ces féroces soldats?	Those ferocious soldiers cry out?
Ils viennent jusque dans nos bras	They come right into our midst
Egorger nos fils, nos compagnes.	To cut the throats of our sons, our wives.

IX.22.
Crockery depicting a cannon, ca. 1789–92.
Courtesy Musée des arts et traditions populaires, Paris, photo: Musées nationaux, Paris.

Refrain
Aux armes, citoyens,
Formez vos bataillons!
Marchons! Marchons!
Qu'un sang impur
Abreuve nos sillons!

. . . .

Stanza 4
Que veut cette horde d'esclaves

Refrain
To arms, citizens,
Form your battalions!
Let us march! Let us march!
Let an impure blood water our
furrows!

. . . .

Stanza 4
What does this horde of slaves
want?

IX.23.
Crockery depicting the Bastille, ca. 1789–91.
Courtesy Musée des arts et traditions populaires, Paris, photo: Musées nationaux, Paris.

De traitres, de rois conjurés?	Traitors, conspiring kings?
Pour qui ces ignobles entraves,	For whom these ignoble shackles,
Ces fers des longtemps préparés? (bis)	These chains prepared so long ago? (bis)
Français! pour vous, ah! quel outrage!	Frenchmen! For us, ah! what an outrage!
Quels transports il doit exciter!	What transports it should excite!
C'est nous qu'on ose méditer	It is us they intend
De rendre à l'antique esclavage!	To return to ancient slavery!

Other commemorative hymns were Rouget de Lisle's "Hymne à l'égalité" (1793), "Hymne à l'humanité" (1795), and "Hymne à la Victoire, déesse d'un peuple." Cherubini, for his part, wrote hymns

IX.24.
Flag of the Revolution, *from Tard-et-Saône, ca. 1789–92.*

to Fraternity (1794), the Panthéon (1794), Combat (1794), Victory (1794), and Youth (1799) and, last but not least, a hymn about "Republican saltpeter." The patriotic hymn involved a transfer of sacrality from religious subjects to human or national concerns, which in the process were meant to acquire superhuman, transcendental value. Clearly this was Gossec's intention when he adapted "O Salutaris Hostia" (O Saving Victim) for the de-Christianizing ceremony at Notre-Dame in brumaire Year II. François de Neufchâteau did the same in his "Hymn to Liberty," which was sung to the music of "Veillons au salut de l'Empire" and later put to Lesueur's music. It reads in part:

O Liberty, holy Liberty!
Goddess of an enlightened people!
Reign today in this sanctuary,
By you this temple is purified!
Liberty! Before you reason chases away imposture:
Error flees, fanaticism is vanquished.
Our gospel is nature
And our cult is virtue.

Love one's country and one's brothers,
Serve the sovereign people,
These are the sacred characteristics,
And the faith of a Republican.
Of a chimerical hell
He does not fear the empty flame;
Of an illusory heaven
He does not wait for false treasures;
Heaven is in peace of soul,
And hell in remorse.[42]

This hymn, sung at the height of the de-Christianization movement in Paris at the Church of Saint-Laurent, is another good illustration of the transfer of sacrality involving on the one hand the desacralization of the Christian worldview and on the other the sacralization of the revolutionary cosmos. It is a hymn because Liberty is considered sacred and is being honored in a desacralized Christian church, one "rebaptized" as a republican temple. It is a religion of humanity (*avant la lettre*), in which the sovereign people are "sacred characters" before whom all must bow. Man worships himself.[43]

A print of Liberty (fig. IX.25) by Pierre-Paul Prud'hon, one of the Revolution's finest artists, explains a great deal of what was intended by the iconographers and lyric composers of the 1790s. Liberty in Prud'hon's print is a woman who has just slain tyranny, represented by a hydra at her feet. Also beneath her lie various human heads, one of which is crowned. Liberty triumphs over the tyranny of monarchy. In her left hand she carries a broken yoke symbolizing the overthrow of oppression, and in her right an ax, instrument of liberation. Liberty stands relaxed and partially bare-breasted, which became a traditional stance. She is free from the normal constraints of working, yet she does not represent license, which would have been a caricature of liberty. Here Liberty is calm, confident, and triumphant,

IX.25.
Pierre-Paul Prud'hon, Liberty, *engraving, ca. 1793.*
Courtesy Musée Carnavalet, Paris, photo: Perrain-Carnavalet.

as she would appear in numerous medals and letterheads of the Republic. In both "La Marseillaise" and this print, Liberty is associated with the bloodshed and combat without which, it was thought, she could not reign.

In the theater, commemorative hymns or perorations to liberty abounded in settings that evoked the sacred past—Greece, Rome, even early modern Switzerland and France—a past of magnanimous actions and freedom-loving gestures. In commemorating these ideals and heroes on stage, the soul is enlarged, elevated to a rarefied atmosphere where it can soar unfettered by human chains.

The old regime's tragic declamation, neoclassical art, and classical education anticipated the discourse, gestures, and actions of republican heroes in the Revolution. The language of tragedy was akin to the rhetoric of the collèges based on Cicero, Plutarch, and the Stoics. Roland Barthes described it as "a properly revolutionary writing. . . . linked more than ever in History to spilled blood."[44] The great classical form depicted crimes, treason, and atrocities in an effort to protect and sacralize liberty. Listen to lines from Antoine-Marin Lemierre's *Guillaume Tell,* a play written in 1766 about the legendary fourteenth-century Swiss hero who defended the Helvetic cantons against the Holy Roman Empire, represented by the bailiff Gessler, to whom Tell had refused to tip his hat. In revenge Gessler commanded Tell, a good bowman, to shoot an arrow through an apple placed on his own son's head.

> I.i. Tell: We have too often preferred glory to virtue.
>
> . . . .
>
> I.i. Tell: Friend, for my country, I immolate myself entirely.
> What does it matter who I shall be among
> posterity
>
> . . . .
>
> I.ii. Tell: There is no compromise with Liberty
>
> . . . .
>
> . . . Humans born free and equal
> have no other yoke to carry than their labors.
>
> . . . .
>
> I.ii. Tell: I will be the first to swear in your hands
> To shed all my blood to change our destinies.
> II.i. Gessler: Patrie and liberté, this double public cry
> Will echo vainly in this sullen people
>
> . . . .

      III.iv. Tell: If my son perishes in such a great danger
                This blood which is so dear to me . . . Heaven
                must avenge.[45]

The themes of tyranny, revolt, sacrifice, and liberty pervaded the French Revolution two decades later. For this reason, *Guillaume Tell* was selected on 2 August 1793, along with *Brutus, Mort de César,* and *Gaius Gracchus,* as the play most suitable for a republican audience. Theaters were subsidized to perform these works.[46]

Marie-Joseph Chénier, who had supported the freedom of theaters as a means of regenerating a people stripped of its ancient rights, was most successful as a playwright during the Revolution. Chénier's *Charles IX,* like Lemierre's *Guillaume Tell,* was set in what was called modern as opposed to ancient history. Neither play manifested the new, indulgent attitude toward medieval chivalry; rather, their message was antimedieval. Both transposed Roman libertarian and tyrannicide values into a modern context. The deliberations that led to the Saint Bartholomew's Day Massacre are the subject of Chénier's play. The massacre occurred during the reign of Charles IX, and in Chénier's version under his orders. Eighteenth-century historians had repudiated the notion that the massacre was premeditated, but the philosophes preferred to believe the worst.

Chénier's play dramatized religious intolerance. *Charles IX* had been censored in 1788, but in 1789 Chénier and others pressed for permission to produce it. His difficulties can be appreciated by a brief inspection of the text. The chancellor, Michel de L'Hôpital, sums up the indictment of "fanaticism":

    Always blood, always sacred crimes,
    Investiture, exile, murders and parricides,
    And the ring of the fisherman ratifying the regicides.
    Must we be astonished if a worn-out people,
    Under the inflexible yoke so many times thrown off,
    Ceaselessly assassinated by the decrees of Rome,
    As soon as the people dare oppose their weakness against her,
    Soon, ardently they hurl themselves into reform
    To stray from an oppressive pontiff.[47]

The language is that of *Brutus,* the *Mort de César,* and *Guillaume Tell,* but the context is wholly different: a medieval Roman ecclesiastic and a Valois king of France replace the Roman tyrants (Tarquin and Caesar). Even Beaumarchais expressed disapproval that the play's premiere took place during the October Days, when the king was being led perilously back to Paris from Versailles. But Chénier used the Saint Bartholomew's Day Massacre to make a powerful, rhetorical statement against church *and* monarchy and in favor of the rights of the people. Revolutionaries considered the play, subtitled "a school for kings," to be the counterpart of the *Mariage de Figaro,* which had been a school for nobility.[48]

If religious fanaticism was the theme of *Charles IX,* social and political oppression was the subject of Chénier's other major revolutionary tragedy, *Gaius Gracchus,* a story of the Roman tribune who sided with the plebs against the patrician class. Addressing the Roman people, Gaius says:

If you crush under your foot patrician pride;
If you can, proud of the plebeian name,
Deaf to the empty prejudices of an ancient nobility,
Imagine your strength and sense their weakness;
All these eternal rights which you have lost,
Will, be assured, one day be returned to you.

Gaius then rejects the urgings of a patrician to submit to the Senate:

This filial respect and this dependence
Could serve the state when Rome in its youth
Believed that with the Tarquins it had chased out all Tyrants;
You will not imitate your ignorant ancestors;
Four whole centuries have increased your knowledge;
You have no need of Patrons nor of Fathers;
But the lands which you have conquered
Must be finally divided up equally.[49]

This commemoration of the Roman revolution was a transparent allusion to the revolutionary present. Inherited authority was discredited, as were social rank and unequal property distribution. Dramatic discourse could easily be as violent and subversive as political rhetoric, because the protective veil of drama allowed greater freedom of speech.

How typical was this tragic discourse of the theaters, which Parisians may have been frequenting in far greater numbers than ever before, particularly after the grant of theatrical liberties (table A.5)? Most republican tragedies were put on at the formerly privileged theaters or new theaters that imitated them, such as the Théâtre de la république or the Théâtre national rue Richelieu. With the exception of the Palais Variété's production of *Guillaume Tell,* the drama recommended by the Committee of Public Safety and the Convention was performed almost exclusively in "high" rather than popular theaters. Indeed, comedy had eclipsed tragedy at midcentury—a phenomenon that vexed Voltaire. Comedies were performed more than twelve times as often as tragedies during the Revolution.

Painting saw a similar attempt to immortalize the great events and figures of the Revolution to inspire the republican present. Perhaps the most famous were those the Convention commissioned David to execute. *The Tennis Court Oath* (fig. IX.9, above) was one huge commemoration. Although the painting was never finished, it was engraved and used to celebrate the founding of the new France. Barère demanded that engravings of David's picture of the young martyr Joseph Bara (fig. IX.26), who refused to shout "long live the king" when he fell into the hands of royalists, be placed outside schoolrooms to inspire young adolescents and children with a similar devotion to the patrie.[50]

The oil portrait *To Marat, David* (fig. IX.27) combines the starkness and severity of David's other paintings in the new context of contemporary history. In a very specific way it commemorates a person whom many considered the incarnation of the Revolution. The transfer of sacrality here is from Michelangelo's pietà of Christ, who gave his life on the cross to save humankind from sin, to a Jacobin cordelier who gave his life for the *menu-peuple,* the sansculottes, to save them from the greed and malevolence of the rich. Christ preached peace and forgiveness, whereas Marat never ceased to cry for an ever larger number of heads. David suppresses the enormous difference between the two, however. Martyrdom effaces Marat's bloodthirstiness, his vindictive denunciations, his obsessive suspiciousness, and his megalomania. None of this is even hinted at in Marat's limp corpse draped pathetically over the side of his bath. We have instead Marat the victim, whose crimes are consumed in revolutionary self-sacrifice. By his death as much by his heroic life he rises to the *hauteur* of the Revolution.[51]

David's Marat is similar to three other depictions by him of revolutionary martyrs: those of Joseph Bara, Agricola Viala, and Louis-Michel Lepeletier de Saint-Fargeau (fig. IX.28, examined in chapter 12). It was as if the Revolution, which had caused so many deaths, could expiate them only by the revolutionaries' own blood. But of course the revolutionaries saw no need to expiate. David, like Marat, endorsed the reign of bloody terror—in fact, David signed over four hundred warrants for arrest issued by the Committee of General Security, of which he was a member. Even more, the erotic rendition of Bara testifies to a

IX.26.
Jacques-Louis David, Bara, *painting, 1794.*
Courtesy Musée Calvet Avignon, photo: Giraudon/Art Resource, New York.

certain necrophilia both on his part and on that of the Revolution, obsessed as it was—from the novels of Ducray-Duminil to the guillotine itself—with death.

Besides the commemorative works of contemporary history, several series of engravings celebrated *événements* (events) of the Revolution. These anticipate the photographs that document later revolutions. In July 1793 Lépine and Claude Niquet l'Ainé published the first *livraison* of a series entitled *Tableaux gravés des principaux événements de la Révolution française.* Another rightly famous series was the *Tableaux historiques de la Révolution française,* engraved by Jean-Louis Prieur Lejeune, Berthault, Jean Duplessis-Berthaux, and Abraham Girardet, who began it in prerevolutionary 1787. A nineteenth-century historian comments that these prints "retrace with great clearness the places and buildings, which were the most moving scenes with the crowds who were the actors and spectators" (figs. VI.6, IX.1, and IX.29). Prieur was arrested and guillotined in the Thermidorean reaction with Antoine Fouquier-Tinville, for whom he had served as a juryman in the revolutionary tribunal. Other series of this genre were Sergent's *Tableaux,* Jean-François Janinet's *Gravures historiques des principaux événements,* and

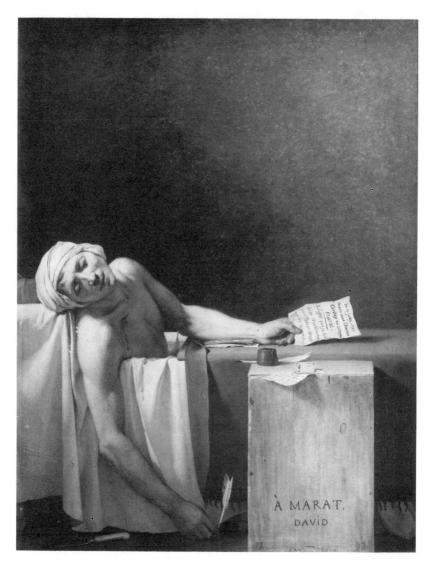

IX.27.
Jacques-Louis David, To Marat, David, *painting, 1793.*
Courtesy Musées royaux des Beaux-Arts, Brussels, photo: Giraudon/Art Resource, New York.

IX.28.
Jacques-Louis David, Lepeletier de Saint-Fargeau,
engraving by Tardieu, ca. 1793.
Courtesy Bibliothèque nationale.

François Bonneville's *Portraits des personnages célèbres de la Révolution* (1796–1802). Numerous artist-engravers had an awareness of history and chose to engrave events they considered epoch-making. The dramatic genre, known as *faits-historiques,* actually signified contemporary events but were judged "historical" because of their momentous character. *Historique* meant something so important that these engravers were under great pressure to cut their plates. The engraver Bervic spent five years before the Revolution engraving the impassible Louis XVI, but revolutionary engravers memorialized events almost as quickly as they occurred. Occasionally, old prints were adapted to new subjects, just as old tunes were put to new words. Both served practical purposes—to speed production and facilitate learning.[52]

Three modes of representation (which could be called three moments were it not for some chronological overlapping) show three ways in which the arts represented the Revolution. The first, reconciliation, is the sweet, affectionate mode in which all citizens are seen as brothers in one patrie. But the excess and urgency of these very

IX.29.
Pierre-Gabriel Berthault, Robespierre Being Led Wounded into the
Antechamber of the Committee of Public Safety, 28 July 1794,
engraving.
Courtesy Library of Congress, photo: John Reynolds.

pleadings of fraternity belie presentiments of conflict. Moreover, themes of conflict with those who oppose the Revolution—say, in Desaugiers's hiérodrame or in the "Ça ira" (which clearly hints that perhaps "ça n'ira pas"!)—actually surface in instances of the conciliatory mode.

The satiric mode occurs most clearly when new distinctions begin to be drawn. The identification of pre-1789 French history as the ancien régime found its theatrical representation in such plays as *Le Convalescent de qualité*, in which a noble who has absented himself from society to recover from illness finds that society unrecognizable when he returns. One can only imagine the delight of a Third Estate audience at this marquis's befuddlement. This satire exposes the incipient attack on the aristocracy, much as the anticlerical prints mark the attack on the clergy and *Le Jugement dernier des rois* parodies the last judgment of Christ, ridding the earth of kings almost simultaneously with their exhumation of Saint-Denis.

The third mode, commemoration, strives to convert the evanescent character of revolutionary events and heroes into something permanent and memorable. It makes the contemporary event historical by conflating present and future with past. The revolutionary generation had an acute sense of the ravages of time—witness the paintings of Hubert Robert. If the Revolution was to avoid being swallowed by Chronos, or by an unwritten history, it had to stem the flow of events and set them in an engraved plate, a painted canvas, a published script, or an old tune. Such works of art would enkindle a republican ardor in those wavering in the present and in descendants of patriots in the future. No, the blood of revolutionary martyrs would not be shed in vain!

Some heroes reached beyond the engraved image to penetrate the Panthéon. Pantheonization raised one above ordinary mortals to quasi-divinity. In dedicating a temple to great men rather than to gods or a saint, the Revolution departed from the Roman precedent by converting its polytheism into an embryonic religion of humanity.

These three modes are not always distinct (David's *Tennis Court Oath* of reconciliation commemorates a great moment in French history). But most artistic works of the Revolution fall into one category or another. Although the Revolution did not dominate the arts statistically, those in power nonetheless used the arts decisively as instruments of revolutionary propaganda.

CHAPTER X

COMMUNICATING

Government in the old regime was considered the agent of a hereditary sovereign who ruled over subjects by virtue of an authority conferred by God: government in revolutionary France was considered an agent of the sovereign people to whom it was responsible and in whose name it exercised authority. Ideally, obedience (of subjects) was expected in the first, trust and spontaneous compliance (of citizens) in the second. But one must not mistake a theoretical contrast for a historical reality. Trust could exist under a monarchy, and fear could exist under a republic.

A comparison of the language of citizen addresses and government decrees in 1789 and 1794 illustrates the change in two forms of communication during the Revolution. The language of denunciation, for example, illustrates what subjects and governors said *about* one another, whereas through oaths—declarations of principle—writers attempted to close the gap between governed and governors. The assemblies and the press were a crucial means of communication between author and audience. And the abbé Grégoire's survey of the use of the French language, and the survival or extinction of dialects and *patois,* demonstrates the National Assembly's attempt to bridge linguistic barriers between citizens and representatives, enlightened and unenlightened, patriots and counterrevolutionaries. By perfecting communication, it was believed that misunderstandings and mistrust would disappear. And malevolence—a sin against the patrie—would be unmasked, punished, or corrected through education.

Addresses, Decrees, and Parliamentary Rhetoric

The *cahiers de doléances* of 1789 were a mixture of formal statements of grievances from parishes, abbeys, academies, and guilds to district baillages and sénéchaussés, where general cahiers of an entire order were drawn up. What do these cahiers tell us about the relationship between electors and king and between electors and deputies? Specific grievances about privileges, feudal dues, commercial barriers, and constitutionalism will be left aside to focus exclusively on communication.

In a small sample of some thirty cahiers of all three orders chosen mostly for illustrative purposes, I have looked specifically at the form of address of subject citizens to their king in an attempt to discover the vocabulary and sentiments communicated.

No body of citizens even remotely desired to see the monarch overthrown in 1789, for the French were devoted to their king. This has led some historians to remark on how little the cahiers anticipated the later events of the Revolution.

The First Estate of Lyons spoke of "bringing to the foot of the throne the homage of respect, of acknowledgment, and of fidelity which inspire all its actions for the best of kings." The clergy of Amiens spoke in similar terms. The clergy of Alençon claimed that such sentiments as these "are engraved in all French hearts" but that "the clergy will always consider it a duty to set an example and to wish most sincerely for the glory and the conservation of His Majesty."

Most of these petitions or demands began with a subjunctive clause, almost never the direct imperative. Their authors still considered themselves subjects even when calling themselves citizens. The subjects of some Third Estate cahiers, like that of Agen, refer to themselves as children before their father: "Let us give ourselves to the sweet hope that the goodness of the king waits for [the deputies] to [whom he will] stretch out a protective hand and receive them with that paternal tenderness which will render him forever the idol of his peoples."[1]

Quasi-feudal expressions of homage mixed with more contemporary expressions of the century. The king, for instance, was often described as *bienfaisant* (beneficent). But, though many cahiers expressed gratitude at being convoked and consulted, these expressions were often combined with the familiar language of contract and rights of the *gens de lois,* who drew up the cahiers and saw the king as existing primarily for the people. This view was ancient, but it was improper to remind the king of this in spring 1789.

The cahier of the Third Estate of Lille suggested that the general interest must prevail over the private, while still recognizing that the beneficent king granted the "National Assembly" (*sic*). The nobles of Metz expressed their relationship to the king in terms of "common interest," not "devotion," and stated that their submission to laws would be proportionate to the protection they received from them. Even the nobility of Agen, which expressed "the most sincere oath of respect of love and of fidelity" to the king, described this feeling as a manifestation of "our patriotism and our veneration." The La Rochellois nobles expressed their attachment to the king in particularly contemporary terms, for they were "so convinced of the powers which they conferred upon him, that they never permitted themselves to raise the least doubt about the authority with which they have invested him." Their king was a deputy king acting under a mandate or contract. This arrangement envisioned future constitutive laws arising from "the consent of the people and the adhesion of the will of the king"—in other words, the constitutional monarchy that France would have between 1789 and 1792. To put matters in those terms during the convocation of the Estates General was audacious.[2]

The nobility of Lille, La Rochelle, and Dijon expressed the new liberties in terms of recovering old ones—not an unreasonable viewpoint if one believed with Tocqueville that the history of the old regime was the suppression of local liberties. For Lille, the mandate of the Estates General was "to reestablish the ancient constitution of the monarchy in which the powers of the prince and the rights of the nation were balanced in the most just equilibrium." For the three estates of Dijon, the issue was "an unexpected return to its ancient existence," possible only if divisions in the estates were surmounted. But a reference to a return to the past could and did mask innovation and criticism of the "present evils."[3]

The silences, too, are noteworthy. Most cahiers of the Third Estate began abruptly by enumerating demands. Although the omission of a preamble does not necessarily imply disrespect, the frequency of these preambles in the clerical cahiers and their frequent absence in the third estate suggest different degrees of respect toward the king.

The list of demands of the Third Estate of Agen was prefaced: "It is indispensable to . . ."; "The king will be supplicated to take into consideration . . ." (a respectful exception); "It should be ordered . . .";

"It is time to return . . ."; "It will be requested . . ."; "Must one for-ever have to . . ."; "It will be legislated . . ."—a blend of indicatives and conditionals. In contrast to these formulas, those of Aix's clergy begin with the respectful expression of a wish in the subjunctive: "Let the king be supplicated . . ."; "Let one represent . . ."; "Let it be ac-corded . . ."; "Let one suppress . . ."; "May the king be very humbly thanked. . . ."[4]

A certain ambiguity about the addressee is evident in these docu-ments. Many authors saw their wishes being carried to the foot of the throne and hence framed their grievances accordingly. But the cahiers were also meant to serve as mandates and instructions for the deputies. The nobility of Agen is more explicit about this than most when it says, "Our will is to limit the powers which our representatives [*commettants*] receive from us," and so it does not hesitate to "order our deputies to demand. . . ." The immediate addressee is the deputy; the remote one is still the king, who most likely would have to approve the demands.[5]

The cahiers varied in the degree of respect and homage they paid to the king. He might still be regarded as supreme sovereign and father of his people, endowed with the power to "accord" satisfaction to his subjects' needs, or he could be seen as receiver of a mandate or partner in a contract whose interests were subordinated to the general interest and who was calling the Estates General to reform inveterate abuses. Demands could be phrased either as firm indicatives, verging on im-peratives, or humble supplications. To the king one expressed wishes, more or less deferentially, but to the deputy, commands.

The crown's form of communicating with subjects before 1789 sprang from the (at least theoretically) absolute nature of its power, which united executive, legislative, and judicial functions in one will. Although royal decrees and edicts had to be registered by the par-lements, in the event of their "remonstrance," a royal *lit de justice* could override their opposition and the parlementaires could be exiled from their seats of jurisdiction. Of course, the crown "communicated" to its subjects through the intendants, through the church, and through the privileged press, notably the *Gazette de France*. In 1789, to over-ride opposition, the king employed not only such traditional au-thoritative channels as the lit de justice but the long-forgotten channel of cahiers.

On 19 November 1787 Louis XVI appeared before the parlement of Paris to register a forced loan of 420 million livres. Keeper of the Seals

M. de Lamoignon, spoke of the king's authority to do this: "To the king alone belongs the sovereign power in his kingdom; . . . he is accountable only to God for the exercise of the supreme power." And when the parlement remonstrated five months later, the king responded: "It was superfluous to speak to me about the law concerning registration and the liberty of suffrage. When I meet with my parlement, it is to listen to discussion of the law that I bring there and to decide for myself about the registration with all the facts before me: that is what I did on 19 November last."[6] The two sides staked their positions in a repetition of a charade of the reign of Louis XV.

In August 1788 the old regime went bankrupt, suspending payments from the royal treasury and calling the Estates General for the following May. The ancien régime had collapsed. The Revolution began when the king's reform efforts failed. He gave in to the wishes of notables, parlementaires, and some clerics. Eventually he capitulated to the Third Estate, which on 17 June 1789 declared itself and those who joined it a National Assembly representing the whole nation. But the language of absolutism did not disappear immediately. Three days after the famous Tennis Court Oath, Louis addressed the moribund Estates General as if nothing had happened: "It is the king's will that the former distinction of the three orders of the state be preserved in its entirety, as essential to the constitution of his kingdom." The "king's will" had hitherto been law.[7] In the Declaration of the Rights of Man and Citizen (August 1789), however, law became: "the expression of the general will; all citizens have the right to concur personally or through their representatives in its formation; it must be the same for all, whether it protects or punishes. All citizens being equal in its eyes are equally admissible to all the honors, positions, and public employments, according to their capabilities and without other distinction than that of their virtues and talents."[8]

By the philosophy of the Declaration, legislators do not have an original authority over citizens but express the will of citizens through a mandate. Communication becomes almost reflexive, the people talking through their representatives to the people. The absolute veto was denied the king in October 1789, and Louis even had difficulty using his suspensive veto, which theoretically overruled the opposition of two legislatures. When in spring 1792 Louis tried to veto legislation affecting refractory priests and émigrés, he helped bring down the monarchy.

Before then, the National Assembly had begun to respond to petitions and protests from citizens. The Assembly's decree of 4 August 1789, more than any other legislation, responded to the grievances of the cahiers. It called for order in the provinces, where peasants, impelled by the Great Fear, were burning châteaux, but it also promised relief: "The National Assembly, considering that the first and most sacred of its duties is to make individual and private interests cede to the general interest, [declares that] the taxes would be much less burdensome for the people if they were distributed equally over the whole citizenry according to their abilities to pay."[9] The contrast between this language and that of the monarchy obscures one point. The king had been a benevolent if authoritarian père du peuple. Until stripped of real power, he continued to swear loyalty to the constitution.

After autumn 1789 communication ceased between sovereign and subject and took the form of decrees between representatives of the national sovereignty and citizens. These had to be read three times at different sessions of the National Assembly, discussed, and voted on. If approved, they went to the king for "sanction," at which time they became "laws." The Assembly had the right to declare war if the king so proposed and—an important right—to decree on budgetary matters without the king's sanction. The decrees reserved for royal sanction were promulgated as follows: "[Louis] by the grace of God, and by the constitutional law of the State, king of the French, To all Present and to come, Salut, The National Assembly has decreed, and We wish and order what follows: . . ." The dual authorship of the decrees reflected the regime's dual nature of authority.[10]

The declaration of war on 20 April 1792 radicalized the Revolution. The Assembly issued decrees almost daily. The king vetoed only occasionally, which was one reason for the outrage when he did. In this time of emergency, the National Assembly frequently used a constitutional provision that allowed deputies to omit the ordinary delays of reading a decree by declaring a "state of urgency": "The National Assembly after having decreed urgency, decrees what follows. . . ." This all circumvented the need for a royal sanction. The language of these decrees was dry and direct, and their number constituted a veritable legislative avalanche, which counterrevolutionaries like Joseph de Maistre ridiculed. Many were really directives of an assembly exercising considerable executive powers. In the first ten days of April, the Assembly drew up no fewer than eighteen decrees. On 3 April Minister of the Interior Roland submitted to the Assembly a list of sixteen decrees that, sanctioned by the king, had become law. The king used

the maximum delay of two months on only one decree; he approved
the rest within two weeks. On 5 April Roland submitted another list of
eleven decrees sanctioned by the king.[11]

The constitution of 1793, drawn up to define the newly created Republic, distinguished between laws and decrees. Decrees concerned
urgent matters, such as national security, public assistance, currency,
and conspiracies; laws concerned more stable things, such as general
administration, taxes, and public instruction. Laws were preceded by a
report and voted on after a fifteen-day delay, and then only provi-
sionally. Once approved by the National Assembly, they would be sent
to all the "communes of the Republic" and approved unless no more
than a tenth of the primary assemblies protested. The law would be
prefaced by the following words: "In the name of the French people,
Year————of the French Republic."[12]

Although approved by a national referendum that July, the constitution of 1793 was never enacted. The decree of revolutionary
government superseded it in December 1793. The Committee of Public Safety, the grand committee of twelve, headed by Robespierre
(fig. x.1), instead issued "orders"—*arrêts,* or decisions—in the name
of the Convention. This established the government of the Jacobin
dictatorship, which was conceived of as perfectly compatible with
popular sovereignty. As Barère put it: "We speak without interruption
of dictatorship; I know of only one that is legitimate, that is necessary and that the Nation wanted, it is [that of] the national Convention;
it is by you that the Nation exercises its dictatorship over itself; and I
believe that that is the only dictatorship which free and enlightened
men can endure." But the Convention had a dictatorial arm in the
Committee of Public Safety, and the roving "representatives on mission" from the Assembly had a power in their departments that was
quasi-absolute. "All is submitted to your power," the representatives
were told in May 1793, "all the civil and military functionaries are
accountable to you." So armed, these representatives could and did
purge local administrations and watch committees and carry out de-
Christianization measures. They executed Convention decrees and
Committee of Public Safety orders, such as those declaring aristocrats
and counterrevolutionaries outside the law and subject to appear before the revolutionary Tribunal.[13]

But the Committee of Public Safety ruled supreme with a bureaucracy of *agents* and *commis.* The committee demanded secrecy, confidence, and speed:

X.I.

Portrait of Robespierre, *engraving from painting by [Pierre Narcisse Baron] Guerin, ca. 1794.*

Courtesy Library of Congress, photo: John Reynolds.

We need a general secretary of great merit, an office of particularly intelligent and patriotic secretaries and agents equally ready to transmit the orders of the Committee to those who must execute them; it is necessary for those who are to execute them to give an account to the Committee within twenty-four hours; we have to determine to whom the orders will be confided and by whom they will be transmitted; we need very reliable couriers attached to the Committee. . . . The Committee must be closed and inaccessible, apart from extraordinary cases, and there must be agents to maintain this aspect of its supervision.[14]

The Committee of General Security had a parallel bureaucracy (although not nearly as large) of commis and agents to arrest suspects. The committees were to know all but were to use extreme caution in divulging their affairs to the public.

Summer 1793 saw resistance to the Jacobin dictatorship from the rightist anti-Jacobin Federalists, whose revolt pitted more than half of France against the Convention, and from the enragés and sansculottes to the left of the Jacobins. The enragés, led by Jacques Roux in the name of two sections of Paris, Gravilliers and Bonne-Nouvelle, and the Cordelier Club fulminated in a manifesto of 25 June 1793:

A hundred times this sacred place has echoed the crimes of egoists and of villains; you have always promised to strike the bloodsuckers of the people. The constitutional act is about to be presented for the sanction of the sovereign [the people]. . . . Have you pronounced the death penalty against hoarders? No. Have you determined in what liberty of commerce consists? No. Have you prohibited the sale of silver money? No. And so! We declare to you that you have not done all for the liberty of the people. . . . Who could believe that the representatives of the French people, who declared war on foreign tyrants, were so cowardly as not to crush those within?[15]

A more intimate, friendly tone, one of confidence, could prevail between the sovereign people and their representatives, particularly between the sansculottes in Paris or the popular societies and the Convention. It was even officially stamped in the universal adoption of the familiar "tu" form, without any trace of condescension, when addressing the sansculottes:

Out of contempt, fanaticism, pride, and feudalism, we have contracted the habit of using the second person plural when we speak to one person. Many evils still result from this abuse; it is an obstacle to the intelligence of the sansculottes, it perpetuates a perverse arrogance and flattery which, under the pretext of respect, brushes aside the spirit of fraternal virtues. . . . I demand [in the name of all my constituents] a decree requiring all French republicans . . . to use the familiar thou [*tutoyer*] . . . on penalty of being declared suspect [of furthering an] inequality among us.[16]

Before dealing with popular addresses that express this intimate relationship between legislator and legislated during the Terror, it is best to turn back to 1789 for a moment and examine how legislators dealt with one another. Hans Ulrich Gumbrecht has offered a persuasive analysis of an evolution of parliamentary rhetoric from the speeches of Mirabeau, which aimed to persuade unconvinced listeners to accept new propositions, to the epideictic discourse of the Mountain (one designation of the Jacobins who sat high on the left of the Convention) in 1793, which presumed unanimity at the outset and confirmed a consensus, although it masked a divergence of interests.[17] The first kind of rhetoric is functional: it is supposed to produce something, namely, a consensus. The second, epideictic, is largely ceremonial: it affirms unanimity and threatens all dissent.

Mirabeau's appeal on 7 July 1789 to recall ministers whose dismissal by the king on 11 July had helped provoke the storming of the Bastille illustrates the first kind of rhetoric. This radical demand, which broke with all tradition, since ministers were responsible to the king alone, had to be couched in language that would preempt opposition. Mirabeau thanked the king for his fatherly solicitude and addressed the deputies tactically as "we," in opposition to the "sinister ministers" (the successors of Jacques Necker), who were referred to as "they." Presumed unanimity was used as a ploy to bring about true unanimity. Controversial propositions, such as the crown's relation to the deputies, were introduced as rhetorical questions: "Have not the people placed the throne between heaven and themselves?" The answer, yes, was quite surprising, since the doctrine of divine right stated that God, not the people, placed the king on his throne. Mirabeau conveyed a major theoretical innovation as accepted wisdom. By introducing the bold new notion of the monarchy in the rhetorical vein, he reduced the chance of a negative response. He circumvented the burden of proof, and his listeners predictably hesitated to disagree with something that appeared to be self-evident. Mirabeau succeeded: Necker and his ministers were recalled. The issue was important. A precedent was established concerning the relationship among king, people, and deputies.

Rhetoric at the beginning of the Revolution was used to obviate proof, to substitute for debate, to short-circuit parliamentary procedure. Listeners were gradually induced to consent to propositions, which, if plainly enunciated from the outset, would never have been approved. Rhetoric broke down resistance by making sudden departures from custom seem less radical.

After the monarchy had fallen, parliamentary rhetoric became less a tool to build unanimity in the Assembly than an expression of the interests of the two principal parliamentary groups—the Girondins and the Jacobins. These, far from being locked in ironclad positions, developed their policies after a series of turnabouts in the debate over such matters as the king's fate. Curiously, the Girondins, in voting for an "appeal to the people" on the fate of the king, who was condemned to death in January 1793, sided with advocates of direct democracy, the form of government the Jacobins officially championed through their alliance with the sansculottes. Their fear of what an appeal to the people might produce, however, belied this. Robespierre had said, "This majority [of the people] has *mœurs* [customs] . . . but it does not have finesse or eloquence."[18]

Between 2 June 1793 and 27 July 1794, parliamentary rhetoric and communication changed, as by now speakers and listeners were presumed to have identical knowledge and convictions. The role of rhetoric as persuasion, with consensus as its goal, was superseded by a discourse in which consensus was the premise and its celebration the end.

But beneath this epideictic function of discourse in the Terror existed divergent interests—of the sansculottes, the indulgents, and the enragés. The addresses after Marat's assassination (13 July 1793) insisted on the need of terror to crush the (Federalist) conspiracy within. These sansculotte demands were couched in such abstractions as "la dignité nationale outragée" (national dignity outraged). Under the veil of a unanimous "nous" and a confidential "vous" lay references to "conspirators who sit still in the national Convention." Hence the threat of more expulsions, prescriptions, and even executions of legislators.[19]

Fear and distrust lurked beneath the assurances of epideictic speech of the triumph of wish over reality, certitude over doubt. The future of the Revolution after the expulsion of the Girondins on 1 June and the murder of Marat was open, and this openness produced anxiety. The Jacobins chose terror, with its suppression of civil liberties, to master this uncertain future and the fear it produced. Epideictic speech, including festival and theater discourse, was effective in its redundancy. It allayed the worries of both speaker and audience.[20]

The addresses of the popular societies to the Convention in January and February 1794, through the tropes and metaphors of republicanism, reveal the new relationship between citizen and government. In light of epideictic discourse's function as assurance (Gumbrecht) and François Furet's insistence on the need to translate Jacobin rhetoric and not take it at face value, the addresses take on new light. To begin with, there are their modes of salutation: "Citoyens représentans," "Représentans," "Citoyens législateurs," "Citoyen président," or simply "Citoyens." The authors and addressees, citizens alike, establish a relationship of equality. The president of the Convention is, moreover, addressed with the familiar "tu." Such familiarity with government officials, with deputies and ministers, would have been unthinkable before 1792 and would become so again after the Terror. In signing off, the authors of these letters used one of several republican expressions: "Salut, Respect, et Fraternité," "Salut et fraternité," "S. et F.," "Vive la République une et indivisible," "Vive la Montagne," or no salutation at all.

These Republican salutations suggest not only equality but an identity of views between constituents and representatives. The addresses of the popular societies criticize the Mountain in no way, the addresses of individuals only occasionally. The Convention rhetoric of classical allusion—to Brutus or Tarquin—was also used in the addresses of the popular societies, where an educated popular teacher could set the tone. The commune of Arnay-sur-Arroux's popular society, for example, wrote: "Following the example of Decius, you have dedicated yourselves to the people without fearing the words of Pyrrhus, and the genius of liberty has inspired you." In tribute to itself, another popular society wrote: "Citizens, the Popular Society of Rebais has just regenerated a region where superstition has long occupied its altars. New Prometheuses, we have stolen a spark of the fire which animates you." Another common ancient symbol of strength was Hercules. As the Popular Society of Montmeillant (Ardennes) put it: "The strength [*massue*] of Hercules with which you are armed and the buckle of Minerva which defends you should not leave your hands until the hydra of aristocracy has been reduced to ashes and there is no more trace of its blood on the globe."[21] The main thrust of these societies was to extirpate the triple foes of the Revolution—kings, priests, and aristocrats, especially kings. The popular society of Arnay-sur-Arroux spoke of "punishing the crimes of the last of our tyrants," and that of Moreau claimed to have "buried royalty long before the death of Capet."[22] Regicide was important even one year after Louis XVI's demise.

The rhetoric of de-Christianization predictably juxtaposed reason and nature against fanaticism and superstition. The Montagnard Society of Estang wrote: "Each day reason makes new progress among us. . . . Imposture, fanaticism, superstition are overthrown and confounded . . . truth alone triumphs. Our priests press forward to abjure all errors, our former churches are either closed or converted into temples of reason destined to instruct people and to make known their rights. Our so-called Saints have come down from their niches, and the silver from the cult is making its way to the Mint. . . . one can say that the [people] have risen to the occasion."[23] And the Society of Franconville-la-Libre proclaimed: "We do not have any temple; but under the vault of the sky and on a simple altar like the truth, we offer to the divinity some acts of bienfaisance and we are persuaded that humanity, union, virtue are also a cult which can please the supreme being."[24]

But the new order was not established automatically, and the popular societies were aware of the rocky road ahead. Plots, subversion, and invasion threatened. The Society of Orthez blamed "machinators, true enemies of the people, [who] have dared to conspire against unity and indivisibility, and these perverse men are the members of the Convention who sit on the right side." After acclaiming the fall of Toulon, the Society of Etaples urged the razing of the city: "This retreat of crowned brigands, which was supposed to become the den of counter-revolution in the Midi, [must] disappear from the ranks of the cities [fig. x.2]. Legislators, we need a great example and severe measures; you have decreed them." (Indeed, Toulon was deprived of its status as capital of the Var until the 1970s.) Speaking of a recent purge of its members, the representative of the people B. Gouly wrote to the Convention from Belley: "The Popular Society has conducted a purge [*scrutin épuratoire*] in which the *messieurs* and those who wanted to appear as such have been taken care of as they should have been."[25]

All these letters were implicitly addressed to the Mountain, the healthy part of the Convention, the true Jacobins who were ever on guard against treason from within and without. These letters thus embellished the imagery of this Mountain, symbol of the Jacobins. The commune of Boulay wrote: "Let us give thanks to the holy Mountain; it has purged the Republic of tyrants and of the principal conspirators which it held in its heart." The popular society of Bapaume wrote: "Let the holy Mountain which you inhabit be still for a time, surrounded with thundering clouds," and the Montagnard Society of Estang broke out into rhapsody: "Achieve Holy Mountain, Achieve the work which you have so happily begun" (fig. x.3). None of these addresses includes a word of criticism, unlike the cahiers of 1789 and unlike the petitions before Jacobin supremacy. The Terror abridged the freedom of the popular societies and the occasional brave individu-

X.2.

J.-B. Regnault, Liberty or Death, *an III [1794–95].*
Courtesy Kunsthalle, Hamburg, photo: © Ralph Kleinhempel.

als who dared to criticize. Jacobinism was predicated on unanimity, unlike politics in the old regime, which was predicated on clear distinctions among subject, sovereign, and the intermediary bodies that linked them. Whereas subjects had been expected to obey, petitions were recognized forms of communication.[26]

In Convention politics, addresses became a form of flattery. No dis-

X.3.
Crockery depicting the Mountain, or the Jacobins, with a pike topped by a
phrygian bonnet, 1793–94.
Courtesy Musée des arts et traditions populaires, Paris, photo: Musées nationaux, Paris.

tance separated constituents from representatives. A powerful soli-
darity united both in a common cause, one fostered by external opposition and internal subversion. The addresses expressed the general
will. The goal was unanimity, a binding of different parts of the Republic. Use of a common language with common tropes was a means
through which the Convention acknowledged these authors. Above
all, authors wanted their addresses to be inserted in the Convention's
Bulletin, if possible with an "honorable mention" as insurance against
unforeseen accusations of sedition, counterrevolution, or moderatism.
The very process by which societies were formed, the scrutin épura-

toire, the imposing model of sister and mother societies, and the practice of fraternization whereby sister societies were compelled to vote in a certain way, guaranteed similar expressions for prescribed political positions. The frequent purging of popular societies by representatives on mission, moreover, gave the lie to the tributes' spontaneity. Dictatorship gave birth to adulation. What appeared to be unanimity might as easily have been a reflex of terror. The addresses of these societies confirm Gumbrecht's explanation of epideictic discourse: the sansculottes are telling the Convention what it already knows and what it wants to hear, with the assurance that they, the popular societies, agree wholeheartedly. Their addresses constitute a kind of incantation.

Denouncing, Informing, Swearing

Not all revolutionary discourse, even during the Terror, was encouraging or reassuring. The dualism of the rhetoric always pitted the healthier part of the Republic, the only true representatives of the general will, against the malevolent, which had to be denounced. Formal denunciations became an essential form of communication during the Terror. Ordinary citizens were encouraged to denounce individuals or groups for words or deeds hostile to the Republic. Even before the Terror—from 1789 on—the targets of denunciations included priests, aristocrats, army officers, municipal officials, hoarders, speculators, immoral persons, and recalcitrant peasants.

Jean-Paul Marat's *Ami du peuple* published innumerable denunciations beginning in September 1789. His stream of accusations were all the more frightening because they were leveled not only against aristocrats and counterrevolutionaries but against supposed agents of the people: the mayor of Paris, Jean-Sylvain Bailly (one of Marat's "modern charlatans") and his city council, elected by "active" citizens. In one of his first issues, 24 September 1789, Marat railed at his readers: "Always vexed, crushed, robbed, will you escape from the hands of royal plunderers only to fall into the hands of popular plunderers?"[27]

For Marat popular insurrection was the motor of democracy. Without it the Assembly would sleep, indifferent to the needs of the people: "Follow the works of the National Assembly, and you will find that it engaged in activity only after some popular uprising, that it decreed good laws only after some popular uprising, and that in times of calm and security, this odious faction never failed to rise up to obstruct the constitution or to pass harmful decrees." Marat (fig. x.4) is the apologist of the Revolution's violence: "The bloody scenes of the 14th of July, the 6th of October, the 10th of August, the 2nd of September . . . have saved France." On 13 November 1789 he denounced "traitors from every quarter," "perfidious enemies" who "assail" him "from every side." He condoned the "right" of every citizen to denounce everyone, from the first minister on down (fig. x.5). Ultimately, he held the authorities, the revolutionary government, the Constituent Assembly, and the town hall responsible: "The government is the mortal enemy, the eternal enemy of the people, and unfortunately this assertion is only too true." In this statement we have the pith and marrow of radical revolution: distrust of *all* authority—except for Marat's own projected dictatorship, which would (at least in theory) be wholly popular. Denunciation was the perennial weapon used against illegitimate authority; it was the raison d'être of *L'Ami du peuple.* The headlines of the issue of 3 September 1790 read: "Counterrevolution begun by the government. . . . Treason of the Blacks [counterrevolutionaries] and the ministers of the National Assembly. . . . Horrible undertakings of the counterrevolutionary [General] Bouillé. . . . Barbarous conduct of the National Guard of Metz. . . . Massacre of the regiment of Châteauvieux and of peaceful citizens of Nancy. . . . Civil war ignited in Lorraine." The response Marat demanded would be counterhorrors—massacres, uprisings, assassinations, a popular dictatorship, and heads, more and more heads.[28]

Marat was an apostle of social, if not class, war, rallying the poor against the rich, taking each occasion of a grain shortage or pension distribution to decry the "delapidators of the people." Impersonating a courtier, he asks: "How can a decorated military man obtain a pension of 400 livres for having shed his blood in defense of the people, and we do not have 15,000 livres for having remained on our sofas." And in another issue, complaining about the property qualifications for the vote, he exclaims, "Fathers of the country! You have laid hold of the goods of the poor to pay for the Sardanapaluses of the court, the favorites of the queen." The Revolution, which Marat believed the people had made, had become but a "painful dream."[29]

Only civil war, not social harmony, could save the Revolution. Nobles, Marat insisted, had abandoned their titles in 1790 only to keep their political power. The Festival of the Federation of 1790, which Michelet later described with quasi-religious exaltation as the highest expression of fraternity, was a sham for Marat, a veil covering discord. After the king's fall in August 1792, Marat laid into the Brissotins, who

X.4.

Marat at the Tribunal, *engraving, 1792–93.*

Courtesy Bibliothéque nationale, photo: Perrain-Carnavalet.

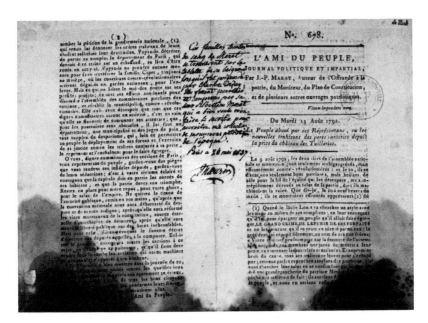

X.5.

13 August 1792 edition of Marat's Ami du peuple, *stained with his own blood from the mortal wound inflicted by Charlotte Corday, 13 July 1793. Courtesy Bibliothéque nationale, photo: Bibl. Nat. Paris.*

had to "bite the dust . . . at least 70,000 more heads are necessary in order to re-establish the republic."[30]

Denunciations could also take the more polite form of a petition. On 29 February 1792 the municipality of Saint-Flour in Cantal addressed the departmental administration to advise it on "prompt means to stop the progress of fanaticism inspired by the nonjuring priests." The Civil Constitution of the Clergy had been administered for a year and had caused deep dissension. The italicized words in the text below identify the vocabulary of revolutionary denunciation:

> Every day the law is *abused* and the enemies of the Constitution ceaselessly invoke it against itself; under the *cover of liberty* [*l'ombre de la liberté*], of religious opinions, our refractory ecclesiastics *fanaticize* the people, and armed with the *destructive* decrees of the *inquisition*, they *lock themselves* in safety in the *private houses* to exercise the functions which they cannot exercise publicly. Clever enough not to be caught in the open, they are wicked enough to preach in *secret* the most *monstrous maxims;* the language of the

stupid people who go to listen to them in their *lairs* teaches us their *antisocial doctrine* [which] they would be incapable of holding without the lessons of their *priests*. . . . The *crime,* although *hidden,* exists nonetheless and we feel only too well its *disastrous effects.* . . . Ah! see to it that the *nonjuring priests* can harm us no longer, count on all our efforts to reinforce you, without forgetting that the object of this petition is extremely *urgent* and that without this enclave of *factious sectaries,* everything would be peaceful.[31]

The language is similar to the description of villains given by Ducray-Duminil, Monvel, and Pixérécourt. This particular denunciation focuses on priests loyal to Rome, who are pictured lurking in private retreats, carrying on secretively in an unsocial manner, and refusing to come out into the public, which has become omnipotent. Crime, as Ducray-Duminil and others showed, always ferments in conventicles, in the cellars of monasteries, in caverns. The revolutionary imagination is obsessed with enclosed space, where private wills conspire against the general will. A patriot must throw light on these recesses of crime.

A second illustration of this phenomenon is the denunciation leveled against M. de Narbonne, minister of war in 1792, just a month before France declared war against Austria. The Assembly was divided over the advisability of such a declaration, partly because of a perceived inadequacy in military preparations. If true, the war might be lost, which many believed was the secret intention of the court, for it needed foreign intervention to restore its authority. The military's weakness was thus seen as a conspiracy rather than as incompetence. The denunciation of Narbonne, whose portfolio had been revoked ten days earlier, came from a municipal officer of the Pyrénées Orientales who complained of the poor defenses along France's Spanish border.

> It is evident that the first duty of M. de Narbonne should have been to put the different fortifications in the best state of defense. If he did not do it, he is a *traitor* worthy of the *ultimate punishment.* . . . In the name of the entire country, I accuse M. de Narbonne, whom I denounce to the Assembly as a traitor, for having until now left Perpignan, this important key to our frontiers with Spain, without any point of defense. This attack is direct and precise: I demand that the former minister of war, M. de Narbonne, be put in a *state of accusation* before the High National Court.[32]

In the old regime, denunciations were the work of *mouchards,* police spies, who ratted on individuals. The Revolution made denunciation a civic duty that citizens had to perform for the safety of the patrie. The surveillance and revolutionary committees, which arose immediately after the overthrow of the king in the municipalities and departments, were given this responsibility by the law of 11 August 1792. Denunciations were originally directed against foreigners but increasingly turned against the French. In the west and other areas of acute turmoil they could lead to confiscations of property, imprisonments, and even the guillotine. Girondins and their sympathizers originally peopled the committees, but after the proscription of the Paris Girondins in June 1793 and the organization of the Terror in September 1793, sansculottes were installed in their place. Such a committee typically included a barber, an innkeeper, a saloonkeeper—people who had frequent opportunity to listen to what others were saying. At Angers one member of a watch committee observed: "Denunciations, which were hateful under the old regime because they served tyranny, have now become legitimate because today they are intended for the good of all."[33] Denunciations were not necessarily made publicly, as was that leveled against Narbonne. Private citizens could denounce one another on the grounds of hearsay or personal observations, making formal declarations against them to surveillance committees or the police, who kept a record of such statements.

The Ministry of the Interior had a team of a dozen agents working the cafés, theaters, and marketplaces of Paris, eavesdropping on citizens, sizing up the opinion of the public, whose loyalty was of the utmost importance to the great committee and to the Convention. The task was not always easy. One agent, Perreire, reported on 2 ventôse Year II (20 February 1794): "Spirit of the cafés.—I entered one of the most frequented cafés of the Maison Egalité [former Palais Royal]. . . . The few persons whom I found ready to speak were as ignorant as I; the others had the air of defending themselves against a question that might be a trap; almost all of them talked about inconsequential things, as if they had no patrie, and were concerned with frivolous games." The informant went on to advocate liberty of opinions in the belief that people would talk freely, but this, of course, overlooked the effect of surveillance. The constitution of 1793, like that of 1791, guaranteed freedom of opinion, but the law of 14 frimaire (4 December 1793), creating the revolutionary government, made the *salut du peuple* a supreme law that preempted civil rights. Commercial freedom was sacrificed to the maximum price on staples in order to provision the cities and the army at a time of shortages and devalued *assignat* currency. The black market, the illegal sale of hard currency, the double price standard (one in paper currency, the other in hard money), the refusal to sell for assignats, the removal of goods from certain districts—all were violations subject to scrutiny by the minister's agents. In the report cited above, Perreire recounted an incident in which a man was found far from the gates of Paris meeting an acquaintance who slipped him a forbidden two-pound loaf of bread. "What can you do to prevent such abuses?" the agent queried. "Shall we search citizens at the gates, as in former times? No, this custom is unworthy of republicans; but we must prevent the bakers from making bread of 2 pounds and punish those whom we find in violation of this law."[34]

These agents made no arrests—they communicated, they informed. They read into what people said, they divined intentions and motives. Their reactions could be positive or denunciatory. Along with the popular societies, the revolutionary and surveillance committees, the Committee of General Security, they acted as the watching eyes (*yeux surveillants*) of the Republic.

Oaths were the converse of denunciations. In denunciations, people ratted on their neighbors to the officials of national sovereignty in the interest of public safety. Oaths, by contrast, were assurances elicited by the authorities from citizens, particularly from citizens whose loyalty was considered questionable. The clergy, with its centuries of allegiance to Rome, however attenuated by Gallicanism, was the most suspect, and from it continual oaths were demanded—no fewer than six between 1790 and 1801.

But clerics were not the only oathtakers. Persons born of one or more foreign parents or persons born abroad also took the oaths of 1790 to foreswear foreign allegiance. The colossal crowd at the Festival of the Federation swore the same oath as did the king, civil servants, and schoolteachers. This was the most important oath of the Revolution, and the words common to all groups swearing it read: "[I swear] to be faithful to the nation, to the law, and to the king and to maintain with all [my] power the constitution decreed by the National Assembly and accepted by the king." Ecclesiastics charged with parishes and dioceses, moreover, swore to "watch over with care the faithful of the diocese, or of the parish which is confided [to me]." After the fall of the monarchy on 3 September 1792, a second oath of fidelity "to liberty and equality" and "to die for the execution of the Law" was administered. After the Terror on 29 September 1795, an oath recognizing "the universality of citizens as sovereign" and a promise of "submission to the laws of the Republic" were taken. And after the royalists' (for many were loyal to the Pretender, the comte de

Provence) electoral returns of Fructidor Year V (August–September 1797) an oath of "hatred to royalty and anarchy" (the twin enemies of the Directory) was demanded. Those who took it were dubbed *les haineux* (the spiteful ones) by their opponents. The Consulate demanded two more oaths, the first a promise of fidelity and obedience to the government, and the second a promise to reveal plots harmful to the state.[35] This was clearly a scaling down of revolutionary oathtaking.

The citizen who took an oath identified his private will with that of the nation as represented by the government. It could be used as a form of coercion to obtain allegiance otherwise not forthcoming. It also made intentions known, for it required citizens to declare themselves publicly at one with the general will. Whereas denunciations were directed at individuals who failed to obey this will, the oath was a solemn swearing of such obedience. It was enshrined in the prerevolutionary and revolutionary paintings of David and the Swiss-born Henry Fuseli. It was an art of patriotism par excellence, a giving of one's self, one's will, to the patrie.

Needless to say, oaths can be modified or annulled, depending upon the taker. This happened in the Revolution in various ways. One method was through mental reservations expressed viva voce while taking the oath, such as an ecclesiastic might place on the oath of 1790, making it contingent on the pope's approval of the Civil Constitution of the Clergy. The second case involved a retraction of the oath by the taker, either because it violated his conscience or because he changed his mind, a not uncommon practice with the oath of 1790. A third involved an individual who took an oath through intimidation—for example, threat of loss of position or of liberty. Such conditions could cloud the very transparency that oaths were supposed to reveal. Hypocrisy, as Benjamin Constant observed, then became a means of personal survival—of blinding the authorities to private thoughts.[36]

Intimately tied to oaths and denunciations was the *carte de civisme,* issued during the Terror as a *laisser passer* in the interior of France, and *passe-portes,* whose history was in large part formed by the French Revolution. A carte de civisme issued by the local revolutionary or surveillance committee attested to an individual's mœurs and patriotism. Passports, which were first issued on a large scale in 1789, were granted only to reliable people who had good reason to leave the country, which would theoretically exclude emigration. Passports and civic cards attested to good standing with the government and were issued by it, unlike the oath, which was sworn by the individual from a formula provided by the government. Together, they purported to reveal how an individual stood in relation to sovereignty. The presence and absence of these attestations (the oath frequently being a condition of the civic card or passport) stamped a citizen as good or bad, patriot or malevolent, and were thus vital signs of communication in a double sense: they informed and they permitted or prevented free circulation.[37]

The Press and Patois

The press informs, persuades, interprets, and watches over the public interest. Whereas police surveillance targets individuals or groups, the press focuses attention primarily at public authorities. It has been recently maintained that the revolutionary press did not really shape public opinion but merely relayed information and points of view—gathered in the Assembly, in the clubs, in popular societies, in cafés and cabarets—to the public. The exact relation between public opinion and the press may never be discovered. Assuming the least original role—that of simply reporting public opinion rather than creating it—is the press insignificant? Is not the transmittal of information and opinion an essential role of communication?

The press took varied forms in France in the 1790s: official organs like *Le Moniteur,* organs of factions or parties like Brissot's *Patriote français,* counterrevolutionary writings like the *Actes des apôtres,* and scientific periodicals that survived the upheaval. Our task is to try to understand the importance of the press in its premodern, but post–ancien régime, form and its connection to the events of the Revolution and to the limits imposed on it by technology, transportation, illiteracy, and poverty.

The Preamble to the Declaration of the Rights of Man and Citizen states that "the contempt of the rights of man are the only causes of public misfortunes and the corruption of governments." Article 11 states that one of the most precious rights of man is "the free communication of his thoughts and opinions. . . . Every citizen can therefore speak, write, print freely, except insofar as he is liable for the abuses of this liberty in cases determined by law."

On 5 July 1788, a year before this declaration, the king's council permitted the free ventilation of opinions in preparation for the Estates General. Over six hundred pamphlets were soon published—an outburst such as France had not seen since the Fronde. Mirabeau and

Brissot defied the remaining restrictions on newspapers during the meeting of the Estates General by publishing, respectively, the *Patriote français* and the *Courrier de Provence*. Volney made his *Sentinel du peuple* the organ of the Breton Club, the precursor of the Jacobin Club.

One authority asserts that copies of over 2,000 French revolutionary newspapers are extant today. Many consisted of just several pages and appeared for only a few issues; nonetheless, this figure represents a staggering amount of print. In 1790, some 335 newspapers were published (not all of them simultaneously). Reading, which foreigners considered widespread in Paris, focused almost exclusively on ephemera—posters, newssheets, pamphlets (fig. x.6). Books, according to Louis-Sébastien Mercier, were "too substantial" for the needs of the times. Newspapers were often literally fleeting; a fifth of them appeared for only one issue, 80 percent for fewer than a dozen. Newspapers belonged to the seventeenth-century tradition of *feuilles volantes* and *canards* more than to the mass media of the late nineteenth or twentieth centuries.[38]

Although general statistics for book publishing are unavailable, due to suppression of the old regime censors, a case study of the family firm of Berger-Levrault in Strasbourg shows that a depression in publishing began in 1789 and ended in 1791, after which there was a "remarkable expansion beginning in 1792, leveling off in 1793." As early as 1789, however, the general characteristics of revolutionary publishing were apparent. Of books published by the firm, 74 percent were in the field of administration. The *livre et société* scholars noticed this trend on a national level, finding that the preponderance of permitted titles were in the social sciences, rather than theology and belles lettres, which had dominated the old regime. During prerevolutionary days the Levraults had the title of "imprimeur de l'Assemblée provinciale." Thanks to their friend Dietrich, municipal officer and then mayor of Strasbourg at the beginning of the Revolution, they received orders from the new municipal government. The sales of Berger-Levrault quadrupled, and the number of its employees increased from sixteen in 1788 to forty at the end of the Revolution. *Placards* (posters) and copies of laws and decrees poured out. The publishers almost always printed a *pièce* rather than a book. Items of over three hundred pages comprised 8 percent of production early in the Revolution but only 2 percent in the period 1791–95, whereas publications of fewer than one hundred pages comprised 75 percent of all production. Political brochures, speeches, and funeral orations doubled; religious texts de-

x.6.
Louis-Léopold Boilly, The Newspapers, *engraving, ca. 1795[?].*
Courtesy Bibliothèque nationale, photo: Lauros-Giraudon/Art Resource, New York.

clined from about 16 percent in 1786–90 to 1 percent during the Directory; and Latin virtually disappeared as a published language.[39]

The growth of ephemera during the Revolution corresponded to the quickening tempo of events, the absence of the leisure and tranquility needed to read a book, and the mandate to rewrite the laws of France

from the national government down to the commune. Tens of thousands of elected officials, never unanimous in their views, wrote hundreds of thousands of pamphlets.

The old regime press, with some forty Parisian and one hundred provincial organs, has recently been considered a more genuine press in terms of its volume, scope, coverage, and quality than was previously thought. It was also—particularly in the foreign French press, such as the *Gazette de Leyde*—more political and oppositional. But the domestic French press was subject to the regime of privilège, to strict censorship, and was generally not permitted to comment adversely on ministerial or royal policy. It was thus rather staid, containing information rather than opinion. Publications of the French revolutionary press, on the contrary, were usually the mouthpiece of one man, frequently a deputy like Brissot or Mirabeau, who made it a "letter to his constituents." It was opinionated, aggressive, and even defamatory toward opponents, no matter how highly placed they were.[40]

The revolutionary process accelerated the division of the national will—a process that had begun in the old regime. The energized Jacobin will under the Terror was not national in comprehension. Under the Directory leaders tried strenuously to create a republican (non-Jacobin) consensus by legal means, but this also failed, and the party of the Directory was obliged to cancel unconstitutionally the royalist electoral returns on 18 fructidor Year V (4 September 1797) and the Jacobin electoral returns of 22 floréal Year VI (11 May 1798) to safeguard its majority.

Mirabeau's *Courrier de Provence* represented the patriot position in 1789, by defending, for example, the massacres at the storming of the Bastille. It could run to as many as eighty pages on a thrice-weekly basis but averaged about thirty pages an issue. Circulated all over France, it was coedited by the future Girondin Etienne Clavière, Etienne Dumont, the abbé Lamourette, and the academician Sébastien-Roch-Nicolas Chamfort.

Brissot's *Patriote français* enjoyed the collaboration of Bancal des Issarts, the abbé Grégoire, Pierre-Louis Manuel, the future leader of the commune, and Jerome Pétion de Villeneuve, the future mayor of Paris. It advocated the abolition of titles, praised ecclesiastical marriages, lampooned bishops, and opposed the veto that Mirabeau wanted to give the king. At four pages, it was considerably shorter than Mirabeau's paper.

To the far left was Prudhomme's *Révolutions de Paris,* invariably long and diverse, and Camille Desmoulins's *Révolutions de France et de Brabant,* which devoted two of its three sections to politics and the third to that staple of old regime publications—book reviews and theater criticism. Prudhomme's newspaper reached fifty-six pages per issue, Desmoulins's a weekly average of forty-eight pages. *L'Ami du peuple* of Marat, which averaged two to eight pages daily, was the most radical of the three "Cordelier" papers, all of which were in print by autumn 1789. In June 1790 the *Père Duchesne* of Hébert, the future enragé, joined the chorus of denunciations led by Marat, but with the distinction of appealing to the sansculottes artisans and salaried workers with vulgar language and frequent profanities. By 1791 the *Père Duchesne* was posing as the "Jacobin Jésus," attacking aristocrats.[41]

To the right of this spectrum was the *Journal de Paris*—reliable, largely unopinionated, "official" in the sense of leaning toward the constitutional monarchy. Many consider Mallet du Pan, a Swiss like Clavière, Dumont, and company, to have been the most astute political analyst of the Revolution. He began his career publishing the *Mercure de France,* and by the end of the Revolution he published the *Mercure britannique.* Such royalist journals as the *Rocambole des journaux,* the *Actes des apôtres,* and *L'Ami du roi,* to which the journalist the comte Antoine de Rivarol contributed, seemed to have been more sarcastic and ironic than the patriot papers, because the Revolution seemed to them to parody the rules both of government and of social organization. The *Actes* ran fifty-five numbers, from spring 1789 into 1790, on a thrice-weekly basis. As Jacques Godechot observed: "Properly speaking, the text of the *Actes* is an extraordinary mixture of epigrams, charades, madrigaux, enigmas, acrostics, riddles, anagrams, all destined to cut down the patriots."[42] *L'Ami du roi* was a continuation of the *Année littéraire* of Elie Fréron, the enemy of Voltaire who in his columns attacked Protestants, Freemasons, and philosophes.

The specialized press of the old regime and its strictly informational papers, *Gazette nationale* and *Petites Affiches,* survived the onset of the Revolution for varying lengths of time. The *Petites Affiches* was published through the decade with its announcements of horses and real estate sales and listings of theater performances. But more specialized papers, such as the *Journal d'histoire naturelle,* were discontinued in 1792, and the learned *Journal des savants* and the *Annales de chimie* ceased publication in 1793. The order of the day was politics, not chemistry, although rather remarkably the *Mémoires* of the Academy of Sciences continued with interruptions throughout the Revolution.[43]

Although freedom of the press had been declared, censorship continued and at times was even stricter than during the old regime (although privilege and prior censorship no longer existed). This was not entirely inconsistent with principle, since the Declaration of Rights of 1789 allowed the legislature to repress abuses of the press. The concept of a general will, moreover, was in itself intolerant of political "factions" and thus inimical to political pluralism. Obscene brochures and prints, frequently mixing politics with pornography, were continually being confiscated in the Palais Royal. But one did not need to be pornographic to be exposed to libel charges. American historian Leonard Levy has shown that freedom of the press in the American states in this period meant freedom from prior censorship but not freedom from subsequent punishment for defamation, such as confiscation of copy and even destruction of presses. In France in May 1792, for instance, the High Court accused Marat of having provoked indiscipline in the army with the 3 May 1792 issue of *L'Ami du peuple*. His papers and possessions were sealed. On 12 August 1792 the Commune of Paris ordered the suspension of all anticivic papers. The writers of *L'Ami du roi*, the *Gazette de Paris*, and the *Mercure de France* were arrested, their presses confiscated and turned over to patriotic journalists. After the Girondins were expelled from the Convention on 31 May 1793, the press of Gorsas, a Girondin (*Courrier des 83 départements*) was broken up by forty men dressed as dragoons. Repression did not become general until after the laws of ventôse (March 1794). During the trial of Louis XVI in January 1793 it was still possible to read rightist papers. After the declaration of the Terror the following September and, even more, after the execution of the Hébertists and the Dantonists in March and April 1794, the clamp on the opposition tightened.[44]

A number of journalists were guillotined, though not solely because of their journalism: Brissot, Gorsas, Carra, Girey-Duplay, Duplain, Charnois, Parisot, Pascal Boyer, Simon Linguet and Camille Desmoulins, then editor of the *Vieux Cordelier*. Marat, of course, was assassinated.[45]

Article 355 of the constitution of the Year III (1795) stated that there could be "no limitation on the liberty of the press" except in circumstances that "make it necessary," an exception that after Fructidor Year V permitted broad censorship. Before that, during the first Directory, some liberty of the press existed, but after Fructidor the Directory found itself torn by a contradiction that has become classic to fledgling democracies: if forced to resort to unconstitutional procedures—such as coups or suppression of basic liberties (for example, that of the press)—in order to survive, how could it still call itself truly representative? Conversely, how could it allow such freedom to be used by royalists or Jacobins for the purpose of overturning the republican regime? The Central Bureau of the Directory took the authoritarian course: it actively supervised the censorship of such papers and journals as the *Quotidienne*, the *Nouvelliste politique*, the *Censeur dramatique*, the *Publiciste,* and the *Journal de Toulouse.* A total of thirty-four papers in Fructidor Year V alone succumbed.[46]

Many papers reappeared under new names to face another round of censorship and surveillance, which could not have happened as easily or as frequently during the Terror. Journalists behaved toward censors like mice toward cats, disappearing and reappearing, trying to avoid the final strike. The government also coopted measures used formerly by the Terror: It assured the loyalty of certain presses (the *Rédacteur,* the *Défenseur de la patrie*) through subsidies and by inserting official articles. A table of such contributions from 26 nivôse to 20 ventôse Year VI (January–February 1798) lists 67 articles given to eleven newspapers, including of course the *Moniteur* (14), the *Rédacteur* (10), and the *Ami des lois* (3) but also the *Journal des campagnes* (1), and the Jacobin *Journal des hommes libres* (3) (even the opposition press could be used). Freedom of the press, then, was not absolute, nor could it have been. One could get something into print more easily during the Directory than before 1787, but if it criticized the government, there were consequences.[47]

Newspapers were the work of fewer than a dozen men, sometimes one man, as in Marat's case. The Stanhope press, capable of turning out six thousand copies a day, was unknown in France. Instead, wooden presses producing only half the volume were the rule. Paper was made of rags and was rough and granular; it was dyed and folded in quarto, octavo, or sixteenmo. With the exception of a few papers, such as the *Moniteur,* French revolutionary newspapers were not the full sheets of modern journalism. Typographical and spelling errors abounded. Subscriptions could vary from seven to fifteen livres a year for the *Feuille villageoise* to thirty-six livres a year for Brissot's *Patriote français*—a fortnight's wages for a Parisian worker. The high cost of production limited circulation drastically, although journalism could be profitable. The editor attended sessions of the Assembly, frequented the usual outlets of gossip and opinion, cafés and clubs, and then sat down to write. Some called themselves *logogrophes,* antecedents of court stenographers. Their minutes are our principal source of information about Assembly debates.[48]

How many people did they reach? One estimate puts press circulation in the old regime at 30,000 to 50,000—that is, a fraction of 1 percent of the population. The figure may have tripled in the Revolution to 150,000. Circulation of individual papers frequently numbered a few hundred copies, rarely above ten thousand. François-Noël Babeuf's *Tribun du peuple* had around 600 subscribers. The press baron of the century, Charles-Joseph Panckoucke, owned several papers totaling 29,000 readers; the Jacobin *Journal des hommes libres* had a circulation of some 3,500; the *Ami des lois* of Sibuet and Bourbon Graves in the second Directory was printed in editions of five thousand copies, and the editor of the *Rédacteur* listed his subscribers at 1,030. The Feuillant Antoine Etienne, editor of the *Journal du soir,* asked commissioners of the Legislative Assembly if he could have five places opposite the tribune for two editors and two copyists, pointing out that his newspaper was "printed every evening at 10,000 copies and read by at least 40,000 persons." He may have inflated his figures to get the places, but his calculation of four readers for every copy was standard. Cafés, clubs, and *cabinets littéraires* supplied multiple readers per subscription. In general the reading audience of eighteenth-century newspapers, even those of Babeuf's *Tribun du peuple,* consisted of the professional bourgeoisie, the clergy, army officers, bureaucrats and officeholders, and *cultivateurs,* or landed proprietors of the countryside.[49]

How much was the *Feuille villageoise,* founded by Joseph-Antoine Cerutti in 1790, an exception to this rule? Set up to win French peasants to the Revolution, it was one of about twenty papers destined for the countryside. In 1790 Cerutti was a moderate partisan of the *monarchien* party, but he moved gradually to the left, eventually embracing de-Christianization. His journal lasted from 1790 to 1795 for one of the longest runs and possibly one of the widest circulations of the decade. Contemporary estimates of its subscriptions range from 8,000 to 16,500, and historians estimate that each copy reached 20 persons. The Committee of Public Instruction subscribed 2,000 communes to the paper, and the department of the Gers subscribed all of its 599 communes in 1793. Only a thorough study of local archives can disclose how deeply it penetrated the countryside through the popular societies and priests, who were encouraged to read it to peasants. In the absence of a subscription list—a rare item for this period—an analysis of some three hundred letters to the editor must suffice.

These letters concern mostly religion (40 percent), for their authors were mainly (57 percent) constitutional priests. A much smaller percentage (22 percent) of reader–letter writers were administrators, and 17 percent of the letters concerned politics. Only 5 percent of authors were peasants and artisans. This does not mean, of course, that peasants did not read the *Feuille villageoise* or have it read to them, but to what extent we will probably never know.[50]

A similar attempt by the minister of the Interior was the *Journal des campagnes,* which aimed to enlighten le peuple in such matters as the "rural economy, the procedures of culture, the construction of country wagons and of plowing instruments, the art of fertilizer and irrigation, the art of sowing and planting, the nourishment of livestock and the perfection of races." The envisaged circulation was 54,000 copies, estimated at an annual cost of 810,000 livres. The prefect of the Basses-Pyrénées in Year IX wondered how peasants, already supporting the schoolmaster and orphans, could pay 25 francs to subscribe to the newspaper. The prefect of Jura reacted similarly, and the paper lasted only a little over two years.[51]

The press did explode in 1787–92, and probably with greater liberty than at any previous period of French history except the Fronde. But the resulting journalistic license led to repression. New restrictions, eventually imposed to check antirepublican papers, grew until the most tightly controlled press of French history emerged under the Empire.

In the general politicization of the French people that occurred after 1789, the press played a great role, if not in originating ideas, then certainly in conveying them to the public. Its history parallels that of the theater. After initial emancipation from censorship and privilege, all the resentments and hatreds of the old regime surfaced. But this was not what the republican authorities wanted, this was not necessarily virtue. Both theater and the press needed direction; the theater particularly since theaters were places of public assembly, and the press because it reached a much broader audience and was more directly political. The restrictions of the Directory foreshadowed the tight controls of the Empire, when only thirteen newspapers were allowed in Paris and one per regional department.

But censorship was not the only cause of restricted communication.[52] Technology, finance, and transportation also played a part. French peasants probably read more about events in Paris during the Revolution than in any previous period of history, but they were neither subscribers nor probably even regular listeners of read newspapers. Barriers to communication were great: a geographical separation of Paris from the provinces and a social separation of the *classes laborieuses* from the *classes savantes*. Only in the cities was there much evidence of wide reading.

One reason for this was the existence of some thirty *patois,* popular Romance languages. In a report to the Convention on the matter on 16 prairial Year II (4 June 1794), abbé Grégoire enumerated the different patois, dialects, and languages: "Bas-Breton, Bourguignon, Bressan, Lyonnais, Dauphinois, Auvergnat, Poitevin, Limousin, Picard, Provençal, Languedocien, Velayen, Catalan, Béarnais, Basque, Rouergat, and Gascon." Only about a sixth (fifteen) of the departments around Paris spoke French exclusively. Elsewhere bilingualism was common. Priests tended to preach mostly in French, but millions of peasants throughout huge expanses of territory did not speak French. How could one hope to forge a national will and spread enlightenment when people did not understand the language of the decrees? Barère, originally a Basque, was concerned in the Convention in 8 pluviôse Year II (27 January 1794) only with the *foreign* languages found in France: Basque, German, Flamand, and Breton. These, he argued, were precisely the languages spoken in the areas of counterrevolution and insurrection: "Federalism and superstition speak Bas-Breton; emigration and hatred of the Republic speak German; counterrevolution speaks Italian, and fanaticism speaks Basque. Let us break these harmful instruments of error."[53]

As early as 1790, Grégoire sent out a questionnaire to local officials, priests, and savants on the nature of the local patois. Eight of these correspondents were in the judicial profession, nineteen were clerics, and fourteen were members of the Jacobin Club; all resided in the areas furthest from Paris, where patois was most common. Historians have interpreted the survey as a war of the ascetic Francophone and bourgeois Aufklärung against the less rational, more naive and friendly peasant language of song and feeling. Patois were considered the refuge of superstition and irrationality. On the whole Patois lacked grammars or dictionaries; a few had some literature—usually poetry or songs and almost never a treatise. The language of learning, even in counterrevolutionary Europe, was French. The language of the "lower people"—around Bordeaux, for instance—was Gascon. A social barrier hampered communication of the Enlightenment and the Revolution below a certain level.

Part of Grégoire's purpose was to inventory these curiosities rather than exterminate them, to uncover their history and morphological connections with Latin and French. His was an anthropological investigation of French subcultures. Grégoire's survey displayed envy of these lowly countryfolk—the answers to many questions revealed a spontaneity, passion, and warmth not found in the educated. But Grégoire also revealed moralizing preoccupations, as, for example, the question whether the patois vocabulary reserved a special place for obscenity and libertinage. Grégoire sought to raise the earthy life of the peasant to one of Reason. He wanted to know about peasants' prejudices, about what "moral effects [the Revolution] had produced in them." "Does one find among them patriotism or only the affections which personal interests inspire?" The peasant uprisings and the conflicts between congregations and curés did not seem to him, as it has to many modern historians, signs of historical progress but "injures grossières" or "outrages" (insults or outrages) that should be replaced by a sane and enlightened patriotism. One respondent, a Bordeaux lawyer named Pierre Bernadau, said, "Destroying patois would not be difficult as long as . . . we could substitute another language for it." The respondent from Alsace, however, felt French linguistic pretensions to be "aristocratic." What we are missing—here as in the letters-to-the-editor of the *Feuille villageoise*—is the peasants' voice.

As a result of Barère's speech in January, the Convention decreed that French be taught in all the outlying departments where foreign languages were spoken; it invited popular societies to translate its decrees into patois. And as a result of Grégoire's survey, the Convention decreed that an effort would be made to give French the character of "the language of liberty" but stopped short of trying to destroy patois. The distance separating peasants from Francophone France had not shrunk.[54]

The French moved rapidly from a language of deference, suited to the hierarchical old regime, to one of familiarity and confidence, which they used in addressing the deputies of the Mountain in Year II. The hierarchy of honorific salutations gave way to the citizen's *tutoyer,* in which all were addressed equally. By contrast, the language of the assemblies, as revealed by Mirabeau's speech, indicated a stratagem to convince the public of unanimity; a reassurance that what is heard is similar to what is already thought. In both cases, parliamentary discourse served to weld a consensus, to establish a confidence to match the intimacy of address. The language of authority, finally, ceased to be an utterance from above but had to originate in the people's will. Although it contained all the absoluteness of the defunct king's pre-revolutionary proclamations, it claimed to speak in the name of a new universal sovereign.

These forms of discourse were soon undermined by others, for discourse rarely goes unchallenged. The language of confidence supposes a union of private wills with the general will. But the French Revolution was a civil war. Informers denounced and exposed the intriguers, the malevolent, the greedy, the self-interested, and the hypocritical to restore confidence in the patrie. In the eyes of the revolutionaries, communication would cease to be a discourse of suspicion about others (the government, malevolent individuals), because, exposed and denounced, the accused would either make amends and reenter society or be excluded from it.

Conspiracy, however, was not the only obstacle to communication. Technological limitations and official censorship checked the press explosion of the 1790s from reaching everyone, as did the recalcitrant patois and dialects and widespread illiteracy. Written French was still far from being a universal means of communication.

The French Revolution was a strange juxtaposition of transparency and distrust, sincerity and misunderstanding. In the end, rhetoric suffocated sincerity, and victims of official virtue were reduced to hypocrisy. Fear crushed the wish for truthfulness. Only when demands for "transparency" abated after the Terror did the possibility of a freer, more authentic expression emerge. Then official revolutionary discourse, like that of the festivals, lost most of its meaning. During the Revolution, the French expressed themselves more voluminously and more volubly than ever before. But passion and politics often deepened old and generated new misunderstandings.

CHAPTER XI

EDUCATING

The central project of the Revolution was education. The transfer of sovereignty from the royal will to the general will demanded new loyalties. According to the sensationalist psychology of the century, this could be achieved only by repetition, by battering the senses with new impressions. "Man is a sensitive being, is led by striking images, great spectacles, profound emotions," contended Mirabeau. French revolutionary festivals emulated Catholic ceremonies, which had effectively used visual and aural aids. Civic funerals for republican martyrs mirrored religious ceremonies honoring saints, a civic calendar replaced the Catholic Gregorian calendar, and a network of secular schools, complete with civic catechisms, substituted for the parish petites écoles and their religious catechism. Besides adapting church institutions for republican purposes, revolutionary pedagogues made use of less obvious pedagogical institutions, such as the theater, the popular societies, and the army. The task was massive, and so too were the means. Old habits were tenacious and could be supplanted by new ones only through repeated exercise. The old *propagandum fidei* (propagation of the faith) supplied the model, and the secular word *propaganda* was born. The very similarity of the revolutionary project to the Catholic mission undoubtedly helped cause their collision. But the differences were only too real; the religion of the Revolution was not simply an inversion of Catholicism but incorporated Protestant, pagan, and libertine elements.[1]

Revolutionary Festivals

Nature and the patrie were celebrated outdoors rather than inside the dank cathedrals where Christians glorified the crucified Christ. The revolutionaries came to agree with Rousseau that Christianity and the patrie were incompatible. "No state," Rousseau argued, "was ever founded without religion serving as its basis . . . [but] far from attaching the hearts of citizens to the state, Christianity detaches them from it and from all earthly things." Rousseau envisaged a civic religion to replace Christianity, and the revolutionaries created one. Historians have debated whether this civic religion was really a religion or simply a political expedient; it recognized a supreme being, but its real object was to bind people to one another and to a republic.[2]

The festivals of classical antiquity—Greek foot and boat races, disk throwing, dancing al fresco—inspired the planners of France's revolutionary festivals, at least in their emphasis on outdoor athletics.[3] The Federations of 1790 to commemorate the storming of the Bastille began outdoors with men braving the elements—rivers, torrents, ice, and snow—as brothers of one patrie. Writing two generations later, Jules Michelet sacralized this new cult with the romanticism of 1848: "Citizens for the first time, and summoned from their remote snowy regions by the unknown name of liberty, they set forth, like the kings and shepherds of the East at the birth of Christ, seeing clearly in the middle of the night, and following unerringly, through the wintry mists, the dawn of spring, and the star of France."[4] The new shepherds announced the birth of the new savior, the nation.

The beginnings of the Federation were provincial and natural. The final celebration in Paris on 14 July was both organized and spontaneous. It included National Guards from all the departments, together with thousands of citizens (the total exceeded 250,000). Tremendous work was needed to plan for this Parisian climax to the provincial celebrations. The champ de Mars in front of the Ecole militaire was transformed into a huge elliptic arena in the center of which rose a huge altar to the patrie. Opposite stood a massive amphitheater where "the majesty of the Nation will reside." A triumphal arch crowned the scene. The manual labor of some ten thousand workers and thousands of men, women, and children of all classes, often working at night, impressed contemporaries by its fraternal spirit. Louis-Sébastien Mercier wrote nostalgically after the Terror: "There has perhaps never been seen in any people this astonishing and forever memorable spectacle of fraternity; I cannot think about it without admiration. . . . It was there that I saw 150,000 citizens of all classes, of every age and sex, forming the most superb picture of concord, of work, of movement and happiness which has ever been shown." Breaching "the code of honor" to work with their hands, citizens shoveled, hoed, and danced to the music of the "Ça ira."[5]

The day of the festival, the cavalry entered, followed on foot by the National Guardsmen and soldiers who in various brightly colored uniforms stood in rows surrounding the amphitheater. Military students and veterans were arranged in front of the altar. Bas-reliefs on the altar represented on one side a beautiful woman dissipating clouds and on the other a warrior pronouncing the oath to the patrie, an oath that Lafayette administered to the crowd. The remaining sides of the altar bore such inscriptions as "Virtue alone makes distinctions" and "The Nation, the Law and the King. The Nation is you, the Law is also you. The King is the guardian of the Law." From appearances the Federation was certainly Christian—what could be more Christian than brotherly love? Talleyrand, moreover, celebrated Mass with some sixty chaplains of the National Guard.

But Mass was said on the altar of the patrie, not on the altar of Christ; it seemed that the sovereignty of man and nation rather than that of God was being celebrated. A horizontal, fraternal concept superseded the vertical, theistic element of the Christian religion. A regime that recognized distinctions only of merit and utility was leveling the hierarchy of Christianity and Christian monarchy. It was probably not accidental that the king's seat in the center of the amphitheater was at the same level as that of the president of the National Assembly. Architecturally, classical motifs (fig. XI.1) overpowered the Christian; the bas-reliefs of the arch of triumph, for example, which resembled Trajan's, represented the French people recovering their liberty.[6] The panoply of visual and aural sensations provided an education in the new patriotic values.

The funeral ceremony a year later to transfer Voltaire's remains (fig. XI.2) to the Church of Saint-Geneviève, recently converted into a pantheon to honor the nation's great men, more explicitly revived pagan ritual in its imitation of classical apotheoses. The iconography of both the ceremony and the frontals of the Panthéon, designed by the sculptor Moitte under the direction of Quatremère de Quincy, were neoclassical palimpsests of pagan mythology. On the sarcophagus there were a sculpted figure of eternal sleep in an antique chair, an Elysian field of immortality, and masked "geniuses" carrying the inverted torches of mourning. The theatrical masks were reminders of

XI.I.

Bas-relief of the Arch of Triumph erected on the occasion of the Festival of the Federation, 14 July 1790, on the Champ de Mars, engraving.
Courtesy Bibliothèque nationale, photo: Bibl. Nat. Paris.

Voltaire's dramaturgy. Like the altar of the patrie, the sarcophagus bore inscriptions to equality, virtue, law, and patrie. The chariot that carried Voltaire's remains was probably designed by David, the marbler Sellier, or Quatremère de Quincy and resembled the style of the Panthéon—antique candelabras, a sacred flame, Victory leaning over the dead hero. Members of the cortège wore togas and followed the chariot, which was twenty-five feet tall, to several stopping points (later called "stations"), among them the Pont Neuf (where the king observed from his window in the Louvre) and the Comédie-Française (where the songs sung and scenes represented by the comédiens were reminiscent of the life of Voltaire). Bad weather—it had also poured furiously during the Festival of the Federation—did not prevent large crowds, perhaps 100,000 persons, from attending.[7]

To remodel the Church of Saint-Geneviève into a pantheon required a series of architectural and iconographical changes and additions. In his report to the National Assembly in late 1791, Quatremère de Quincy, the building's administrator, detailed some of the changes he envisaged: an inscription—"To great men / the Country / in recognition"—placed on the fronton, where a woman representing the

patrie would replace the existing angels and clouds. Five bas-reliefs of the life of Saint-Geneviève would go; as Quatremère insisted, "You must search to destroy every kind of equivocation which can harm our religion." "Our religion" was of course the religion of antiquity, "which has become the Religion of the Arts and Artists." The "philosophical Pantheon" was "the Emblem of this truly philosophical religion to which all people must rally: this religion is Morality." The paganism of Quatremère and his artistic generation was less limited to allegory than was the pagan allegory of their Christian predecessors. The revolutionaries clearly did not resurrect a literal belief in pagan divinities, but they did make a cult of the self-sufficiency of human virtue. Their deities were more literally anthropomorphic than those of the ancients!

In a report of 22 October 1793, Quatremère made clear that the building should educate the common man in this religion: "It was from simple motifs of the building, and not in vague generalities, that I wanted to draw the subjects of decoration. I wanted everything to be clear and within the reach of all." The bas-reliefs underneath the peristyle were dedicated to the Declaration of Rights (this one by

XI.2.
Order of the Cortège for the Removal of Voltaire's Remains,
Monday, 11 July 1791, *engraving.*
Courtesy Bibliothèque nationale, photo: Bibl. Nat. Paris.

Boichot), to Public Instruction (by Lesueur), to the New Jurisprudence, to Patriotic Devotion, and so on. The nave and other parts of the interior represented the Enlightenment and its component sciences. For Quatremère, the Panthéon was "a *simulacre* of the *Patrie,* this veritable idol of the People, and the true divinity of the Temple which it has chosen for itself."[8]

The Panthéon held the bodies of men whom the Republic declared worthy of immortality—Mirabeau (until 1793), Voltaire, Lepeletier de Saint-Fargeau (until Thermidor), Marat, Rousseau (after Thermidor), and Descartes. Lepeletier was assassinated the day after he voted for the king's death. His body, nude to the waist, was transported on a funeral litter to the pedestal of the dismantled statue of Louis XIV, Place Vendôme, and from there to the Panthéon. His livid, bloody corpse was decorated with laurels and a civic crown.[9]

Marat, ironically, did not receive the honors of the Panthéon until after the Jacobin dictatorship collapsed, but on his death he was given a hero's funeral akin to that of Lepeletier. Marat's body was wrapped in a wet sheet—he had been murdered while bathing on 13 July 1793. He was exposed before burial at the Cordelier courtyard, and his heart was interred in the Luxembourg Gardens. "His burial," David insisted as planner, "would have the simplicity appropriate for an incorruptible republican."[10]

The cult of Marat spread throughout France during the next year. In a ceremony at Langres his bust joined those of Brutus, Voltaire, Rousseau, Franklin, and Lepeletier. Several plays commemorated his "martyrdom," and he was even likened to Jesus, notably in the *Révolutions de Paris.* But the de-Christianizing comparison—"Jesus is a prophet and Marat is a God"—would desacralize Jesus more than it sacralized Marat. Jesus, according to Léonard Bourdon, was "only a man . . . a friend of the people . . . the first sansculotte." As Albert Soboul has rightly maintained, the borrowings from Catholicism did not "imply an attitude of veneration" or constitute a real religiosity.[11]

The assassination of Marat marked a crisis in the Republic, for the assassin, Charlotte Corday, was linked to the Federalist revolt, which since that spring had grown to immense proportions. Soon over two-thirds of France was in revolt, including the cities of Lyons, Marseilles, and Bordeaux (and also the Vendée), and parts of Normandy (Caen) and Brittany. Although much of this insurrection was soon quelled, it formed the backdrop for David's grandiose festival of 10 August 1793, the anniversary of the overthrow of the monarchy, honoring the unity and indivisibility of the Republic.

David's plan, presented in the name of the Committee of Public Instruction, envisaged a vast procession involving representatives of the primary assemblies of the eighty-six departments, the president of the Convention (the *bon vivant* ex-noble, Hérault de Séchelles), popular societies, the Convention, and a mass of citizenry. The procession began at what had become the habitual starting point, the Place de la Bastille, and proceeded through four stations, including an *arc de triomphe* on the boulevard des Italiens. On the Place de la Révolution, a "goddess of the French," a statue of Liberty, was constructed on a pedestal of the symbols of royalty. The statue itself was to contain three thousand doves, which, as they flew off carrying the message "We are free! Imitate us" on little banners attached to their feet, were to symbolize the free ascent of the soul.[12]

The festival appropriated ancient Catholic ritual, as in the drinking from the cup of regeneration, reminiscent of Catholic communion (as well as Hellenic ritual), and the sharing of a "frugal repast" on the grass in the champ de Mars, perhaps recalling the miracle of the loaves and fishes. Finally, the mountain erected in the champ de Mars harkened back to Mount Sinai, as well as to a Masonic mountain symbol and from there into popular imagery (see fig. IX.3). The self-sacrifice of patriots who swore to "defend unto death" the new constitution and the motto "liberty, equality, or death" captured the pagan "pro patria mori," as well as the Christian idea of martyrdom. One historian of art, Anita Brookner, has observed that David's success with the festival was due to his "brilliant and instinctive manipulation of familiar actions and associations." The old symbols were reemployed in a civic religion. This transfer was what the revolutionaries understood by "education"; today it might be termed "reeducation."

To commemorate the festival, David had a medal struck in its honor. On one side it depicted a statue of Nature spewing out the waters of regeneration, on the other a statue of Hercules, representing the French people, standing on the debris of the statues of kings recently removed from Notre-Dame.[13]

The Festival of Unity, or the Reunion, as it came to be called, did not prevent the declaration of the Terror on 5 September. Nobles and clergy were the Terror's principal victims. Both had been subjected to harassment and ridicule since 1789, and former clerical sectors of influence—education, charities, hospitals, and so on—had been secularized. But strict de-Christianization—eradication of Christianity—began in late September 1793 and lasted through the winter.

The festivals of the Revolution were half-secular, half-pagan counterparts of Christian ceremonies of the Mass, baptism, and burial. Rousseau, David, and Quatremère de Quincy all contributed to the iconography and choreography of these festivals. Their basic thrust was to focus on the patrie and its great men rather than on Christ, His mystical body, and the king. Humanity was being taught to reach less to some being above and beyond than inward to the self and outward to all people to find a human greatness. This was not yet, or not primarily, atheistic humanism à la Ludwig Feuerbach, who urged men to return into themselves and repossess their alienated (upreaching) humanity; deism was to be the religion of Robespierre and the Republic. But the object of worship in this religion was more civic and human than transcendental. As the Greek adage put it, man was "the measure of all things." For Rousseau there could be no worship that took man away (alienated) from the city. Christianity, he felt, was culpable precisely because it created a dual allegiance, one divine, one human, thereby splitting man's loyalties. The classical city, with its identity of the civic and the religious, was far better. What better symbol of the apotheosis of man could there be than the Panthéon, the shrine to great men, desanctified of its original Christian iconography?

De-Christianization

The representatives-on-mission (conventionnels sent to the departments) and the interior "revolutionary armies" were the principal agents of de-Christianization in the provinces, where the movement began. One of them, Marc-Antoine Baudot, wrote from Toulouse that "the revolutionary army is today the watchword, and with this word we convert thousands of political sinners by the minute." In the Oise and elsewhere, "apostles of reason" were sent into the countryside to "convert" peasants to philosophy and Jacobinism. Jacques-Léonard Laplanche, from Bourges, spoke of the need to "strike out against bad priests"; but when Fouché, an ex-Oratorian representative-on-mission in the Nièvre, established the model of de-Christianization for the country, all priests, not just bad priests, became its designated victims.

Fouché preached against celibacy; he ordered priests to marry, to adopt a child or nourish an old man, and to wear only secular garb outside their "temples." He denied the immortality of the soul and inscribed the words "Death is an eternal sleep" on the portals of the cemeteries of the Allier. Funeral biers in Moulins were draped in cloth representing "sleep." Holbach contended that belief in the immortal soul was the raison d'être of priests. Abolish that belief, Fouché seemed to be adding, and you abolish the priesthood. Christian names of children were supplanted by Roman names—children and towns were called Brutus in civic baptisms. Fouché's own daughter received the name Nièvre.

On 23 brumaire (13 November 1793), a month into de-Christianization, the churches of the Allier were closed and the guillotine was installed in the public square of Moulins. Allier had won favor as a "juring" department in 1790–91 when 426 of its 484 priests had taken the oath. But de-Christianization made no distinction between those who did and those who did not: priests were expected to abdicate the priesthood, if not abjure the faith. In 1793 only 58 priests of Allier refused to abdicate or give up the functions of the priesthood. In France as a whole, an estimated 15,000–20,000 of the 130,000 clerics (in 1789) abdicated between October 1793 and March 1794. In Lyons almost 100 priests became victims of the Terror; throughout France 920 were guillotined or otherwise executed. After 1792 noncompliant clerics more commonly were deported. The south and southeast alone saw well over a thousand deportations (500 from the Aveyron, 218 from the Hérault, 304 from the Gard, 60 from Chambéry). The lightest punishment was imprisonment. In the Aveyron, 206 were incarcerated. As it turned out, more priests emigrated than abdicated. Nationwide there were 25,000–40,000 emigrations and an estimated 20,000 abdications, in the southeast 6,000–7,000 emigrations and 4,228–4,471 abdications.[14]

The entire purpose of this movement was to eradicate what the philosophes and their followers considered "a superstition" or "the infamous thing." Its elimination would make way for the reign of reason. Where the philosophes hesitated to use anything but persuasion, which they directed only toward the literate, the de-Christianizers of Year II did not hesitate to resort to force to insure that the same "truth" was accepted by all.

The de-Christianizing "festivals" were often more traditional than David's, for they recalled the carnival-like burlesque rather than classical antiquity. Such was the *promenade des ânes,* part of a traditional charivari used against violators of community mores in which the victim rode backward on a donkey. This masquerade was used in 1792 against the wives of anti-Jacobin *chiffonistes* in Arles and was re-employed in Year II on the occasion of the recapture of Toulon, when mannequins of the king of England, the king of Spain, and the pope were burned in "lent" amid civic communions. In these de-Christianizing promenades a donkey often wore the bishop's miter. Charivaris were usually accompanied by autos-da-fé of paintings from local churches and priests' vestments. At Manosque in Provence and at Draguignan, confessionals and other objects of the cult were consumed by fire.[15] These masquerades were no longer simply carnavalesque but revolutionary. They were no longer playful suspensions of the rules but intentional sacrilegious acts. By and large, de-Christianization took the place of carnivals, which virtually disappeared in the 1790s. What had been community amusement in the old regime became spiteful persecution in the Revolution.

How voluntary were the letters by which priests formally abdicated their priesthood? Some acts of abdication were accompanied by formal "abjurations" or acts of apostasy. In these a priest could proclaim his long-standing wish to be defrocked and to embrace the torch of reason and the Revolution, which he would then claim to have supported from the beginning. The letter of the curé Verneau of Saint-Nizier (district of Autun) dated 21 brumaire Year II (11 November 1793) is an example of just such a "philosophical" abdication:

> Citizens,
> My principles are those of a republican; I must reenter the class of citizens, and I abjure today the profession of priest. . . . The principles of Philosophy ought to be raised upon the remains of prejudice; these are my motives for resignation.
>
> These documents [the letters of priesthood] which you receive with this letter are the titles of error and intolerance; may they be put to flames; that is my wish. . . .
>
> *Salut et fraternité*[16]

There is some evidence that clerics occasionally used form letters to abdicate. Priests could fill in the blanks and they knew pretty much what they were expected to say, which casts doubt on the authenticity of many statements. Priests acted under fear. Batches of signatures on one particular day and the coincidence of abdications following the passage of de-Christianizing measures leave their legitimacy in question.[17]

But some abdications were genuine. Virlez of Nimelles, from the district of Auxerre in the Yonne, explained his motives for abdicating: "Placed at my graduation from collège by my parents in one of the monasteries which existed then . . . I became a priest, it was part of my duty. . . . Today, now that the free man recovers the entire dignity of his being, he feels that there is no need of an intermediary between the divinity and him[self] in order to become accustomed to the exercise of virtues." The specificity of this confession rings true. The protestations had a different tone. Clerics alleged that they never wanted to be priests, that they never believed what they preached, that they no longer wanted to stand apart from the general citizenry, that the priesthood represented a "prejudice" which they renounced in favor of philosophy and reason, and that the priesthood was contrary to the Revolution.[18]

If a priest married as well as abdicated, the authorities could boast a surer conquest, since without marriage priestly functions could be resumed at any time. The figure of 6,500 married priests for the whole of France has been advanced by Michel Vovelle. Of some 1,500 Parisian priests, 194 married during the Revolution and 410 abdicated. Elsewhere the proportion is lower; in the Gers, only 23 of some 300 priests married.[19]

The dossiers of Cardinal Caprara, who was appointed by Rome in 1802 to examine the petitions of abdicators and married clerics who sought reunion with the church, provide a retrospective look at de-Christianization. Nationwide, the total number of requests for absolutions was 3,224: in the southeast approximately 60 percent retracted their abdications, of which approximately one-half resumed their priestly functions and roughly one-third remained laicized. Almost all of the petitioners gave fear and weakness as motives of their infidelity. One married a blind aunt, "an imbecile since childhood . . . to protect myself from plenty of miseries." Another referred to himself as having been "struck by the horrors of death of the Terror. . . . The supplicant did this act of cowardice only to save himself from death." A third "tried to smother a passion which was stronger than myself." Many expressed "the tears of a sincere penitence."[20]

Taking into account the external forces in Year II and the desires for reinstatement in Year X (1801–2), it seems clear that the campaign to de-Christianize was unsuccessful. The vast majority of priests did not abdicate; more preferred emigration, deportation, imprisonment, or even the guillotine. Many others who did abdicate returned furtively to their functions a few days later, and still more chose formally to reintegrate themselves with the church in 1802. Some historians question whether the church in truth lost any worthy servants.[21]

The geography of de-Christianization has been studied by Richard

Cobb and Michel Vovelle. Cobb lists the following departments as having undergone vigorous de-Christianizing activities: the Nord, Morbihan, Loiret, Allier, Nièvre, Isère, Drôme, Ariège, Haute-Garonne, Gironde, and Bas-Rhin. Vovelle distinguishes between an area of early and massive de-Christianization in the Allier to the Saône-et-Loire and the Ain, including the Nièvre and Cher, and an area of late but significant de-Christianization to the south in the Hérault, Gard, Bouches-du-Rhône, Vaucluse, Var, and Drôme. The principal areas affected were the center, the Rhône Valley, and the southeast. To a considerable extent these areas coincide with the areas of Red republicanism in 1848 described by M. Agulhon, as well as with the map of religious practice and nonpractice drawn by Canon Boulard. To a lesser extent they coincide with areas studied by T. Tackett where there were many clergy who took the oath from 1790 to 1791. Areas whose clergy had in the main refused the oath, such as in the west, experienced little de-Christianization. Further, in some areas of high abdications the network of Jacobin clubs had been densely established by 1791.[22]

Resistance to de-Christianization can be understood in terms of age, sex, and geography. Abdicating priests averaged fifty years of age. Younger priests with fewer memories of the old regime were more inclined to be faithful than older ones, just as younger deputies in the councils of the Directory tended to be more royalist than their older counterparts. Likewise, women seem to have been more active than men in opposing the de-Christianizing missions of representatives and the revolutionary armies. In many towns they physically tried to impede the stripping or closing of the churches, as in Conflans, Nogent-sur-Marne, Romainville, Noisy-le-Sec, Augervilliers, Villetaneuse, La Villette, Vincennes, Laon, and Auxerre. Instances of Catholic worship—*fêtes Dieu* in June, midnight Mass on Christmas 1793—and their resurgence after Thermidor 1794 seem to indicate that for many of the French de-Christianization was an aberration.

Many French men and women wanted their curé and patriotism, or a curé patriote like the priest in Radet and Desfontaines's play *Au retour* or the real priest of Fourqueux near Mantes whom several hundred people tried unsuccessfully to save from the guillotine in nivôse Year II (June 1794). A more counterrevolutionary village, La Ferté Gaucher, demonstrated with cries of "Vive la religion Catholique! A bas les Jacobins! Nous aurons nos curés! Nous voulons la Messe les dimanches et fêtes!" (Long live the Catholic religion! Down with the Jacobins! We will have our priests! We want Mass on Sundays and feast days!) These instances of resistance may have been isolated, but they were not infrequent. In the Midi, Vovelle concludes that the departments of the Aveyron, Lozère, Ardèche, Haute-Loire, Cantal, Puy-de-Dôme, Gard, and Hérault successfully escaped efforts at de-Christianization. On a more general geographical level, as has been noted, the areas of good communication (the Rhône Valley) fell prey to de-Christianizing forces more easily than did the mountainous areas (the massif Central). Towns with sansculotte populations tended to welcome the movement more than did the countryside, where the "apostles of reason" sent out to "convert" the peasants usually met with failure.[23]

The Festival of Reason in Notre-Dame on 20 brumaire (10 November 1793) has come to symbolize the Parisian de-Christianization movement. The archbishop of Paris abdicated on 7 November and over four hundred priests followed suit. Churches were closed. On 10 November Chaumette and Hébert of the Paris Commune visited the Convention and instigated a ceremonial procession to Notre-Dame of musicians, soldiers, and young girls girded with tricolored ribbons and garlands of flowers who followed a goddess of Reason, Mlle Maillard, a singer of the Opéra. The Convention declared Notre-Dame a Temple of Reason, and a hymn to Liberty composed by Chénier, with music by Gossec, was sung:

> Descend, O Liberty, daughter of Nature:
> The people have recaptured their immortal power:
> Over the pompous remains of age-old imposture
> Their hands raise thine altar.
> . . . .
> Thou, holy Liberty, come dwell in this temple
> Be the goddess of the French.

Antoine-François Momoro, a Hébertist, described in the *Révolutions de Paris* the Temple of Reason erected atop a Jacobin mountain inside Notre-Dame. "To philosophy" was inscribed on the façade of the Temple, and participants sang republican "songs of happiness" which, he claimed, did not "wail" like church music. A "beautiful woman" was chosen to represent Reason and Liberty, rather than a statue, so that she would not become an idol: "There is one thing that one must not tire telling people," Momoro explained, "Liberty, reason, truth are only abstract beings. They are not gods, for properly speaking, they are part of ourselves." Momoro's cult of reason was an explicit religion of man, in line with the civic religion of man of Rousseau, Quatremère de Quincy, and David.[24]

Mona Ozouf has characterized the Festival of Reason in Paris as "reasonable reason," as distinguished from the wild masquerades of the southwest and the early spontaneity of the May festivals and of the Federation. It was perhaps a step toward the order, discipline, and sclerosis of the Directory festivals. Ozouf sees a great similarity between the Festival of Reason, which celebrated Liberty as much as Reason, and the Festival of the Supreme Being seven months later. This may have been the case in Paris and elsewhere in the months following its inauguration, but the inaugural Festival of Reason in Notre-Dame left no impression of rationality on the memories of contemporary observers. Indeed, tales of its raucousness may have contributed to Robespierre's opposition to de-Christianization in December 1793. Durand Maillane recorded in his *Histoire de la Convention nationale* that he "did not attend the more than scandalous scenes which took place in the Church of Notre-Dame, where an actress of the Opéra was incensed as a divinity, and I must say, at least half of the conventionnels refused to attend." Louis-Sébastien Mercier gave the most lurid account in his *Nouveau Paris*. The goddess Reason, he wrote, used the tabernacle as her pedestal, cannoneers stood as acolytes, the cathedral was filled with trumpet blasts, and participants removed their culottes and blouses to dance the carmagnole in the sanctuary. Licentious laughter emerged from the side altars, which were covered with curtains. At Saint-Eustache a great gourmand feast and a ball were held in the Chapel of the Virgin, giving rise to further alleged depravities at night. However much those details are the workings of Mercier's imagination after his imprisonment during the Terror, it was evident that the Festival of Reason was a scandal.[25]

On 29 November Robespierre lashed out against de-Christianization in the Convention, declaring that it was never intended that Catholicism be outlawed and that abdications in fact did nothing to check priests. Moreover, he said, "atheism is aristocratic." The motives of the de-Christianizers, Anacharsis Cloots, Léonard Bourdon, François Desfieux, Balthazar Proli, Jacob Pereira, and Hébert, were suspect. The scandalous scenes, he felt, played into the hands of France's enemies by associating the country with irreligion and barbarism. Frontal attacks on religion would only trigger frontal resistance.[26]

Robespierre's influence was such that the de-Christianization movement rapidly slackened after he guaranteed the liberty of cults on 9 frimaire (29 November), although churches remained closed. A week later Robespierre again denounced coupling liberty with irreligion, for this would make liberty "odious" and would fuel the counterrevolutionary revolt in the Vendée.[27]

From November 1793 to June 1794 Robespierre followed a consistent line of argument: atheism plays into the hands of counterrevolution; there is a good indication that God exists and that the soul is immortal; even were these beliefs false (and it was not up to the Convention to make metaphysical declarations), it would be necessary to hold them, for without them the Republic could not endure. Presiding over the Festival of the Supreme Being on 20 prairial (8 June 1794), which crowned his efforts, Robespierre testified publicly to the social utility of religion.[28]

That festival (fig. XI.3) was held in the National Gardens (the Tuileries), where a mountain was erected (for the last time), stands built, houses decorated, and members of the Convention assembled on the platform built for them. Many members suspected Robespierre of having made himself the new pontiff. The Incorruptible spoke to the French of their great accomplishments, of their distance—by virtue of the Enlightenment and the Revolution—from primitive man and subjugated Europeans. The existence of God and the immortality of the soul, even if "but dreams . . . would still be the finest of all the conceptions of human intelligence." The cult of the Supreme Being would strike a double blow—against both the conspiracy of atheism and the "fanaticism" of priests. This festival, though it may have contributed to the downfall of Robespierre, has been called the most successful of the Revolution.[29]

On 20 September 1793, after nine months of study, the Committee of Public Instruction recommended a new republican calendar to the Convention. Twenty-one September 1792, the autumnal equinox and the day of the Republic's founding, would mark the beginning of the new republican time: "The sun passed from one hemisphere to the other on the same day in which the people, triumphing over the oppression of kings, passed from a monarchical government to a republican government." This famous day, it appeared, would replace the birth of Christ as the beginning of time, and all future dates would be counted from the first year of French liberty. The year 1789 was already taken by many as the first year of French liberty, but a proposal in 1793 to count backward from that year was not accepted. The term *ancien régime* for dates before 1789 would have to suffice.[30]

Gilbert Romme explained the proposed calendar and Fabre d'Eglantine later worked out some of the nomenclature, but the substitution of

XI.3.
Festival of the Supreme Being, 8 June 1794, *engraving.*
Courtesy Bibliothèque nationale.

a "rational" calendar based on natural principles for one based on "superstition" was no simple matter. The indivisibility of the solar year by lunar months has always been the principal problem of calendar making: the solar year is about 365.25 days long, whereas 13 lunar months of 28 days each equals 364 days. The Gregorian calendar takes account of this discrepancy by having 12 months of different lengths (30, 31, and 28 days) and a quadrennial leap year with an extra day. Romme proposed a regular scheme: 12 months of equal (30-day) duration, to which extra days would be added at the end of the year. Although these months were also not lunar, they had the advantage of being divided decimally like the metric system, to which the calendar was compared. A week would last ten days, the tenth day (the *décadi*) would be a day of rest, and each day would be divided decimally. Thus "the bizarre inequality of months" would be eliminated, the days of the week could be counted on one's fingers, watches would tick every 100,000th part of the day, or as often as the heartbeat of an average-sized man walking at a brisk pace!

This decimal division of the day (fig. XI.4) was not much used outside certain administrative circles (such as Marseilles); decimal watches were extremely rare. The names for the days proposed by Fabre d'Eglantine, who used agricultural and botanical terms to substitute for saints' days, never took hold, but his seasonal names for the months of the year did come into use. Thus vendémiaire, brumaire, and frimaire signify the fall harvest, fog, and cold of autumn; nivôse, pluviôse, and ventôse the snow, rain, and wind of winter; germinal, floréal, and prairial the germination, flowers, and meadows of spring; and messidor, thermidor, and fructidor the summer harvest, heat, and fruit of summer. The days of the week were given decimal names (*primidi, duodi, tridi,* and so on), but only the tenth day, décadi, was much used. Since the twelve thirty-day months did not equal the solar year, five days were added at the end of the summer called *sans-culottides.* The extra day on leap year was called a *franciade,* the sole Gallic element in this otherwise natural standard that Fabre felt would "enlighten the entire human race."[31]

Habit and religion were the great enemies of the new calendar. The Fabre report did not envisage making the observance of décadi obligatory for anyone but administrators. But as early as Year II, aggressive representatives-on-mission, like Dartigoeyte in the Haute-Garonne, acted against "do-nothing citizens" who rested on Sunday instead of the décadi. Plans for décadi celebrations were made several times by such legislators as Chénier and by the Committee on Public Instruc-

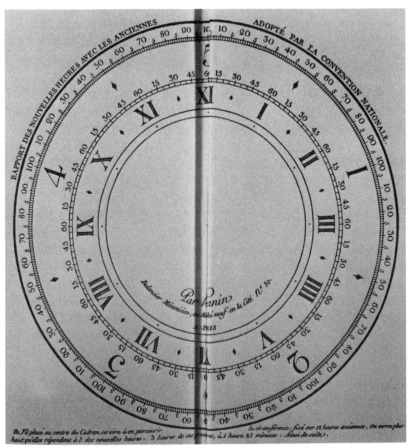

XI.4.
Concordance of New and Old Hours Adopted by the National
Convention, *in J. Guillaume,* Procès-verbaux du Comité d'instruction
publique de la Convention nationale, *2:893.*

tion, as well as by Robespierre in his speech on "religious and moral
ideas." Robespierre proposed honoring Nature, Humanity, the French
People, Glory, Misfortune, Benefactors of Humanity, Martyrs of Liberty, Stoicism, Frugality, Filial Piety, Old Age, Industry, and on and
on. Although this proposal was decreed, it was never enforced, and it
was left to the Daunou Bill eighteen months later to settle on seven
celebrations as opposed to Robespierre's thirty-six. They were Youth
(10 germinal, fig. XI.5), Marriage (10 floréal), Recognition (10 prairial), Agriculture (10 messidor), Liberty (9 and 10 thermidor—the
date of Robespierre's execution), and the Aged (10 fructidor). The

XI.5.
Poster announcing celebration of the national Festival of Youth,
Department of the Rhône.
Courtesy Bibliothèque nationale, photo: Bibl. Nat. Paris.

seasonal element was made to match the cycles of life—youth and marriage in the spring, old age with the harvest. In addition, several commemorative festivals were designated: the foundation of the Republic (1 vendémiaire, fig. XI.6), the fall of the Bastille (14 July), the overthrow of the monarchy (10 August), the execution of the king (21 January).[32]

XI.6.
Festival of the Foundation of the Republic, 1 vendémiaire an III
[22 September 1794], *engraving.*
Courtesy Bibliothèque nationale, photo: Bibl. Nat. Paris.

The new calendar was largely a failure, for it was associated with
the de-Christianization of the Terror and with lifeless ceremonies
in which local officials intoned dull precepts of republican morality.
After Thermidor these were unpopular with the disillusioned and re-
Christianized populations. By the time the calendar was enforced, entire segments of the citizenry had become bored or disgusted with the
Republic, and many had returned to the Catholic cult.

During the first Directory (October 1795–September 1797) the history of the calendar was a history of infractions. In the theaters, singers of the counterrevolutionary "Réveil du peuple" drowned out the
patriotic "Chant de départ"; *muscadins* ripped up liberty trees in public
squares; and "Monsieur dimanche" abstained from the festivals that
"Citoyen décadi" continued to observe. Calendars in almanacs began
once again to list saints' days in the Gregorian calendar, and without
giving the republican equivalent. Market days kept to the old week,
dances moved from the décadi to Sunday, and worship began anew on
Sundays in the reopened churches. The royalist elections, which
threatened to overthrow the Directory in August 1797 and were an-

nulled in the coup d'état of 18 fructidor Year V (4 September 1797), saw a new wave of republican legislation—on schools, on priests, and on the décadi. A decree of 14 germinal Year VI (4 April 1798) made the observance of the décadi obligatory at a time when the calendar was in disrepute. Local popular festivals to dedicate a church or statue (*dédicasses*) and rowdy patronal festivals (*kermesses*) of the old regime persisted or had reappeared since the Terror. Churches that had returned to Catholic worship were made to share as "temples" for the new deistic religion of theophilanthropy of the Director Louis-Marie La Revellière-Lépeaux. In republican towns like Toulouse, the décadi was strictly observed by the authorities, who gathered at eleven o'clock in the town hall and proceeded in military procession to the "temple," where a copy of the *Bulletin des lois* and announcements were read, speeches made, music played, and patriotic hymns sung. Throughout France these ceremonies fell on deaf ears and stony faces. Teachers, pupils, and public officials were expected to attend, but the general public held back.[33]

In general, enforcement of the calendar and the décadi ceremonies during the Directory came as a response to challenges from the left and right to the Thermidorean constitution. These were particularly strong during the crises of Years V, VI, and VII. The commemorative festival now became "the school of the citizen"; the Revolution was to be sustained through a repetition of patriotic memories and moral injunctions. The essential irony of the calendar was underlined: born to create a new time, it had continually to repeat itself simply to survive. The festival had to legitimize the conquests of the Revolution and bind people who had recently been fighting one another. Thus the festival of 31 May celebrating the elimination of the Girondins was dropped when the Revolution moved to the right. Men and events of the Terror were forgotten in an attempt to placate enemies; fail-safe days like the fourteenth of July were chosen instead. In contrast to the festivals at the beginning of the Revolution, spontaneity ceased. Public celebrations became petrified and formal. Festivals anodized the Revolution they had originally been intended to commemorate. When the tenth of August was invoked it was without allusion to the killing that had brought it about.[34]

The debate surrounding the law of Boissy d'Anglas providing again for the liberty of cults offers information on the background of calendar observance. Passed on 3 ventôse Year III (21 February 1795), inspired partly by Boissy d'Anglas's Protestantism, it was actually more restrictive than emancipatory in spirit. No cult was to be "troubled," but no minister was to be salaried, thus separating church and state. Neither exterior manifestation of the cult nor any endowment of churches was allowed. Of the law's twelve articles, two were permissive and ten prohibitive. Priests were closely watched during the Directory, particularly after the Eighteenth of Fructidor, when they were deported by the hundreds for failure to take an oath of hatred of royalty (prompted by the royalist election returns in 1797, which scared republicans) or for other causes. Ecclesiastical publications were censored—the *Annales de la religion,* for example—for disapproving of divorce. Educational legislation of the period was anticlerical.

But the permission to open churches and hold services was enough to spur a Catholic revival. Lambert, a deputy in the Côte d'Or's Council of Five Hundred, reported on a trip he had made through seven or eight departments in the east: "Everywhere I observed that the general mass of people would never familiarize itself with our *décadaire* system, although infinitely superior to the old calendar; that our tridi are, for the ignorant on the one hand and the ill-intentioned on the other, a continual object of derision; that Sundays and feast days are observed more regularly than ever, for the sole reason that they depend on religious principles." Elsewhere Lambert observed that if you go forth as "apostles of reason," the country inhabitants "look at you with all your pompous phrases either as charlatans . . . or as insane people whose brain is delirious and more worthy of pity than of anger." Deputy Audrein, in support of the Freedom of Cults Bill but not of Boissy d'Anglas's version, pointed out that 20 million of France's 26 million people were Catholic.[35]

A large proportion of the urban political elite embraced an anti-clericalism quite foreign to most working people (with the exception of sansculotte militants) who had not been exposed to the Enlightenment and whose exposure to de-Christianization during the Revolution had only reinforced their religious convictions. It was to this problem, among others of a similar nature, that the pedagogy of the Revolution was addressed.

Republican Pedagogy

The paramount objective of French revolutionary pedagogy was not only to instruct people in the elements of reading, writing, and arithmetic but to educate them in the principles of republicanism. The term *instruction* in French is quite distinct from *éducation*—

the latter means a total education of the person, the formation of character, whereas the former means imparting information and skills. True, the committee concerned with these matters in the Convention was called the Comité d'instruction publique, and the titles of plans the conventionnels submitted to it used the term *éducation* only a bit more than *instruction*. But these plans were divided over the number of levels national education should have and whether it should be entirely common, mixing all classes together, or have a track system separating children with different abilities and social destinies. Questions of secularity, obligation, gratuity, and state monopoly versus "free" education, in which a private and even religious sector would be allowed to exist, were also hotly debated. The efforts of the conventionnels in planning the education of the Republic have been compared by R. R. Palmer, the historian of these plans, to the efforts of Penelope weaving her cloth by day and unweaving it at night to avoid making a choice. Scores of plans were proposed, a few were approved, only two were effected.[36]

Among those approved but never implemented was the plan of the slain Michel Lepeletier, presented by Robespierre on 13 July 1793 to the Convention, which never enacted it. It was a more complete plan of éducation than any other because it concerned the total child. Children were to be separated by law from their parents at age five and placed in one of twenty thousand boarding schools across the nation until age twelve. An entire regeneration would be effected under the "yoke" of a "precise rule" regulating every minute of the day in industrious and useful tasks. "Continually under the eye and in the hand of an active surveillance each hour will be marked for sleep, meals, work, exercise, relaxation; the whole regime of living will be invariably regulated; gradual and repeated tests will be fixed; the genres of physical activity will be designated, gymnastic exercises will be indicated; a salutary and uniform regulation will prescribe all these details and a constant and smooth execution will guarantee every good effort." The schools were to teach a universal but no particular religion (in this sense it was less than total). In their free time, however, students could go to a temple and learn a religion. Education would be given without charge, the rich paying for the poor, but the children were also expected to help support the schools. Some, Lepeletier deemed, would go on to secondary and higher education—that is, have instruction, which would "become the exclusive possession of a small number of members of society because of differences of occupations and talents."

In contrast, *éducation nationale,* or primary education, was obligatory for all.[37]

Public surveillance and republican indoctrination were the Revolution's chief educational innovations. In Lepeletier's Spartan model, a rotating council of fifty-two fathers would, by their supervision, insure that "all who must compose the Republic will be cast into a republican mold." All children would wear the same clothes and have the same instruction, and schools would become the seedbeds of republican citizenry. Republican education would be achieved less by moral lessons than by Spartan physical and practical training. France was at war, and good citizenry consisted as much in technical know-how and bodily fitness as in sound opinions. Lepeletier planned to seize hold of the coming generation, wrest it from the tutelage of parents, and with a tough regimen make it thoroughly republican. Education would combat the lassitude and delinquency of the public.[38]

A far less coercive plan of public instruction, that of the playwright, painter, and deputy Gabriel Bouquier, was proposed just after the peak of de-Christianization. The law of 29 frimaire Year II (19 December 1793), passed a week after Bouquier's proposal, provided for a national primary education that proclaimed éducation open to all—that is, permitted to anyone who wanted to open a school, which allowed clergy to continue teaching, contrary to an earlier law of 7 brumaire that excluded them. Bouquier's provision paralleled the law of 19 frimaire on religious liberty. Proscribing "all idea of academic corps, of scientific society, of pedagogic hierarchy" (that is, the subsidized upper tiers of Condorcet's five-level system of education), Bouquier nonetheless allowed higher institutions of learning to exist freely, without public subsidy. The intermediate levels of secondary education were to be provided for by "popular societies, theaters, civic games, military evolutions, and national and local festivals." Similar to Lepeletier in objective if not in method, Bouquier's plan sought to turn out good soldiers, robust laborers, and loyal republicans with the help of state-paid teachers and state-approved textbooks. Like Lepeletier's plan, the law of 19 frimaire provided for supervision but by the "municipality or the section," as well as by "fathers, mothers, tutors or guardians and . . . all the citizens." The teacher could be denounced if he should teach "maxims contrary to the laws or to republican morality." But Bouquier's plan was nevertheless far less total, less a matter of éducation and more a matter of instruction than was Lepeletier's.[39]

The "elementary books of knowledge absolutely necessary to form citizens," in Bouquier's plan, would be approved by the Committee of Public Instruction and would consist of "the Rights of Man, the Constitution, the Tableau of heroic and virtuous actions." The idea of state textbooks had been put forth in former reports on education by Talleyrand and especially by Condorcet. Condorcet's plan had mandated textbooks of high quality, appropriate for the young, and easy and agreeable to read. The Lakanal and Lepeletier plans of 1793 incorporated this idea, and on 25 September the Convention declared that it would publish "each day a sheet which will present to the nation the heroic traits of the French who are in uniforms of Liberty and the moral virtues which serve as the bases of truly democratic Republics." Although not exactly a textbook, it was a moral and civic instruction for the armies, the municipalities, and the popular societies, as well as the schools.

On 10 nivôse (30 December 1793), under the editorship of the radical Jacobin Léonard Bourdon, the publication appeared under the title *Recueil des actions héroïques et civiques des républicains français*; 80,000 copies were printed. The issues would relate the early events of the Revolution, depicting civic heroism. "Sometimes this will be a trait of disinterestedness; a heroic action will follow it which will be followed by a sentiment of filial piety." The Convention intended to substitute this book in the schools for the catechisms and livres bleus, "inflaming [the students] with the desire to imitate the virtues of the founders of the Republic." The third issue had 150,000 copies; the fifth and final issue appeared on 13 messidor (1 July 1794).[40]

The first experiment with a text of moral and civic instruction was followed by a concours on 3 pluviôse Year II (22 January 1794) for the best "elementary books," in which anyone could compete. The idea, proposed by Lakanal on 13 June 1793, was taken up by the Lepeletier plan and promulgated at Grégoire's insistence the following winter (3 pluviôse, or 22 January 1794). Not wholly satisfied with the submissions for the concours, the Committee of Public Instruction picked scientists and men of letters to compete. Bernardin de Saint-Pierre was charged with morality, Joseph-Louis Lagrange and Adrien-Marie Legendre with arithmetic and geometry, Edmonde Mentelle with geography, and so forth. But on 4 brumaire Year IV (26 October 1795), at the beginning of the Directory, prizes were nonetheless awarded to a number of the original contestants: Charles-François Lhomond for *Eléments de grammaire française*, André-Joseph Panckoucke for *Grammaire élémentaire et mécanique*, J.-B. Sarret for *Eléments d'arithmétique* based on Condorcet's notes, Aubin-Louis Millin for *Eléments d'histoire naturelle,* Poisson de La Chabeaussière for *Principes de morale républi-caine,* Paul Turquin and Deligny for an *Art de natation,* and an illus-trated natural history by Antoine-Nicolas Duchesne and Auguste-Savinien Leblond entitled *Portefeuille des enfants.* On 11 germinal the Council of Ancients approved this motion and made it law. All these works strove not only to abridge adult knowledge for children but to simplify it. Duchesne and Leblond's *Portefeuille des enfants,* for instance, stated that "the best way to succeed with children is to show them a picture and to tell them a story," and Lhomond, in his grammar, sought to be "brief, clear and factual." The objectives do not seem revolutionary in retrospect, but the authors felt that they were bridg-ing the gap between both generations and classes of citizens, bringing the latest knowledge and methods of learning to those accustomed to the livres bleus, the almanacs, and the Catholic catechisms, and doing so in an effective manner. From the survey of primary schools in Year VI, initiated by François de Neufchâteau, it is evident that the republi-can catechisms were by far the most widely disseminated of the gov-ernment's elementary textbooks; of these, the most popular was La Chabeaussière's, which was republished eight times by 1800 and forty times by the end of the nineteenth century.[41]

Written for children in question-and-answer form, like its Catholic antecedents, it avoided their dryness by the use of quatrains. Some-what skeptical, deist, and Rousseauist-spiritualist answers to such questions as "Who are you?" "What is God?" and "What is the soul?" were substituted for those formerly dedicated to the Christian myste-ries. Sacrifice for the patrie replaced the sacrifice of the Mass. Service to humanity replaced the individual relationship of man to God. Hu-man virtues such as courage, friendship, study, and work, to which thirty-eight of the fifty-two questions were devoted, left no space for the Christian theological virtues of faith, hope, and charity.

The classical curriculum of the collèges left its mark on the cate-chisms of La Chabeaussière and others of the Revolution. Chemin-Dupontès's catechism mentions the "three hundred new Brutuses" who testified before the Convention of their willingness to sacrifice their children should any of them conspire against equality. Bulard cites the Spartans at Thermopylae, Boissel admires the rigor of Solon's and Lycurgus's legislation. La Chabeaussière echoes Seneca's quest for simplicity: "The wisest is he who desires the least." The convention-nel Lanthenas appeals for a Romanlike "public censorship and encour-agement of good moeurs, Republican moeurs." Sansculottes could now profit from the elite passion for ancient mores, popularized by the speeches of Camille Desmoulins and some subsidized productions of Voltaire's *Brutus* and *Mort de César*. This reinvigorated, heroic, and civic morality, geared to replace the more private Christian ethic, found its principal inspiration in classical antiquity.

But the debt to Christianity was greater than to classical antiquity, at least superficially. Chemin-Dupontès's *Morale des sans-culottes de tout âge, de tout sexe, de tout pays, de tout état, ou Evangile républicain* (Paris, Year II) was silent on dogma but claimed that the law of nature "is found in the Bible and the Gospel . . . as well as in the republican Constitution. Moses and Jesus were also as good sansculottes as our Montagnard deputies." This sentiment was echoed by L.-M. Henriquez's close imitation of the words of the "revolutionary from Judea." Chemin-Dupontès's definition of charity, which most authors had secularized as *bienfaisance*, was a close paraphrase of Paul's classic definition in *Corinthians* 1.13. Jesus' exhortation to love one's enemies and Paul's that women remain submissive to their husbands were reproduced almost verbatim. Although Jesus' divinity and resurrection were not mentioned, some of the most specifically Christian precepts of Gospel morality were reiterated for a sansculotterie that was not thoroughly de-Christianized.

Sacrilegious parodies of Catholic forms, rituals, and doctrines were far more frequent. Where the church was the "community of the faithful" in the Catholic catechisms of 1791–92, Gerlet's patrie was an equally mystical "communion of citizens." Pierre Gallet's *Le Véritable Evangile* (Paris, 1793–94) gives natural accounts of all Jesus' miracles but adds a sanction on divorce, unlike most revolutionary catechisms. Other authors provided republican equivalents of the Decalogue, the six commandments of the church, the seven deadly sins (usually the same as the Catholic seven), the seven sacraments, and even a creed in which sansculottes sit at the right hand of the Father.

The Enlightenment provided the language and commonplaces (for example, the natural religion of "Moses, Jesus, Mohammed") for these authors, who saw little need to cite sources. Virtually every tenet of Enlightenment morality can be found—Rousseauist attention to the heart for moral inspiration, praise of the bourgeois virtues of propriety, conjugal love, study, and work, and condemnation of libertinage, drunkenness, gambling, superstition, swearing, and fortune telling. As early as 1785 such virtues as virility, steadfastness, force, and courage were also emphasized. Unlike the philosophes, these authors denigrated the passions as sources of human misery.

The secular catechisms, gospels, commandments, and credos were used for anti-Christian or non-Christian purposes. Christian forms were filled with a de-Christianized content. Revelation, the divinity of Jesus, supernaturally binding precepts, and the promise of salvation were all jettisoned. A vague, impersonal promise of immortality remained in the Rousseauist catechisms, but it was quite distinct from the Christian heaven, the holy family, and the communion of saints. Man was once again *homo sibi relictus*—left to his own resources—or, rather, left to republican institutions, to the state. The catechism followed the old Christian practice of reaching and shaping the child, but, as Lepeletier put it, "in a republican mold," not in the Christian faith. Miracles and sacraments were out; instead, a religion of morality, in which everything focused on human virtue, prevailed. Like the religion of the Panthéon and the religion of Reason, the republican catechism fostered a religion of man, above all, a morality.

The concours ended in brumaire Year IV (autumn 1795). The Council of Five Hundred finally awarded prizes to La Chabeaussière's catechism (the only one designated to be printed at public expense), to Bulard's *Instructions élémentaires sur la morale républicaine,* and to Henriquez's *Epîtres et évangiles du républicain.* Ministers of the Interior during the Directory sent numbers of copies, with strong recommendations, to local administrations for use in the elementary schools.[42]

François de Neufchâteau's survey[43] of Year VI (1797–98) provides significant information on the ideological character of teachers and textbooks. Prompted by recent royalist election returns and by the subsequent coup d'état of Fructidor Year V (August 1797), Neufchâteau seems to have wanted to attack electoral prejudice by deracinating it in the schools. He wanted to know how many schools and what kind of schools—public or private—there were in each canton. He was also interested in knowing the "principles" of the teachers, what books they used (republican or traditional), what level of "fanaticism" prevailed. The answers are available for both types of schools in only eleven departments; in all but the Loir-et-Cher, private schools outnumbered public two to one. Surprisingly, many public school teachers used such ancien régime texts as the *Imitation of Christ,* often because of parents' demands, whereas in numerous private schools teachers used republican books. Distinctions between the two systems cannot be too sharply drawn; the inroads that republicanism made on the primary level were limited, although perhaps not so limited as contemporaries and historians have maintained.

The Directory's surveillance of teachers forced some of them out of the classrooms; others were made to adopt republican textbooks through fear. Citoyenne Duffan, an ex-nun in Labastide, in the Gers, after reading the report of the inspectors' visit to her school, claimed, "One would think oneself transported to those unfortunate times when the Terror hovered over all France."[44]

"Fanaticism" was recorded in roughly one-third of all public schools where such information is available. In Epzig, in the canton of Barr (Bas-Rhin), the teacher refused to introduce the books "approved by the Convention." In twenty-one communes of Lautrebourg, the schoolmasters taught religion and arithmetic only in German. In the canton of Arleux, in the Nord, "the majority of teachers are not republican," according to the municipal agent; the teachers neither fought "fanaticism" nor observed the *fête de la jeunesse*. In five departments (the Bas-Rhin, Charente, Gers, Nord, and Puy-de-Dôme), forty-three public schools used textbooks approved by the Convention, whereas twenty-eight were reported as not using them, refusing to use them, or using books of the old regime.[45]

In contrast, a civic republican spirit was often evident in the private schools (in 115, or 44 percent, of 259 cases). In Nogaro (the Gers), a former nun made her students address one another as "citoyen" or "citoyenne" and refused to employ corporal punishment, in accordance with the new pedagogy. At Pont Lévy (Loir-et-Cher), Citizen Chapolin, master of a pensionat, taught Bulard's *Catéchisme de morale républicaine*. His students recited the *Rights of Man,* wore the republican cockade, and observed the republican calendar. Sister Duffan found republicanism and Christianity perfectly compatible: "I think that any Christian," she wrote, "can attend the festivals of the décadi as long as the orators do not indulge in any diatribe against the Christian religion." Her aim was to form "*bonnes chrétiennes et bonnes républicaines* . . . for I am far from thinking these two titles incompatible. . . . I find in the Gospel the most pure maxims of the republican code and I will always make it the basis of my education."[46]

Those who did adopt republican textbooks did not always do so voluntarily. The period after the Eighteenth of Fructidor has been called the second Terror. Although it never inspired the same fear as the Great Terror, it republicanized culture with lesser forms of intimidation and compulsion, which like the earlier ones met with considerable resistance.

The Revolution's project of education and its project of de-Christianization were inextricable. The irrational, *carnavalesque* character of the latter risked making it disrespectable. But this did not mean that de-Christianization by more peaceful means was abandoned. For

Robespierre a new cult of the Supreme Being would replace Christianity. For his successors after Thermidor, the return to religious tolerance involved suspending priests' salaries and prohibiting external manifestations of cult. In a country where public means of support had been removed with the abolition of the tithe and the confiscation of church property, salaries had been quite important. Their discontinuation created an effect quite different from the more positive effects of separation of church and state in the United States. For one intent of the Boissy d'Anglas law of 1795 was to assure that Catholicism would never regain its former strength. Indeed, this second antireligious policy may have brought about a decline of religious practice in some places in certain milieux more effectively than the de-Christianization of the Terror, because its effects were gradual and thus less perceptible. The real decline in religion during the Revolution may have come about as a result less of outright persecution than of the interruption of the sacraments, which in locales without priests were not dispensed for a generation. Some Frenchmen forgot what the sacraments were, others never learned.

As for education proper, the same secularizing tendencies prevailed. In the primary public and private schools, the survey-inquest of Year VI aimed at replacing Catholic primers with republican ones. In the central secondary schools, the old regime Christian curriculum was deliberately abandoned for a more "ideological" or philosophical one. Certainly one educational aim of the Revolution was to de-Christianize the nation.

To this end the revolutionaries were right to view education as a polymorphous experience capable of being acquired through work and play, war and peace, prose and pageantry. It was an education paradoxically closer to its Catholic antecedent, with the capital substitution of patrie for God and nation for church. This was the religion of a Michelet in the 1840s, when more explicit pantheisms held sway over many romantics. But the faith of the republicans of the 1790s was not atheistic: its center of gravity had simply shifted from a transcendent God to an immanent humanity.

The conversion of the Church of Saint-Geneviève into a pantheon of great men will always remain the symbol of the revolutionary faith. It remained close enough to its Christian origins to be twice rededicated to its original patron in the nineteenth century. This proximity, this confusion, remains an indelible trait of contemporary French civilization, which celebrates on one day in the summer the storming of the Bastille and a month later the Assumption of the Virgin.

The republican school had links to its Catholic predecessor, but it announced the arrival of the secular public school, instrument of the state in shaping young minds with propaganda useful to its survival. What separated 1789 from 1917 and 1933 was its greater earnestness. Propaganda and revolution were not yet reduced to techniques. "Ideology" was not yet admittedly "ideological" but rather science. The republican still revered his objects of belief. He was still a naive "true believer" rather than a cynical worshiper of power. The idea that morality was nothing more than a function of the state would have been repugnant to him, because he believed in natural law and an objective standard of right rather than in one that only served some political utility. This belief distinguished the republican from the totalitarian.

Educating through Theater

Although schools were the natural organs of education, a wide view of education would repeatedly define theater as a "school of civicism and republican mores." But theater audiences were far less well behaved than schoolchildren; their obstreperousness was notorious long before the Revolution. Attempts had been made to curb them, to prevent them, for instance, from sitting on stage. Long before the Revolution, observers like Grimm noticed what they regarded as a vulgarization of audiences in elite theaters, which now included day laborers, cook boys, hairdresser helpers. Of course the boxes still seated aristocrats, but when the aristocracy emigrated, the boxes were often converted into seats for le peuple. Saint-Just wrote in his *Institutions républicaines*: "We begin to see today citizens who work only three days a year. Formerly, the nobility, the court, filled up the theaters: the latter is banished, the former is not very numerous; and still the theaters have the same luxury. Who are those then who parade there if it is not those who worked in former times?"[47]

The revolutionaries wanted to educate this public through entertainment, but first they had wanted a free theater. This freedom, however, resulted in a breakdown of all restraints; caricatures of priests, nuns, and monks, which had been banned from the stage in the old regime (Tartuffe was a layman), were now prominently displayed as objects of ridicule. Further, plays with no apparent ideological or moral message—such as Louis Anseaume's *Les Deux Chasseurs et la laitière* (1763) or Pierre-Jean-Baptiste Desforges's *Le Sourd, ou L'Auberge pleine* (1790)—were overwhelmingly popular. Convent "garbage" (anticlerical satires) and frivolous or pastoral comedies were not what the revolutionaries had in mind when they spoke of a regenerated theater.

Before theaters were subjected to prior censorship, the Committee of Public Safety, in the person of Georges-Auguste Couthon, stipulated that "incivic" theaters be purged and that all theaters perform weekly Chénier's *Gaius Gracchus,* Voltaire's *Brutus* and *Mort de César,* and Lemierre's *Guillaume Tell.* In his intervention in the Convention of 2 August 1793, Couthon referred to "an infinity of plays filled with allusions injurious to liberty, and which have no other aim than to deprave public spirit and moeurs." Neither aristocrats nor kings could be portrayed favorably. The tragedies of Corneille and Racine virtually disappeared from the repertory; the word *rois* (kings) was changed to *lois* (laws). But it was difficult to satisfy the Committee of Public Safety; even some radical plays, like the *Jugement dernier des rois,* mysteriously disappeared from the repertory after only twenty-two performances. Official orders may have been responsible, for such plays were the work of Hébertists or ultrarevolutionaries, who Robespierre felt were trying to discredit the Revolution by their excesses.[48]

Censorship, which had been abolished with theater privilege in 1791, was gradually reintroduced. It was first entrusted to the municipalities to keep public order and eventually to the Commission d'instruction publique in April 1794 to purge repertories. Prior submission of scripts was then reimposed. As we have seen, stringent controls were imposed on religious practice after it had been proclaimed free by the Declaration of Rights in 1789. Education was also presumably free, but the republican controls over schooling said otherwise. State "censorship" fell first on religion, next on education, and finally on the theaters.

The convocations of numerous theater directors on charges of incivism before the Committee of Public Safety between 29 July and 10 August 1793 and again between 20 and 25 January 1794 suggest how seriously the government wished to purify repertories. By 6 pluviôse Year II (25 January 1794) virtually all the theaters of Paris had been convoked. Whatever freedom remained to directors in choosing their repertories was removed by the institution of prior censorship (1 April 1794).[49]

Before then, as we have seen, the Ministry of the Interior had its agents roaming through Paris, eavesdropping, observing, and writing reports for the minister. Often they were reassured by enthusiastic throngs, as for instance when watching any one of the five plays about the recapture of Toulon performed in late 1793 and early 1794. This proved the good health of public opinion (*esprit public*), the agents' primary concern. But frequently what they saw was distressing: plays that had nothing to do with the Revolution, or worse, counterrevolutionary plays; audiences that took patriotic lines from an actor's mouth and twisted them into incivic meanings (which left censorship helpless); disturbances by audiences divided in their reactions; incidents that required police or military intervention. All this proved a heightened need for the *police des théâtres* and for the censorship of repertories. But how hard that was. On 5 October 1793 Chénier put on his play *Timoléon* at the Théâtre de la République—a play about a Greek statesman and dictator. Chénier was ostensibly obeying the wishes of the government, which wanted classical tragedy celebrating the heroic, republican virtues, but Chénier's tyrant was a republican (perhaps really a French republican), not a king. Legouvé made similar use of a classical tyrant in his *Epicharis et Néron,* premiered in early February 1794 and performed again on the night of Ninth Thermidor. The allusions to Robespierre and the Twelve were obvious, and both plays were recalled.[50]

Theaters and scripts were harder to strip of all "traces of feudalism and royalty" than were churches and castles, or so it seemed, because live audiences reacted to live actors, whose tone of voice and facial expressions could not be censored. "Educating" thus became very difficult, and with the Ninth of Thermidor, when Robespierre fell, the repertory gradually assumed an anti-Jacobin tone. Censors had the difficult task of watching for a resurgence of Jacobinism, which frequently took the form of singing the *Chant du départ* before performances and preventing the counterrevolutionary *Réveil du peuple.* Police interventions to put down these two feuding contingents were far more frequent between 1794 and 1800 than during the Terror.[51]

To educate in this pandemonium (fig. XI.7) was not easy, and the repertories after 1794 became both more classical in elite theaters and more poissarde in many popular theaters. These were the years of Mme Angot, but her allusions to politics were no longer republican propaganda as such, for satire was coming into its own. In short, the Directory failed to make the theater a school—so much so that the lament of republicans like Chénier about the quality of theater was common by Year VI. When the minister of the Interior later began his survey of schools to counteract fanaticism, the playwrights dreamed of an Institut dramaturgique that would allow them to lift drama out of the morass of bad taste and vulgarity. Democratization in theater had

XI.7.
[Louis-Léopold] Boilly, The "Rixe" of the Muscadins, or the Arrest of
the Singer Garat, *painting, ca. 1794–95.*
Courtesy Musée Carnavalet, Paris, photo: Lauros-Giraudon/Art Resource, New York.

begun before the Revolution and was at odds with éducation during it,
for neither the Chapelier Law nor revolutionary censorship was able
to make drama a "school of civicism and republican moeurs." *Gaieté*—
which one could translate here as sheer fun, pleasure, or diversion—
thwarted the efforts of the educators.[52]

Clubs and Garrisons

The revolutionaries' notion of education was far more
polymorphous than our own, encompassing theaters as well as schools,
garrisons as well as clubs. Their idea of education was also more ideological and political than the liberal ideal of free inquiry.

The Masonic lodges had established the principle of free association
for the pursuit of knowledge, virtue, and fraternity on no grounds
other than commonly shared beliefs. These beliefs were quasi-secular,
quasi-religious, but entirely independent of ecclesiastical hierarchy.

They formed the basis of a new mode of association. The Jacobin societies that followed in their steps were not so much their genealogical descendants as a new manifestation of the same phenomenon of secular association. For Augustin Cochin, who analyzed the principles of these organizations in *Les Sociétés de pensée et la démocratie moderne,* the philosophes were a sect with their own corps of initiates organized throughout Europe in a République des lettres, constituting a fanatical hatred of the Christian religion. The substance was entirely in the principle of association itself. "Society" had become an idol: "The secret of union, the law of progress, moreover, lay in the fact of association itself." Democracy, which substituted a societal form of government for a personal one, became a school in itself. The Jacobin clubs were the principal instruments of political acculturation that some hundred thousand Frenchmen received between 1790 and 1799. They supplanted the monks, the Dominican Jacobins, whose name they adopted and in whose library and refectory they met. Many of the over two thousand Jacobin clubs that sprang up by the end of 1793 in the provinces also met in former convents or other "national property" confiscated from the church. To view Jacobinism as a religion, as has Crane Brinton, has displeased many French revolutionary historians, but the Jacobins themselves spoke of their patriotism as "a religion." Listen to Camille Desmoulins in the *Révolutions de France et de Brabant:*

> In the propagation of patriotism, that is to say of philanthropy, this new religion which is destined to conquer the universe for itself, the club, or the Jacobin church seems to be called to the same primacy as the church of Rome in the propagation of Christianity. Already all the clubs or assemblies or churches of patriots which are forming everywhere solicit at birth its correspondence, write to it as a sign of communion. The society of Jacobins is the nation's true committee of investigation, and less dangerous to good citizens than that of the Assembly, where denunciations and deliberations are made public, [but] much more formidable to the bad, because it embraces every nook and cranny of the 83 departments in its correspondence with the affiliated societies. It is again the great inquisitor which frightens aristocrats. It is also the great prosecutor which corrects abuses and comes to the help of all citizens.

In prairial 1794, the denounced president of the Jacobin club of Apt cleared himself by going to the tribune "to teach his religion on this subject" and to testify to his "well-known patriotism." The Grand

Orient was the other model of the Jacobin network. According to Desmoulins: "[The Jacobin Club] is the Grand Orient, the metropolitan to
which all the Jacobins, all the friends of the constitution in the 83
departments, correspond." Even so, the Jacobins closed down the
Grand Orient in 1793 as the de-Christianizers (fig. XI.8) tried to close
down the Church.[53]

For Frenchmen unaccustomed to participating in government, belonging to the Jacobins was an educational experience. Parisian society
consisted largely of deputies of the Assembly who formed "the party"
loyal to the constitution, or at least their interpretation of it, whence
their original appellation: Society of the Friends of the Constitution.
Most members were middle-class, but, particularly in the provincial societies, artisans and shopkeepers were numerous and made up
slightly less than one-fourth of membership—clergymen, merchants,
and members of the liberal professions accounted for two-thirds. Members were nominated from the floor and had to be scrutinized (*épuré*)
for civicism before being admitted. Many clubs were large, and in the
spring of 1794 even such small ones as that of Apt could admit a dozen
new members in one day. Provence was thick with the Jacobin network: Aix had 736 members in 1791, Marseilles 1,800 in August 1790.
Elections were a form of practicing democracy; a "bureau" was required of every club, and election of its president, secretary, and treasurer occupied many meetings. To speak, members had to "be given
the floor," and although meetings occasionally resulted in brawls, the
ritual required each to wait his turn and then intone a discourse in
patriotic jargon. This was one of the Revolution's several experiments
with direct democracy.[54]

Committees were the essence of the democratic experience. In them
Jacobins learned to assume special responsibilities, such as sending a
deputation on visits—to the municipality, to the local surveillance
committee, to the representative-on-mission, or to the "national agent"
responsible for the local economy—and to prevail on those visited to
adopt a particular course of action. A key committee was the correspondence committee, which handled the mail from Paris and from the
affiliated societies, opened the newspapers to which the society subscribed, and decided which would be read at the next meeting. Vigilance committees that kept watch over local inhabitants were the earli-
est forms of surveillance in such towns as Bar-le-duc and Dunkirk,
where anxiety over security was more acute than in the interior. Meetings lasting several hours could be called as often as four times a week.
The educational nature of the societies sprang from their probable

XI.8.
Society of the Friends of the Constitution, Otherwise Known as the Jacobin Club, *engraving.*
Courtesy *Bibliothèque nationale.*

origins as cabinets de lecture more than from their connections to the Masonic lodges or academies. One author likens their "correspondence" to the news network of the Jansenist *Nouvelles Ecclésiastiques* of the old regime. In the reading rooms of these societies, reading aloud and in private was the principal means by which Jacobin democracy spread to the professional classes and literate artisanate.[55]

Below the network of predominantly middle-class Jacobin clubs with fairly steep membership fees were popular societies founded to educate the people, for the most part artisans and shopkeepers— butchers, bakers, water porters, fruit vendors, greengrocers, and their wives and children. The first and foremost of the Parisian societies was the Société fraternelle des Jacobins, founded in February 1790, which occupied the Jacobin library after the senior club moved to the refectory at the end of 1791. Others included the Société des amis des droits de l'homme, the Société fraternelle des amies des droits de l'homme, the Ennemis du despotisme, the Société des nomophiles, and several fraternal societies of specific quartiers. The founder of the Société fraternelle des Jacobins was a schoolmaster who envisaged the role of his society in strictly educational terms—so much so that he was forced to leave when in early 1791 the society adopted the policy of the senior societies of active policing, surveillance, and denunciations. These societies admitted women, unlike the Jacobin clubs. On their entrance they were obliged to swear to use the Declaration of the Rights of Man and Citizen to teach their children to read—a practice that the republican catechisms of the Year II formalized in print. The societies went beyond instruction of the illiterate to the surveillance and denunciation that Marat urged on them. The language of the sansculottes of Year II shows a good grasp of the ideology of egalitarianism but not the qualities of educated men: moderation, impartiality, good judgment, detachment. The Société des indigents wrote to the Société patriotique de la section de Luxembourg with candor and humility about their limitations: "Our title, which is a real fact, indicates to you that we do not have the time to instruct ourselves, to participate with our insights in your deliberations, but we will come there to be able to report to our Society within the limits of our intelligence."[56]

The popular societies and the Jacobin clubs were distinct groups, but so parallel that frequently their rules overlapped. The same political ritual adhered in both societies—electing members, after 1791 by a *comité épuratoire,* reading minutes, reading newspapers, drafting addresses, delivering, printing, and distributing speeches, making formal denunciations, and holding meetings of committees of correspondence and surveillance. The popular societies were almost deferential in their imitation of the Jacobin clubs. The whole process was an éducation in political participation, in stretching the web of concern from the corporation or ville to the nation and Republic. Like the Jacobins, many were federated (in a Comité central des sociétés patriotiques), attended one another's meetings in deputations, and shared their minutes. Through frequent communication and through the patriotic content of the entrance oaths, the popular societies broke down the separatist barriers of corporations and *compagnonnages* and strove to create a true fraternity. The Committee of Public Safety on one occasion told the popular societies that they were "in some manner the professors of a new instruction."[57]

Denunciations and illiteracy, ignorance and violence clearly undermined these democratic aspirations. The popular societies and Jacobins attempted to establish a democracy. But theirs was virtuocracy that could fall into the worst crimes—sacrilege, false testimony, fratricide, pillage. (Witness the representatives Javogues in the Rhône and Carrier at Nantes.) Education can only be understood to mean what

Jacobinism pretended it to mean, not what it usually conveys. Democracy was spoiled, not saved, by the Terror. According to Cochin, its machine—its vast network of committees and correspondence—obscured personal responsibility and decision making and made actions that would appear personally reprehensible seem collectively justifiable. Denunciation, to choose the most important Jacobin activity, became an independent, ritualized art, fueled by fear perhaps, but perpetuated independently of its cause. Where cause for denunciation was lacking, one was found, for a Jacobin is by definition a vigilante.

Such a picture of the Jacobins may jar with an impression of naive earnestness on the part of sansculotte members of the popular societies—their pitiful attempts to read, to behave "constitutionally," to serve the patrie. But these societies also deteriorated. After the springtime youthfulness of 1790 and 1791, they dropped to the level of the ugly, vindictive comités révolutionnaires of Year II (see fig. IX.19). By then the popular societies lacked the generous and conciliatory spirit needed to be truly national and democratic, and they degenerated into a dominant faction.[58]

But where the popular societies were invariably patriotic, carrying out purges on their less loyal members, the army at the very beginning of the Revolution was not. Almost the entire officer corps was aristocratic at the time of the oath following Varennes. When war broke out in spring 1792, numerous regiment commanders emigrated. Troops were divided between those friendly to the Jacobins and popular societies and those loyal to the royal army. Gaining the army's loyalty was critical to the Constituent Assembly and led it to allow soldiers to take part in the political life of the clubs and elect their own petty officers. Democracy thus reached the army only to a slightly lesser degree than it reached the clubs and popular societies. The enrollment of patriotic volunteers in 1792 and 1793 and their "amalgamation" with the infantry of the royal army helped create a patriotic force of *défenseurs de la patrie*. The *levée en masse* of 1793, however, brought in thousands of peasants who had no desire to march hundreds of miles from their homes to risk their lives for a republic that was requisitioning their crops and livestock. Desertions were easy and numerous. An education appropriate to the army was needed to insure that these soldiers would fight more effectively and perform the civilian services taken over by the army—surveillance, purges, requisitions. Soldiers were not yet fully citizens; they had to be made such.[59] The military doctrine of the Revolution put great stock in morale, bravery, and the will to fight. The conventionnel Merlin de Thionville wrote in May 1792: "It is not the fright of punishments that can motivate the soldiers of the patrie, it is the burning passion of liberty; the sentiment of glory and honor has always made heroes, and the fear of punishments has never produced anything but slaves."[60]

Generals could instill this love of country and desire for triumphs by haranguing troops, painting the enemy in dark colors as "satellites of tyrants." They could appeal for obedience by describing their own magnanimity. But in Year II the most orthodox doctrine was that of autodiscipline, the military application of the doctrine of the general will. Saint-Just observed in the Terror that "it is not only the number and discipline of soldiers that must give you victory; you will obtain it only by virtue of the progress which the republican spirit has made in the army. The word 'command' is improper; for to whatever degree one observes the law, you do not command. There is therefore no real command except the general will and the law." Fighting was not the execution of orders but the carrying out of the innermost sentiments of a citizen to defend the patrie of which each was a part. One obeyed because one was the author of the general will through the social contract.[61]

Military journals had sprung up under the ministry of Duc Etienne-François de Choiseul. By 1793 several journals had come into existence, such as the *Journal de l'armée des côtes de Cherbourg* and the Jacobin *Avant Garde* of the army of the Pyrénées-Orientales. These journals of individual armies attempted to familiarize homesick peasants with their new environment. But these journals were novel in that they were intended for the troops rather than for the *état major*—a sign in itself of democratization. Jacobin newspapers sent mailings from Paris to soldiers to read in their spare time. The *Feuille de salut public,* the official organ of the Terror, was also distributed. The number of copies mailed was limited—probably under twenty thousand (four of the papers accounted for ten thousand)—but each copy was widely circulated. After the fall of Robespierre, Carnot published the *Soirée du camp.* Although it had a short life, it was the first national military journal intended for the troops. Imitating the popular style of the defunct *Père Duchesne,* Carnot tried to win the confidence of the soldiers by his conversational tone, speaking to them as the Old Good-Hearted Sargeant, addressing them as his "comrades in the army of the Republic." This journal was followed by the *Journal des défenseurs de la patrie,* another national military journal that came out when the Jacobin political newspapers were canceled after Thermidor.[62]

The *Journal des défenseurs de la patrie* was founded in part to combat Babeuf's Conspiracy of the Equals of 1796. Like the governments of the Republic, Babeuf wanted to win the army, to make it an instrument of politics. "Soldiers of the People?" Babeuf wrote to the armies, "For whom and for what do you fight? . . . Is it to fortify the Republic of invaders, of speculators, of . . . oppressors? Is it to come back to languish from hunger and from misery under their yoke?" The army risked being corrupted by both democratic and Caesarean propaganda during the Directory, and in Year II it was the task of Carnot and his *Journal des défenseurs de la patrie,* edited by Joseph Lavallée, to continue the civic education of soldiers as best possible. Although the army of the Directory became subordinate, not fraternal, to the government and the alliance of soldiers and people was abandoned, the stress on virtue and on love of nation and liberty survived in this newspaper as an inspiration for combat.[63]

The commanders of the Republican armies also instilled loyalty in their troops in other ways. When camps were close to towns with theaters, soldiers viewed performances of patriotic plays. Like the popular societies, the armies also took an active part in the civic festivals. On these occasions, officers, like mayors in the cities, harangued their troops. And in a negative sense, the Terror "educated" the army through its civil commissioners and military tribunals, which were ready to denounce and prosecute embezzlement, mismanagement of funds, pillage, desertion, and incivicism. Through surveillance, soldiers were forcibly educated to live up to the high expectations of citizen soldiery.

The letterheads of bulletins and decrees, and the *mots d'ordres* of each unit, which changed daily, included: "Virtue, bravery, triumph," "Rome, Cato, Virtue," "Armed Forces, Friendship, Fraternity," "Revolution, Convention, Obedience," "Love, Respect of the Laws," "People, Property, Respect," "Heroic Actions Rewarded." By such slogans, soldiers were reminded of what it was they were fighting for.[64]

How much of the republican military education did the soldiers imbibe? J.-P. Bertaud, who has studied several hundred letters from soldiers at the War Archives at Vincennes, has found that some soldiers of the Puy-de-Dôme and Indre expressed sentiments of the purest patriotism: "It would be better to die than to cede an inch. Our cause is just, we will uphold it as we always have to the very last drop of our blood." Or again, "The armies of the Republic are doing well, and soon the tyrants will be confounded." But only fifteen in several hundred of the letters of the Indre mirrored these sentiments. The rest of the soldiers complained of lacking food and supplies or hoped to get a "Piedmontese bullet" in the gut so as to be freed from the hardships of war. A less drastic solution, and one common on the frontiers, was to drink. It is safe to say that the patriotic education and memories of Valmy, Fleurus, and Lodi had a profound effect on some soldiers but failed to inflame the hearts of many others.[65]

CHAPTER XII

EPILOGUE

THE CULTURAL

CONSEQUENCES

OF THE REVOLUTION

The French Revolution was an explosion. What remained of the ancien régime and revolutionary culture—religion, schools, theaters, works of art—when that explosion had subsided? What changed and what survived from the distant and immediate past? How many Frances resulted from the shattering (if exhilarating) experience of the 1790s?

The Short-Term: The Revolution

A violent political upheaval like the French Revolution could not have been expected to give birth to many durable cultural creations. Chained to the interests and passions of factions, culture served political ends. It failed to rise far enough above the circumstantial to gain a place beyond its century, a universality. The thousands of brochures, pamphlets, committee minutes, satirical songs, parodies, caricatures, and newspapers, the revolutionary calendar and the festivals, the two-score Parisian theaters, the oaths of the constitutional church, the hundreds of pedagogical plans, the thousands of clubs and popular societies and sections, the revolutionary nomenclatures—many of these were disintegrating by the time Napoléon razed them; others, like the Institute's Class of Moral and Political Sciences and the central schools, died a violent death. Little of an institutional nature remained of the cultural upheaval of the 1790s after the turn of the century. Notable exceptions were the Louvre, elements of the Napoleonic codes, and the metric system.

The Revolution did not leave a culture of its own behind largely because it negated the culture of the old regime rather than creating a new one. Culture had become too implicated in the nexus of social-political interests and passions. This involvement made the survival of revolutionary creations precarious, since culture presumes transcendence of the immediate in order to pass on something universal to successive generations. Those projects universal in scope—for example, the metric system—survived if they did not conflict with vital cultural traditions. The revolutionary conquest of space within France succeeded (the division of France into departments), but the reorganization of time (apart from the basic division of history into ancien régime and Revolution) did not, the calendar of the saints being more perdurable than the lands of the church.

The legacy most proper to the Revolution, as Maurice Agulhon and Lynn Hunt have so forcefully pointed out, was democratic republicanism, which was embraced by a large segment of the middle classes, the working class, and regional sections of the peasantry. The difficult, bloody birth of republicanism in the Revolution, however, made it unacceptable to many of the French and to most Europeans in the first half of the nineteenth century. The Republic meant Terror, and Terror meant war with Europe. This republicanism had to throw off its origins, learn to coexist with more moderate forms of government in the Restoration and the July Monarchy. Secularism, individual liberties, a broad suffrage, public education, free trade, and economic progress constituted the ideals of the republican consensus rather than a definite form of government. Most republicans of the nineteenth century accepted the Revolution of 1789 without the Jacobin trappings.[1]

Most significant about this republican legacy was politics itself—elections, campaigns, voting, with all the options this implied. Participation in local and national elections involved progressively more and more of the French people after 1848, including by 1875 a broad peasant support for the Third Republic. Republicanism was the most enduring consequence of what was above all a political revolution in 1789. Political passion substituted for folkways, popular culture, and religion, although in 1848 and for a long time afterward it was en-tangled with them. Politics evolved into a new form of popular cul-ture—led by the elite but to which the elite had to bow deeply if it wished to stay in power. The mass citizenry would not be entirely literate until the First World War, whence in part the ironic ambiva-lence of those whom George Armstrong Kelly called Parnassian liber-als—Tocqueville, Renan, Flaubert—at the mid-nineteenth century.[2]

The second most significant cultural consequence of the Revolution stemmed from the abolition of corporations in 1791. The state dis-solved and absorbed the corporate church, academies, theaters, and schools, with their privileges, charters, and endowments. The revolu-tionary replacements followed no one pattern but took varied forms—outright proscription of the church and academies in Year II, free competition of theatrical enterprise, albeit with supervision, and a half-hearted national organization of schools, successful primarily on the secondary and higher levels. The beneficiary of this successful war on ancien régime corporatism was the state as much as the citizen. Tocqueville was correct: the Revolution enhanced the centralization of the old regime, because the state stepped into the vacuum the old corporations had left. The state harnessed the church through the Concordat (and the Organic Articles appended to it) more tightly than before 1789. The church, for example, no longer held the assemblies of the clergy as it had in the old regime. Theaters had to be authorized and plays censored, with only brief interludes of liberty, throughout the nineteenth century. Napoléon censored the book, periodical, and pamphlet press, and this censorship continued with brief interruptions of liberty (1830–34, 1848, 1870–74) until censorship was abolished for all but the theater in 1881.

The university monopolized education on all levels; it conceded to congregations and private bodies the right to teach on the primary and secondary levels. Where the church, in the old regime, had been a loose confederation of religious orders and bishops that dispensed education, after the Revolution the state was sovereign over education, though with the cooperation of congregations and religious orders throughout the nineteenth century. Religious influence survived in many ways—in the bishop as grand master of the university during the Restoration, in the battle over Jesuit presence in the educational system in the July Monarchy, in the primary and secondary schools run by religious orders, and in the teaching of Catholicism in the pub-lic schools even after the Guizot law of 1833. But the state theoretically was at the helm, and when the Falloux law of 1850, which favored

Catholic education, caused enrollment in Catholic secondary schools to increase, anticlerical republicans grew worried.[3]

Change was easily enacted. As minister of education in 1879 and 1881, Jules Ferry, a Freemason like many of his cominsters in the Third Republic, secularized state education by passing three laws in two years, a feat made simple by the state control over the entire educational establishment. What changed with Ferry was not so much state control but the enforcement of a secularization that the university had not yet implemented. The regime was the first republic to take hold since the Revolution, not because it was democratic but because it was conservative—the regime "that divides us the least."[4] The republicanism of the regime consisted almost entirely in elections and in enforcing the secular pedagogy in thousands of schools throughout the nation. There was a real throwback to 1795—to the principles of the textbooks of the Convention, to the secular catechisms. The rest had already been dismantled.

But perhaps the greatest galvanizer in early nineteenth-century France was the Bonapartist myth, which painted the emperor as having "organized the Revolution" and as having been a friend of peace for fifteen years, not only within France but throughout Europe. He had, the myth claimed, been forced into endless war by the intransigence of Great Britain. For the average Frenchman after 1815— veterans on half-pay, peasants, workers—Napoléon was *the* exciting personality. Besides his military prowess, it was he, after all, who had proclaimed: "Every Frenchman could say under my reign, 'I shall be a minister, a marshall of France, a grand officer of the Empire, duke, count, baron, if I deserve it, even king.'"[5]

By establishing electoral colleges composed of the six hundred wealthiest citizens of each department, Napoléon effectively eviscerated France of political life; but he also brought internal peace, limitless careerism, and military adventure abroad. To France he brought peace, to Europe war, to France equality in exchange for political liberty, to Europe a modicum of internal political liberty in exchange for subordination to France. Napoléon synthesized the egalitarianism of the Revolution with the authority and centralization of the old regime. He accentuated the second and attenuated the first, all without civil war and terror.

The appeal of religion for Napoléon was largely political: "In religion," he said, "I do not see the mystery of the Incarnation but the mystery of the social order."[6] He made use of religion because it taught respect of authority and resignation to one's lot, which seemed the logical alternative to the democratic envy of sansculotterie. Not that Napoléon eschewed promotion and opportunity. He and his regime exemplified it in spectacular fashion. But when he restored the nobility and established the Legion of Honor, rank became neither a right nor a grace but an award—something to be both deserved and conferred. (He alone gained his title when he took his crown from the pope.) This model was far closer to the fledgling meritocracy at the end of the old regime than to the popular democracy of Year II.

Waterloo eclipsed Bonapartism. The threat of a recrudescence of European war that Napoléon's restoration would mean was, to most contemporaries, one of the fears that kept the Bourbon Restoration alive. If Charles X had ruled in the same style as his brother, Louis XVIII, the Restoration would doubtless have lasted longer. Most of the French in 1815 were looking for peace and a degree of comfort they had sacrificed during a generation of war. But the Bonapartist prestige loomed over every government from 1815 to 1848, promising adventure and glory at the right moment to all who might be bored.

Peace and the repose of nations, as Metternich put it, were the prevailing aspirations of statesmen during the first half of the nineteenth century. Napoléon satisfied it domestically for the French and fell because he failed to satisfy it on the Continent. The foreign conflicts of the Revolution were tolerated far longer than the national fratricides. Boulevard and metro names in Paris still commemorate the glories of the Empire whereas, with few exceptions, the Revolution has been effaced from French toponymy.[7]

The Revolution's principal legacies were the Revolution itself and the memory of it, which has not completely faded in two hundred years. Through the first half of the nineteenth century, this memory was largely a nightmare—a fear of the Terror's recurrence. Most politicians and historians incorporated revolution in their work to exorcise it, neutralize it, make it tolerable. But however much they excoriated it, it would not go away. It was for Tocqueville an ever-present menace that would surface every fifteen or twenty-five years. It had been there since 1814 for Destutt de Tracy, following on the heels of the Napoleonic "counterrevolution," and he shuddered to think where it would lead, "republican" that he was. Felicité-Robert de Lamennais prophesied that France would rapidly fall "to the last degree of weakness and misfortune" and would become "the theater of a new revolution" before the century was out.[8] For the romantic Pierre-Simon Ballanche, however, it would lead to a complete social regeneration—a *palingénésie sociale*. To Maistre it signaled a revolt of the nations against

God, which called for the pope's restoration as an arbiter between subjects and sovereigns.[9] For Louis Bonald, the Revolution that had begun with a declaration of the rights of man would end with a declaration of the rights of God. And for Michelet it *was* a religion: the climax of the people's march through history, when justice would replace grace.[10]

From revolutionary "faith" were born the numerous nineteenth-century religions of humanity (including Comte's)—religions that made humanity an object of cult. The Revolution's impact on the explosion of history in the nineteenth century has yet to be fully examined, but it is unmistakable. A new messianism, the Revolution staked out a new beginning and a new end of time—the overthrow of the old regime and the establishment of a free, fraternal, egalitarian society. If for historians the Revolution did not begin time anew, as for the authors of the revolutionary calendar, they often found it the central event toward which the previous centuries of suffering, gradual emancipation, or democratizing centralization had led. The force of the French Revolution dictated a historical reconsideration of tradition. A historical outlook and historical mindset became the salient features of nineteenth-century thought.

The widows, sons, and daughters of the sansculottes and Jacobins who had been deported, shot, or guillotined carried the Revolution into the nineteenth century. Richard Cobb describes them: "The irreconcilables [widows] nourished the coming generation on a mixed diet of reverence, revenge, romantic republicanism, and the purifying beauties of violence. . . . *La veuve* Sijas, *la veuve* Loys, *la veuve* Babeuf, *la veuve* Le Bas, saw to it that their sons never forgot."[11] These "intransigent priestesses at revolutionary shrines . . . retained the militaristic chauvinism of Jacobinism." The humble wives of sansculottes lived in "the hutments of the Gros Caillou in the former Section des Invalides" juxtaposed painfully and dangerously with the rich of the faubourg Saint-Germain. They grouped together in "cellars and cafés," where they were tracked by the police; they passed onto the next generation the hopes of 1793. The historian Gabriel Monod heard a Breton widow, with whom he lodged, praise her father for his continuing loyalty to the ideals of 1793, expecting the Revolution to reappear with every new outburst from 1814 to 1848. This old man died during the Second Empire, paraphrasing Zachary: "O sun of 1793, am I going to die thus without ever again seeing your rays?"[12] This revolutionary faith became a tradition. To quote Cobb again: "In 1830, 1848, and 1871 the militant would be acting the same old play over and over again, publishing the same old play over the same old titles, and many of the *insurgés* of the Trois Glorieuses had a second go in the June Days, many of the women of the Commune were the wives or the widows of the *proscrits de juin.*"[13]

But does this memory, this tradition, with its ritual reenactments and respect of fallen martyrs, make a culture? Small, fragmented, and fractured as it was, it constituted more a subculture than a national culture. Perhaps it can be called a counterculture, but at the present state of research it remains a question whether these latter-day revolutionaries communicated sufficiently among themselves to constitute a counter- or subculture. Was there a revolutionary network beneath a layer of conservative "bien pensants" of the party of order? It is possible that the 27,000 arrested following the coup d'état of Louis Napoléon in December 1851 constituted a corps of "red" Republicans who linked the egalitarianism of 1789 with that of 1871 and after. But more work is needed on whether enough of a network existed to make up a microsociety, a counterculture descending from the sansculottes of 1793. Determining this goes beyond the scope of the present work.

The term *revolutionary culture* may imply mutually contradictory ideas—of subversion and of transmission. If the values of the Revolution had been established and transmitted, the culture of 1789–93 would no longer have been revolutionary, for the desire to overthrow established values and institutions would have ceased to exist. This, roughly, has been the situation in France since 1880: the Republic is firmly established, the Fourteenth of July is a national holiday, and the "Marseillaise"[14] is no longer a battle hymn but now a national anthem (1879). The Republic was anodized, successfully distanced from the Terror and the war; it had become as bourgeois as France. At last the Revolution had ended!

The Medium-Term: Enlightenment and Romanticism

If the memory of the Revolution became a quasi-tradition in the nineteenth century, so did the Enlightenment. The Idéologues survived the Revolution to publish several major works: the *Rapports du physique et du moral de l'homme* (1802) of Cabanis, the *Eléments d'idéologie* (1801–15) of Destutt de Tracy, and the *Essai sur les garanties individuelles* . . . (1817) of Daunou. Repeated publications of the works of the Enlightenment philosophes, with Tracy as active protagonist, penetrated the corners of the globe. That Enlightenment was still "critical," in Comte's sense of the word. Because of the persistence of the Revolution *and* tradition, it helped to create the "moral anarchy" that characterized the nineteenth century; an anarchy brought about by the conflict over fundamentals.[15]

Although idéologie and philosophie remained at war with altar and throne, a new order was attempted, one based on self-interest and the maximalist, felicific principle that the greatest good is the greatest happiness of the greatest number. This respect for the interests of society, which bordered on reverence, was already evident in the Enlightenment (and, in very different ways, with Comte and Marx) and became first sociology and then socialism. For the main thrust of ideology had been to rivet attention on human ideas as the "proper study of mankind" rather than on the study of Being itself (namely, metaphysics). The sequel to the Enlightenment was thus the science of society rather than the science of man in the singular or of the knowledge of God (ethics, metaphysics). "We have a metaphysics about many things," Charles Comte de Rémusat wrote in 1842, "except metaphysics itself. . . . We live in a period in which the study of society has the edge on the science of man."[16]

The absence of any integrated, organic culture after the disorder that followed the Enlightenment and the Revolution indicated to Auguste Comte the deep malaise that beset French society. The organic worldview of medieval Christianity had been disturbed. Comte was no true partisan of the Middle Ages, believing neither in the transcendent nor in the natures, forms, and essences of medieval metaphysics. But his admiration for the social and cultural order of the Middle Ages led him to pine for a similar order, stripped of both the supernatural and the metaphysical, reconstructed on the ruins of the old. To Comte the Enlightenment was a dissolvent and the Revolution a disruption, but he accepted their promise of human perfectibility within an immanent world context. He approached the problems of society with reason alone; in that he was a philosophe. But he wrote from this side of 1789—the side that had learned the cost of corrosive criticism.[17]

Likewise, classicism survived the French Revolution in the studios—such as those of Girodet and Ingres—and in the Ecole des Beaux-Arts.[18] Neoclassicism lost the revolutionary implications that Jacques-Louis David had given it. Nineteenth-century classical images lacked David's dramatic tension. Art became academic art—routine, school-like, pedantic, uncreative. Although that description is often undeserved, the pulse of French art was beginning to throb outside the academy. Part of this new life sprang from the revolutionary rights of man and the individualism (particularly in expression) that they sanctioned. Freedom of expression seemed to dash against the wall of academicism when it came to the artist's choice between a sketch and a finished work, for the unfinished was thought to express spontaneity and individuality. The academy was the bastion of classical authority, and with the Revolution it represented oppression, the Bastille of the arts. Restored in 1816 after having been demolished by David and others in 1793 and reinvigorated by the Hellenic revival of the 1830s following the Greek war of independence, it survived other Restoration institutions only to lose influence again after 1863.[19]

Three expressions of eighteenth-century culture—the Enlightenment, the metric system, and neoclassicism—survived into the nineteenth century but met different fates. The Enlightenment and neoclassicism struggled with romanticism only to succumb to its late nineteenth-century incarnations—the irrationalist movements that alienated artists from mimesis, or fidelity to nature. The metric system, in contrast, assumed the opposite: that the language of quantity should be universal, that human diurnal use of space and weight should conform to a natural standard accessible to all, the circumference of the earth. The thrust of the Revolution was more carefully preserved by this metric standardization, but its mathematical rationalism was counteracted in the nineteenth century by the explosion of the psychic, an expression of boundless individualism.[20]

Mal du siècle, a lassitude and boredom that sprang from disillusion with the Revolution's promise of metaphysical, moral, and political regeneration, dominated the early nineteenth century. In turn, the unbounded individualism and supreme egoism of Napoléon unleashed unbelievable energies and expectations in soldiers and civil servants. Waterloo, then, must also be considered a cause of the despondency about the future of France and the French. Nineteenth-century ennui definitely resulted from letdown—anxiety approaching despair—in sharp contrast to the restless excitability of the eighteenth century. Pierre Barbéris, a Marxist historian of the mal du siècle, sees it springing from the "greatest depths of French consciousness, shaken by the crumbling of the old regime," as well as by disappointment in the Revolution. French society was in disarray, due to the collapse of the old moral foundations and the failure of the new ruling class to provide an adequate moral substitute. The bourgeois Revolution, he writes, was at once "liberating and incomplete." And yet the century moved on: "The mal du siècle is conscious of being carried forward in a movement whose direction is not seen." The eighteenth century "sapped the foundation of beliefs and left profoundly critical habits." The moral and intellectual anarchy attacked by Comte was perhaps one cause of this mal du siècle.[21]

Malaise also sprang from the unlimited vistas of social ascent that the Revolution opened up, a progression of which Stendhal was well aware.[22] Tocqueville called it the democratic disease of envy, which feeds on the little advantages of neighbors rather than on the traditional, more insurmountable walls. Those walls might keep their occupants relatively immobile, but they also keep them relatively content. After 1830, because society had been set in motion, class conflict became important, for out of the vertical and lateral mobility, up the rungs of the social ladder and across from villages to cities, came a profound dislocation.[23]

In this respect, the nineteenth-century career manuals indicting ambition and industrial and business occupations as dangerous to one's health, one's sanity, and one's happiness can be compared to spates of laws that condemn a crime. Neither guarantees that the proscribed item will be avoided. It is entirely possible that the problem of ambition contributed to mal du siècle. The Revolution gave rise to the *homme nouveau*; the nineteenth century inherited a burgeoning activity, an ambition, a hope of achievement and of progress toward some indefinite perfectibility, followed by frustration and bitterness when these proved unattainable.[24]

In 1818 Montloisier ridiculed the liberal litany "increase of enlightenment, spirit of the century, power of the times, progress of civilization." In 1857 Flaubert parodied the Enlightenment in one of its devotees, the druggist Homais of *Madame Bovary*. Following Homais's advice, Charles Bovary performs a surgical operation on a clubfooted mail clerk, and the operation is written up as a triumph of medicine. A few days later the poor fellow's foot must be amputated. Here is disillusionment with self-congratulatory "virtucrats" who are in truth no more than fatuous pedants. In *Nausea* (1937), Sartre satirized every descendant of eighteenth-century humanism.

Flaubert was certainly the most eloquent witness to the democratic disappointment in the Revolution of 1848 (*L'Education sentimentale*), but Balzac was also a keen observer of the mal du siècle, so much so that Engels felt that the best way to study the reality of the July Monarchy was to read this Catholic traditionalist. For Balzac, postrevolutionary France was consumed by greed and ambition, which, far from producing dazzling Napoleonic adventures, resulted in a profound ugliness. Sizing up the meaning of Balzac's lifelong commentary on greed, Emile Faguet, the late nineteenth-century literary critic, wrote that the hope in a future life "in which the social edifice has been supported for eighteen hundred years because expectations of the absolute were placed beyond the grave are now placed in the worldly paradise of luxury and unlimited enjoyment. . . . [One must] harden the heart and mortify the body in order to get hold of fleeting possessions just as formerly men suffered lifelong martyrdom in order to ensure their eternal welfare—such now is the general thought." To Balzac, far from producing "beautiful people," the materialism of his generation produced caricatures of humanity, much like those of Honoré Daumier.[25]

The Long-Term: Popular Culture and Christianity

The Revolution had a minimal effect on the material environment of France. Little building occurred in Paris, even with the Napoleonic creations, after the eighteenth century. How could the French build when they were busy attending meetings and festivals? Moreover, no industrial revolution accompanied the political revolution. If anything, the immediate material consequences of the civil and foreign wars were what they are in almost every civil and foreign war: devastation, dislocation, and disruption of industry. The environment regressed. Listen to the prefects of 1800 trying to apprise Napoléon of the economic and social situation of their departments. General Emmanuel Roergas de Serviez of the Basses-Pyrénées reported that the handkerchief and wool industries, which employed six thousand persons before the Revolution, were reduced in 1790 to twelve hundred employees. This was not, it is true, all due to the Revolution; the peace treaty with England in 1783 and the interruption of commerce with Spain in 1790 also contributed. But the Revolution did reduce the industry to four hundred looms. Vandalism had laid waste to the educational establishments, hindering "the progress of public instruction." The Bas-Rhin, observed the prefect Jean-Charles Laumond, had only 146 master weavers, as opposed to almost 1,800 before the war. The Revolution had "destroyed some fortunes, displaced a great number of persons." Peyre of the Lot-et-Garonne wrote of the decline in the manufacture of Indian cloth fabrics and tobacco manufactures and of a general "afflicting languor," a "general misery" throughout the department. Luçay of the Cher commented on the stagnation of cultivation, the impassability of many roads, and depopulation. Almost everywhere brigandage threatened communications. In sum, far from experiencing a breakthrough from a feudal to a capitalist economy, France was less prosperous, safe, and developed immediately after the Revolution than before the economic crisis of 1788.[26]

Popular culture proper displayed remarkable continuity with the old regime. The observers of the Académie celtique in the Empire had little trouble describing ancient folklore—festivals, superstitions, occultism, astrology, rites of passage, ancient fears and hopes—in the present tense. Nor did Arnold van Gennep find that these customs had disappeared in the early twentieth century. The survival of such folkloric traditions has been recorded by Lawrence Wylie for the Vaucluse and by Pierre-Jakez Hélias for Brittany. All this revealed a post-Enlightenment scientific understanding of popular culture rather than the former Enlightenment disdain.[27]

The Celtic folklorists of the Empire did not provide—though the prefects and priests did—insight into moral and psychological effects of the Revolution: effects underlying or undermining the stability of popular beliefs. Prefects were vocal on this point. Serviez wrote that peasants were "limited to routine, and sacrifice to their habits and prejudices the improvements of fertile territories where agriculture is a science." The reports of commissioners and municipal officials to the survey of Year VI on education also stressed how much peasants were bound by "old routines." No profound agricultural revolution, in spite of the sale of some common land, accompanied the French Revolution. Attachment to communal lands stayed strong into the mid-nineteenth century. The equal inheritance laws, only slightly modified by Napoléon, caused property to be divided and redivided through the nineteenth century and guaranteed the survival of a larger small-landholding peasantry. The *veillée* and collective dances did not die out until after the railroad had linked the country to the city in the second half of the century.[28]

Prefects not only witnessed the inveteracy of peasant ways, they also noted a disruption of the spirit of work, of the artisans in particular and of the classes laborieuses in general. As Laumond of the Bas-Rhin wrote, the Revolution had offered "to the man of the people, to the worker, ideas of individual independence which he had not known before, and provoked in general an 'irritation' of classes, which time alone could calm, in bringing men back to the habit of work. All these causes have necessarily contributed to the stagnation of manufactures." What might seem like emancipation to some modern historians this prefect interpreted as regression. In summarizing the effects of the Revolution, Laumond noted that everyone wanted to step out of their previous positions. Even the rich were unwilling to undergo difficult self-discipline, like mining, and sought instead quick fortunes through speculation. Fewer workers in every field were active, and those who did work were either old or demanded higher pay. In spite of these faults, Laumond found the Alsatian population as happy and willing to dance and sing as ever! Philosophy, he felt, had made absolutely no inroads in this territory. A popular culture was emerging that abandoned the difficult, even oppressive, aspects of traditional work and retained the more pleasurable ones of song and dance. Yet people adopted goals born with the Revolution, such as higher pay and quick success.[29]

The prefect of the Loire-Inférieure, Jean-Baptiste Huet de Coetlizan, was even more ambivalent about the moral and psychological changes among le peuple. They have acquired, he wrote, "an infinity of new habits, of dissipations, and of debauchery, until then unknown: little prepared for philosophic institutions, they have not distinguished liberation [*affranchissement*] from independence, liberty from insubordination, insolence from equality." In spite of this, he continues, the vicissitudes of the Revolution have not "been able completely to corrupt their natural goodness, nor cause them to lose their love of work, their love of justice, their respect for the law and for their property."[30]

These reports reveal a real problem: the insubordination, indiscipline, and anxiety of the classes laborieuses, particularly in the cities. Although confréries and religious practices continued among urban workers for at least half a century, the Revolution, by abolishing the corporations and by prohibiting workingmen's associations, ignored workers' genuine needs and probably made them less willing to accept their subordinate stations. Dormant after 1795, the worker movement reawoke after 1830. By then worker dissatisfaction threatened the notables.[31]

Similar observations of general decline can be found in the records of the Catholic religion. These are not as systematic as they would be after 1848, but Gabriel Le Bras, the dean of religious sociology in France, who studied the available documents, referred to the "subversion révolutionnaire." The schism resulted in a decline of religious practice. Yves-Marie Hilaire has called the Revolution a true "rupture in history and in geography of [religious] beliefs in France." This rupture took, as one form, the suspension of religious practice by a large part of the population for ten years—the absence of baptisms, the suspension of feast days, the abolition (in law) of Sunday leisure, and, finally, the virtual halt in ordinations to the priesthood. The church of France had never faced a crisis of these proportions. In 1815 priestless parishes dotted the landscape, particularly in the Parisian basin, the Marne and Oise valleys, and Champagne. De-Christianization and the general delapidation of the church had taken its toll. For this reason, the Mission of France was formed.[32]

The postrevolutionary mission movement was created by a former Jesuit, le Père Pierre-Joseph Picot de Clorivière, who in 1790 founded the Société de cœur de Jésus. In 1794 a parallel mission, the Pères de la foi, was founded in Belgium. The missions were active during the Empire until Napoléon quarreled with Pius VII over his divorce from Joséphine and in 1809 prohibited all missions. When the Catholic church became the state religion in 1814, the Jesuits were restored and a Société des prêtres des missions de France was formed under Clorivière's direction. It was complemented by the work of the Congrégation, founded in 1801 and organized in 1814 under the name Société des bonnes œuvres. Individual missions involved from eight to thirty priests. Most were too young to have known the church of the old regime, but many had lived as children in the Revolution. This made them far more zealous than their old regime counterparts. They generally had little advanced education, since seminaries had been closed, and this contributed to the simplicity, exaggeration, and rigidity of their vision.

The bishop and the prefect would invite the missionaries into a diocese, and the bishop would formally give them the mission to preach. In 1815 they preached in Angers, Nantes, Laval, Beauvais, Poitiers, and Caen—the areas affected by the insurrections of the Vendée and *chouannerie* in northwest France, where Catholicism was strong. Fifty dioceses received missions in 1815, and between 1821 and 1823 eighty of the hundred-odd dioceses of France were visited. Some 1,200 to 1,500 missions were preached during the Restoration.

A mission lasted five or six weeks. Preaching would begin before sunrise and continue after working hours into the night, often in frigid, dank churches. Attendance seems to have been remarkably high, often several thousand. Local authorities assisted in the opening procession in town and at the concluding ceremony, usually the planting of a Calvary cross in the public or cathedral square.

These priests delivered a basic message of repentance and renewal—repentance for disobeying the commandments during the Revolution and afterward (the missionaries deplored the moral state of the French even in 1814). They never minced words, never flattered, but preached the "last things"—death and judgment, the pains of Hell. They even visited open graves to impress listeners, many of whom had not been to Confession or Communion for years and thus needed to repent and return to the sacraments. They upbraided one for infidelity, another for drunkenness, another for theft; many were told to make public acts of expiation. Blasphemy, sacrilege, and the profanation of Sunday had become common, particularly during the Revolution. Usury (along with ambition and self-interest, à la Balzac) had become uncontrolled, and these priests persisted in teaching church doctrine. In everything, they tried to link worship and communion with tradition.

Return to the sacraments was essential. Priests spent five hours and more at a time hearing confessions. None had been formally heard in the Vendée since 1791. The rate of return to Communion of men whose main obstacle was fear of what others would think ("human respect"), was between 250 and 300 per department, that of women roughly double, a statistical sign of the rural feminization of piety. Marriages and baptisms that had been performed irregularly by constitutional clergy were often revalidated. Although Rome had recognized the sale of church property in 1801, the missions did not hesitate in some cases to encourage purchasers to make restitution. In 1816 the "impious works" of Voltaire and Rousseau were burned. Even dancing and Carnival came under the missions' censure, which caused a falling out with one bishop who felt that dancing should not be so categorically condemned.

These preachings obviously went against the grain of liberal Restoration France; the liberals, free of the Napoleonic oppression, were trying to steer the Restoration as close to 1789 as possible. Any questioning of the revolutionary settlement on church property and secular marriage, any threat of a closer union of throne and altar instantly raised the liberals' hackles. The mission clergy were all royalists, but they did not talk much of politics. They were nevertheless accused of doing so, not so much in the public missions as in the more private confréries that frequently resulted from them. Their cries of "Vive la

France! Vive le Roi!" rather than the liberals' "Vive la Charte!" convinced many that the union of throne and altar would clericalize France anew. The liberal press questioned the good faith of these priests and accused them of political ambitions or cupidity. But the priests came from humble origins and their way of life offered little in a material way, so little, in fact, that the bourgeois reversed eighteenth-century practice and kept their children from joining the clergy. Clerical attachment to the Bourbons, of course, is unquestioned—theirs was the recognized government, the one that would "restore France to God and God to France" (fig. XII.1). Beyond that and the traditional impingement of politics on moral questions (like those relating to property), clerics were apolitical. But in many towns the mere announcement of a mission could trigger sharp opposition.

France, like any country, needed missionary activity, conversion and repentence, but in 1814 the need was greater than ever. From the missionary perspective, the Revolution had been a grand moral truancy beyond the ordinary failings of human weakness, one requiring the restoration of all moral life as well as of political legitimacy. The missions were thus not simply a continuing or long-term response but a specific answer to the revolutionary crisis.[33] How successful were they? Their reconquest of France was partial and fragile. Many areas lacked missions, and the people often resisted missions, sometimes with violence. The favorable memory of the Revolution and the disenchantment with Catholicism was strong, particularly if it entailed property or revolutionary practice. A new wave of official anti-Catholicism accompanied the July Revolution. The constituents of 1848, in a survey on agricultural and industrial work that involved religion, broke down religious practice geographically: the Pyrénées region, the massif Central, the Breton West, and the northern and eastern frontiers were strong; the southwest, center-west, and southeast were weak; and the center, the Parisian basin, was very weak. But the main thrust of working-class de-Christianization resulted from the Revolution of 1848, the June Days, and industrialization.[34] The irreligious 1793 had provoked a religious renaissance after Thermidor. It took the religious utopian revolution of 1848 to de-Christianize the working class.

The Mission of France revitalized religious practice, but not completely, because it aroused the animosity of those notables and intellectuals who were unreconciled to the church. They, the offspring of Voltaireanism, led the nineteenth-century anticlerical battles which effectively secularized the state by the end of the century and in 1905 separated church and state. Like the separation of 1795, this partition

XII.I.

Long Live the King! or Speculators and Politicians Foiled, *engraving,*
ca. *1814.*

Courtesy Library of Congress.

met a spontaneous resistance from sizable groups, which guaranteed
the survival of an independent church.

The long-term indeed persisted. The physical environment of
France remained largely unchanged by the generation of Revolution
and Napoleonic wars. The social structure was also altered little during

these years. The religious revivals of 1795, the Empire, and the Restoration created a France of more vibrant belief than in the previous century.

Much that is attributed to the cultural revolution of Year II in fact grew out of the Enlightenment, the neoclassical revolution of the eighteenth century, and the preromantic sensibility that continued long after the Revolution had ended. The Académie des sciences morales et politiques, restored in 1832, continued the Enlightenment's investigations of man and society, whereas the Ecole des Beaux-Arts protected classicism until mid-century. The roman noir and the roman rose were still flourishing in the 1840s. Ducray-Duminil and Bernardin de Saint-Pierre continued to be widely read.

But the Revolution did leave its mark, most visibly in politics and political culture: the practice and ethos of republicanism; the new networks of friendships and associations; the dream of an education that could belong entirely to the city of man. This legacy of the revolutionary struggle certainly marked the long-term (*longue durée*).

Can a key be found to these myriad connections that comprise the culture of the French Revolution? We have discovered it in what we call the "religion of humanity," in which all coalesces around the sacred rights of the individual and the collectivity of the nation, the holder of sovereignty. The abolition of the corporations meant that nothing could exist between these two terms, and the war against the church meant that nothing could stand above this human sovereignty. Even the cult of the Supreme Being was worship of a god useful to the civic world of man. For Quatremère de Quincy this was a religion of morality, as exemplified in his pagan iconography of the Panthéon. That structure was "a simulacre of the Patrie, this veritable idol of the People, and the true divinity of the Temple which it has chosen for itself." It was the ancient liberty of which Benjamin Constant spoke— a liberty that sought fulfillment in the human and civic. If the Revolution possessed one cultural continuity with past and future it was a religion of humanity that was symptomatic of a more general Western immanentism in which God is sought in man, nature, and society rather than in any transcendental order.

The anticlerical victory was never complete and should not obscure the strength of nineteenth-century Catholicism, as the passage of the Falloux law of 1850 testified. The church received strength by the saints of the century—the curé d'Ars,[35] Bernadette of Lourdes, Thérèse of Lisieux—to whose shrines millions would flock during the next century.

The sins of the Revolution were to be expiated by the erection on

Montmartre of the gleaming shrine Sacré-Cœur, which dominated Paris.[36] Far across the Seine on Mount Sainte-Geneviève stands the Panthéon, dedicated to the great men first apotheosized by the Revolution. The two loom over Paris from their respective heights, contending for (and sharing) the loyalties of those who struggle below.

APPENDIX A

STATISTICS ON MUSIC

AND THEATER

TABLE A.I

Most frequent themes in first lines of revolutionary songs and hymns

Theme	Frequency of Occurrence
Supreme Being	95
Liberty	82
Peace	67
Marat	65
Reason	59
Republic	56
Tuileries	54
Tenth August	48
Louis Capet (XVI)	47
Lepeletier	45
National Convention	44
Liberty Tree	43
Victory	42
Fourteenth of July	41
Versailles	40
Jacobins	40

TABLE A.2

Plays performed during the Revolution

Date of Composition	Plays	Performances
1630–1700	81	3,217
1701–1750	126	4,518
1751–1788	581	19,884
1789–1799	1,691	39,965

TABLE A.3

Forty-five most performed playwrights of the Revolution

Rank	Author	Performances
1	Beaunoir, R.	1,891
2	Barré, P.-Y.	1,865
3	Molière, J.-B.	1,800
4	Guillemain, C.	1,524
5	Dorvigny, L.	1,264
6	Monvel, J.-M.-B.	1,172
7	Cuvelier, T. de	1,154
8	Dumaniant, J.-B.	1,107
9	Patrat, J.	1,090
10	Gardel, M.	1,077
11	Picard, L.-B.	1,076
12	Pigault-Lebrun, C.	1,073
13	Radet, J.-B.	929
14	Arnould, J.-F.-M.	843
15	Maurin de Pompigny	835
16	Lazzari	834
17	Marsollier des Vivétières	831
18	Gabiot de Salins	818
19	Anseaume, L.	774
20	Léger, F.-P.-A.	738
20	Voltaire, F.-M.-A.	738
22	Beffroy de Reigny	706
23	Hoffman, F.	686
24	Desforges, P.-C.	685

TABLE A.3
(*continued*)

Rank	Author	Performances
25	Dubuisson, P.-U.	658
26	Caron de Beaumarchais	598
27	Regnard, J.-F.	577
28	Deschamps, J.	570
29	Destouches, P.-N.	563
30	Sedaine, M.-J.	533
31	Dejaure, J.-C.-B.	522
32	Desfontaines, F.-D.	497
33	Marivaux, P.	488
34	Demoustier, C.	454
35	Guillard, N.	453
36	Dancourt, F.	449
37	Ribié, C.	437
38	Destival de Brabant	393
39	Claris de Florian	384
39	Rousseau, J.-J.	384
41	Audinot, N.	381
42	Sedaine, S. de	365
43	Legrand, M.-A.	358
44	Baurans, P.	332
45	Marmontel, J.-F.	332

Note: Figures do not include 16,600 performances of plays by anonymous authors

TABLE A.4

Performances of plays with revolutionary and nonrevolutionary titles

Year	Revolutionary	Nonrevolutionary
1789	74	6,447
1790	274	6,980
1791	962	7,369
1792	665	6,544
1793	1,437	7,213
1794	2,443	4,872
1795	814	6,223
1796	721	9,775
1797	220	8,496
1798	338	7,936
1799	240	6,642
Total	8,188	78,497

TABLE A.5

Performances of comedies and tragedies by theater, 1789–1799

Theater	Comedies	Tragedies
Théâtre de la nation	2,183	710
Académie de musique	243	654
Théâtre italien	5,259	839
Théâtre Feydeau	2,018	129
Théâtre Louvois	861	50
Théâtre Molière	843	62
These and other unlisted theaters combined	41,307	3,415

APPENDIX B

PROSOPOGRAPHY OF
THE CULTURAL ELITE

The intellectual and cultural changes of the period 1750–1820, though often radical, were generally peaceful. So were most of the cultural elite who lived into the Revolution and witnessed or even led the upheaval. Some—David, Chénier, Maréchal, Marat, François-Jean-Baptiste Topino-Lebrun—expressed themselves with violent language at critical moments. And the acerbic criticism of such others as Mercier or Beaumarchais may have done as much to hasten the destruction of cultural privilege. But a study of the lives of some two hundred prominent playwrights, poets, journalists, painters, philosophers, educators, clerics, and musicians shows a certain incongruity between the relatively comfortable origins or acquired positions of these men before the Revolution and the enormity of disruption of ancien régime culture after 1789. The moderate behavior of most of these men, moreover, fails to account for the outcome. Most members of this elite who came from humble backgrounds were recognized and rewarded early in their careers, like the painters David, Prud'hon, and Barthélemy. But the Catholic church, the educational system, and the academies themselves were all abolished. Two explanations of this discrepancy are in order. First, the disruption was the work of a relatively small number of distinguished individuals in unison with a greater number of undistinguished, even anonymous, artists, artisans, and men of letters who do not enter the sample. Second, destruction often came from outside—from the Assembly or Convention and from such leaders as Mirabeau, Barère, and Fouché—rather than from artists and writers.

A prosopography of these 200-odd culturally prominent individuals[1] includes the 30 most performed living playwrights of the Revolution and the 33 members of the salon of the princesse de Salm, which met from the Directory into the Empire and included such figures as Houdon, the editor Amaury Duval, and the ideologue Ginguené. To these groups were added 142 individuals chosen from among academicians, painters, architects, engravers, journalists, scientists, and legislators (table B.1).

These men were somewhat older (between 39 and 40) on average in 1789 than the average member of the Convention (age 35). At the height of the Terror this cultural elite was almost 45, whereas members of the Committee of Public Safety were only 36. The former tended to come from the north of France (134 out of 190 whose birthplace is known, or 70 percent); 67, or just over one-third (35 percent) were born in Paris and fewer than one-third (56, or 29 percent) were born south of the Geneva–Saint-Malo literacy line established by historians. The high percentage of northerners and low percentage of Parisians is almost identical to those of a list of men of letters composed by a police inspector, Joseph d'Héméry, around 1750.[2] The capital probably exercised an even greater attraction over aspiring men of letters in the provinces than it did over restless peasants or bourgeois. Although many of the most distinguished of this list—David, Firmin Didot, Mercier, Beaumarchais—were Parisians by birth, such others as Condorcet, Rétif de la Bretonne, Grétry, Bernardin de Saint-Pierre, and Pigault-Lebrun were not.

The social-professional origins of 146 fathers of this elite who could be identified seem more popular than the 1750 list of Héméry, yet the majority were respectable (table B.2). Eleven were of noble lineage, including Condorcet, Saint-Lambert, Destutt de Tracy, Châteaubriand, Sade, Florian, Constance de Salm, Talleyrand, Ginguené (poor noble), and Quatremère de Quincy (*anobli*). Seven had fathers who occupied high administrative posts, among them three painters, Hubert Robert, F. Gérard, and A.-L. Girodet, as well as the nobles above. Seven had fathers who were military officers, including A.-J. P.-Ségur and Destutt de Tracy. Five fathers were magistrates in high courts, including the father of playwright Marsollier des Vivétières. Another six had fathers who were either minor officials on sovereign courts (Debucourt) or officials in lower courts. Only four served in the lower ranks of the administration, but there were some fourteen lawyers (*avocats*) and three notaries—such as the fathers of Charles Nodier and Cabanis. Six were doctors' sons, and five were sons of *négociants* or *commerçants*

TABLE B.1
Professions of members of the cultural elite

Writers	44
Playwrights	38
Painters	28
Scientists	15
Musicians	14
Legislators/administrators	14
Clerics	10
Philosophes/savants	10
Cultural administrators	6
Engravers	6
Sculptors	4
Architects	4
Academicians	3*
Antiquarians	3
Publishers/printers	3
Doctors	2
Actors	2
Theater directors	2
Total	208

*Over 40 academicians have been listed under other categories; second professions are not listed

(Chénier's father had been a commerçant in Constantinople, and Lavoisier's father had become wealthy in commerce). The industrial-commercial world was weakly represented in the cultural elite (in proportion to officeholding), as it was in the political leadership of the Revolution as a whole. Passing from the urban to the rural bourgeoisie, three fathers were *agriculteurs* (including those of Gossec and Rétif de la Bretonne).

The domestic and artisanal world is better represented in this sample than in Héméry's list: Regnault, Méhul (whose father was a maître d'hôtel), and Houdon (whose father was a *valet de chambre*). Five parents were shopkeepers: Olympe de Gouges's mother sold perfume, the father of Panckoucke, the press baron, was a bookseller, Chamfort was the adopted son of a grocer (*marchand-épicier*), David's father was a haberdasher and his mother's father a stonecutter. Twelve more were artisans' sons, including Prud'hon, Dupont de Nemours,

TABLE B.2
Professions or occupations of fathers of the cultural elite

Clergy (Protestant)	1
Titled nobility	20*
Administration	
High	7
Low	4
Justice	
High courts	5
Low courts	6
Lawyers	14
Notaries	3
Doctors/dentists	6
Business/high commerce	5
Manufacturing	1
Merchants	9
Rentiers	8
Artists, actors,	
musicians, writers	22
Scientists	2
Teachers	3
Cultivateurs	3
Shopkeepers	5
Artisans	12
Peasants	2
Servants	3
Miscellaneous	5**
Total	146

*Includes 7 who were also military officers
**Includes father of the playwright Louis-François-Archambault Dorvigny
(1742–1812), who may have been Louis XV

the abbé Maury, Topino-Lebrun, the engraver Sergent, and the chemist abbé Haüy.

A tabulation of individuals that had achieved recognition before the Revolution and those that received recognition only after 1789 places 126, or almost two-thirds, in the former category, whereas 69 had to wait for the Revolution to be recognized. The cultural elite appears to have been significantly democratized before the Revolution began. Of children of shopkeepers, only Olympe de Gouges achieved recognition after 1789, and of artisans, all but Mme Dufrenoy (a member of the salon de Salm) and Topino-Lebrun became important after 1789 (Topino-Lebrun was too young for earlier recognition). Charles-Simon Favart, the son of a *pâtissier,* was a recognized librettist of opéras-comiques before the Revolution (and he died before the Terror). David, Chamfort, and Haüy were all members of different royal academies before the Revolution.

Recognition before 1789 did not preclude adverse treatment during the Terror (in some cases it brought it about). The philosophes, the Encyclopédistes, and their followers, it has been argued, had little responsibility for the Revolution, since most of those who survived either emigrated, were imprisoned, or were guillotined.[3] Our cultural elite experienced the same adversity, although many still contributed significantly to the Revolution. Some, like Fabre d'Eglantine, Rabaut Saint-Etienne, Momoro, Claude Payan, and Charles Ronsin, were guillotined *because* of their involvement; others, like Destutt de Tracy (who was imprisoned), had withdrawn and had unsuccessfully tried to hide their ties to the past. Adversity affected just under half of this sample. Twenty-three emigrated, 4 committed suicide, 19 were executed, roughly the same proportion as in the Convention, which suggests how sensitive and provocative statements in the arts and letters could be during the Revolution. Another 25 were imprisoned and 17 denounced, visited, or watched as suspects.

Clearly, during the Revolution ideas were dangerous—not only counterrevolutionary ideas, such as those of Châteaubriand or Mallet du Pan (who expressed them in emigration)—but revolutionary ones, too, for the vast majority of these men embraced the Revolution, even if only moderately. The blade of justice could fall on those who considered themselves oracles of the Revolution. Victimization need not imply absence of participation or hostility, but most of these men were not ultra-revolutionary. They went about their business and did not concern themselves overly about the exigencies of Republican *vertu.*

ABBREVIATIONS

SOURCES

A.D.	Archives départementales
A.N.	Archives nationales
A.P.	*Archives parlementaires de 1787 à 1860: Recueil complet des débats legislatifs et politiques des chambres françaises,* Paris, 1st ser. (1787–1799), ed. J. Mavidal and E. Laurent, 82 vols. (Paris, 1862–1913)
B.M.	British Museum
B.N.	Bibliothèque nationale
L.C.	Library of Congress
PVCIPCN	*Procès-verbaux du Comité de l'Instruction publique de la Convention nationale,* ed. James Guillaume, 7 vols. (Paris, 1891–1907)

PLAYS

a	act	pr	prose
c	comedy	sc	scene
dr	drama	tr	tragedy
mus	music	v	verse
pant	pantomime		

NOTES

INTRODUCTION

1 Albert Soboul made this distinction in a letter to the author.

2 The distinction is Benjamin Constant's in "De la liberté des anciens comparée à celle des modernes," lecture of 1819 printed in *Cours de politique constitutionnelle,* 2 vols. (Paris, 1872), 2:539–60, cited and analyzed in Stephen Holmes, *Benjamin Constant and the Making of Modern Liberalism* (New Haven and London, 1984), chap. 2. Constant dates modern liberty with the Reformation. It likely dates from at least Augustine, who has been called "the first modern man." *The City of God* clearly differentiates between a transcendental and a secular realm.

3 Albert Camus, *L'Homme révolté (The Rebel)* (Paris, 1951).

4 This is at least my reading of the section on Christianity in Hegel's *Philosophy of History,* ed. C. J. Friedrich (New York, 1956), esp. pp. 324, 333.

5 Momoro, in *Révolution de Paris,* accounting for the festival of 20 brumaire Year II (10 November 1793) in Notre-Dame, reproduced in *PVCIPCN,* 2:806.

6 Albert Soboul, *La Civilisation et la Révolution française,* 3 vols. (Paris, 1982), 2:191; 440,000–490,000 casualties for the wars of the 1790s and 880,000–970,000 for the Empire for a total loss of 1.3–1.4 million. These figures are taken from J. Dupâquier, *La Population française au XVIIᵉ et XVIIIᵉ siècles* (Paris, 1979). The figures for the Terror are based on Donald Greer, *The Incidence of the Terror during the French Revolution* (Cambridge, Mass., 1935). Recent estimates of the repression in the Vendée put the killing at 15 percent of the population of 800,000. See Reynald Secher, *Le Génocide Franco-Français* (Paris, 1986), cited in Richard Bernstein, "The French Revolution: Right or Wrong?" *New York Times Book Review,* 10 July 1988, p. 27.

7 Lynn Hunt, *Politics, Culture, and Class in the French Revolution* (Berkeley, 1984), pp. 181ff.

1. PARIS MILIEU AND CULTURAL INSTITUTIONS

1 *Gallic Wars,* trans. H. J. Edwards (London, 1930), 7.57–58; Hemingway, *A Moveable Feast* (New York, 1964), pp. 44–45. See also F. Hoffbauer, *Les Rives de la Seine* (Paris, n.d.).

2 Alan Williams, *The Police of Paris, 1718–1789* (Baton Rouge, 1979), pp. 21, 63, 65, table 1; Daniel Roche, *Le Peuple de Paris: Essai sur la culture populaire au XVIIIe siècle* (Paris, 1981), pp. 19–21. No one knows the population of Paris in 1789 with certainty. Based on contemporary estimates, Roche says "less than 800,000." Marcel Reinhard puts it between 576,000 and 800,000 (*Nouvelle histoire de Paris: La Révolution, 1789–1799* [Paris, 1971], pp. 117–18). Louis-Sébastien Mercier's treasurehouse entitled *Le Tableau de Paris* puts the figure at 700,000 (12 vols. [London and Hamburg, 1781–88], 1:30). On the environment of Paris in 1789, see also Jeffrey Kaplow, *The Names of Kings* (New York, 1972).

3 Jean Tulard, *Nouvelle histoire de Paris: Le Consulat et l'Empire* (Paris, 1970), pp. 9–25.

4 Reinhard, pp. 176–77, chap. 2; Mercier, 1:112–17.

5 Mercier, 1:112–17, 103–6, 176–78, 50–53.

6 Howard C. Rice, Jr., *Thomas Jefferson's Paris* (Paris, 1976), p. 13; Roche, pp. 18–19.

7 Roche, chap. 4; Rice, chaps. 2, 4; Reinhard, pp. 166ff.

8 Reinhard, pp. 90–91; Williams, pp. 259–60; Roche, pp. 159–61, table 26.

9 Reinhard, pp. 251–52; Rice, pp. 4–5.

10 James A. Billington, *Fire in the Minds of Men: The Origins of the Revolutionary Faith* (New York, 1980), pp. 24–33; Robert Isherwood, *Farce and Fantasy: Popular Entertainment in Eighteenth-Century Paris* (New York, 1986), chap. 8; Rice, chap. 2.

11 Hoffbauer, p. 45; Rice, pp. 28–29.

12 Reinhard, pp. 169–70.

13 Rice, pp. 19–21, 45–49, 68–69; Roche, pp. 16–19.

14 Rice, chaps. 4–5; Roche, pp. 17–18. For building in provincial cities in the 18th century, see J.-C. Perrot, "Les Rapports sociaux et villes au xviiie siècle," in *Ordres et classes: Colloque d'histoire sociale, Saint-Cloud, 24–25 mai 1967,* ed. D. Roche and C.-E. Labrousse (Paris, 1973), p. 151.

15 James A. Leith has analyzed in detail various plans to redesign Paris during the Revolution, but virtually none of these plans was implemented: "All these bold projects . . . were only 'paper architecture,' destined never to be completed because of the financial problems and turbulence of the period, but this does not strip them of their historical significance" ("Symbolizing a New Era: Some Architectural Projects under the Constituent and Legislative Assemblies," typescript, p. 7). On later plans, see also his "Desacralization, Resacralization, and Architectural Planning during the

French Revolution," *Eighteenth-Century Life* 7 (1982): 74–84. "All these projects remained paper architecture" (p. 82).

16 *Almanach Royal* (1789), pp. 494–98, 539–41.

17 Randy Bailey, *French Secondary Education, 1763–1790: The Secularization of the Ex-Jesuit Collèges,* American Philosophical Society, *Transactions* 68, pt. 6 (1978); R. R. Palmer, *The Improvement of Humanity: Education and the French Revolution* (Princeton, 1985), chap. 2. See below, chap. 7.

18 *Almanach Royal* (1789), pp. 494–99ff.; *Almanach Royal* (1786), pp. 675–80; *Almanach Royal* (1788), pp. 696ff.; *Almanach National* (1798), p. 591. There were 179 censors listed in thirteen fields. Cf., on incidental 18th-century cases during the Revolution, Archives de la Préfecture de Police de Paris, AA; Mercier, 1:67–70, 158–59, 177; 2:151–55; 3:66, 75; 6:51–55; D. S. Packer, "La Calotte and the Eighteenth-Century Vaudeville," *Journal of the American Musicological Society* 32 (1970): 82–83.

19 Stephen Botein, Jack R. Censer, and Harriet Ritvo, "The Periodical Press in Eighteenth-Century English and French Society: A Cross-Cultural Approach," *Comparative Studies in Society and History* 23 (1981): 470; Mercier, 2:132–34; 3:75.

20 Mercier, 1:67–70, 158–59, 177; 2:151–55; 3:66, 75; 6:51–55; *Almanach Royal* (1789), pp. 499ff.; *Almanach Royal* (1786), pp. 675–80; *Almanach Royal* (1788), pp. 696ff. Carla A. Hesse's authoritative piece, "Economic Upheavals in Publishing" (in press), puts the number of printers before the Revolution at thirty-six.

21 See Alice T. Bowers, "Allusions to the Private Life of Louis XIV in the Dramatic Literature of the Seventeenth Century" (Ph.D. diss., University of Missouri, 1968), on dramatic allusions (not always honorable) to the king's life; Robert M. Isherwood, *Music in the Service of the King: France in the Seventeenth Century* (Ithaca, 1973), pp. 40ff.; and Joseph Klaits, *Printed Propaganda in France under Louis XIV: Absolute Monarchy and Public Opinion* (Princeton, 1976), p. 14.

22 Pierre Goubert, *L'Ancien Régime,* 2 vols. (Paris, 1969, 1973), 1:chap. 9; 2: chap. 8; Emmanuel Le Roy Ladurie, *Carnival in Romans* (New York, 1979), pp. 350–51. On the society of orders, see Roland Mousnier, *Les Institutions de la France sous la monarchie absolue, 1588–1789,* 2 vols. (Paris, 1974), vol. 1. Thomas Edward Brennan, *Public Drinking and Popular Culture in Eighteenth-Century Paris* (Princeton, 1988). Mercier, 2:173ff.; Tocqueville, *The Old Regime and the French Revolution,* trans. Stuart Gilbert (New York, 1955), pt. 2.

23 Daniel Roche, *Le Siècle des lumières en province: Académie et académiciens provinciaux, 1680–1789,* 2 vols. (Paris, 1978), 1:chap. 1; *Almanach Royal* (1789), pp. 539–41.

24 *Almanach Royal* (1789), pp. 539–41; Roche, *Le Siècle des lumières,* 1:9, 15.

25 Roche, *Le Siècle des lumières,* 1:173; "The academic ideal privileges a social

and intellectual aristocracy" (ibid., 1:197ff.); 2:216ff.; Augustin Cochin, *Les Sociétés de pensée et la démocratie moderne* (Paris, 1978); François Furet, *Penser la Révolution française* (Paris, 1978), pt. 2:chap. 3.

26 Roche, *Le Siècle des lumières,* 1:11, 30, 98ff., 111, 136–81. On the Société royale de médecine, see below, chap. 2; Roger Hahn, *Anatomy of a Scientific Institution: The Academy of Sciences, 1666–1803* (Berkeley, 1971).

27 Roche, *Le Siècle des lumières;* Foucault, *The Order of Things* (New York, 1973; orig. publ. Paris, 1966). On French "classical" culture, see the excellent book by W. L. Wiley, *The Formal French* (Cambridge, Mass., 1967).

28 Margaret Jacob, *The Radical Enlightenment: Pantheists, Free Masons, and Republicans* (Boston, 1981), pp. 155–76, 267ff.; Roche, *Le Siècle des lumières,* 2:419; Ran Halévi, *Les Loges maçonniques dans la France d'ancien régime: Aux origines de la sociabilité démocratique* (Paris, 1984), pp. 87–88; R. Robin, "La Loge Concorde à l'Orient de Dijon," *Annales historiques de la Révolution française* 197 (1969): 440ff. See also the excellent discussion of Freemasonry in connection with the academies in Roche, *Le Siècle des lumières,* 1:60ff., 260–78.

29 Halévi, pp. 22–27, pt. 2 passim. Most of the foundations were made in the south before 1750, in the northwest between 1750 and 1760, in the south and east in the 1760s and 1770s, and throughout France in the 1780s. The social composition of the lodges was more military than the academies.

30 Halévi, chap. 1.

31 Roche, *Le Siècle des lumières,* 1:25; Roger Picard, *Les Salons littéraires et la société française, 1610–1789* (Paris, 1943), chaps. 3, 2, and pp. 147–241 passim. The academies were often linked in origin to the salons and to the sociétés or chambres de lecture.

32 Edmond and Jules Goncourt, *The Woman of the Eighteenth Century,* trans. Jacques Le Clercq and Ralph Roeder (New York, 1927), pp. 258–59.

33 Alan Kors, *D'Holbach's Coterie: An Enlightenment in Paris* (Princeton, 1976), chaps. 1, 7, 8, 9.

34 Quoted in Picard, p. 241.

35 Henri Peyre, "The Influence of Eighteenth-Century Ideas on the French Revolution," *Journal of the History of Ideas* 10 (1949): 73–74.

36 Bertier de Sauvigny, *Nouvelle Histoire de Paris: La Restauration, 1815–1830* (Paris, 1977), pp. 333–34.

37 Ibid., pp. 334–43.

38 Ibid., pp. 344–50.

39 Ibid., esp. pp. 351–84. See chap. 8, n. 36, below, on monastic libraries. The author of the document cited there indicates that 5,000–6,000 monasteries opened their libraries to the public before the Revolution throughout France. The subject deserves further investigation.

40 Edouard Herriot, *Madame Récamier,* trans. Alys Hallard, 2 vols. (New York, 1906), chaps. 2, 3; Robert Bied, "Salons, athénées et Institut: Essai

sur le pouvoir culturel à Paris de 1780 à 1830," *L'Information historique* 44 (1982): 73ff.

41 Emmet Kennedy, *A Philosophe in the Age of Revolution: Destutt de Tracy and the Origins of "Ideology"* (Philadelphia, 1978), chap. 7; Maurice Agulhon, *Le Cercle dans la haute bourgeoisie, 1810–1848* (Paris, 1977).

42 David H. Pinkney, *The Decisive Years: France, 1840–47* (Princeton, 1986), pp. 3–4.

II. THE RHYTHM OF POPULAR CULTURE

1 Marc Bloch, *Les Caractères originaux de l'histoire rurale française* (Paris, 1931), pp. 155–72; cf. Pierre Goubert, *The Ancien Régime: French Society, 1600–1750* (New York, 1973), chap. 4; Jacques Godechot, *Les Institutions de la France sous la Révolution et l'Empire,* 2d ed. (Paris, 1968), p. 109. "Peasants" (as well as land) were a diverse lot, for they included free landowners (*laboureurs* or *cultivateurs*), tenant farmers (*fermiers*), sharecroppers (*métayers*), the payers of feudal dues for land they held on a hereditary basis (*censitaires*), and day laborers (*journaliers* or *manoeuvriers*).

2 Bloch, pp. 172–94; Georges Lefebvre, *Les Paysans du Nord pendant la Révolution française* (Paris, 1972; orig. publ. 1924), p. 320; Alexis de Tocqueville, *The Ancien Régime* (New York, 1955), pt. 2: chaps. 2, 3, 7, 9, 10; Albert Babeau, *Le Village sous l'ancien régime,* 3d ed. (Paris, 1882), pp. 382–87.

3 Goubert, chap. 4 and passim.

4 Maurice Agulhon, *The Republic in the Village: The People of the Var from the French Revolution to the Second Republic* (Cambridge, 1982), chap. 2; Bloch, chap. 2 and pp. 184–90, plate 6; Georges Frèche, *Toulouse et la région Midi-Pyrénées au siècle des lumières (vers 1670–1789)* (Toulouse, 1974), chaps. 8–10.

5 Bloch, pp. 131–54, 201–2 and chap. 6; Frèche, pp. 471–76; Louis Bergeron, *France under Napoleon* (Princeton, 1981), pp. 80–81; Lefebvre, pp. 31, 94, 349, 407; Georges Dupeux, *La Société française, 1789–1970* (Paris, 1972), pp. 111–16; Theodore Zeldin, *France, 1848–1945: Ambition, Love and Politics* (Oxford, 1973), p. 146; Frèche, chaps. 6, 7; Tocqueville, *Ancien Régime* pt. 2: chap. 1; Emmanuel Le Roy Ladurie, *The Peasants of Languedoc* (Urbana, 1974); Kennedy, *A Philosophe,* p. 8.

6 Bloch, pp. 21–25; Frèche, chaps. 7, 10.

7 Bloch, chap. 4, p. 134; Le Roy Ladurie makes the distinction between these three types of peasant protests (*Carnival in Romans,* chap. 13); Hilton Root, "Challenging the Seigneurie: Community and Contention on the Eve of the French Revolution," *Journal of Modern History* 57 (1985): 652–81, esp. 658–63 on seigneurial reactions; Camille Labrousse, *La Crise de l'économie française à la fin de l'ancien régime* (Paris, 1944), p. xxiv; and see

Robert Forster, *The House of Saulx Tavannes* (Baltimore, 1977), pp. 66–108, for an account of one duchal seigneurial reaction.

8 Bloch, p. 232; Lefebvre, pp. 232–35; Agulhon, *Republic,* pp. 24–48; André Thuilliery, *Économie et société nivernaises au début du XIXe siècle* (Paris, 1974), chap. 1; cf. [J.-B. C. L. Comte de] Luçay, *Description du département du Cher* (Paris, an X [1802]), p. 20. For an account emphasizing conflicts between the peasant community and the seigneur, see Root, pp. 652–81.

9 Mercier, 1:14, 112.

10 Lefebvre, *The Great Fear* (New York, 1973), pp. 67–74; Edward Shorter, *The Making of the Modern Family* (New York, 1977), pp. 44–53.

11 Lucienne A. Roubin, "Savoir et art de vivre campagnard," in Jacques Beauroy, Marc Bertrand, and Edward Gargan, eds., *The Wolf and the Lamb: Popular Culture in France from the Old Regime to the Twentieth Century* (Saratoga, Calif., 1977), pp. 93–100.

12 Jules Michelet, *Histoire de la Révolution française,* ed. Gérard Walter, 2 vols. (Paris, 1952), 1:intro., pt. 2; Tocqueville, *Ancien Régime,* pt. 2:chap. 1; Furet, *Penser la Révolution française,* pp. 132–34.

13 J. P. Goubert, "L'Art du guérir: Médecine savante et médecine populaire dans la France de 1790," *Annales, ESC* 32 (1977): 919.

14 *Histoire de la Société royale de médecine de Paris avec les mémoires de médecine et de physique médicale,* 10 vols. (Paris, 1776–89), 6: pt. 2: 248, 78–80; 6: pt. 1: 152–54, 200n, 149n.

15 J. Léonard, *La France médicale au XIXe siècle* (Paris, 1978), pp. 22–24ff.

16 Ibid., pp. 26–29; Zeldin, p. 27.

17 Léonard, p. 43.

18 Zeldin, p. 30.

19 Michel Vovelle, *La Mentalité révolutionnaire* (Paris, 1985), pp. 34–37. See also on the diffusion of the *Encyclopédie,* Robert Darnton, *The Business of Enlightenment: A Publishing History of the Encyclopedia, 1775–80* (Cambridge, Mass., 1979), chap. 6.

20 Le Roy Ladurie, in *Histoire de la France rurale,* ed. Georges Duby and Armand Wallon, 4 vols. (Paris, 1975–76), 2:509ff.

21 François Furet and Jacques Ozouf, *Lire et écrire: L'Alphabétisation des français de Calvin à Jules Ferry,* 2 vols. (Paris, 1977), 1:38, 69–96; Le Roy Ladurie, *Histoire de la France rurale,* 2:520–21.

22 Furet and Ozouf, 1: chaps. 1, 2.

23 J. Quéniart, *Culture et société urbaines dans la France de l'Ouest au XVIIIe siècle,* 2 vols. (Lille, 1977), 1:112–24.

24 Roche, *Le Peuple de Paris,* pp. 209, 206; Roche, *Le Siècle des lumières,* 1:190.

25 Robert Mandrou, *De la culture populaire au XVIIe et au XVIIIe siècles* (Paris, 1964); Roger Chartier, "Culture as Appropriation: Popular Cultural Uses in Early Modern France," in *Understanding Popular Culture: Europe from the Middle Ages to the Nineteenth Century,* ed. S. L. Kaplan (Berlin, 1984), pp. 229–53.

26 Chartier, "Culture as Appropriation," "Popular Reading Strategies in Early Modern France, 1530–1660," and "Uses of Reading from the Mid-Seventeenth Century to the Revolution" (workshop at the Folger Library, Washington, D.C., 29 April, 1 May 1985); Rétif de la Bretonne, *Vie de mon père*, ed. Gilbert Rouger (Paris, 1970), p. 10, engravings entitled *Lecture de la Bible* and *Lecture du Soir*.

27 R. Muchembled, *Culture populaire et culture des élites dans la France moderne* (Paris, 1978), pp. 348–66; Chartier, "Culture as Appropriation," pp. 250–52; P. Burke, "The Classical Tradition and Popular Culture in Early Modern Europe," in *Les Intermédiaires culturels: Actes du colloque de Centre méridional d'histoire sociale, des mentalités et des cultures, 1978* (Paris, [1981]), pp. 237–44.

28 Mandrou, pp. 48–49.

29 Robert Darnton, *The Great Cat Massacre: And Other Episodes in French Cultural History* (New York, 1984), pp. 29, 53.

30 Paul Delarue, *Le Conte populaire français*, 3 vols. (Paris, 1957–76), 1:101–3; Eugen Weber, "Fairies and Hard Facts: The Reality of Folk Tales," *Journal of the History of Ideas* 42 (1981), pp. 93–113.

31 Mandrou, pp. 43–49.

32 Rétif de la Bretonne, pp. 9–10.

33 Mikhail Bakhtin, *L'Oeuvre de François Rabelais et la culture populaire du moyen âge et sous la Renaissance* (Paris, 1970); Le Roy Ladurie, *Histoire de la France rurale*, 2:510–17; Norbert Elias, *The Civilizing Process: The History of Manners* (New York, 1978).

34 Packer, "La Calotte," 82–83.

35 Neal R. Johnson, "Almanachs français et mentalités collectives au dix-huitième siècle," Fifth International Congress on the Enlightenment, *Transactions*, in *Studies on Voltaire and the Eighteenth Century* 191 (1980): 1023–30, and a fuller unpublished version by the same title.

36 The almanacs cited were consulted at the Musée des arts et traditions populaires, Paris.

37 Roger Chartier's observation, conversation with author in April 1985.

38 A.N. F⁷ 3488: Nord.

39 Mercier, 2:152; Michel Vovelle provides evidence of a certain amount of popular de-Christianization in Provence based on a decline of pious intentions mentioned in wills (*Piété baroque et déchristianisation en Provence au XVIIIᵉ siècle: Les Attitudes devant la mort d'après les clauses des testaments* [Paris, 1973], p. 51). Some have found this conclusion to be flawed on the grounds that the decline in question could reflect a shift in devotions rather than de-Christianization proper, or the attitudes of the notaries who drew up the wills rather than those of testators (Bernard Plongeron's view). See also, however, Le Roy Ladurie, who argues for the existence of popular de-Christianization in certain areas of Provence, the north, and Normandy (*Histoire de la France rurale*, 2:510–17). On the almanacs and

the Enlightenment, see chap. 4, below, and Geneviève Bollème, *Les Alma-nachs populaires au XVIIe et XVIIIe siècle: Essai d'histoire sociale* (Paris, 1969), esp. p. 93.

40 On festivals see: Yves-Marie Bercé, *Fête et révolte: Des mentalités populaires du XVIe au XVIIIe siècle* (Paris, 1976); Alain Faure, *Paris Carême prenant: Du carnaval à Paris au XIXe siècle* (Paris, 1978); Muchembled, pp. 124, 158–88; Michel Vovelle, *Les Métamorphoses de la fête en Provence de 1750 à 1820* (Paris, 1976); Maurice Agulhon, *Pénitents et francs-maçons de l'ancienne Provence* (Paris, 1968), and *La Société méridionale: Confréries et associations dans la vie collective dans la Provence orientale à la fin du XVIIIe siècle,* 2 vols. (Aix-en-Provence, 1966); Philippe Goujard and Claude Mazauric, "Dans quel sens peut-on dire que la Révolution française fut une révolution cul-turelle?" *Europa: Revue d'études interdisciplinaires* (Canada) 2 (1978): 35–65.

41 Darnton, *Great Cat Massacre,* p. 120.

42 Ibid.

43 *Mémoires de l'Académie celtique,* 6 vols. in 3 (Paris, 1807–12), vols. 2–5. Examples of patron saints are Joseph (carpenters, cabinetmakers), Eloi (farmers, cultivateurs, ironsmiths, muleteers), Blaise (carders), Madeleine (gardeners), Mark (vintners, grapegrowers), Honoré (bakers), and Barbe (artillerymen).

44 Aubin-Louis Millin, *Voyage dans le Midi de la France,* 4 vols. (Paris, 1807–11), 3:332–33.

45 Archives de la Préfecture de Police (Paris), AA, *220, 269; 184,* 296; *72,* 69; *138,* 198. I am grateful to Keith Baker for his comment at the 1980 AHA convention on the Saint-Antoine incident.

46 A.N. F¹⁹ 5541; cf. AF^{iv} 1897.

47 Faure, pp. 74, 61.

48 The theory of a rift between popular and elite culture at the end of the Enlightenment advanced by Peter Burke, *Popular Culture in Early Modern Europe* (New York, 1978), has been challenged by Michèle Root-Bernstein in *Boulevard Theater and Revolution in Eighteenth-Century Paris* (Ann Arbor, Mich., 1984), and by Robert M. Isherwood, *Farce and Fantasy: Popular En-tertainment in Eighteenth-Century Paris* (New York, 1986).

INTRODUCTION TO PART II

1 The expression is Pierre Chaunu's in *La Civilisation de l'Europe des lumières* (Paris, 1971).

III. ENLIGHTENMENT AND CHRISTIANITY

1 Jean Gaulmier, *L'Idéologue Volney, 1757–1820: Contribution à l'étude de l'ori-entalisme en France* (Beirut, 1951), pp. 214, 226; Volney, *La Loi naturelle ou*

Catéchisme du citoyen français, ed. G. Martin (Paris, 1934).

2 Destutt de Tracy, *Analyse raisonée de "l'Origine de tous les cultes ou Religion universelle": Ouvrage publié en l'an III, par Dupuis Citoyen français* (Paris, an XII [1804], p. 160.

3 Rousseau, *Émile* (1762), bk. 4.

4 Sir Isaac Newton, *Mathematical Principles of Natural Philosophy and His System of the World,* ed. Florian Cajori, trans. Andrew Motte (Berkeley, 1946), "General Scholium," pp. 545–46.

5 *Dictionary of Scientific Biography,* s.v. "Laplace."

6 Ibid., pp. 308–9; Laplace, *Exposition du système du monde,* 2 vols. (Paris, an IV [1796]), 2:chap. 6.

7 Roger Hahn, *Laplace as Newtonian Scientist: A Paper Delivered at a Seminar on the Newtonian Influence Held at Clark Library,* 8 April 1967 (Los Angeles, 1967), esp. pp. 15–17.

8 Diderot, *Pensées sur l'interprétation de la nature,* in *Oeuvres complètes,* ed. J. Assézat and Maurice Tourneux, 20 vols. (Paris, 1875–77), 2:11; Michel Foucault, *The Order of Things* (New York, 1973; orig. publ. 1970), pp. 226–32, chaps. 3, 5.

9 *Dictionary of Scientific Biography,* s.v. "Lamarck"; Georges Gusdorf, *La Conscience révolutionnaire: Les Idéologues,* vol. 8 of *Les Sciences humaines en occident* (Paris, 1978), pp. 429–50.

10 *Système des animaux sans vertèbres* (Paris, an IX [1801]; Brussels, 1969), p. 11.

11 *Histoire naturelle des animaux sans vertèbres,* ed. G. P. Deshayes, H. Milne Edwards, 2d ed., 11 vols. (Paris, 1835–45), 1:113, 145, 135. This text is that of the first edition (1815–22) except for the notes. See Lamarck, "Discours d'Ouverture" (an X [1802]), cited in Gusdorf, p. 432; Lamarck, *Système analytique des connaissances positives de l'homme* (Paris, 1820), pp. 154–55.

12 *Rapports du physique et du moral de l'homme,* 2 vols. (Paris, an X [1802]); Martin Staum, *Cabanis, Enlightenment, and Medical Philosophy in the French Revolution* (Princeton, 1980), p. 4; Kennedy, *A Philosophe,* p. 114; Destutt de Tracy, *Projet d'éléments d'idéologie* (Paris, an IX [1801]), p. 224.

13 Cabanis, "Lettre à F* sur les causes premières," in *Oeuvres philosophiques,* 2 vols. (Paris, 1956), 2:264.

14 Ibid., p. 274; Laplace, *Exposition du système du monde,* quoted in Henri Gouhier, *Les Conversions de Maine de Biran* (Paris, 1947), p. 183.

15 Destutt de Tracy, pp. 38, 35. See Emmet Kennedy, "Destutt de Tracy and the Unity of the Sciences," *Studies on Voltaire and the Eighteenth Century* 171 (1977): 223–39; Condillac, *Traité des sensations* (1754), in *Oeuvres,* ed. Georges Leroy, 3 vols. (Paris, 1947–51), 1:222.

16 Destutt de Tracy, "Memoires sur la faculté de penser," *Memoires de l'Institut national, Classe des sciences morales et politiques,* 4 vols. (Paris an VI [1798]–an XI [1804]), 1:323–24.

17 Kennedy, *A Philosophe,* pp. 33–37; Jean A. Perkins, *The Concept of the Self*

in the French Enlightenment (Geneva, 1969); Diderot, *Rêve d'Alembert,* in *Oeuvres,* 2:160–73; Gustave Lanson, *Voltaire,* trans. Robert A. Wagoner (New York, 1966), p. 24; Destutt de Tracy, *Analyse raisonnée,* pp. vii–viii.

18 Condorcet, *Esquisse d'un tableau historique des progrès de l'esprit humain,* ed. O. H. Prior (Paris, 1933); Keith Michael Baker, *Condorcet: From Natural Philosophy to Social Mathematics* (Chicago, 1975), chap. 2; Condillac, *Essai sur l'origine des connaissances humaines* (1746), pt. 2.

19 Condorcet.

20 Jean-Marc-Gaspard Itard, *The Wild Boy of Aveyron,* trans. and ed. George and Muriel Humphrey (New York, 1962), p. xxi. Itard's account was published as *Rapports et mémoires sur le sauvage de l'Aveyron* (Paris, 1884). All references are to the Humphreys' translation.

21 Ibid., pp. xxiii, 6.

22 Ibid., pp. 36, 52ff. For a detailed analysis of the wild boy of Aveyron, see Harlan Lane, *The Wild Boy of Aveyron* (Cambridge, 1976).

23 Lucien Febvre, "Civilization: Evolution of a Word and Group of Ideas," in *A New Kind of History: From the Writings of Lucien Febvre,* ed. Peter Burke (New York, 1973), p. 230; J. G. A. Pocock in conversation with the author about Gibbon; see his "Superstition and Enthusiasm in Gibbon's History of Religion," *Eighteenth-Century Life* 8 (1984): 83–94.

24 Kennedy, *A Philosophe,* pp. 37, 48–50, 59, 143, 232, 333, 217, 207; Destutt de Tracy, *Principes logiques; ou, Recueil de faits relatifs à l'intelligence humaine* (Paris, 1817), p. 88; Tracy to C.-F. Lacroix, 15 December 1816, MS, Bibliothèque de l'Institut, no. 2396.

25 R. R. Palmer, *Catholics and Unbelievers in Eighteenth-Century France* (Princeton, 1939), pp. 33–35; Bernard Plongeron, "Recherches sur 'l'Aufklärung' catholique en Europe occidentale (1770–1830)," *Revue d'histoire moderne et contemporaine* 16 (1969): 555–605; Plongeron, *Théologie et politique au siècle des lumières (1770–1820)* (Paris, 1973), quotation on p. 144; Dale Van Kley, *The Jansenists and the Expulsion of the Jesuits from France, 1757–1765* (New Haven and London, 1975).

26 Harvey Chisick, *The Limits of Reform in the Enlightenment: Attitudes toward the Education of the Lower Classes in Eighteenth-Century France* (Princeton, 1981), p. 277.

27 Harry Payne, *The Philosophes and the People* (New Haven and London, 1976), p. 7; Chisick, chap. 1 passim.

28 Payne, pp. 1, 25, chap. 7; Chisick, pp. 185–97.

29 Payne, p. 1; Chisick, pp. 84, 95–100, 108–15. R. Chartier et al., *L'Education en France du XVIe au XVIIIe siècle* (Paris, 1976), chaps. 2, 3 passim.

30 Chisick, p. 275.

31 [Diderot, Alembert, et al.], *Encyclopédie, ou Dictionnaire raisonnée des sciences, des arts et des métiers,* 35 vols. (Paris, 1751–80), 12:476 and end vols.

32 A.N. F^15 227.

33 Ibid.

34 Peter Burke, *Popular Culture in Early Modern Europe* (New York, 1978), pp. 270–81; Agulhon, *Pénitents et francs-maçons,* pp. 18, 147, 152, 159.

35 Abbé Grégoire, *Essai sur la régénération physique, morale et politique des juifs* (Metz, 1789; reprint, Paris, 1968), pp. 188–89; T. Tackett, *Priest and Parish in Eighteenth-Century France* (Princeton, 1977), pp. 86–95, 161–64.

36 Jean-Jacques Tatin, "Relation de l'actualité, réflexion politique et culte des grand-hommes dans les almanachs de 1760 à 1793," *Annales historiques de la Révolution française* 261 (July–September 1985): 307–16, and Emmet Kennedy, "Neues und Altes in der 'Massenliteratur' der Revolutionszeit," in *Die Französische Revolution als Bruch des gesellschaftlichen Bewusstseins: Vorlagen und Diskussionen der internationalen Arbeitstagung am Zentrum für interdisziplinäre Forschung der Universität Bielefeld, 28. Mai–1. Juni 1985,* ed. Reinhart Koselleck and Rolf Reichardt with Erich Pelzer and Michael Wagner (Munich, 1988), pp. 305–10, hereafter cited as *Arbeitstagung Bielefeld;* Chisick, pp. 154–55; Emmet Kennedy, "The French Revolutionary Catechisms: Ruptures and Continuities with Classical, Christian, and Enlightenment Moralities," *Studies on Voltaire and the Eighteenth Century* 199 (1981): 353.

37 Ruth Necheles, *The Abbé Grégoire: The Odyssey of an Egalitarian* (Westport, Conn., 1971), p. xii; *Biographie uneversalle,* s.v. "Grégoire"; Paul Pisani, *Répertoire biographique de l'épiscopat constitutionnel (1791–1802),* s.v. "Grégoire"; Arthur Hertzberg, *The French Enlightenment and the Jews* (New York, 1968), esp. pp. 273–86.

38 Grégoire, *Essai sur la régénération . . . des juifs.*

39 A. Gazier, *Etudes sur l'histoire religieuse de la Révolution française d'après des documents originaux et inédits* (Paris, 1887), pp. 30–31, 36.

40 Grégoire, *Lettre aux citoyens de couleur et de nègres libres de Saint-Domingue et des autres îles françoises de l'Amérique* [8 June 1791], pp. 3, 13; Grégoire, *De la liberté de conscience et de culte à Haiti* (Paris, 1824), esp. p. 2. Grégoire here quotes Paul's *Letter to the Ephesians,* 4.5.

IV. THE QUEST FOR SIMPLICITY

1 Witold Kula, *Les Mesures et les hommes* (Paris, 1984), p. 179, chaps. 19–21 passim.

2 Adrien Faure, *Les Origines du système métrique* (Paris, 1931), pp. 34–83 passim, esp. p. 78; *Dictionary of Scientific Biography,* vol. 15 (Supplement), s.v. "Laplace," p. 335. M. de La Condamine, *Journal du voyage fait par ordre du Roi à l'Equateur, servant d'introduction à la mesure des trois premiers degrés du méridien* (Paris, 1751); Prieur Duvernois, *Instruction sur le calcul décimal, appliqué principalement au nouveau système des poids et mesures à l'usage de ceux qui savent l'addition, la soustraction* (Paris, an III [1794–95]), *Nouvel instruction sur les poids et les mesures . . .* (Paris, an III [1794–95]), p. 51, and *Rapport sur*

l'exécution des lois relatives aux poids et mesures (25 germinal an VI [14 April 1798], Conseil des Cinq Cents), p. 2; Kula, chap. 22.

3 Charles Coulston Gillispie, *Science and Polity at the End of the Old Regime* (Princeton, 1980), pp. 113–16; *Dictionary of Scientific Biography,* s.v. "Cassini."

4 François Benoît, *L'Art français sous la Révolution et l'Empire: Les Doctrines, les idées, les genres* (Paris, 1897), chaps. 2, 3; Daniel Wildenstein, comp., *Louis David: Recueil de documents complémentaires au catalogue complet* (Paris, n.d.), no. 677.

5 Benoît, chaps. 2, 3; C. Gabillot, *Hubert Robert et son temps* (Paris, 1895), p. 16.

6 Franklin M. Biebel, "Fragonard and Madame du Barry," in *The Garland Library of the History of Art,* vol. 10: *Rococo to Romanticism, 1700–1850* (New York, 1976), pp. 51–70 (reprinted from *Gazette des Beaux-Arts* 56 [1960]); Gabillot, pp. 18–26. David's energy and severity gave new life to an enfeebled school. He was both heir to and creator of the neoclassical tradition. The grand style of historical paintings had been encouraged officially by the directors of royal buildings, such as Lenormant de Tournehem, and by the marquis de Marigny. Marigny commissioned such neoclassical architects as Ange-Jacques Gabriel, who designed the place de Louis XV (Concorde), and Jacques-Germain Soufflot, who designed the Church of Sainte-Geneviève, later to become the Panthéon. Marigny also commissioned neoclassical paintings.

7 Johann Joachim Winckelmann, *Recueil des lettres sur Herculanéum à Pompeii, à Caserte et à Rome* (Paris, 1784), esp. p. 278.

8 [Johann Joachim] Winckelmann, *History of Ancient Art,* trans. G. Henry Lodge, 4 vols. (Boston, 1849–73), 2:15, 5; L. D. Ettlinger, "Winckelmann," in *The Age of Neo-Classicism, [Catalogue of] the Fourteenth Exhibition of the Council of Europe [held at] the Royal Academy and the Victoria Albert Museum, London, 9 September–19 November 1972* (London, 1972), pp. xxx–xxxiv.

9 Winckelmann, *History of Ancient Art,* 2:136, 138, 146.

10 Ibid., 2:147.

11 Ibid., 2:136, 50, 112–14, 122–23, 218.

12 Hugh Honour, *Neoclassicism* (Harmondsworth, 1971), pp. 60ff.

13 Barthélemy, *Voyage du jeune Anarcharsis en Grèce,* 2d ed., 7 vols. (Paris, 1789), 4:465, 6:8–14, 178, 1:vii–viii, 104. Over forty complete editions and twenty-five abridged editions of this work appeared by 1900.

14 Winckelmann in Lorenz Eitner, *Neoclassicism and Romanticism, 1750–1850: Sources and Documents,* 2 vols. (Englewood Cliffs, N.J., 1970), 1:11, 14, 9.

15 Antoine Schnapper, *Jacques-Louis David* (New York, 1980), p. 11; Honour, pp. 22–23; Norman Bryson, *Tradition and Desire: From David to Delacroix* (Cambridge, 1984), pp. 6ff.; Michel Laclotte, "J.-L. David, Reform and Revolution," in *The Age of Neo-Classicism,* pp. lxvii–lxxi.

16 Eugène Delacroix, *Journal,* 3 vols. (Paris, 1932), 3:271.

17 Wildenstein, no. 677.

18 Seymour Howard, *A Classical Frieze by Jacques-Louis David: Sacrifice of the Hero: The Roman Years* (Sacramento, Calif., 1975); Wildenstein, no. 88.

19 Bryson, chap. 3.

20 Thomas Crow, "Painting and Pre-Revolutionary Radicalism in France," *Art History* 1 (1978): 426, 428, 429, 433.

21 Tom Crow, *Paintings and Public Life in Eighteenth-Century Paris* (New Haven and London, 1985); Philippe Bordes, *Le Serment de jeu de paume* (Paris, 1983), pp. 21–23, 53, 230.

22 Robert L. Herbert, *David, Voltaire, "Brutus," and the French Revolution: An Essay in Art and Politics* (New York, 1973), pp. 125, 59–61.

23 Crow, *Paintings and Public Life,* p. 185.

24 Jean-Marie Pérouse de Montclos, *Etienne-Louis Boullée, 1728–1799* (New York, 1974), pp. 1–28; Emil Kaufmann, *Three Revolutionary Architects: Boullée, Ledoux, Lequeu,* in American Philosophical Society, *Transactions,* n.s., 42, pt. 3 (1952): pp. 430–50 passim, 449.

25 Montclos, pp. 1–28; Kaufmann, pp. 459–88.

26 *Essai sur l'art,* ed. J.-M. Pérouse de Montclos (Paris, 1968), p. 47 (available in English translation by Helen Rosenau); Kaufmann, pp. 465, 488.

27 Quoted in J. C. Lemagny, ed., *Visionary Architects: Boullée, Ledoux, Lequeu* (Houston, 1968), p. 26; Kaufmann; Montclos.

28 For architects of the Revolution proper, see James Leith, "Desacralization, Resacralization, and Architectural Planning during the French Revolution," *Eighteenth-Century Life* 7 (1982): 74–84, which has some fine reproductions of plans; Lemagny, p. 54.

29 Quoted in Louis Reau, *Houdon,* 2 vols. (Paris, 1964), 2:425.

30 H. H. Arnason, *The Sculptures of Houdon* (New York, 1975). This work contains reproductions of Houdon's work.

31 Houdon, *Réflexions sur les concours en général et sur celui de la statue de Jean-Jacques Rousseau en particulier* (n.p., n.d.), pp. 7, 13; Arnason.

32 Georges Giacometti, *La Vie et l'œuvre de Houdon,* "Preface" by Camille Mauclair, 2 vols. (Paris, 1929), 1:76, ii, iii, 111.

33 Camille Mauclair in ibid., 1:i–iv; Giacometti, 1:75; Louis Reau, "Houdon sous la Révolution et l'Empire," *Gazette des Beaux-Arts* 66 (1924): 59–86, denies that Houdon retired during the Revolution.

34 Albert Boime, *The Academy and French Painting in the Nineteenth Century* (London, 1971), p. 36, chaps. 1, 2 passim; [Jean-Auguste-Dominique] Ingres, *Ecrits sur l'Art,* ed. Raymond Cogniat (Paris, 1947), pp. 40, 38, 19.

35 *The Grand Prix de Rome: Paintings from the Ecole des Beaux-Arts, 1797–1863,* ed. Philippe Grunchec (Washington, D.C., 1984), pp. 18–28, 54–55, 64, 77, 98, 116–17.

V. FROM SENSIBILITY TO TERROR

1 Paul Hazard, *The European Mind, 1680–1715,* trans. J. Lewis May (New York, 1963; orig. publ. Paris, 1935); Nannerl O. Keohane, *Philosophy and the State in France: The Renaissance to the Enlightenment* (Princeton, 1980), pp. 338–43; Lionel Rothkrug, *Opposition to Louis XIV: The Political and Social Origins of the Enlightenment* (Princeton, 1965), chap. 5; Howard Mumford Jones, *Revolution and Romanticism* (Cambridge, Mass., 1974); E. Thomas Noonan, *The Dark Side of the Enlightenment* (Cambridge, Mass., 1984).

2 Young, *Night-Thoughts,* illus. William Blake, ed. Geoffrey Keynes (Cambridge, Mass., 1927), lines 72–81, 447–56. See n. 27, below, on Young's influence on France.

3 Maurice Lévy, *Le Roman gothique anglais, 1764–1824* (Toulouse, 1968), chap. 2. Lionel Gossmann, *Medievalism and the Ideologies of the Enlightenment: The World and Works of La Curne de Sainte Pelaye* (Baltimore, 1968).

4 Burke, *Philosophical Enquiry into the Origin of Our Ideas on the Sublime and the Beautiful,* ed. James T. Boulton (Notre Dame, Ind., 1968; orig. publ. 1958), p. 44.

5 Ibid., pp. 60, 63, 58, 39.

6 Diderot, *Salons* (1767), 3:165–66, quoted in Richard A. Etlin, *The Architecture of Death: The Transformation of the Cemetery in Eighteenth-Century Paris* (Cambridge, Mass., 1984), p. 101.

7 *Julie, ou la Nouvelle Héloïse,* ed. Michel Launay (Paris, 1967), bk. 3, letters 20, 16, and passim; bk. 4, letter 17.

8 Darnton, *Great Cat Massacre,* pp. 236, 243, 244, chap. 6 passim.

9 André Monglond, *La France révolutionnaire et impériale: Annales de bibliographie méthodique,* 10 vols. (Grenoble, 1930–78), vols. 1–4. Roughly twice as many pages (60) list Rousseauian titles as religious ones (31).

10 *Du théâtre, ou Nouvel Essai sur l'art dramatique* (Geneva, 1970; orig. publ. Amsterdam, 1773), pp. 2, 8–10; Mercier, *Tableau de Paris,* 4:91–92.

11 Mercier, *Du théâtre;* Félix-Alexandre A. Gaiffe, *Le Drame en France au XVIIIᵉ siècle* (Paris, 1910), p. 93.

12 Friedrich Grimm, *Correspondance littéraire,* vol. 7, quoted in Gaiffe, p. 144; Oddly, these attitudes coincided with a popularization of the audiences of the grand theaters and were in marked contrast to attitudes of popular audiences on the boulevards. See also [Friedrich M. Baron] Grimm, *Correspondance philosophique et littéraire,* ed. M. Tourneux, 16 vols. (Paris, 1877–82), 10:341.

13 On sensibility in France, see Pierre Trahard, *Les Maîtres de la sensibilité française au XVIIIᵉ siècle,* 4 vols. (Paris, 1931–33), and Gaiffe; Chisick, *Limits of Reform,* pp. 225–38.

14 Mercier, *Tableau de Paris,* 2:168.

15 *Les Deux Petits Savoyards,* 1a c pr mus Dalayrac (1789), in *Collection des théâtres français* (Senlis, 1829), v. 62, sc. 4, 5, 6, 18. All records of numbers of performances are taken from the Kennedy-Netter Theater Project, a count of performances between 1789 and 1799.

16 F. Talma, *Mémoires de Lékain, précédés de réflexions sur cet acteur et sur l'art théâtral* (Paris, 1825; reprint, Geneva, 1968), p. xix; Talma, *Reflections on the Actor's Art* [Paris, 1826], ed. Sir Henry Irving (New York, 1915), p. 19.

17 Diderot, *Oeuvres,* ed. La Pléiade (Paris, 1951), "Entretiens sur le Fils Naturel," p. 1242, "Réponse à Mme. Riccoboni," p. 1313.

18 Diderot, *Paradoxe sur le comédien,* in *Oeuvres,* p. 1071.

19 Rousseau, *Lettre sur la musique française* (n.p., 1753), pp. 42, 4, 16, 91.

20 Quoted in William Weber, "La *musique ancienne* in the Waning of the Ancien Régime," *Journal of Modern History* 56 (1984): 78.

21 *An Eighteenth-Century Musical Tour in France and Italy,* ed. Percy Scholes (London, 1959), pp. 18, 17.

22 Weber, p. 83.

23 Ibid.; Kennedy-Netter Theater Project; see also firsthand account of music of the comic-opera in Andre Grétry, *Mémoires, ou Essais sur la musique,* 3 vols. (Paris an V [1797–98]), 1:18, 49–51, 178.

24 Charles B. Paul, "Music and Ideology: Rameau, Rousseau, and 1789," *Journal of the History of Ideas* 32 (1971): 395–401, quotation on p. 400.

25 Paul Henry Lang, "French Opera and the Spirit of the Revolution," *Studies in Eighteenth-Century Culture* 2 (1972): 97–112, quotation on p. 97.

26 Ibid., pp. 108–12.

27 Grétry, 1:18, 49–51, 114, 125n, 178, and 1–126 passim.

28 Ibid., 1:370.

29 Ibid., 1:105–6, 287, 388; 2:138; 3:456; Winton Dean, "Opera under the French Revolution," *Proceedings of the Royal Musical Association* 94 (1967–68): 80.

30 Edward J. Dent, *The Rise of Romantic Opera* (Cambridge, 1976), pp. 47–62.

31 Ibid., pp. 62–68.

32 Ibid., pp. 71–77.

33 René Brancour, *Méhul, biographie critique* (Paris [1912]).

34 Pierre de Nolhac, *Hubert Robert, 1733–1808* (Paris, 1910), pp. 1–88; Gabillot, *Hubert Robert.*

35 Diderot, *Salon de 1767,* quoted in Nolhac, p. 41.

36 Grimm, quoted in *Dictionnaire de biographie française,* s.v. "Baculard d'Arnaud"; Lawrence Marsden Price, "The Relation of Baculard d'Arnaud to German Literature," *Monatschefte für Deutsche Unterricht* 37 (1945): 151–60; Robert Dawson, *Baculard d'Arnaud: Life and Prose Fiction,* 2 vols. (Oxford, 1976), esp. 1:407; R. Hermans o. p. m., "Un Temoin inattendu de l'influence de Baculard d'Arnaud en Allemagne: Le Père Girard (1765–1850)," *Neophilologus* 35 (1951): 51.

37 *Fanni ou Paméla, Histoire anglaise,* in Baculard d'Arnaud, *Oeuvres,* 6 vols. (Paris, an XI [1803]), vol. 1; see Fernand Baldensperger, *Etudes d'histoire littéraire* (Paris, 1907), pp. 55–109, on Young's *Night-Thoughts* in France. Arnaud was a friend of the translator Le Tourneaux. Hans Jürgen-Lusebrink, "Mémoire pour la fille Cléreaux (Rouen 1785)," *Studies on Voltaire and the Eighteenth Century* 208 (1982): 323–72, esp. 330, 334, 340, 346–47; cf. the notice in the *Journal de Paris,* 21 December 1789, about the Association de bienfaisance judiciaire and its distribution of medals to acquitted criminals. Millin, in *Voyage dans le Midi,* 3:385, cites a play by Blanc Gilles, *La Bienfaisance de Louis XVI.*

38 *Paul et Virginie,* ed. Pierre Trahard (Paris, 1964), pp. 101, 122, 103, 151, 202, 174, 228–29.

39 Ibid., editor's intro., pp. xxvii–xxxi; cf. Favière's theatrical adaptation, *Paul et Virginie,* 3a c mus Kreutzer (Paris, 1791). Dawson, *Baculard d'Arnaud,* 1:367; Trahard, ed., *Paul et Virginie,* pp. xxv, xliv. *Werther* was published in France in 1776, 1777, 1792, and in one dateless edition before a spate of editions between 1840 and 1860.

40 *Alexis, ou La Maisonnette dans les bois,* 4 vols. (Grenoble, 1789), 4:75; Grimm, quoted in *Dictionnaire de biographie française,* s.v. "Baculard d'Arnaud." For another cavern and female corpse, see Marsollier des Vivétières's *Camille, ou Le Souterrain,* 3a c pr mus (Paris, 1791).

41 R. D. Mayo, "Ann Radcliffe and Ducray-Duminil," *Modern Language Review* 36 (1941): 501–5.

42 Ducray-Duminil, *Coélina, enfant du mystère,* 6 vols. (Paris, an VII [1799]), 5:124; 1:51, 70, 15.

43 Alexis Pitou, "Les Origines du mélodrame français à la fin du XVIIIᵉ siècle," *Revue d'histoire littéraire de la France* 18 (1911): 256–66.

44 Ibid., pp. 268–70; Arnould-Mussot, *L'Héroïne américaine,* pant, 3a (Paris, 1786).

45 Larmartelière, *Robert, Chef de brigands,* dr, 5a pr (Paris, 1793); Pitou, pp. 272–73; Arnould-Mussot, *Forêt noire, ou L'Enfant naturel* (English trans. *Forêt Noire, or Maternal Affection: A Serious Pantomime in Three Acts* [Boston, 1796]).

46 Pitou, pp. 280ff.; Maurice Descotes, *Le Public de théâtre et son histoire* (Paris, 1964), chap. 7.

47 Argens, *Thérèse philosophe, ou Mémoires pour servir à l'histoire de D. Dinag et de Mademoiselle Eradice,* new ed. (London, 1785), pp. 7, 29, 110; Sade, *Justine, ou Le Malheur de la vertu,* ed. Georges Bataille (Paris, 1955).

48 Ronald Paulson, *Representations of Revolution, 1789–1820* (New Haven and London, 1983), pp. 220–21.

49 Saint-Just, *Organt,* in *Oeuvres, discours, rapports, institutions républicaines,* ed. Gratien (Paris, 1946), pp. 63–84; for complete text and helpful introduction to this poem, see Charles Vellay, *Oeuvres complètes de Saint-Just,* 2 vols. (Paris, 1908), 1:1–216, esp. nn. 1, 2, 215–16; Norman Hampson, *Will*

and Circumstance: Montesquieu, Rousseau, and the French Revolution (Norman, Okla., 1983), pp. 244–45.

50 *Institutions républicaines* in *Oeuvres,* ed. Gratien, pp. 279–321.

51 Ibid.; Trahard, *La Sensibilité révolutionnaire, 1789–1794* (Paris, 1936), p. 6.

INTRODUCTION TO PART III

1 Kant, *Foundations of the Metaphysics of Morals and What Is Enlightenment?,* trans. Lewis White Beck (Indianapolis, 1959), p. 85. The integration of the Republic of Letters on the social professional level into the old regime was considerable, as with the coterie d'Holbach and the Encyclopedists. On the moral and intellectual plane, there was considerable disintegration (Michael P. Fitzsimmons, "Privilege and Polity in France, 1786–1791," *American Historical Review* 92, no. 2 [April 1987]: 269–95). I am indebted to Daniel Boorstin for suggesting the title for Part III.

VI. THE MEN AND THE INSTITUTIONS (1): CHURCH AND SCHOOLS

1 Tocqueville stated: "The Church was hated not because its priests claimed to regulate the affairs of the other world but because they were landed proprietors, lords of manors, tithe owners, and played a leading part in secular affairs" (*The Old Regime and the French Revolution,* pt. 1, p. 6); see R. R. Palmer, "Man and Citizen: Applications of Individualism in the French Revolution," in *Essays in Political Theory presented to George H. Sabine,* ed. Milton Konvitz and Arthur E. Murphy (Port Washington, N.Y., 1972; orig. publ. 1948), pp. 130–52.

2 Oliver G. Welch, *Mirabeau: A Study of a Democratic Monarchist* (New York, n.d.), pp. 229–30; Talleyrand's motion of 10 October on ecclesiastical property is in Paul Beik, ed., *The French Revolution* (New York, 1970), pp. 114–19; Holmes, *Benjamin Constant,* chap. 1; Godechot, *Institutions,* p. 178. Peter Gay used the apt term *modern paganism* in his *The Enlightenment, an Interpretation: The Rise of Modern Paganism* (New York, 1966).

3 Godechot, pp. 51–52; Jefferson to John Rutledge, 2 February 1788, in *Papers of Thomas Jefferson,* ed. Julian P. Boyd, 1st ser., 21 vols. (Princeton, 1950–83), 12:557.

4 On the Gerle proposal, see Timothy Tackett, *Religion, Revolution, and Regional Culture in Eighteenth-Century France: The Ecclesiastical Oath of 1791* (Princeton, 1986), pp. 210–18.

5 Richard Tuck, *Natural Rights Theories: Their Origin and Development* (Cambridge, 1979); Otto Friedrich von Gierke, *Natural Law and the Theory of Society, 1500 to 1800* (Boston, 1957).

6 Godechot, p. 51.

7 Ibid., pp. 52–55; Hertzberg, *Enlightenment and Jews;* Marcel Marion, *Dictionnaire des institutions de la France au XVIIe et XVIIIe siècles* (Paris, 1972; orig. publ. 1923), s.v. "voeux."

8 Godechot, p. 257. See Archives de la Préfecture de Police de Paris, AA, *81,* 138, for a seizure of an antimonastic pamphlet.

9 Archives de la Préfecture de Police, Section Butte de Moulins, April 1791, AA *83.*

10 Text copied in ibid., AA *266,* 81.

11 Beik, p. 137; Ludovic Sciout, *Histoire de la Constitution civile du clergé et de la persécution révolutionnaire, 1790–1801* (Paris, 1887), p. 63; the text of the first two titles of the Civil Constitution are on pp. 39–46.

12 Monique Cottret, "Aux Origines du républicanisme Janséniste: Le Mythe de l'Eglise primitive et le primitivisme des lumières," *Revue d'histoire moderne et contemporaine* 31 (1984): 99–115; Beik, pp. 139–42.

13 Constitution Civile, title II, arts. 18, 19, in Sciout, p. 43.

14 Cornwell Barnham Rogers, *The Spirit of Revolution in 1789: A Study of Public Opinion as Revealed in Political Songs and Other Popular Literature at the Beginning of the French Revolution* (Princeton, 1949), pp. 80, 85ff.; *Procès-verbaux de l'Académie de peinture et de sculpture,* ed. Anatole Montaiglon, 10 vols. (Paris, 1875–92), 10:37. Louis accepted the tricolor, and later the constitution. He was called "le bourgeois de Paris."

15 Tackett, pp. 44ff.

16 Bernard Plongeron, *Les Réguliers de Paris devant le serment constitutionnel: Sens et conséquences d'une option, 1789–1801* (Paris, 1964), pp. 427ff.

17 Philippe Sagnac, "Etude statistique sur le clergé constitutionnel et le clergé réfractaire en 1791," *Revue d'histoire moderne et contemporaine* 8 (1906): 97–115; Tackett, chap. 2, app. 2, 3.

18 Tackett, chaps. 4, 5, 7.

19 Ibid., chaps. 3–5, 7, on the clerics' own explanation of their choice.

20 *Catéchisme catholique, dans lequel on traite sommairement de l'Eglise, des devoirs réciproques de l'Eglise et de l'Etat, de la nouvelle Constitution du Clergé, du schisme, des règles à suivre à l'égard des Intrus et des schismatiques,* 3d ed. [1791], p. 24; *Catéchisme nouveau et raisonné à l'usage de tous les catholiques français* [1793–94].

21 *Catéchisme d'un curé intrus* (Paris, 1791), p. 6. This and other Catholic catechisms form part of the library of the comte Alfred Boulay de la Meurthe, now part of Harvard's Widener Library. Examples of the few constitutional catechisms found are *Catéchisme de la véritable église par un curé du Département de l'Ain* (Lyons, 1792), *Le Catéchisme du curé constitutionnel, tiré du journal intitulé les loisirs d'un curé déplacé* (Paris, 1791), and the *Catéchisme d'un curé intrus,* 3d ed. (Paris, 1791), most likely a parody of the Catholic catechism by the same title.

22 Le Coz to Pope Pius VI, 19 March 1791, and Le Coz to Municipality of

Rennes, 11 April 1791, in *Correspondance de Le Coz, évêque constitutionnel d'Ille et Vilaine,* ed. le P. Roussel, 2 vols. (Paris, 1900–1903), 1:212, 237.

23 "Les propos 'incendiaires' du curé Jacques Benoît," *Annales historiques de la Révolution française* 39 (1967): 400–401.

24 Luc-François Lalande, *Instruction pastorale . . . pour le Saint Temps de carême* (Paris, 1792), pp. 11–12.

25 Louis XVI à l'Assemblée constitutionale, 26, 29 December 1790; *Louis XVI, Marie Antoinette et Madame Elisabeth: Lettres et documents inédits,* ed. F. Feuillet de Conches, 6 vols. (Paris, 1864–73), 3:319; 4:465.

26 *Bref du Pape Pie VI à S.E.M. Cardinal de la Rochefoucault au sujet de la Constitution Civile du Clergé* [n.p., 10 March 1791], pp. 13–14. On these briefs and the Civil Constitution in general, see *Dictionnaire de théologie catholique,* vol. 3 (Paris, 1908), s.v. "Constitution civile de clergé." For a more general discussion of church-state relations during the Revolution, see André Latreille, *L'Eglise catholique et la Révolution française,* 2 vols. (Paris, 1946, 1950).

27 *Bref du Pape Pie VI à S.E.M. Cardinal de la Rochefoucault,* p. 17.

28 *Bref du Pape à tous les cardinaux, archevêques, évêques au clergé, et au peuple de France* [13 April 1791].

29 Godechot, pp. 237–38, 241–43, 253–54; Holmes, chap. 1.

30 Pierre Chevallier, *Le Panthéon* (Paris, 1977), pp. 3, 13.

31 Mercier, *Tableau de Paris,* 3:97; cf. 5:37–39.

32 Ibid., 3:74; in Madame Roland, *Mémoires,* ed. Paul de Roux (Paris, 1966), she describes the Sunday catechism lessons she received as a child as follows: "We repeated by heart the gospel of the day, the epistle, the prayer and chapter of the catechism indicated for the assignment of the week." The curé had an assistant but reserved for himself "questions on the heart of the matter" (pp. 206–7).

33 Bailey, *French Secondary Education, 1763–1790;* R. R. Palmer, *The Improvement of Humanity: Education and the French Revolution* (Princeton, 1985), pp. 55–56.

34 Alembert, s.v. "Collèges," in *Encyclopédie, ou Dictionnaire raisonné des sciences, des arts et des métiers,* 35 vols. (Paris, 1751–80), 3:635; Mercier, *Tableau de Paris,* 1:103–6.

35 Mirabeau quoted in Howard Clive Barnard, *Education in the French Revolution* (Cambridge, 1969), p. 67.

36 E. Allain, "L'Enquête scolaire de 1791–1792," *Revue des questions historiques,* n.s., 6 (1891): 143–203; D. Julia, *Les Trois Couleurs du tableau noir: La Révolution* (Paris, 1981), p. 172.

37 Allain, pp. 165, 149; J. Rives, *Dîme et société . . .* (Paris, 1976).

38 Ibid., pp. 175–83.

39 R. R. Palmer, *The School of the French Revolution: A Documentary History of the Collège of Louis-le-Grand and Its Director Jean-François Champagne, 1762–1814* (Princeton, 1975), pp. 88, 101, 104, 108–14.

40 *PVCIPCN,* 1:333; Palmer, *School,* p. 129.

41 Palmer, *School,* p. 127; Archives de la Préfecture de Police, AA, *200,* 552–55, 566–67, 570–71, 574–76, 583–84.

42 *PVCIPCN,* 1:568.

43 See the origins of the debate at the time of the Ferry laws in Albert Duruy, *L'Instruction publique et la Révolution* (Paris, 1882), which is favorable to the educational work of the Revolution, and Ernest Allain, *L'Oeuvre scolaire de la Révolution, 1789–1802* (Paris, 1882), which is not.

44 For a more complete analysis of this plan see chap. 11, below; *PVCIPCN,* 3:56–62.

45 Palmer, *Improvement,* p. 251; the survey is published in *PVCIPCN,* 6:899–910. Figures in the text are my tabulation of the survey.

46 The Daunou proposal is printed in Célestin Hippeau, *L'Instruction publique en France pendant la Révolution* (Paris, 1881), pp. 470–86.

47 E. Kennedy and M. L. Netter, "Les Ecoles primaires pendant le Directoire," *Annales historiques de la Révolution française* 243 (1981): 3–38.

48 Félix Rocquain, ed., *L'Etat de la France au dix-huit Brumaire* (Paris, 1874), pp. 194–95.

49 Fourcroy gives the reason for this decline in school attendance: "Besides the bad conduct, the immorality and drunkenness of many of these [teachers], it seems certain that the lack of instruction on religion is the principal motive which prevents parents from sending their children to these schools: they prefer to send them to private teachers whom they like to pay better, because they hope to find a better instruction, purer morals and the principles of religion to which one gives great importance in the department of the Manche" (in Rocquain, p. 194).

50 On the central schools, see R. R. Palmer, "The Central Schools of the First French Republic: A Statistical Survey," in *The Making of Frenchmen: Current Directions in the History of Education in France, 1679–1979, Historical Reflections* 7, nos. 2, 3 (1980): 223–47, and *Improvement,* pp. 242–57. M. M. Compere, "Les Professeurs de la République: Rupture et continuité dans le personnel enseignant des écoles centrales," *Annales historiques de la Révolution française* 243 (1981): 43; Palmer, *Improvement,* pp. 242–57 passim; Dominique Julia et al., *Atlas de la Révolution française,* vol. 2: *L'Enseignement* (Paris, 1987), pp. 40–45; Wilhelm Frijhoff and Dominique Julia, *Ecole et société dans la France d'ancien Régime: Quatre Exemples; Auch, Avallon, Condom et Gisors* (Paris, 1975), pp. 14ff.; D. Julia and P. Pressly, "La Population scolaire en 1789: Les Extravagances statistiques du ministre Villemain," *Annales ESC* 30 (1981): 3–38.

51 Julia, *Atlas,* pp. 40ff.; Palmer, *Improvement,* pp. 242–57 passim; Harvey Chisick, "Institutional Innovation in Popular Education in Eighteenth-Century France: Two Examples," *French Historical Studies* 10 (1977): 51–52.

52 Palmer, *Improvement;* Albert Troux, *L'Ecole centrale à Besançon, an IV–an XI* (Paris, 1926), chap. 6.

53 Palmer, *Improvement,* p. 249; Troux, chap. 6.

54 Stendhal, *Vie de Henry Brulard,* in *Oeuvres intimes,* ed. Henri Martineau (Paris, 1955), chap. 23.

55 Marcel Guy, "Trois siècles d'histoire d'un enseignement secondaire de province: Le Collège, l'école centrale, le lycée d'Albi, 1613–1950" (MS, Toulouse, [c. 1965]), p. 79.

56 Palmer, *Improvement,* pp. 244, 242–56 passim; Julia, *Atlas,* chap. 3; Troux, pp. 100–101.

57 Troux, pp. 194–200; Palmer, *Improvement,* p. 256.

58 Stendhal, chap. 23; Troux, pp. 191–92; Palmer, *Improvement,* pp. 243, 255–56; Kennedy, *A Philosophe,* pp. 84–97.

59 Julia and Pressly, "Population scolaire"; Destutt de Tracy, Observations sur le système actuel de l'Instruction publique (Paris, an IX [1800–1801]), pp. 2, 5, 62–63.

VII. THE MEN AND THE INSTITUTIONS (2): THEATERS, ACADEMIES, AND SCIENTIFIC COMMITTEES

1 For a full discussion of the end of old regime theatrical privilege and popular entertainment, see Root-Bernstein, *Boulevard Theater,* chaps. 1, 2.

2 Mercier, *Tableau de Paris,* 3:123, 133.

3 Robert Isherwood, "Entertainment in the Parisian Fairs in the Eighteenth Century," *Journal of Modern History* 53 (1981): 30–32; Maurice Descotes, *Le Public de théâtre et son histoire* (Paris, 1964), chap. 7; Root-Bernstein, p. 15, plate 2. The least expensive seating was in the pit.

4 For the text of the Chapelier report and law, see *A.P.* 13 January 1791, 22:210–14.

5 Ibid., 212.

6 Joseph-Nicolet Guyot, *Grand vocabulaire français,* vol. 23 (1772), p. 313, quoted in Root-Bernstein, p. 17.

7 Olympe de Gouges, *Adresse aux représentants de la Nation,* and *Mémoire pour Madame Gouges contre la Comédie française* (n.p., n.d.); Jean-François Cailhava, *Mémoire . . . en réponse à des défenses faites par les comédiens françois aux directeurs du Théâtre du Palais Royal, de jouer ses pièces* (Paris [1790–91]), p. 2.

8 *Observations pour les comédiens français sur la pétition adressée par les auteurs dramatiques à l'Assemblée nationale* (Paris, 1790), pp. 20–21.

9 Caron de Beaumarchais, *Réponse de l'agent général des auteurs dramatiques à son correspondant de la ville de S. . . .* (Paris, n.d.), p. 6.

10 *Pétition des auteurs dramatiques qui n'ont pas signé celle de M. de la Harpe* (Paris, 1790), cited in Jacques Herissay, *Le Monde des théâtres pendant la Révolution, 1789–1800* (Paris, 1922), pp. 48–53.

11 The *Journal de Paris* (1791–93), *Moniteur* (1789–94), and *Petites Affiches* (1789–99) printed theater listings and of course names and addresses of theaters regularly.

12 Claude Alasseur, *La Comédie-Française au dix-huitième siècle, étude économique* (Paris, 1967), table 12; A. Pougin, *L'Opéra comique pendant la Révolution de 1788 à 1801 d'après des documents inédits . . .* (Paris, 1891), pp. 26, 37–40, 52, 69, 93, 124; Albert de la Salle, *Les Treize Salles de l'Opéra* (Paris, 1875), pp. 144–48; Le Roux, *Rapport sur l'Opéra présenté au corps municipal le 17 août 1791* (Paris, 1791), p. 22; budget of Théâtre de l'égalité, in A.N. AD[viii] 44[3]; Root-Bernstein, app., fig. 3.

13 A. Pougin, *Un Directeur d'Opéra au dix-huitième siècle, L'Opéra sous l'ancien régime, l'Opéra sous la Révolution* (Paris, 1914), p. 111.

14 See Sigismond Lacroix, ed., *Actes de la Commune de Paris pendant la Révolution,* 16 vols. (Paris, 1894–1916), 1:284–85, 2:286–87, 7:200–225, for the *Charles IX* affair, as well as A. Pougin, *La Comédie-Française et la Révolution* (Paris, n.d. [1902]), which reprints numerous documents relating to the controversies of the Comédie-Française. On 18th-century scholarship on the Saint Bartholomew's Day Massacre, see Herbert Butterfield, *Man on His Past* (Cambridge, 1955; reprint 1979), pp. 172–73n.

15 Quoted in Pougin, *La Comédie-Française,* p. 103.

16 L. Henry Le Comte, *La Montansier: Ses aventures, ses entreprises, 1730–1820* (Paris, n.d.), p. 142. For performances, see the Kennedy-Netter Theater Project.

17 Le Comte, pp. 144, 147, 210–11.

18 Cited in Daniel and Guy Wildenstein, *Louis David: Recueil de documents complémentaires au catalogue complet* (Paris, n.d.), nos. 515, 581; *Journal des spectacles,* 29 September 1793, p. 710.

19 Hérissay, pp. 255–74, 47–53, 108–13, 184–95, 197–274.

20 See the police reports on the Théâtre Feydeau, B.N. MS Fr. 7005.

21 See police reports on theaters during the Directory in A. Schmidt, *Tableaux de la Révolution française publiés sur les papiers inédits du département et de la police secrète de Paris,* 3 vols. (Leipzig, 1867–70); on Robespierre, see A.P., 22:216.

22 M.-J. Chénier, *Motion d'ordre sur les théâtres* (Paris, 8 frimaire an VI [28 November 1797]) in A.N. AD[viii] 45[2], p. 21; Hérissay, pp. 367–69.

23 Mauduit Larive, *Réflexions sur la décadence du théâtre* (n.p., n.d.), in A.N. AD[viii] 45[2].

24 Porthiez [de l'Oise], *Opinion sur les théâtres, 2 germinal an 6* [22 March 1798] (n.p., n.d.), p. 6, in A.N. AD[viii] 45[2]; Amaury Duval, *Observations sur les théâtres* (n.p., n.d.), p. 2.

25 Marc Regaldo, *Un Milieu intellectuel: La Décade philosophique, 1794–1807,* 5 vols. (Paris, 1976), 3:1358–70; *Règlement pour les théâtres, 8 juin 1806,* in A.N. AD [viii] 44 [3]. For the provincial theater, which underwent much of the same turbulence as Parisian theater, see the excellent treatment by Henri Lagrave et al., *La Vie théâtrale à Bordeaux des origines à nos jours* (Paris, 1985), vol. 1 (chapter by Marc Regaldo, "La Période révolutionnaire").

26 Roche, *Le Siècle des lumières,* 2:437, 387; 1:211, 233, 287; Martin S. Staum, "The Class of Moral and Political Sciences, 1795–1803," *French Historical Studies* 11 (1980): 374.

27 Gillispie, *Science and Polity in France,* pp. 290–329; Marat to Roume de Saint-Laurent, 20 November 1783, in *Correspondance de Marat,* ed. Charles Vellay (Paris, 1908), p. 36.

28 Robert Darnton, *Mesmerism and the End of the Enlightenment in France* (New York, 1970; orig. publ. 1968), pp. 6–7, chap. 1 passim.

29 Ibid., pp. 62–74, 97.

30 Mercier, *Tableau de Paris* 2:120–25.

31 Darline G. Levy, *The Ideas and Careers of Simon-Nicolas-Henri Linguet: A Study in Eighteenth-Century French Politics* (Urbana, Ill., 1980), pp. 173–74. According to Elizabeth Eisenstein, Babeuf also unsuccessfully sought entrance to the academy.

32 Hahn, *Anatomy of a Scientific Institution,* chap. 4.

33 *PVCIPCN,* 2:250–55; 1:87–91; 2:258.

34 Anita Brookner, *Jacques-Louis David* (New York, 1980), p. 87; Quatremère de Quincy, cf. *A.P.,* 34:280–84; J.-L. Jules David, *Le Peintre Louis David, 1747–1825: Souvenirs et documents* (Paris, 1880), pp. 93, 103; David Lloyd Dowd, *Pageant Master of the Republic: Jacques-Louis David and the French Revolution* (New York, 1969; orig. publ. 1948); Wildenstein, no. 395.

35 *Procès-verbaux de l'Académie de Peinture et Sculpture, 1648–1793,* ed. Anatole de Montaiglon, 10 vols. (Paris, 1875–92), 10:25–26, 31–35, 39; Dowd, p. 32; David, pp. 66–82; and for quotation, Henry Lapauze, ed., *Procès-verbaux de la Commune Générale des Arts . . .* (Paris, 1903), p. 2.

36 Lapauze, 26 nivôse an II [17 January 1794], p. 202.

37 On the Academy of Sciences and its competitors and successors, see Hahn, chaps. 6, 7.

38 *PVCIPCN,* 3:56.

39 Ibid., 3:236–42, lxxxiii. One response to the abolition of the academies was the proposal on 15 November 1793 for a "Point Central des Sciences, Arts et Métiers," which would consist of a network of scientists and artisans eligible for membership simply on the basis of some scientific or artisanal work and which would be organized in local primary assemblies. Parisian centralization was to be guaranteed by nomination of members from a "general directory of arts," itself drawn from the Paris local assembly (*A.P.,* 79:262–63).

40 Joseph Fayet, *La Révolution française et la science, 1789–1795* (Paris, 1960), chap. 4; Hahn, chap. 11; Palmer, *Improvement,* pp. 197–220 passim on scientists and education.

VIII. VANDALISM AND CONSERVATION

1 Biographical information on the members of the commission is taken from Michaud, *Dictionnaire de biographie universelle,* and Amat et al., *Dictionnaire de biographie française.* For an account of Alexandre Lenior's Musée des monumens, see Christopher M. Greene, "Alexandre Lenoir and the Musée des Monumens Français during the French Revolution," *French Historical Studies* 12 (1981): 200–222. On vandalism, see Gabriele Sprigath, "Sur le vandalisme révolutionnaire," *Annales historiques de la Révolution française* 52 (1980): 510–35, and Bronislaw Baczko, "Le Complot Vandale," *Le Temps de la réflexion* 4 (1983): 195–242. I am grateful for suggestions made by the Washington Group of Old Regime French Historians and to Dr. Daniel Sherman for suggestions for revising this chapter. For the Commission on Monuments's final *compte-rendu,* see n. 22, below.

2 "Instructions concernant les chasses, reliquaires et autres pièces d'orfèvrerie provenant du mobilier des maisons écclésiastiques et destinés à la fonte," Papers of the Commission des monumens (on which the account below is largely based), A.N. F^{17}.

3 Stanley Mellon, "Alexandre Lenoir: The Museum versus the Revolution," *The Consortium on Revolutionary Europe: Proceedings* (Athens, Ga., 1979), p. 80.

4 *PVCIPCN,* 4:1002, 5:166–67. Romme uses the term *vandals* in denouncing spoliation. Grégoire elaborated: "By an exaggeration supposedly republican or by a movement more worthy of vandals than of Frenchmen, under the pretext of pursuing *fleurs de lys,* the monograms of kings, the coats of arms, medals, and all which can remind us of overthrown tyrants, have been taken from citizens and broken, precious engravings have been seized from print merchants. The engraving of the execution of Charles I was torn up because it bore an escutcheon. The engraving of liberty conquered by William Tell met the same fate. Our libraries, our collections, our art repositories are threatened" (J. Guillaume, "Grégoire et le vandalisme," *La Révolution française* 41 [1901]: 159). On 9 October 1793, Chénier had referred to "Vandals and Visogoths who may take the place of your silence" ("suppléant à votre silence"), ibid., p. 158. Grégoire made three reports on *vandalism* (a word he coined) after Thermidor: (1) 14 fructidor an II (31 August 1794) in ibid., pp. 176–80, 242–68; (2) 8 brumaire an III (29 October 1794) in *PVCIPCN,* 5:166–67 (extracts); and (3) 24 frimaire an III (15 December 1794) in *PVCIPCN,* 5:294–97 (extracts), *PVCIPCN,* 2:658.

5 "Instruction sur la manière d'inventorier et de conserver dans toute l'étendu de la République tous les objets qui peuvent servir aux sciences et à l'enseignement proposé par la Commission temporaire des arts et adopté par le Comité d'instruction publique de la Convention nationale," in A.N. F^{17A} 1045^2, pp. 67–68, also excerpted in *PVCIPCN,* 3:549.

6 A.N. F^{17} 1035, liasse G. "Troisième Rapport sur le vandalisme" (24 frimaire an III [14 December 1794]), *PVCIPCN,* 5:295; Baczko.

7 A.N. F^{17} 1036^A; *Procès-verbaux de la Commission temporaire des arts,* ed. Louis Tuetey, 2 vols. (Paris, 1912, 1917), 23 July 1794; Pulhod and Moreau to Leblond, secretary of Commission of Monuments, 1 September 1793, A.N. F^{17} 1036^b, liasse U; F^{17} 1039^A, ds. 1.

8 A.N. F^{17} 1036^b; F^{17} 1039^a, 1039^A ds. 1.

9 *PVCIPCN,* 1:89; A.N. F^{17} 1036^b, liasse Z, liasse U, no. 2.

10 A.N. F^{17} 1036^A, pièce 16.

11 Secretary of Commission of Monuments to Minister of Interior, 16 November 1792, in A.N. F^{17} 1039^A, ds. 16; F^{17} 1036^A.

12 A.N. F^{17} 1039, ds. 16.

13 Article on excavations in *New York Times,* 4 May 1977, p. A2; Alain Erlande-Brandenburg, "Les Sculptures de Notre-Dame de Paris récemment découvertes," *Le Petit Journal des grandes expositions,* n.s., 46 (1977); M. Fleury, "Histoire d'un crime," in *Les Rois retrouvés* (Paris, 1977), pp. 15–20; L.-S. Mercier, "Figures de portrait de Notre-Dame," in *Paris pendant la Révolution (1789–1798), ou Le Nouveau Paris,* new ed. (Paris, 1862). I am grateful to Vivian Chakarian for this translation and for research assistance on this chapter and chaps. 6 and 7.

14 *Révolutions de Paris,* 182, 29 Dec. 1792–5 Jan. 1793, p. 83; cf. Jacques Saint-Germain, *La Seconde Mort des rois de France* (Paris, 1972), pp. 162–63.

15 *A.P.* 1 August 1793, 70:103.

16 Saint-Germain, p. 170; A.N. F^{17} 1035^A; F^{17} 1036^A, pièce 91; F^{17} 1036^A, pièce 112.

17 A.N. F^{17} 1035^A, 10 September 1793; *PVCIPCN,* 2:610–11; A.N. F^{17} 5.

18 Saint-Germain, pp. 182–89. Quotations are from documents published in Jean F. E. Robinet, *Le Mouvement religieux à Paris pendant la Révolution,* 2 vols. (Paris, 1898), 2:498, 482, 484.

19 Alexandre Lenoir, "Notes historiques sur les exhumations faites en 1793 dans l'abbaye de Saint Denis," in *Description historique et chronologique des monumens de sculpture,* 6th ed. (Paris, an X [1802]), p. 345. On Henry IV, see ibid., pp. 340–42, and Saint-Germain, p. 219.

20 A.N. F^{17} 1036^A. Madame de Maintenon was exhumed from her grave at Saint-Cyr. I am grateful to Elborg Forster for this information.

21 Lenoir, "Notes historiques sur les exhumations."

22 *Procès-verbaux de la Commission temporaire des arts,* 1:57; *PVCIPCN,* 3:171–82.

23 A.N. F^{17} 1039, ds. 11; F^{17} 1036^b, liasse T, no. 77, for Marly. For the com-

mittee's self-defense, see its *Compte rendu à la Convention nationale par la Commission supprimée des monumens, et servant de réponse au rapport du Comité d'instruction publique* (Paris, an II [1794]).

24 A.N. F^{17} 1039^b, ds. 11; F^{17} 1035^A, ds. 4; F^{17} 1039^a, ds. 11.

25 Quoted in Pierre Riberette, *Les Bibliothèques françaises pendant la Révolution, 1789–1795* (Paris, 1970), p. 19.

26 *PVCIPCN,* 4:121–23.

27 Ibid., 2:798.

28 Ibid, p. 799.

29 Ibid., 4:127.

30 Ibid., 2:799.

31 A.N. F^{17} 1035, ds. 5, no. 56.

32 *PVCIPCN,* 4:126; Riberette, p. 117; F. V. Mulot, *Mémoire sur l'état actuel de nos bibliothèques, lu au Lycée des arts dans sa 50ème séance, le 30 nivôse an 5ème* [19 January 1797], p. 39; *L'Art de l'estampe et la Révolution française, Musée Carnavalet, 27 juin–20 novembre 1977,* intro. Pascal de la Vaissière (Alençon, 1977), p. 4.

33 A.N. F^{17} 1039^A, ds. 11; on book burning, R. Cobb, *Les Armées révolutionnaires: Instrument de la Terreur dans les départements,* 2 vols. (Paris, 1961, 1963), 2:662.

34 Riberette, p. 101.

35 Ibid., p. 105.

36 Benjamin Bois, *La Vie scolaire et les créations intellectuelles en Anjou pendant la Révolution, 1789–1799* (n.p., n.d. [1928–29]), p. 160. The "Observations d'un citoyen de Lille, relatives à la Conservation des livres, tableaux, estampes manuscrits, statues et choses précieuses en tout genre qui existent dans tous les Départements du Royaume et notamment dans celui du Nord" [Year II] by B. Brovellios [*sp.?*], municipal officer of Lille, department of the North (n.d., in A.N. F^{17} 1036), in chap. 5 makes several things clear: (1) That the means to ward off ignorance could be found in the former religious houses, for example, in the *chapitre* of Saint-Pierre in Lille; (2) That these resources should be pooled and located in one former religious house or national property of Lille, where instruction could be given; (3) That a librarian's staff should be created at municipal expense; (4) That this would allow one to recoup the losses of the Revolution, for the libraries of the religious houses were "open formerly to the public" and these houses numbered five to six thousand throughout France. One library should be built in every capital of each of the 530 or 540 districts of France (clearly a modest aim compared to the monastic library infrastructure of the old regime or to the ten public libraries in Lille before 1789). Schools should be established in the same places; and (5) It is essential to unite the instruments of instructions in one place, but in the smaller towns one could furnish libraries with the same books that can be found "ten times over" in the houses of the religious. This document and the above

analysis of the Bibliothèque d'Angers demonstrate that the principal sources for the holdings of the new municipal libraries were the libraries of the former religious houses. As my former student Cristel MacDonald showed in an excellent seminar paper ("The French Revolution and Its Central Libraries"), the republican authorities, such as Benezech, stressed the importance of *selection* from these monastic holdings. A simple transfer of the *fonds* of one into the collection of the other was unthinkable. A censorship like Doumergue's "index of reason" had to republicanize and secularize these libraries. As Angers proves, this was not always (perhaps not "usually") done. The card catalogs of municipal libraries are the proof.

37 Paul Priebe, "From Bibliothèque du Roi to Bibliothèque Nationale: The Creation of a State Library, 1789–1793," *Harvard Library Bulletin* 17 (1982): 405.

38 M. Edgar Boutaric, "Le Vandalisme révolutionnaire: Les Archives pendant la Révolution française," *Revue des questions historiques* 12 (1872): 348.

39 Ibid., pp. 351–52.

40 Ibid., p. 373.

41 Ibid., pp. 325–96 passim.

42 André Blum, *Le Louvre* (Paris, 1946), pp. 140, 104–40, chaps. 6, 7. The Luxembourg housed some paintings in the eighteenth century and the palace was open to the public three hours a day, two days a week, before the Revolution (Cecil Gould, *Trophy of Conquest: The Musée Napoléon and the Creation of the Louvre* [London, 1965], pp. 19–20).

43 Blum, p. 147; *A.P.*, 26 May 1791, 26:472; *La Commission du Muséum et la création du Musée du Louvre (1792–1793): Documents recueillis et annotés par Alexandre Tuetey et Jean Guiffrey*, in *Archives de l'art français*, n.s., 3 (1909): 1–2; Blum, pp. 151–52.

44 *Commission du Muséum*, pp. 6–28, 53, 102–4, 122, 128, 213, 222–25; A.N. F^{17} 1036^A, pièce 115, liasse 2, pièces 59, 76. The duc d'Orléans's Toulouse residence yielded two Veroneses, one Cortona, and one Poussin. From the collection of the duc de Penthièvre, a Bourbon, came Veronese's *Antony and Cleopatra*, Guercino's *Combat of the Romans and the Sabines*, and Pietro Cortona's *Romulus and Remus*—none of which can be found in the December 1793 catalog of the collection of the Louvre. Madame du Barry's château of Louveciennes was visited on 19 December 1793 and surrendered some Vernets, Vien's *The Merchant of Love* and *The Flight of Love*, and Fragonard's *The Night*. Paintings taken from the émigré Vasse were Titian's *The Virgin and Saint Catherine*, Fragonard's *A Landscape on Wood*, and Hubert Robert's *Ruins of Italy* (drawings). But Angivillers had the most remarkable paintings: Tintoretto's *Jesus in the Tomb with Angels*, Guercino's *Marriage of Saint Catherine*, and Rembrandt's *Pilgrims of Emmaus* and *Old Man and a Young Man*, together with about nine paintings from the French School—Lagrénées, Hubert Roberts, a Vien, and Le Nains among them.

From the Italian School came thirty-four paintings, from the Flemish and Dutch schools sixteen paintings, and from the French School thirty-five paintings, six sculptures, and nine engravings.

45 L. Courajod, *Alexandre Lenoir, son journal, et le Musée des Monuments français,* 3 vols. (Paris, 1886–88), 2:154.

46 *Commission du Muséum,* p. 125; for the November inventory of the museum see ibid., doc. no. 216.

47 Quoted in Charles Saunier, *Les Conquêtes artistiques de la Révolution et de l'Empire* (Paris, 1902), p. 22; *Commission du Muséum,* pp. 298–99.

48 *Le Conservatoire du Muséum national des arts au Comité d'instruction publique, le 7 pluviôse de la 3ᵉ année républicaine* (n.d., n.p.), in British Library, Pamphlets on the French Revolution, nos. 1527–29, p. 6. On David, see n. 50, below.

49 *Commission du Muséum,* nos. 49, 50; Gould, pp. 25, 20.

50 Lebrun's pamphlet is in "Pamphlets on the French Revolution," no. 529; David's first report on the museum is in *Commission du Muséum,* no. 206, quotation on p. 356.

51 David, "Second Rapport sur la nécessité de la suppression de la Commission du Muséum . . . 27 nivôse an II [16 January 1794]," in *Commission du Muséum,* p. 368.

52 Saunier, p. 26; Gould, chap. 2.

53 Gould, pp. 4, 46, chaps. 2–4 passim; Saunier, p. 26. See also Paul Wescher, *Kunstraube unter Napoleon* (Berlin, 1976).

54 Jules David quoted in Biver, *Fêtes révolutionnaires,* p. 127.

55 *Le Conservatoire du Muséum national des arts au Comité d'instruction publique,* p. 6.

56 Alexandre Lenoir, *Déscription historique et chronologique des monuments de sculpture réunis au Musée des monuments français,* 5th ed. (Paris, an VIII [1799]), app.

57 Louis-Pierre Deseine, *Opinion sur les musées, où se trouvent retenus tous les objets d'arts, qui sont les propriétés des temples consacrés à la religion catholique* (Paris, an XI [1802–3]), p. 5.

58 Ibid., p. 41.

IX. THE FINE ARTS AND THE REVOLUTIONARY IMAGINATION: MUSIC, ART, AND DRAMA

1 James A. Leith, *Media and Revolution: Eight Talks for CBC Radio* (Toronto, 1968), and *The Idea of Art as Propaganda in France, 1730–1799* (Toronto, 1965); Conrad Donakowski, *A Muse for the Masses: Ritual and Music in an Age of Democratic Revolution* (Chicago, 1977), esp. p. 34.

2 Constant Pierre, *Les Hymnes et les chansons de la Révolution* (Paris, 1904), p. 49; this source was used to compile table A.1. Cf. James Leith, "Music as

an Ideological Weapon in the French Revolution," *Canadian Historical Association Annual Report, 1966* (Ottawa, 1967), p. 139.

3 All the chart material on theater is here reproduced from E. Kennedy, "Traitement informatique des repertoires théâtraux pendant la Révolution française," in "Traitements informatiques de textes du 18eme siècle," S.A.M.J. Chouillet, ed., *Textes et documents,* ser. 7 (1984) (INa LF-CNRS-ENS, Saint-Cloud): 43–60. The statistics are the product of a count of theater performances recorded in the *Journal de Paris* and *Moniteur* for the period 1789–94 and the *Affiches annonces et avis divers* for the period 1795–99 done by the research team of E. Kennedy, M. L. Netter, S. Lambrakopoulos, and N. Roberts. The data (86,000 records) is recorded on IBM computer tape, and the charts here are the result of computer sorting.

On Beaunoir, see Robert Isherwood, *Farce and Fantasy: Popular Entertainment in Eighteenth-Century Paris* (New York, 1986), p. 196.

4 Kennedy-Netter Theater Project.

5 Stanley Idzerda, "Art and the French State during the French Revolution" (Ph.D. diss., Western Reserve University, 1951), tables in app.

6 Leith, *Idea of Art,* app., pp. 173ff.

7 Cited in *French Painting, 1774–1830: The Age of Revolution* (Detroit, 1975), p. 110. My own investigation in the Desloynes Collection of the Cabinet des Estampes confirms these conclusions.

8 William Olander, "Pour transmettre à la posterité: French Painting and Revolution, 1774–1795" (Ph.D. diss., New York University, 1983).

9 See chap. 11, below, and Michelet, *Histoire de la Révolution française,* 3: chap. 11.

10 During the Great Fear of July 1789, peasants rose up in many regions of France and ransacked châteaux for hated feudal registers; some châteaux were burned, and aristocrats were maltreated and a few killed. The October Days of 5 and 6 October 1789 witnessed the march on Versailles of the women of Les Halles, Paris, to demand bread of the king and to force the royal family from Versailles and back to the Tuileries.

11 Constant Pierre, *Histoire du concert spirituel, 1725–1790* (Paris, 1975).

12 Biographical information on composers is taken from *The New Grove Dictionary of Music and Musicians,* ed. Stanley Sadie, 20 vols. (New York, 1980).

13 Rogers, *Spirit of Revolution in 1789,* pp. 13–20; Lynn Hunt, *Politics, Culture, and Class in the French Revolution* (Berkeley, 1984), chap. 3, plates 5, 17, pp. 61–64, 118–19.

14 See texts reproduced in Pierre, *Hymnes et chansons,* pp. 185–89. Citations to the Bible are Desaugiers's.

15 See the eyewitness account published in Reinhard, *Nouvelle Histoire de Paris,* pp. 416–18; Pierre, *Hymnes et Chansons,* pp. 197–99.

16 Kennedy-Netter Theater Project.

17 Donakowski, pp. 34–51. Donakowski underscores this use of the sacred and the "mythopoeic" for patriotic purposes—"how to utilize Christian mythopoesis in a new synthesis" (p. 308). Enlisting music could be more easily effected in the Catholic Latin nations, he continues, where a particularly strong musical tradition exists. Rather than simply transferring sacrality, Donakowski sees revolutionary music emerging from sacred music as the ancient Greek chorus emerged from Greek religious ritual. On the Festival of the Federation, see chap. 11, below.

18 See the excellent discussion of the "Ça ira" in J. Tiersot, *Les Fêtes et les chants de la Révolution française* (Paris, 1908), pp. 18–25. I am greatful to Isser Woloch for bringing my attention to the different versions of this song. For an English translation of still another version see James A. Leith, "Music for Mass Persuasion during the Terror," unpublished text to accompany a tape of revolutionary music and a slide show, translation I.

19 Bordes, *Le Serment du jeu de paume*, p. 38. This is a first-rate, definitive study of this unfinished painting.

20 Ibid., chaps. 3–5 passim.

21 Dorvigny, *Janot, les battus paient l'amende* (1779), to which Robineau de Beauvoir responded, *Jeanette, ou les battus ne paient pas l'amende*, 1a c pr (1780), and Sedaine, *Richard Cœur de Lion*, 3a c pr and v mus (1784).

22 Dezède and Mantauffel, mus Louis-François Faur, *Auguste et Théodore, ou les deux pages*, 2a c pr, "melée de chant" (Paris, 1789, 1824), 2.7.

23 Ibid. An engraving of the period, *Un trait de Bienfaisance du Roi*, by Philippe-Louis Débucourt illustrates the same themes as in *Auguste et Théodore*.

24 Beffroy de Reigny, *Nicodème dans la lune, ou La Révolution pacifique*, folie, 3a pr, "melée d'ariettes et de vaudevilles" (Paris, 1791), 1.1.

25 Ibid., 1.2.

26 Ibid., 1.13.

27 Ibid., 3.1.

28 See various natural images of revolution discussed in Paulson, *Representations of Revolution*.

29 Leith, "Music for Mass Persuasion," translation I.

30 Ibid., translation II.

31 Pierre Barbier and France Vernillat, *Histoire de France par les chansons*, 8 vols. (Paris, 1956–61), 4:125, 131.

32 Ibid., pp. 209, 153, 134–40, 234–44.

33 Pascal de la Vaissière, *L'Art de l'estampe et la Révolution française* (Paris, 1977), quoting M. Jacquemin, who "assures us that engravings with a traditional imagery disappeared by the millions" (p. 4) and that F. Meyer, *Fragmente aus Paris* says, "The merchants themselves burned their collections" (p. 6) out of fear of Robespierre. This subject deserves further investigation.

34 Fabre d'Eglantine, *Le Convalescent de qualité*, 2a c v (Paris, 1791), 1.13, 2.5, 2.4.

35 Jean-Baptiste Radet, *Le Noble Roturier*, 1a c, "melée de vaudevilles" (Paris, an II [1794]), 1.4.

36 Louis-Benoît Picard, *Les Visitandines*, 3a c, music by Devienne (Paris, 1792), 1.8, 2.3.

37 Pigault-Lebrun, *Les Dragons et les bénédictines*, 1a c pr (Paris, 1823; orig. publ. an II [1794]); *Les Dragons en cantonnement, ou la suite des bénédictines*, 1a c pr (Paris, 1823; orig. publ. an II [1794]).

38 Maurice Albert, *Les Théâtres des boulevards, 1789–1848* (Paris, 1902), pp. 122, 133, and chaps. 5, 6 passim. It is this fare that merited the term *ordure*, "garbage."

39 Joseph Aude, *Cadet Roussel, ou le Café des aveugles*, 2a (Paris, 1793), 1.2.

40 Sylvain Maréchal, *Le Jugement dernier des rois prophétie en un acte et en prose* (Paris, an II [1793]), sc 3; Kennedy-Netter Theater Project, for number of performances. Daniel Hamiche's estimate of 100,000 spectators throughout France appears to be unfounded as it is unsubstantiated by a count of performances in and outside Paris (*Le Théâtre et la Révolution: La Lutte des classes au théâtre en 1789 et en 1793* [Paris, 1973], p. 176).

41 Billington, *Fire in the Minds of Men*, pp. 59–61; Pierre, *Hymnes et chansons*, pp. 223ff.

42 Leith, "Music for Mass Persuasion," paragraphs 40–41, my translation.

43 See chap. 11. The religions of humanity were a vogue in the romantic 1840s.

44 Roland Barthes, *Le Degrée zéro du l'écriture* (Paris, 1953), p. 34.

45 Lemierre, *Guillaume Tell* (Neufchâtel, 1776), 1.1, 1.2, 2.1, 3.4.

46 In commemorating a legendary champion of Swiss liberty, the revolutionaries of the Committee of Public Safety hoped to kindle a love of liberty in the hearts of republicans. Actually it was in such former privileged theaters as the Théâtre de la nation (Comédie-Française), where Voltaire's *Mort de César* and Lemierre's *Guillaume Tell* were most performed (twenty-two and fourteen times, respectively), that this drama had the greatest impact. But for a few productions in popular theaters, this drama was the *apanage* of the bourgeois notables of the Revolution.

47 Marie-Joseph Chénier, *Charles IX, ou L'Ecole des rois*, 5a tr v (Paris, 1790), 3.2.

48 Hamiche, p. 62. At the première of *Charles IX* Danton is said to have shouted: "Figaro killed the nobility and *Charles IX* will kill royalty."

49 M. Chénier, *Gaius Gracchus* (Paris, 1793), 1.4, 2.2.

50 Bordes; Wildenstein, no. 763.

51 See Frank Paul Bowman, "Le Sacré Cœur de Marat," in *Les Fêtes de la Révolution: Colloque de Clermont-Ferrand (juin 1974)*, ed. Jean Ehrard and Paul Villaneix (Paris, 1977), pp. 155–79. See below, chap. 11; on Lepeletier,

see Wildenstein, nos. 410, 427; Albert Soboul, "Sentiment religieux et cultes populaires pendant la Révolution: Saintes patriotes et martyrs de la liberté," *Annales historiques de la Révolution française* 148 (July–September 1957): 193–213.

52 *PVCIPCN,* 4:280–82; Jules Renouvier, *Histoire de l'art pendant la Révolution considérée principalement dans les estampes* (Paris, 1863), chap. 2.

X. COMMUNICATING

1 *A.P.* 3:599; 1:675–708, 690; cf. 1:718, 526.

Even Régine Robin (*La Société française en 1789: Semur-en-Auxois [Paris, 1970]*, pp. 269, 310–15, 234–67, and conclusion), for whom the 133 cahiers of the baillage of Semur-en-Auxois, Burgundy, were the "ultimate form of popularisation of the philosophy of the enlightenment," states contradictorily that "those who expect to find in the cahiers the distant echo of great philosophical struggles of the century are guilty of a grave misunderstanding." Radical antiseigneurial statements were made in Semur: the new seigneur, in particular, was often seen as the king's opposite, representing rapacity as opposed to the monarch's mercy and justice. Expressions of love and veneration for the king counterbalanced statements of radical dissatisfaction with the old regime. These cahiers called for a rectification of the old regime rather than a revolution. The doléance showed the desire to obtain relief from the addressee rather than the will to take matters into one's own hands. Robin insists that the demands of these cahiers amount to revolution and not reform but qualifies this by stating that this revolutionary will attempted to save rather than destroy the old regime. If so, how could it have been revolutionary?

Two years later, George Taylor ("Revolutionary and Nonrevolutionary Content in the Cahiers of 1789: An Interim Report," *French Historical Studies* 7 [1972]: 484ff., 491–94) systematically analyzed over 700 general baillage and parish cahiers chosen nationwide. Taylor ranked his cahiers according to revolutionary content. The least revolutionary, "nearly apolitical," cahiers mention only local problems and "show no capacity for projecting problems or the solutions on a national scale. . . . [There is no] discernible thought that the social and political structure should or would be changed." In category four, by contrast, he found "new, rational, constitutional principles—those found in the Declaration—foreign to the traditional sanctions of the Old Regime." Taylor concluded that on balance the cahiers are *not* revolutionary. Those on the parish level state grievances without envisaging solutions, and many baillage grievances that do envision change couch their wishes not in Enlightenment language but in that of old regime France.

2 *A.P.*, 3:532, 471, 762; 1:679.

3 Ibid., 3:526, 111.

4 Ibid., 1:686–93.

5 Ibid., 1:680–81.

6 Beik, *French Revolution*, pp. 2–4; William Doyle, *The Origins of the French Revolution* (Oxford, 1980), pp. 43–52, 113–14.

7 Beik, p. 73.

8 Article 6, in ibid., pp. 95–96.

9 Beik, p. 90.

10 Constitution of 1791, chap. 3, sec. 1, arts. 1, 2; chap. 4, sec. 1, art. 3, in Godechot, *Les Constitutions de la France depuis 1789* (Paris, 1970), pp. 50–57.

11 *A.P.*, 41:107–8, 102, 222; Ferdinand Brunot, *Histoire de la langue française*, 13 vols. to date (Paris, 1905–), 9: pt. 2, 778, s.v. *urgence*.

12 Godechot, *Institutions*, pp. 86–87.

13 Quoted in Marc Bouloiseau, *Le Comité de salut public (1793–1795)*, 2d ed. (Paris, 1968), pp. 19, 26.

14 Ibid., p. 39.

15 John Hardman, ed. *French Revolution Documents*, vol. 2: *1792–1795* (London and New York, 1973), pp. 135–37.

16 Ibid., pp. 132, 133.

17 Hans Ulrich Gumbrecht, *Funktionen parlamentärischer Rhetorik in der französischen Revolution* (Munich, 1978). I am grateful to Tamara Schoenbaum for her complete and careful abstract of this book.

18 Ibid., pp. 86–90.

19 Ibid., pp. 101, 107.

20 Ibid., pp. 109–20.

21 *A.P.*, 83:1, 9; 84:240. Four days of the Convention's numerous printed addresses have been chosen: 16, 17, 18 nivôse an II (5, 6, 7 January 1794), and 15 pluviôse an II (3 February 1794).

22 Ibid., 83:1, 24.

23 Ibid., 83:28, 6.

24 Ibid., 84:15 pluviôse, no. 1.

25 Ibid., 83:71, 4, 70, cf. 80, 25.

26 Ibid., 83:2, 6, 28, 73, cf. 78.

27 Marat, *Ami du peuple*, 25 September 1789, p. 131; cf. 30 September 1789, p. 174.

28 Ibid., 11 November 1789, p. 53; *Journal de la République française*, 29 September 1792, p. 4; *Ami du peuple*, 13 November 1789, p. 67; 31 December 1789, p. 5; 3 September 1790, p. 1.

29 *Ami du peuple*, 16 June 1790, p. 5; 30 June 1790, p. 2.

30 Ibid., 16 July 1790, p. 2; cf. 23 June 1790, p. 8; *Journal de la République française*, 1 December 1792, p. 5.

31 *A.P.*, 41:35; my emphasis.

32 Ibid., 41:31; my emphasis.

33 John Black Sirich, *The Revolutionary Committees in the Departments of France* (Cambridge, Mass., and New York, 1971; orig. publ. 1943), pp. 59–68.

34 Pierre Caron, *Paris pendant la Terreur: Rapports des agents secrets du ministre de l'intérieur,* 7 vols. (Paris, 1910–78), 4:239.

35 Godechot, *Institutions,* pp. 49, 260, 261, 263, 274, 422, 431, 529–32, 710, 715.

36 Holmes, *Benjamin Constant,* pp. 121–22.

37 Godechot, *Institutions,* pp. 49, 260, 261, 263, 274, 422, 529–32, 710, 715.

38 Albert Soboul and Gundala Gobel, "Audience et pragmatisme du Rousseauisme: Les Almanachs de la Révolution, 1788–1795," *Annales historiques de la Révolution française* 234 (1978): 610, 635; Jack Richard Censer, *Prelude to Power: The Parisian Radical Press, 1789–1791* (Baltimore, 1976), p. 9, table 1.1. Much of the following section is based on Jacques Godechot's contribution on the revolutionary press in Claude Bellanger et al., *Histoire générale de la presse française,* 5 vols. (Paris, 1969–76), 1:pt. 3, p. 405, chart on p. 436. For the old regime background, see Botein, Censer, and Ritvo, "Periodical Press in Eighteenth-Century English and French Society," pp. 463–90. The figures for the provincial press stand corrected by Sgard; see n. 40, below.

39 Frédéric Barbier, *Trois cent ans de librairie et d'imprimerie: Berger-Levrault, 1676–1830* (Geneva, 1979), pp. 190–203, 253–362, 510–32. For an excellent account of the revolutionary crisis in publishing and the multiplication of Parisian printers-publishers in the 1790s, see Carla A. Hesse, "Economic Upheavals in Publishing" (in press).

40 Louis Trenard, in Bellanger, vol. 1, pt. 2; Jean Sgard breaks down the provincial press into "périodiques," of which there were forty, and "affiches" (modeled on the *Petites Affiches* of Paris, doubtless), of which there were sixty-five (*La Presse provinciale au XIIIe siecle* [Grenoble, 1983], p. 4). Compare Jack Censer's paper "Die Presse des Ancien Regime im Übergang: Eine Skizze," in *Arbeitstagung Bielefeld,* pp. 127–52.

41 Godechot, in *Histoire générale,* 1:424–29, 451–61; Censer, *Prelude to Power.*

42 Godechot, in *Histoire générale,* 1:476, 463–64, chap. 4 passim.

43 Hahn, *Anatomy of a Scientific Institution,* pp. 272–73; cf. Godechot, in *Histoire générale,* 1:492–99.

44 Alexandre Tuetey, *Répertoire général des sources manuscrites de l'histoire de Paris pendant la Révolution française,* 11 vols. (Paris, 1880–1914), 4:401–2, 8:no. 2189; J. Popkin, "The French Revolutionary Press . . . New Perspectives," *Eighteenth-Century Life* 5 (1979), and "The Royalist Press in the Reign of Terror," *Journal of Modern History* 51 (1979): 685–700.

45 Godechot, in *Histoire générale,* 1:508–9.

46 A.N. F⁷ 3450.

47 A.N. AFⁱⁱⁱ 45.

48 Godechot, in *Histoire générale,* 1:435; Melvin Edelstein, *La Feuille Villa-*

geoise: Communication et modernisation dans les régions rurales pendant la Révolution (Paris, 1977), p. 63.

49 Popkin, "French Revolutionary Press," pp. 96, 103 n. 23, 104 n. 26; A.N. AF^{iii} 45, for the *Ami des lois;* Tuetey, 1:60; Godechot, in *Histoire générale,* 1:438–39.

50 Edelstein, pp. 27, 68–69, 81.

51 A.N. F^{18} 12; Godechot gives the title of this journal as *Journal des campagnes et des armées* (in *Histoire générale,* 1:535). It would seem to merit study.

52 On the press under Napoléon, see André Cabanis, *La Presse sous le Consulat et l'Empire* (Paris, 1975). Hugh Gough's *Newspaper Press in the French Revolution* (Chicago, 1988), reached the author too late to be consulted.

53 Grégoire, "Rapport sur la nécéssité et les moyens d'anéantir les patois et d'universaliser l'usage de la langue française," 16 prairial an II [4 June 1794], in Michel de Certeau, Dominique Julia, and Jacques Revel, *Une Politique de la langue: La Révolution française et les patois* (Paris, 1975), p. 301, and B. Barère, "Rapport du Comité de salut public sur les idiomes," in ibid., p. 295. On the subject of the Revolution and patois, see Patrice L.-R. Higonnet, "The Politics of Linguistic Terrorism and Grammatical Hegemony during the French Revolution," *Social History* 5 (1980): 41–69, and Martyn Lyons, "Politics and Patois: The Linguistic Policy of the French Revolution," *Australian Journal of French Studies* 18 (1981): 264–81.

54 Certeau, Julia, and Revel, pp. 58, 68–71, 186, 14, 189, 276, 278, 283.

XI. EDUCATING

1 Mirabeau quoted in Erhard and Villaneix, *Fêtes de la Révolution,* p. 191; Brunot, *Histoire de la langue française,* 9: pt. 2, 628; A. Aulard, *Le Culte de la raison et le culte de l'être suprême, 1793–1794: Essai historique* (Darmstadt, 1975; orig. publ. 1892); Aulard, *Christianity and the French Revolution,* trans. Lady Frazer (London, 1966; orig. publ. 1927); A. Mathiez, *Les Origines des cultes révolutionnaires, 1789–1792* (Paris, 1902). Mathiez, I feel, was basically correct about the indigenous nature of revolutionary religiosity.

2 Rousseau, *Social Contract,* ed. Lester G. Crocker (New York, 1967), bk. 4, chap. 8, pp. 140, 142; William R. Everdell, "The Rosières Movement, 1766–1789: A Clerical Precursor of the Revolutionary Cults," *French Historical Studies* 9 (1975): 23–36.

3 Harold T. Parker, *The Cult of Antiquity in the French Revolution* (New York, 1965; orig. publ. 1937), pp. 131–38, 140, 145, 161–62.

4 Michelet, *Histoire de la Révolution français,* 1:328; English trans. Charles Cocks (Chicago, 1967), p. 351.

5 Marie-Louise Biver, *Fêtes révolutionnaires à Paris* [a collection of documents] (Paris, 1979), pp. 18–20, chapter entitled "1790," passim.

6 Ibid.

7 Ibid., pp. 35–44; Dowd, *Pageant Master of the Republic,* pp. 44–51.

8 Marie-Louise Biver, *Le Panthéon à l'époque révolutionnaire* [a collection of documents] (Paris, 1982), pp. 18–20, 124, 101–2, 112.

9 Biver, *Fêtes,* pp. 57–61.

10 Ibid., pp. 61–62.

11 Frank Paul Bowman, "Le Sacré Cœur de Marat," in Erhard and Villaneix, *Fêtes de la Révolution,* pp. 155–79. Bowman argues against any real appropriation of the cult of the sacred heart of Jesus in the cult of Marat. A. Gazier, "Grégoire et l'Eglise de France, 1792–1802," *Revue historique* 15 (1881): 72n.; Albert Soboul, "Sentiment religieux et cultes populaires pendant la Révolution: Saints, patriotes et martyrs de la liberté," *Annales historiques de la Révolution française* 148 (July–September 1957): 193–213.

12 Biver, *Fêtes,* pp. 68–77; Hunt, *Politics, Culture, and Class,* pp. 96–98.

13 Brookner, *David,* p. 107; *PVCIPCN,* 2:290–91. The medal of David differs from the engraving reproduced in Hunt, p. 97, in that the latter has Hercules crushing the hydra of federalism (Hunt, p. 99). On the débris of royalty see chap. 9, above.

14 Hardman, *French Revolution Documents,* pp. 152–53; Mlle Rebouillat, "Les Abdicataires du Département de l'Allier," in *Les Prêtres abdicataires pendant la Révolution française,* ed. Marcel Reinhard, in *Actes du Quatre Vingt-Neuvième Congrès national des Sociétés savantes (Lyon, 1964),* Section d'Histoire moderne et contemporaine I (Paris, 1964), pp. 141–82; Michel Vovelle, *Religion et Révolution: La Déchristianisation de l'an II* (Paris, 1976), pp. 19, 71. Donald Greer, *The Incidence of the Terror during the French Revolution: A Statistical Interpretation* (Cambridge, Mass., 1935), p. 165, and *The Incidence of the Emigration during the French Revolution* (Cambridge, Mass., 1951), table 8, p. 132. Maurice Dommanget, "Le Symbolisme et le prosélytisme révolutionnaire à Beauvais et dans l'Oise," *Annales historiques de la Révolution française* 5 (1928): 442–56. A more recent survey of the question, Jean de Viguerie's *Christianisme et Révolution: Cinq Leçons d'histoire de la Révolution française* (Paris, 1986), pp. 160–62, estimates that two-thirds of the constitutional clergy abdicated (the same figure of twenty thousand, however). The original figure of twenty thousand is Pierre de la Gorce's based on his survey of 148 of France's 562 districts. Viguerie puts the figure for emigration of the clergy at 40,000 (pp. 132–33).

15 Fabio Sampoli, "A Popular Traditional Punishment in a Revolutionary Context: The Promenade des Anes in Arles," *Proceedings of Eighth Annual Meeting of the Western Society for French History* 8 (1980): 205–19; Vovelle, *Religion,* pp. 195, 127–28.

16 A.N. F^{19} 893.

17 Cobb, *Armées révolutionnaires,* 2:664–65, chap. 6 passim; Vovelle, *Religion,* pp. 238–39ff.; Sr. M. L. Fracart, "Les Abdicataires dans les Deux-Sèvres," in Reinhard, *Prêtres abdicataires,* p. 189.

18 A.N. F^{19} 893.

19 Vovelle, *Religion,* p. 109; Philippe Bordes, "Les Abdicataires du département du Gers," in Reinhard, *Prêtres abdicataires,* pp. 105, 110.

20 A.N. AF^{iv} 1898, ds. 1, 9; AF^{iv} 1897; Vovelle, *Religion,* pp. 142–43; B. Plongeron, "Les Prêtres abdicataires parisiens," in Reinhard, *Prêtres abdicataires,* pp. 56ff.

21 Bordes, "Les Abdicataires," pp. 107–8.

22 Cobb, 2:672–73, 683–84ff.; Vovelle, *Religion,* pp. 25, 38, 297–98; Tackett, *Religion, Revolution, and Regional Culture,* pp. 53–54, figs. A, B; M. Agulhon, *Republican Experiment,* pp. 105–6. Map of Abbé Boulard in G. Le Bras, *Etudes de sociologie religieuse,* 2 vols. (Paris, 1955–56), 1:324.

23 Cobb, pp. 668 n. 98, 669, and chap. 6 passim; Vovelle, *Religion,* pp. 285, 289–96. Compare chap. 10, above.

24 Beik, pp. 269–71; *PVCIPCN,* 2:805–6; Plongeron, "Prêtres abdicataires parisiens," in Reinhard, *Prêtres abdicataires,* pp. 34ff.

25 Mona Ozouf, *La Fête révolutionnaire, 1789–1799* (Paris, 1976), pp. 114ff.; Hardman, p. 366; Mercier, *Le Nouveau Paris,* 4:115–20, quoted in Biver, *Fêtes,* pp. 78–79.

26 Robespierre, *Oeuvres,* ed. M. Bouloiseau and A. Soboul, 10 vols. (Paris, 1910–67), 10:193–99.

27 Ibid., 10:237, 235.

28 George Rudé, ed. *Robespierre* (Englewood Cliffs, N.J., 1967), p. 70.

29 Biver, *Fêtes,* pp. 87–96; R. R. Palmer, *Twelve Who Ruled* (Princeton, 1967; orig. publ. 1941), pp. 327–34; Robespierre, *Oeuvres,* 10:462–65.

30 *PVCIPCN,* 2:442.

31 Ibid., 2:443–44, 877; M. Meinzer, "Der Französische Revolutionskalender und die 'Neue Zeit'" in *Arbeitstagung Bielefeld,* pp. 23–60; James Friguglietti, "The Social and Religious Consequences of the French Revolutionary Calendar" (Ph.D. diss., Harvard University, 1966), chap. 1.

32 Robespierre, *Oeuvres,* 10:463–64; Friguglietti, pp. 37, 73n.

33 Friguglietti, pp. 77–78, 108, 116–17.

34 M. Ozouf, "De Thermidor à Brumaire: Le Discours de la Révolution sur elle-même," *Revue historique* 253 (1970): 31–66; R. Koselleck's comments on calendar at Bielefeld Symposium, May 1985.

35 [Charles] Lambert, *Sur la liberté des cultes* (Paris an III [1795]), and *Lambert à ses collègues, en réponse à différentes objections sur la liberté des cultes* (n.p., an III [1795]); [Yves-Marie Audrein], *Un cinquième mot du Citoyen Audrein, ou Réponse à Pautrizel, représentant du peuple . . .* (Paris, n.d. [1795]), p. 5; Dauchez [d'Arras], *Sur la liberté des cultes* (Paris an V [1796–97]), puts the proportion of Catholics to the general population at eighteen-twentieths. Compare Grégoire, *Sur la liberté des cultes* (25 frimaire an III [15 December 1794]), p. 7, who compares the French situation with the greater religious liberties obtained in the U.S. Constitution. See A.N. F^7 3449 on *Annales de la religion* [an VI].

36 Palmer, *Improvement,* p. 177.

37 Ibid., pp. 138ff.; Lepeletier, "Plan d'éducation nationale de Michel Lepeletier," in *PVCIPCN,* 2:42, 34–60 passim.

38 *PVCIPCN,* 2:50.

39 Ibid., 3:56–62, 191–96.

40 Ferdinand Buisson, *Nouveau dictionnaire de pédagogie et d'instruction primaire*
(Paris, 1911), s.v. "livres scolaires," pp. 1048–49.

41 Ibid., pp. 1051, 1052, 1055. The following section on catechisms is reproduced with permission of the Voltaire Foundation from my "French
Revolutionary Catechisms: Ruptures and Continuities with Classical,
Christian, and Enlightenment Moralities," *Studies on Voltaire and the Eighteenth Century* 199 (1981): 353–62, where the references can be found.

42 Jean Morange and Jean-François Chassaing, *Le Mouvement de réforme de
l'enseignement en France, 1796–1798* (Paris, 1974), p. 136; Survey of Primary Schools known as "L'Enquete de l'an VI" by François de Neufchâteau, Year VI (1797–98), departmental archives; cf. n. 43 below.

43 The following section can be found developed at greater length in
E. Kennedy and M. L. Netter, "Les Ecoles primaires sous le Directoire,"
Annales historiques de la Révolution française 243 (1982): 3–38.

44 A.D. Gers L 392.

45 A.D. Bas-Rhin 1 L 1515; A.D. Nord L 4803; Kennedy and Netter, "Les
Ecoles primaires," table 9.

46 A.D. Gers L 392; A.D. Loir-et-Cher, L 768; A.D. Bas-Rhin 1 L 1515;
Kennedy and Netter, "Les Ecoles primaires," table 2.

47 John Lough, *Paris Theater Audiences in the Seventeenth and Eighteenth Centuries*
(London, 1972; orig. publ. 1957), chap. 3; Maurice Descotes, *Le Public de
théâtre et son histoire* (Paris, 1964), chap. 7. Descotes's chapter is one of the
best pieces on the theater public during the Revolution. See also Grimm,
Diderot, and Raynal, *Correspondance littéraire, philosophique et critique,* 16
vols. (Paris, 1877–82), 10:341; La Harpe, *Correspondance littéraire* (Paris,
1820), letter 181; Saint-Just, ed. Gratien, *Oeuvres,* p. 299.

48 For censorship of revolutionary theater, see Victor Hallays Dabot, *Histoire
de la censure théâtrale en France* (Paris, 1862), pp. 145–220, and A. Lieby,
"La Presse révolutionnaire et la censure théâtrale sous la Terreur," *La
Révolution française* 45 (1903): 306–53, 447–70, 502–29; ibid., 46 (1904):
98–128; A.P. 70:134–35 (2 August 1793). Pierre Caron, ed., *Paris pendant
la Terreur: Rapports des agents secrets du ministre de l'intérieur,* 7 vols. (Paris,
1910–78), vol. 7, s.v. "Spectacles," "Théâtres."

49 Tuetey, *Répertoire,* 9:321; 10:316.

50 Caron, *Agents secrets;* Marvin Carlson, *The Theater of the French Revolution*
(Ithaca, N.Y., 1966), pp. 175, 199, 208, 181. *Epicharis et Néron* was first performed 3 February 1794. *Timoléon* had its first full performance 11 September 1794.

51 A. Lieby, "L'Ancien Répertoire sur les théâtres de Paris à travers la réaction thermidorienne," *La Révolution française* 49 (1905): 146–75, 193–319. On the "Reveil du peuple," see chap. 7, above.

52 See chap. 7, above.

53 Augustin Cochin, *Les Sociétés de pensée et la démocratie moderne* (Paris, 1978; orig. publ. 1921), p. 18; Furet, *Penser la Révolution française,* pp. 212ff.; Camille Desmoulins in *Révolutions de France et de Brabant* 63 (n.d. [1791]): 495–96; Michael Kennedy, *The Jacobin Clubs in the French Revolution: The First Years* (Princeton, 1982), p. 6; *Révolutions de France et de Brabant* 41, p. 57. "Procès-verbaux du Club Patriotique des amis de la Constitution . . . séante à Apte, département des Bouches du Rhône," Bibliothèque munici-pale de Marseilles, MS 1373; on the sociétés of Provence and their old regime antecedents, the confréries, see Agulhon, *Pénitents et francs-maçons,* and Marie-Hélène Froeschlé-Chopard, "Pénitents et sociétés populaires du Sud-est,"*Annales historiques de la Révolution française* 268 (1987): 117–57. On the size of Jacobin membership, see M. Vovelle, "Jacobinism," in *His-torical Dictionary of the French Revolution, 1789–1799,* ed. Samuel F. Scott and Barry Rothaus, 2 vols. (Westport, Conn., 1985).

54 M. Kennedy, pp. 81–83, chaps. 2, 4 passim. "Procès-verbaux . . . Apte"; "Registre des délibérations de la Société populaire et Montagnard de Provins," Bibliothèque municipale de Provins . . . [3 nivôse an II– 10 ger-minal an III], MS 185. See also ibid. partially published in Justin Bellanger, *Les Jacobins peints par eux-mêmes: Histoire de la société populaire et montagnarde de Provins, 1791–1795* (Paris, 1908).

55 M. Kennedy, pp. 81–83, chaps. 2, 4 passim; "Procès-verbaux . . . Apte"; "Registre . . . Société populaire de Provins."

56 Isabelle Bourdin, *Les Sociétés populaires à Paris pendant la Révolution* (Paris, 1937), pp. 418–19, 132–34.

57 Circular letter of the Committee of Public Safety to the Sociétés popu-laires, November 1793, in Hardman, p. 370.

58 Bourdin, pp. 14, 16, 30–31. On the Jacobin clubs of the Directory, see the complete and elucidating study by Isser Woloch, *The Jacobin Legacy: The Democratic Movement under the Directory* (Princeton, 1970), esp. pt. 2. Woloch finds the social composition of the Directory Jacobins to have been more egalitarian than those of the Terror.

59 Lt. Col. Hartmann, *Les Officiers de l'Armée royale et la Révolution* (Paris, 1910); J.-P. Bertaud, *La Révolution armée: Les Soldats et la Révolution française* (Paris, 1979).

60 Marc Martin, *Les Origines de la presse militaire en France à la fin de l'Ancien Régime et sous la Révolution, 1770–1799* (Paris, 1975), p. 198.

61 Ibid., p. 197.

62 Ibid., chaps. 5–7; J. Godechot, *Les Commissaires aux armées sous le Directoire,* 2 vols. (Paris, 1941), 1:234.

63 Martin, chap. 7, p. 277.
64 Bertaud, p. 214.
65 Ibid., pp. 218–23.

XII. EPILOGUE: THE CULTURAL CONSEQUENCES OF THE REVOLUTION

1 Maurice Agulhon, *The Republican Experiment, 1848–1852* (Cambridge and New York, 1983), pp. 2–3; Hunt, *Politics, Culture, and Class,* chaps. 1–3; Cheryl B. Welch, *Liberty and Utility: The French Ideologues and the Transformation of Liberalism* (New York, 1984), chaps. 1, 3, 5. I am indebted to Michel Vovelle's reflections on revolutionary time and space, expressed at the Bielefeld Symposium on revolutionary culture, 28 May–1 June 1985.
2 Agulhon, *Republican Experiment;* George Armstrong Kelly, "Parnassian Liberalism in Nineteenth-Century France: Tocqueville, Renan, Flaubert" (paper communicated to author).
3 Theodore Zeldin, *Conflicts in French Society: Anticlericalism, Education and Morals in the Nineteenth Century* (London and Paris, 1970); Raymond Grew and Patrick J. Harrigan, "The Catholic Contribution to Universal Schooling in France, 1850–1906," *Journal of Modern History* 57 (1985): 223–24. The main expansion of Catholic education occurred between 1850 and 1863, coinciding with the religious revival of the Second Empire. See Yves-Marie Hilaire, "La Pratique religieuse en France de 1815 à 1878," *Information historique* 25 (March–April 1963): 57–69; *Grande encyclopédie,* s.v. "censure, livre."
4 Adolphe Thiers in 1871.
5 Quoted in A. L. Fisher, *Bonapartism* (Oxford, 1908), p. 71; J. Lucas-Dubreton, *Le Culte de Napoléon, 1815–1848* (Paris, 1960); Alan B. Spitzer, *Old Hatreds and Young Hopes: The French Carbonari against the Bourbon Restoration* (Cambridge, 1971).
6 Conseil d'Etat (1806), quoted in J. Christopher Herold, *Mind of Napoleon: A Selection of His Written and Spoken Words* (New York, 1955), p. 105.
7 The prevalence of the Bonapartist myth is well described by Lucas-Dubreton: "On every occasion: in literature, journalism, theater and in the street, it hatches in the cafés in the public balls, in the secret conventicles" (p. 118).
8 Stanley Mellon, "Nineteenth-Century Perceptions of Revolution," Consortium on Revolutionary Europe, 1750–1850, *Proceedings* (1975): 1–12; Tocqueville, *Recollections,* trans. George Laurence, ed. J. P. Mayer and A. P. Kerr (New York, 1971), p. 83. Writing about the February Revolution of 1848, Tocqueville notes: "Here was the French Revolution starting again, for it was always the same one"; Félicité de Lamennais to l'abbé Jean,

23 July 1814, in *Oeuvres inédits,* ed. A. Blaize, 2 vols. (Paris, 1866), 1 : no. 63; E. Kennedy, *A Philosophe,* chaps. 6, 8.

9 Pierre-Simon Ballanche, *Essais de palingénésie sociale,* 2 vols. (Paris, 1827– 29). Joseph de Maistre, *Du Pape dans son rapport avec l'Eglise catholique,* in *Oeuvres complètes,* 14 vols. (Lyons, 1884), vol. 2. Compare Maistre's statement in *Essai sur le principe général des constitutions politiques:* "Never before the eighteenth century has there been in the heart of Christianity, an insurrection against God; never especially has one seen a sacrilegious conjuration of all talents against their Author; but this is what we have seen in our days" (*Oeuvres complètes,* 1 : 305).

10 Michelet, *Histoire de la Révolution française,* 1 : intro.; see Stanley Mellon, *The Political Uses of History: A Study of Historians in the French Restoration* (Stanford, 1958); James Billington, *Fire in the Minds of Men,* bk. 2; Frank E. Manuel, *The Prophets of Paris* (Cambridge, Mass., 1962), pp. 164–68, 268–74.

11 Richard Cobb, *The Police and the People: French Popular Protest, 1789–1820* (Oxford, 1970), p. 169.

12 Quoted in Frank Kafker and James Laux, *The French Revolution: Conflicting Interpretations,* 2d ed. (New York, 1976), p. 246; Cobb, *Police and People,* p. 169. This is the main thesis of Billington.

13 Cobb, *Police and People,* p. 170.

14 *Grande Larousse encyclopédique,* s.v. "Marseillaise."

15 E. Kennedy, *A Philosophe,* chaps. 6, 8, epilogue.

16 Welch, *Liberty and Utility,* chap. 5; Charles de Rémusat, *Essais de philosophie,* 2 vols. (Paris, 1842), 1 : 1, 2.

17 Comte, *Introduction to Positive Philosophy* (Indianapolis and New York, 1970), and *Cours de philosophie positive,* 6 vols. (Paris, 1830–42).

18 See chap. 4, above.

19 Boime, *The Academy,* chaps. 1, 2.

20 See chap. 4, above.

21 Pierre Barbéris, *Balzac et le mal du siècle,* 2 vols. (Paris, 1970), 1 : 32–35, 42, 49.

22 Stendhal, *Mélanges d'art et de littérature* (Paris, 1869), quoted in Barbéris, *Balzac,* 1 : 43.

23 Barbéris, 1 : 35–41.

24 Theodore Zeldin, *France, 1848–1945: Ambition and Love* (Oxford, 1979), pp. 87–112.

25 Emile Faguet, *Balzac* (New York, 1974; orig. publ. 1918), p. 59.

26 [General Emmanuel G. R. de] Serviez, *Statistique du departement des Basses Pyrénées* (Paris, an IX [1800–1801]), pp. 129, 24–30; Jean-Charles Laumond, *Statistique du département du Bas-Rhin* (Paris, an X [1801–2]), p. 90; Peyre, *Statistique du département du Lot-et-Garonne* (Paris, an X [1801–2]), pp. 24–27; Luçay, *Description du département du Cher* (Paris, an X [1801–2]),

pp. 20, 55, 57. Richard Cobb, *Paris and Its Provinces, 1792–1802* (London, 1975).

27 Gennep, *Manuel de folklore français contemporain*, 9 vols. (Paris, 1938–58), 1:24–25; Lawrence Wylie, *Village in the Vaucluse* (New York, 1964; orig. publ. 1957); and Pierre-Jakez Hélias, *The Horse of Pride: Life in a Breton Village*, trans. and abr. June Guicharnaud (New Haven and London, 1980).

28 Serviez, p. 49; for the school survey of Year VI, see Kennedy and Netter, "Les Ecoles primaires"; Edward Shorter, "The Veillée and the Great Transformation," in Beauroy and Gargan, *The Wolf and the Lamb*, pp. 127–40; Eugen Weber, *From Peasants into Frenchmen: The Modernization of Rural France, 1870–1914* (Stanford, 1976).

29 [Jean-Charles-Joseph] Laumond, *Statistique du . . . Bas-Rhin*, p. 90.

30 J.-B.-Cl.-R. Huet de Coetlizan, *Statistique . . . de la Loire inférieure* (Paris, an X [1801–2]), p. 13.

31 See William Sewell, *Work and Revolution in France: The Language of Labor from the Old Regime to 1848* (Cambridge, 1980), chaps. 4, 8. Sewell places the development of class consciousness in the July Monarchy and finds the old regime compagnonnages conserved in the first decades of the nineteenth century. The conditions for class struggle, however, were created, he finds, by the abolition of the corporations by the Le Chapelier law of 1791.

32 Hilaire, pp. 57–69, quotation on p. 58.

33 Abbé Ernest Servin, *Les Missions religieuses en France sous la Restauration 1815–1830*, vol. 1: *Le Missionaire et sa mission* (Paris, 1948).

34 Hilaire, pp. 60–64; Tackett, *Religion, Revolution, and Regional Culture*, p. 299: "Patterns first engraved in the countryside in 1791 would thus be perpetuated into the nineteenth century and, beyond the Industrial Revolution and the economic modernization of the French countryside, well into the twentieth century" (H. Godin and Y. Daniel, *France, pays de mission* [Paris, 1943], p. 9).

35 Philippe Boutry, "Un sanctuaire et son saint au XIXe siècle: Jean Marie Baptiste Vianney, curé d'Ars," *Annales ESC* 35 (1980): 353–79.

36 Alexander Sedgwick, *The Third French Republic, 1870–1914* (New York, 1970; orig. publ. 1968), p. 15.

APPENDIX B. PROSOPOGRAPHY OF THE CULTURAL ELITE

1 I selected 208 men for their cultural prominence, such as appearing at the top of the Kennedy-Netter Theater Project listings of the fifty most performed authors during the Revolution (authors who died before the Revolution were excluded), being members of the salon of the princesse de Salm in the Directory and Consulate, or being otherwise culturally promi-

nent. Principal sources were: J. Fr. Michaud, *Biographie universelle ancienne et moderne,* 45 vols. (Graz, 1966–70; orig. publ. 1843–65); *Dictionnaire de biographie française;* Emmanuel Bénézit, *Dictionnaire critique et documentaire des peintres, dessinateurs et graveurs de tous les temps et de tous les pays,* new ed., 8 vols. ([Paris], 1948–57); *New Grove Dictionary of Music and Musicians,* ed. Stanley Sadie, 20 vols. (New York, 1980); *Dictionary of Scientific Biography;* Robert Bied, "Salons, Anthénées et Institut: Essai sur le pouvoir culturel à Paris de 1780 à 1830," *L'Information historique* 44 (1982): 73–74; Samuel F. Scott and Barry Rothaus, *Historical Dictionary of the French Revolution,* 2 vols. (Westport, Conn., 1985).

2 Darnton, *Great Cat Massacre,* chap. 4.

3 Frank A. Kafker, "Les Encyclopédistes et la Terreur," *Révue d'histoire moderne et contemporaine* (1967): 284–95.

INDEX

202; literacy rates under, 35; Voltaire's admiration for, 55; criticism of, 105; corpse of, 209; mentioned, 15

Louis XVI: obedience to, 18; music at court of, 118; and edict of *1787* on Protestants, 147; and emancipation of Jews, 148; and Civil Constitution of the Clergy, 153; corpse of, 207; as "father of people," 238–39, 294–98; engraving of, 246; mentioned, 9, 296–98

Louvre: salons of, 14; as public museum, 23, 220–34; great masters of, 103; mentioned, 375

Lully, Jean-Baptiste, 15, 117

Luxembourg Palace: gardens of, 11; as museum, 229; before Revolution, 431

Lyons: literacy in, 38; cahier of, 294; in revolt, 336

Maggiolo, Louis, 35–38. *See also* Literacy

Maistre, Joseph de, xxvii, 19, 298, 378–79, 445 *n*9

Mal du siècle, 382–83

Malesherbes, Chrétien-Guillaume de Lamoignon de, 148

Mandrou, Robert, 41

Marat, Jean-Paul: David's portrait of, xxi, 286–87; academic aspirations of, 185–86, 188; commemorated in songs, 236; assassination of, 303; *L'Ami du peuple,* 308–11, 320, 322; cult of, 336; and popular societies, 369; mentioned, xxi, 397

Maréchal, Sylvain, xxiv, 259, 275–76, 292, 363, 397, 435 *n*40

Mariage de Figaro (Beaumarchais), 285

Marie-Antoinette, 118, 123, 179–80

Marivaux, Pierre, 20, 176

"Marseillaise," xxi, 123, 241, 277–279, 283, 380

Marseilles: literacy in, 38; in revolt, 336; mentioned, 28

Marsollier des Vivetières: 106, 113, 114, 253–54, 398

Marx, Karl, 26, 112, 381

Masonic lodges. *See* Freemasonry

Materialism, 64–65, 117

Mathiez, Albert, 439 *n*1

Maximum General, 313–14

Medicine, popular, 4, 33–35

Méhul, Etienne-Nicolas: *Euphrosine, ou Le Tyran corrigé,* 22; "Chant du départ," 123; *Adrien, empereur de Rome,* 123; hymns, 241; mentioned, 122, 239, 399

Melodrama, 135–36

Mercier, Louis-Sébastien: *Du théâtre, ou Nouvel essai sur l'art dramatique,* 112; *Tableau de Paris,* 113, 187; on drama, 114; as critic of Catholic schooling and cathechisms, 155–56; on theaters, 171; on statuary of Notre-Dame, 206; on literacy, 317; mentioned, 169, 330, 397, 398

Mercure de France, 244, 321–22

Mesmer, Franz, 186

Metaphysics, 381

Michelet, Jules: on old regime and revolution, 263; on Festival of Federation, 330; and Revolution, 379; mentioned, 33

Millin, Aubin-Louis, 49, 356–57

Ministry of Interior, 216, 313–14

Mirabeau, Honoré-Gabriel-Riquetti, comte de: Houdon's sculptures of, xxii, 96, 100; in Panthéon, xxv, 336; and nationalization of church property, 146; and emancipation of Jews, 148; death of, 155; plan of national education, 157; rhetoric of, 302; *Courier de Provence,* 320; on senses, 329; mentioned, 302, 397